THE STATE OF THE EUROPEAN UNION

Pearson
Education

We work with leading authors to develop the
strongest educational materials in law,
bringing cutting-edge thinking and best learning
practice to a global market.

Under a range of well-known imprints, including
Longman, we craft high quality
print and electronic publications which help
readers to understand and apply their content,
whether studying or at work.

To find out more about the complete range of our
publishing please visit us on the World Wide Web at:
www.pearsoneduc.com

THE STATE OF THE EUROPEAN UNION

Edited by

John A. Usher

Longman

An imprint of **Pearson Education**

Harlow, England · London · New York · Reading, Massachusetts · San Francisco
Toronto · Don Mills, Ontario · Sydney · Tokyo · Singapore · Hong Kong · Seoul
Taipei · Cape Town · Madrid · Mexico City · Amsterdam · Munich · Paris · Milan

Pearson Education Limited
Edinburgh Gate
Harlow
Essex CM20 2JE
England

and Associated Companies throughout the world

Visit us on the World Wide Web at:
http://www.pearsoneduc.com

First published 2000

ISBN 0 582 36991 6

British Library Cataloguing-in-Publication Data
A catalogue record for this book is available from the British Library

Library of Congress Cataloging-in-Publication Data
A catalog record for this book is available from the Library of Congress

10 9 8 7 6 5 4 3 2 1
04 03 02 01 00

Typeset by 35 in 10/12pt Plantin
Printed and bound by T.J. International, Padstow, Cornwall, UK.

CONTENTS

CONTENTS

LIST OF CONTRIBUTORS

Professor T. St John Bates
Clerk of Tynwald, Isle of Man
Director of the Centre for Legislative and Parliamentary Studies, University
of Strathclyde

Mrs Christine Boch
Advisor on EC Law to the Scottish Parliament

Dr Gisbert Brinkmann
Ministry of Social Security, Federal Republic of Germany

Professor Noreen Burrows
Professor of European Law, University of Glasgow

Dr Caitríona Carter
Lecturer, Europa Institute, University of Edinburgh

Peter Cullen
Lecturer, Europa Institute, University of Edinburgh

Professor Alan Dashwood
Professor of European Law, University of Cambridge

Professor Carlos Esplugues
Professor of European Law, University of Valencia

Professor Jan H. Jans
Director, Europa Instituut, University of Amsterdam

Professor Joseph A. McMahon
Professor of Law, Queen's University of Belfast

Andrew Scott
Senior Lecturer, Europa Institute, University of Edinburgh

Professor John Usher
Salvesen Professor of European Institutions
Director, Europa Institute, University of Edinburgh

Professor Stephen Weatherill
Jacques Delors Professor of EC Law, University of Oxford

Dr Stephen Woolcock
London School of Economics

TABLE OF CASES

German Courts

United Kingdom Courts

TABLE OF STATUTES

Regulations

Decisions

Conventions and treaties

INTRODUCTION

The Europa Institute of the University of Edinburgh opened as the Centre of European Governmental Studies in November 1968, the moving force behind its creation being Professor J.D.B. Mitchell, the first holder of the Salvesen Chair of European Institutions. Its thirtieth anniversary therefore fell in 1998, at a time when the Treaty of Amsterdam had been signed, economic and monetary union was about to commence, and the debate about enlargement to include Central and Eastern European countries in the European Union was well-advanced – not to mention the domestic issue of the creation of the new Scottish Parliament. It therefore seemed particularly appropriate to mark the thirtieth anniversary of the Europa Institute with a conference examining the state of the European Union, and this book contains the revised texts of papers presented at that conference.

The book starts with overviews of the European Union from internal and external perspectives. Internally, Professor Weatherill mounts a critical investigation of the developing idea of flexibility, while Christine Boch takes a fresh look at the long-established concept of direct effect. Externally, Professor Dashwood's paper examines the framework of the common foreign and security policy, while Professor McMahon looks at what is widely recognized as one of the fundamental problems of enlargement to include Central and Eastern European States, the common agricultural policy.

The social and environmental issues emphasized in the Amsterdam Treaty are considered in the next three chapters. Professor Jans considers the extent to which protection of the environment has become a pervasive issue in EC law, Professor Burrows examines the new employment chapter and social provisions introduced by the Treaty of Amsterdam, and Dr Carter gives a critique of the 'European Social Model'.

The establishment of the Scottish Parliament in effect underlies the two chapters concerned with the implementation of Community law. Professor St John Bates looks at the domestic implementation of Community law in the context of devolution, and Dr Brinkmann discusses the problems of implementation of Community law in a federal system from a German viewpoint.

The next two chapters consider cooperation between Member States outside the Community framework. Professor Esplugues examines the Convention in the area of private international law, notably the 1968 Brussels Convention on jurisdiction and the enforcement of judgments in civil and commercial matters, and Peter Cullen looks at the criminal law aspects of the Third Pillar of the European Union.

The final section of the book turns to matters of a more economic nature. Dr Woolcock's chapter looks at the role of the EU in the international trading system, and the remaining two chapters examine economic and monetary union from different perspectives: Andrew Scott considers its impact at the regional level from an economist's point of view, and I myself endeavour to give a lawyer's perspective.

Although Professor J.D.B. Mitchell was a lawyer (and three of the four directors of the Institute/Centre have been lawyers) his concern from the outset was that there should be an input from economics and political science, and this disciplinary diversity is reflected in the chapters by Dr Carter, Andrew Scott, and Dr Woolcock.

The Europa Institute (in its guise as the Centre of European Governmental Studies) can claim to be the longest-established specialist institute of its kind in the United Kingdom, and can also claim to have had a considerable influence on the development of European Community and Union studies. In particular, all the contributors to the 1998 Conference, and to this volume, have a direct association with the Institute, whether as former members of staff in, or teaching courses in, the Institute (Professor St John Bates, Dr Brinkmann, and Professor Dashwood), as academic visitors holding fellowships in the Institute (Professor Jans), as former postgraduate students in the Institute (Professor Burrows, Professor Esplugues, Professor McMahon, Professor Weatherill and Dr Woolcock) or as staff in the Institute at the time of the Conference (Christine Boch, Dr Carter, Peter Cullen, Andrew Scott and myself). I am most grateful to all of them for so willingly participating in this venture.

However, the hope of all the contributors is that this book will be found useful in its own right as a contribution to the discussion on the state of the European Union.

John A. Usher
Europa Institute
University of Edinburgh
November 1999

1

FLEXIBILITY OR FRAGMENTATION: TRENDS IN EUROPEAN INTEGRATION

Stephen Weatherill

I AIMING HIGH

In 1891, Sir Hugh Munro published his 'Tables of Heights over 3,000 feet' in the *Journal of the Scottish Mountaineering Club* (SMC). As the first trustworthy attempt to compile a reliable list of the mountains of Scotland, it commanded great interest. Munro died in 1919 while working on revisions to his list. The 3,000 foot contour was essential to inclusion, but he left no precise definition of what he regarded as a mountain for the purposes of his list and what he excluded from mountain status as a mere subsidiary top of a nearby, higher summit. Nevertheless, his list has captured the imagination of hillwalkers and the quest to climb all the 'Munros' enjoys widespread popularity. However, Munro's original list has not survived untouched. Taken into the care of the SMC, it has been periodically revised. Some amendments reflect improvements in surveying. If a hill is shown to fall short of the 3,000 foot mark, it must be deleted; if it is found to possess the necessary altitude, it is entitled to insertion. But other changes reflect subjective assessments of whether a particular top enjoys sufficient distinctive character to deserve classification as a true Munro. In the absence of any hard-and-fast rules bequeathed by Munro himself, and given that the SMC does not seem to be content to treat the list extant on Munro's death as immutable, the list of Munros has altered at the margins according to the predilections of the SMC-appointed editors. In 1997, the first revision since 1990 was published.[1] The total number of Munros has risen from 277 to 284. Eight summits are added; one is deleted. The magnificent Five Sisters of Kintail range in the far west of Scotland now carries not two, but three, Munros, by virtue of the elevation of Sgurr na Carnach. Sgurr Dearg, on the Isle of Skye, one of

---

[1] D. Bearhop (ed.), *Munro's Tables*, SMC, 1997.

Munro's orginal choices, is now obliterated from the Tables. The hills, of course, have neither gained nor lost height. Nor have they been re-surveyed. The changes represent attempts to achieve consistency at the margin between true Munros and mere subsidiary tops which was created, but never explicitly defined, by Sir Hugh Munro himself.

The adjustments have attracted fierce criticism. 'There is absolutely no logic to the latest batch of changes',[2] according to one observer; another considers that '[T]he SMC are no longer fit custodians of the list'.[3] But who is to say what constitutes a mountain? Sir Hugh Munro chose not to. The core definition of the Munro remains elusive, depriving debate of a benchmark.

What is the core of the European Union? Like that of the Munros, it is rather hard to find, and it is simply not available in a single, immutable source. Yet it is vital to establish a benchmark in order to measure the validity of revisions made to the Treaty, which, according to the heroic claims of the European Court, constitutes nothing less than the constitutional charter of a Community based on the rule of law.[4] Failing such a basis for examination of what has been done, first at Maastricht, now at Amsterdam, there is a risk of hurling allegations of destruction of the dreams of the architects of the system which reflect mere subjective aspiration, tending to suppress constructive debate about why we concern ourselves with the fate of the EU at all.

II   FLEXIBILITY OR FRAGMENTATION

'Common rules for a common market' offers an appealingly simple slogan for judging legal development in the European Community. One would readily suppose that maintaining uniformity in the application of EC law would be central to realization of the system's economic and political objectives. After all, in the absence of a level playing field, what can prevent the system sliding towards fragmentation and, ultimately, the restoration in Europe of economic, and perhaps also political, division? Uniformity of application offers itself as a candidate benchmark for determining whether changes to the system fulfil its historical aspirations, albeit perhaps with a dash of necessary flexibility, or whether instead they constitute impulses towards fragmentation which will ultimately tear the Union apart.

Departures from the notion of the uniformity of the Community legal order are to be observed. In this chapter, I will demonstrate that in some respects such departure is not only inevitable, it is entirely desirable. But, I will then proceed to examine other manifestations of the thirst for flexibility which threaten the core values of the system. I pay special attention to the provisions on 'closer cooperation' which are one of the main innovations of

---

[2] Roger Smith, 'Munro Madness', *The Great Outdoors*, October 1997, 14.
[3] Richard Webb, *The Angry Corrie*, Issue No.33, Sept.–Oct. 1997, 10.
[4] E.g. Case 294/83, *Les Verts v Parliament* [1986] ECR 1339; Opinion 1/91 on the draft Agreement on a European Economic Area [1991] ECR I-6079.

the Treaty of Amsterdam (which was agreed in 1997, but which will enter into force only on ratification by all fifteen EU member states in accordance with domestic constitutional requirements). Overall, my thesis is that the EC legal order, and the EU as a polity, is perilously close to casting itself adrift of its anchors of constitutional stability. It has become forbiddingly difficult to understand. This prompts me to propose the elaboration of a 'constitutional document' capable of providing a foundation for principled discussion about the nature and purpose of a system which is, in the past decade as never before, dominated by the incremental process of Treaty revision in the wake of intergovernmental conferences.

III FLEXIBILITY

A helpful example of soundly motivated adjustment of the notion of 'common rules for a common market' is provided by the decline in the pre-eminence of orthodox notions of pre-emption as the constitutional norm governing the impact of Community legislative intervention on national competence. Traditional notions would hold that once a particular field has been occupied by EC rules, national competence to maintain or introduce more intense forms of regulation is excluded.[5] This is plainly an important means of securing common rules for a common market; the Community rule sets both the floor and the ceiling for permissible regulatory intervention and a level playing field is created, free of oddities on the territories of particular member states caused by diverse national choices. This pattern is central to the construction of a single market and it has been, and in many respects remains, highly significant in EC law and policy. But this clean-cut transfer of competence from member states to Community is, increasingly, plainly only one possible constitutional outcome of EC legislative action. Widely visible is the rise of the technique of minimum harmonization, whereby the EC sets a standard which must be introduced into the legal orders of the member states but which allows the member states to introduce stricter rules in the field should they so wish. The EC rule sets the floor, below which member states may not descend, but the ceiling is not set by EC secondary legislation. The ceiling is formed by primary EC law.

The technique of minimum harmonization may be identified in individual legislative measures, including those adopted in the heartland of the internal market project under Arts 94 and 95 of the EC Treaty. For example, a series of Directives harmonizing national laws governing the protection of economic interests of consumers explicitly permit member states to maintain or introduce rules for the protection of their consumers which are more stringent than those required under the Directive, notwithstanding the damaging impact on the process of levelling the commercial playing field. A 1985

---

[5] E.g. Case 5/77 *Tedeschi v Denkavit* [1977] ECR 1555; Case 60/86 *Commission v UK* [1988] ECR 3921; Case C-83/92 *Pierrel SpA v Ministero della Sanita* [1993] ECR I-6419.

Directive on Doorstep Selling, which envisages a cooling-off period and a right of withdrawal for consumers entering into a contract on the doorstep, has been interpreted by the Court as not precluding a French ban on the practice of doorstep selling, by virtue of the minimum formula contained even in a Directive based on Art. 94 EC.[6] More generally, specific Treaty provisions stipulate that legislative action adopted in the field set minimum EC rules only, which may be exceeded by stricter national rules. Article 153 on consumer protection and Art. 176 on EC environmental protection both permit more stringent national measures of protection provided only that they comply with primary EC law, encompassing most significantly the Treaty rules on free movement of goods.

The technique of minimum harmonization has much to commend it.[7] It has the pragmatic advantage that it improves the chances of securing support in Council for legislative proposals, for it offers member states some flexibility in stepping beyond an agreed EC standard. Were classic notions of field occupation applicable, the legislative log-jam would be intense, even in the post-Single European Act days of widespread Qualified Majority Voting in Council. At a more principled level, minimum harmonization offers the prospect of a more gradual, and a more informed, process of harmonization, whereby experiments in innovative regulation are permitted of individual member states, which may indicate a desirable up-grade in the level of regulation mandated by EC rules. Such opportunities are lost under the stifling impact of exhaustive harmonization. More generally, minimum harmonization is testimony to the pressures injected into the EC's policy-making structure as a result of its own success. The EC has expanded to a remarkable extent in recent times: expansion here refers to both functional and geographic expansion. Amid that process it has drawn into its sphere of influence a range of interests that cannot adequately be served by a one-dimensional insistence on negative law; the law that stops member states from doing things that will harm free trade. It is today not conceivable to deny the role of the EC in showing a measure of respect for national measures which may affect trade patterns yet which possess a cultural and social resonance extending beyond a superficial characterization as mere trade barriers. For the Court, that may be seen, *inter alia*, in the balance it draws between the competing interests of market integration and national choices about market regulation in its *Cassis de Dijon* formula.[8] In the legislative arena, the inevitable spillover of trade policy into environmental policy, consumer policy and social policy makes it unfeasible to deny the validity of the EC's own role in

---

[6] Dir. 85/577 *OJ* 1985, L372/31 as interpreted by the Court in Case 382/87 *Buet* [1989] ECR 1235. Other Directives in this area adopted under Arts 100/100a which contain a minimum clause include Dir. 84/450 (misleading advertising) and Dir. 93/13 (unfair terms in consumer contracts). See, generally, Weatherill, *EC Consumer Law and Policy*, Harlow, Longman, 1997.

[7] Stuyck, 'Patterns of Justice in the European Constitutional Charter: minimum harmonisation in the field of consumer law' in Kramer, Micklitz and Tonner (eds), *Law and Diffuse Interests in the European Legal Order*, Baden-Baden, Nomos, 1997.

[8] Case 120/78 [1979] ECR 649.

making its own choices about the thrust of regulatory endeavour (controversial though the detail may be). Minimum harmonization is part of the expanding EC's attempt (on several fronts) to place market integration alongside – not above – other legitimate objectives of the member states and the EC.[9] The EC is performing regulatory functions in ever wider fields in ever more member states, and 'the more competences the Community is acquiring, the less exclusive will be its jurisdiction'.[10]

Adjustments are inevitable under the pressures of geographical and functional expansion. And this is already the key to understanding why 'common rules for a common market' is inadequate in plotting Community policy-making. The EC is bent on much more than creating a common market[11] and its rule-making must reflect that multi-functionalism.

IV OPT-OUTS AND FRAGMENTATION

It is possible elsewhere to identify trends that are less desirable, or at least less openly managed and targeted. Although flexibility is far from novel in the historical development of the EC,[12] there are recent manifestations of an unwillingness to work within, and constructively to adjust, the EC structure in response to the pressures of expansion. Whereas it is possible to portray minimum harmonization as an exercise in adapting orthodox Community expectations in the light of the increasing load placed on the system, there are noticeable temptations to treat the load as too heavy and to evade the system. These trends include:

(a) In the (Maastricht) Treaty on European Union:[13]
    (i)   the Social Policy Protocol-plus-Agreement, commonly described as the UK's opt-out, although in precise legal terms better described as an opt-in by all the other member states to a special, though legally ambiguous, arrangement;[14]
    (ii) the structure of economic and monetary union, which offers to the United Kingdom and to Denmark the freedom not to participate in the third stage even if they comply with the economic convergence criteria stipulated by the Treaty.

---

[9] Weatherill, *Law and Integration in the European Union*, Oxford, Clarendon Press, 1995, chapter 5, 'Pre-emption and Competence in a Wider and Deeper Union'.

[10] Reich, 'Competition between Legal Orders: A New Paradigm of EC Law', 29 CMLRev. (1992), 861–896, at 895.

[11] Article 2 EC asserts the establishment of a common market as a means to other ends, not an end in itself.

[12] Usher, 'Variable Geometry or Concentric Circles: Patterns for the European Union' 46 ICLQ (1997) 243; C-D. Ehlermann, *How Flexible is Community Law? An Unusual Approach to the Concept of 'Two Speeds'*, (1984) 82 Michigan Law Rev 1274.

[13] For a sustained critique of the Treaty, see Curtin, 'The Constitutional Structure of the Union: a Europe of Bits and Pieces', 30 CMLRev (1993) 17.

[14] Whiteford, 'Social Policy after Maastricht' 18 ELRev (1993) 202.

Both instances serve as examples of disagreement about the nature and intensity of common policy-making within the EC, resolved by allowing a dissentient minority entirely to stand aside. Far from a managed response to the inadequacy of seeking common rules for a common market amid a complex multi-functional entity, which is how I have portrayed minimum harmonization, far indeed from a transitional period in which states agree to reach the same destination at different times, these arrangements instead act as an outright denial of common rules and a lurch towards competition between the regulatory choices of a big and a small bloc of member states.

(b) The Schengen system has operated in a formal sense outside the EC system. Through it, some member states propose to move faster to a common goal of 'open borders', frustrated by the dogged unwillingness of some member states to proceed within the framework of EC law. The Schengen arrangements are stated not to compromise the integrity of EC law, but it is not easy to see how they could not result in some level of discrimination between nationals of different member states.

(c) The Treaty of Amsterdam contains some significant sector-specific manifestations of fragmentation. The most contentious aspects of the post-Amsterdam arrangements are located in the new Title on 'Visas, asylum, immigration and other policies related to free movement of persons' which is dedicated to the progressive establishment of a freshly minted political slogan, 'an area of freedom, security and justice'. By virtue of Art. 2 of the Treaty of Amsterdam, which amends the EC Treaty, this Title is inserted as a new Title IV in the EC Treaty. The Title comprises Articles 61–69 EC. It is built around a five-year timetable for dismantling internal borders. The Title in the EC Treaty is home to modified versions of material allocated to the 'third pillar', on Justice and Home Affairs, by the (Maastricht) Treaty on European Union. This suggests that Amsterdam saw a triumph of EC institutional and constitutional method over the species of intergovernmentalism found in the non-EC EU. However, that jubilant communautaire perspective should be tempered by awareness that the new Title, although part of the EC Treaty, is marked by some aspects which are alien to the EC system, including usurpation of the Commission's exclusive right of initiative[15] and curtailment of the role of the European Court of Justice under (a version of) the preliminary reference procedure.[16] For present purposes, it is especially remarkable that special provision is made in Protocols to the Amsterdam Treaty for Denmark, the United Kingdom and Ireland.[17]

---

[15] Art. 67(1), ex Art. 73o(1), EC.
[16] Art. 68, ex Art. 73p, EC.
[17] Den Boer, 'Justice and Home Affairs Cooperation in the Treaty on European Union: More Complexity Despite Communautarization' 4 MJ (1997) 310; Labayle, 'Un espace de liberté,

Provision for an opt-out from the planned opening of borders to people is secured. As with the Maastricht social policy arrangements, this invites criticism from the perspective of inequality of treatment. The Amsterdam pattern envisaged for the incorporation of the 'Schengen *acquis*' into the structure of the Union is especially peculiar, most of all in relation to Denmark. It is envisaged that international law obligations will arise between Denmark and the other member states in so far as Denmark chooses to apply in its national law a Council measure building upon the Schengen *acquis*. This seems 'truly bizarre'.[18] Broadly, the possibility that three member states may, in different ways, enjoy effective exclusion for an indefinite period from the pattern of open borders envisaged in the new Title seems to contradict basic expectations surrounding the integrity of the EC legal order. It is possible that pursuit of the area of freedom, security and justice will do for the mobility of people what the internal market did for the mobility of manufactured goods. But the new patterns are strewn with open questions about how, if at all, to reconcile such fragmentary momentum with cherished notions of common purpose.

In the wake of Amsterdam, one could contend, perhaps plausibly, that such rupture in orthodox method represents no more than the price that had to be paid to secure the agreement of the member states to make the fundamental decision to transfer the body of material relevant to securing unrestricted free movement of persons from a non-EC pillar and (in the case of Schengen) from outwith the EU altogether across into the EC pillar. Moreover, an instinctive distaste for the hesitation exhibited by the 'stand aside' states may reflect no more than majoritarian bias. Treaty amendment depends on unanimous agreement among the member states, so failure to reach agreement on deeper common patterns of integration can as readily be interpreted as apt protection of recognized minority interests as it can be treated as curmudgeonly denial of majority preferences.

Without it being necessary to resolve these complex questions relating to the nature of the European polity, there is on any reading reason for anxiety about the injection of an alarming degree of intransparency into the system. Admittedly, these rather different manifestations of 'fragmentation' operate in different ways and for different reasons and with different consequences.[19] But my main concern is the unmanaged nature of the process and the fearsome difficulty involved in attempting to make it intelligible. This bundle of

---

de securite et de justice' 33 RTDE (1997) 813; Monar, 'Justice and Home Affairs in the Treaty of Amsterdam' 23 ELRev (1998) 320.

[18] Editorial comments, 'The Treaty of Amsterdam: Neither a bang nor a whimper', 34 CMLRev (1997) 767; see also Barents, 'Some Observations on the Treaty of Amsterdam', 4 MJ (1997), 332, 343: '. . . one may ask if Denmark does not already have one leg outside the Union'.

[19] Stubb, 'The 1996 Intergovernmental Conference and the management of flexible integration', 4 JEPP (1997) 37 discusses different models.

choices about opt-outs and fragmentation is not underpinned by a core definition of what the EU is seeking to achieve.

V CLOSER COOPERATION UNDER THE AMSTERDAM TREATY

In this light, the new provisions on closer cooperation to be introduced by the Treaty of Amsterdam are of major potential significance. For they attempt to establish a framework within which new endeavours falling within the scope of EU competence may be pursued by some, but not all, member states. They are, then, initimately connected with the quest to identify what is central to the EU's mission and, accordingly, deserving of protection from splinter groups.

Under the Amsterdam Treaty, a new provision has been inserted into the EC Treaty as Art. 11. It provides as follows:

1. Member States which intend to establish closer cooperation between themselves may be authorised, subject to Articles 43 and 44 of the Treaty on European Union, to make use of the institutions, procedures and mechanisms laid down by this Treaty, provided that the co-operation proposed:
(a) does not concern areas which fall within the exclusive competence of the Community;
(b) does not affect Community policies, actions or programmes;
(c) does not concern the citizenship of the Union or discriminate between nationals of Member States;
(d) remains within the limits of the powers conferred upon the Community by this Treaty; and
(e) does not constitute a discrimination or a restriction of trade between Member States and does not distort the conditions of competition between the latter.
2. The authorisation referred to in paragraph 1 shall be granted by the Council, acting by a qualified majority on a proposal from the Commission and after consulting the European Parliament.

If a member of the Council declares that, for important and stated reasons of national policy, it intends to oppose the granting of an authorisation by qualified majority, a vote shall not be taken. The Council may, acting by a qualified majority, request that the matter be referred to the Council, meeting in the composition of the Heads of State or government, for decision by unanimity.

Member States which intend to establish closer cooperation as referred to in paragraph 1 may address a request to the Commission, which may submit a proposal to the Council to that effect. In the event of the Commission not submitting a proposal, it shall inform the member states concerned of the reasons for not doing so.
3. Any Member State which wishes to become a party to cooperation set up in accordance with this Article shall notify its intention to the Council and to the Commission, which shall give an opinion to the Council within three months of receipt of that notification. Within four months of the date of that notification, the Commission shall decide on it and on such specific arrangements as it may deem necessary.

4. The acts and decisions necessary for the implementation of cooperation activities shall be subject to all the relevant provisions of this Treaty, save as otherwise provided for in this Article and in Articles 43 and 44 of the Treaty on European Union.

5. This Article is without prejudice to the provisions of the Protocol integrating the Schengen acquis into the framework of the European Union.

Articles 43 and 44 of the (re-numbered, post-Amsterdam) Treaty on European Union operate as a type of master provision, to which both these procedures for closer cooperation in the EC Treaty and their kin in (what was) the 'Third Pillar' governing Cooperation in Justice and Home Affairs[20] are subject. Article 43 of the Treaty on European Union, formerly Article K.15 TEU, provides

1. Member States which intend to establish closer cooperation between themselves may make use of the institutions, procedures and mechanisms laid down by this Treaty and the Treaty establishing the European Community provided that the cooperation:
(a)   is aimed at furthering the objectives of the Union and at protecting and serving its interests;
(b)   respects the principles of the said Treaties and the single institutional framework of the Union;
(c)   is only used as a last resort, where the objectives of the said Treaties could not be attained by applying the relevant procedures laid down therein;
(d)   concerns at least a majority of Member States;
(e)   does not affect the *acquis communautaire* and the measures adopted under the other provisions of the said Treaties;
(f)   does not affect the competences, rights, obligations and interests of those Member States which do not participate therein;
(g)   is open to all Member States and allows them to become parties to the cooperation at any time, provided that they comply with the basic decision and with the decisions taken within that framework;
(h)   complies with the specific additional criteria laid down in Article 11 of the Treaty establishing the European Community and Article 40 of this Treaty, depending on the area concerned, and is authorised by the Council in accordance with the procedures laid down therein.

2. Member States shall apply, as far as they are concerned, the acts and decisions adopted for the implementation of the cooperation in which they participate. Member States not participating in such cooperation shall not impede the implementation thereof by the participating Member States.

Article 44 of the Treaty on European Union, formerly Article K.16 TEU, provides:

1. For the purposes of the adoption of the acts and decisions necessary for the implementation of the cooperation referred to in Article 43, the relevant institutional provisions of this Treaty and of the Treaty establishing the European Community

---

[20] Art. K.12 TEU, becoming Art. 40 TEU in the re-named post-Amsterdam Title, Provisions on Police and Judicial Co-operation in Criminal Matters.

shall apply. However, while all members of the Council shall be able to take part in the deliberations, only those representing participating Member States shall take part in the adoption of decisions. The qualified majority shall be defined as the same proportion of the weighted votes of the members of the Council concerned as laid down in Article 205(2) of the Treaty establishing the European Community. Unanimity shall be constituted by only those Council members concerned.

2. Expenditure resulting from implementation of the cooperation, other than administrative costs entailed for the institutions, shall be borne by the participating Member States, unless the Council, acting unanimously, decides otherwise.

These provisions will doubtless stimulate a wealth of detailed comment. It is not the purpose of this chapter to conduct an intricate textual examination of the criteria that must be satisfied or of the envisaged institutional supervision. Nor am I concerned to interrogate the implications for institutional dynamics of the ghoulish revival of a procedure akin to the Luxembourg Compromise, now rooted in the Treaty, rather than lurking murkily, influencing its operation from the shadows. Yet, at a general level, the attraction of this procedure is plain. It seems to promote managed and non-exclusionary deepening of collaborative endeavour by most, but not all, member states. Variation occurs sector-by-sector, diminishing the risk of a generally applicable deep rift between hard core states and an outer rim. The opportunity for advance other than at the pace of the slowest members of the convoy seems especially vital in the light of the next load to be placed on the EC/EU system, enlargement to the East. In this sense, these new provisions on closer cooperation could be regarded as the key to resolving the 'widening or deepening' debate – they promise both, albeit at the (now inevitable) price of abandoning the uniformity of application of the law. But the criteria are very demanding. What really does *not* 'affect' EC policies, actions or programmes (Art. 11(1)(b))? what does not constitute a discrimination or a restriction of trade between member states and – in particular – what does not 'distort the conditions of competition between the [member states]' (Art. 11(1)(e))? It was mentioned above that the EC adopted in 1985 a Directive on Doorstep Selling,[21] which envisages a cooling-off period and a right of withdrawal for consumers entering into a contract on the doorstep. It is stated in the recitals to this Directive that it was adopted because disparity between national legislation in the field 'directly affects the functioning of the common market'. If Art. 11(1)(e)'s insistence that closer cooperation must not distort the conditions of competition between the member states is read in in the same way in which the EC was prepared to treat disparity between national laws on Doorstep Selling, then there can be little anticipation of regular deployment of the Amsterdam provisions on closer cooperation.

The thickening patterns of mutual interdependence among the member states make it implausible that closer cooperation between some will not affect the others in some form. The new provisions appear to be based on

---

[21] Note 6 above.

assumptions of a static relationship between policy sectors, which is entirely at odds with the intertwining evolution of EC activity. The conditions may be applied in a rather pliable manner (by the political and, should the occasion arise, judicial institutions). Failing that, they seem apt to preclude most, if not all, imaginable forms of closer cooperation by most, but not all, member states.[22] It has been said that the new arrangements simply follow up, and provide a planned framework for, the type of flexibility that was in any event embraced at Maastricht, but, in fact, several of these criteria would seem *not* to be satisfied by the Maastricht innovations applicable to social policy and to EMU. For example, the Social Policy Protocol-plus-Agreement could readily be analysed as incompatible with principles of equality and undistorted competition in the EC. It may be concluded that the Amsterdam provisions on closer cooperation are more important for their message about a mood of determination not formally to abandon deepening for widening rather than for their precise formal legal meaning or even for their operational utility.

VI THE FEAR OF INTRANSPARENCY

A broader anxiety lurks beneath this discussion. The EU has become a highly complex, (in some respects) state-like entity.[23] Is it any longer intelligible to those on whose behalf it is supposed to act, the peoples of Europe who were converted by the Maastricht Treaty on European Union into the Citizens of the Union? What is its appeal? A simple example of the problem is provided by the invention at Maastricht of a European Union, which, on closer inspection, lacks a single pattern but rather comprises (at least) two very distinct forms of legal and political animal, the familiar EC model and the less ambitious, quasi-intergovernmental non-EC EU model which is used for cooperation between the member states in the areas of foreign and security policy and justice and home affairs. It is a disturbing symbol of the intransparency surrounding the whole enterprise that a question as simple as

---

[22] Langrish, 'The Treaty of Amsterdam: Selected Highlights' 23 ELRev (1998) 3 offers as projects capable of complying with the conditions 'further integration in areas such as culture, education or public health so long as any benefits or schemes established were open to all Union citizens'. See also, emphasizing the narrow scope of permissible closer cooperation, Favret, 'Le Traite d'Amsterdam: une revision a minima de la Charte constitutionnelle de l'Union europeenne' 33 CDE (1997) 555, 595–600; Constantinesco in 'Les clauses de cooperation renforcee' 33 RTDE (1997) 751; Ehlermann, 'Engere Zusammenarbeit nach dem Amsterdamer Vertrag: Ein neues Verfassungsprinzip?' 32 EuR (1997) 362; Shaw, 'The Treaty of Amsterdam: Challenges of Flexibility and Legitimacy' 4 ELJ (1998) 63; Edwards and Philippart, 'Flexibility and the Treaty of Amsterdam: Europe's New Byzantium?' (1997) Cambridge, CELS, Occasional Paper 3; Gaja, 'How flexible is flexibility under the Amsterdam Treaty?' 35 CMLRev (1998) 855. For a still broader perspective, see Walker, 'Sovereignty and Differentiated Integration in the European Union', forthcoming.

[23] There is no call here to enter the debate about the nature of the system; for a doorway see Nelsen and Stubb (eds), *The European Union: Readings on the Theory and Practice of European Integration*, 2nd ed. (Lynne Rienner, 1998). *Cf* Stone, Sweet and Sandholtz, 'European integration and supranational governance' 4 JEPP (1997) 297; Laffan, 'The European Union: a distinctive model of internationalization' 5 JEPP (1998) 235.

'How is the EU different from the EC?' can be answered only with great difficulty (and even then only assuming a patient listener already well-informed about the EC).

There is a sort of delayed reaction to EU expansion. It is hard to believe that there has been anything more radical done to the EC system since the injection of Qualified Majority Voting in Council by the Single European Act (SEA), entering into force in 1987. That swept aside the legislative log-jam caused by unanimity; that propelled the EC forward in a number of policy areas; that prepared the enduring tension between the member states' desire to get more decided (which dictated surrender of the veto) and the fear that what might be decided would be damaging to individual states' interests (which dictated the growth of other strategies for controlling the process[24]). Yet the SEA created barely a murmur of protest. It is hard to regard the Treaties of either Maastricht or Amsterdam as carrying any implication for the relationship between EC and state powers which is remotely as penetrating. A lot of the criticism of the EC system found rather close to the surface of the grudging acceptance by the Bundesverfassungsgericht in 1993 that Germany could ratify the TEU in accordance with its constitution could not convincingly be directed at the TEU at all.[25] It was mostly past history. This was especially true of the remarks directed at the EC's open-handed approach to competence. This does not deprive the Bunderverfassungsgericht's comments of general significance, nor of their danger to the integrity of the EC legal system should the claim to *Kompetenz-Kompetenz* be acted on (in Germany or elsewhere[26]), but it does suggest that there must be a passage of time before the EU finds itself obliged to explain itself. One might say much the same of the Danish 'No' to the Maastricht Treaty, delivered in the 1992 referendum. It seems more probable that this was a cry of vexation aimed at 'Europe', meaning 40 years of increasingly complex institutional and constitutional fare culminating in the indigestible text of the TEU, than at the impact of the Maastricht Treaty itself. Moreover, the academic criticism of the activist Court that has become popular in some quarters in the 1990s has been largely directed at decisions from many years previously, in some instances by writers apparently little troubled at the time by these incidents of alleged judicial opportunism. The Court's decisions have not changed in the interim, though their impact may have done, given trends towards geographical and functional expansion in the EU. They attract a delayed reaction.

Criticism of the Maastricht Treaty, and now the Amsterdam Treaty, is not really about either Treaty. It represents a delayed reaction – a criticism, even a fear, of the accumulation of intransparency and citizen fatigue.

[24] Weatherill, *Law and Integration in the European Union*, Oxford, Clarendon Press, 1995, chapter 5.
[25] In English, *Brunner v European Union Treaty* [1994] 1 CMLR 57.
[26] See Slaughter, Sweet and Weiler, 'The European Courts and National Courts: Doctrine and Jurisprudence', Hart Publishing, 1998.

VII   BEYOND THE COMMON MARKET: SLOGANS AND CATCHPHRASES

What I diagnose here is a wide-ranging expansion of EU activity (gauged both functionally and geographically) which has bred a need for rather grander, yet more politically charged, fundamentals than the 'simple' pursuit of 'common rules for a common market'. Slogans that have been bandied about amount to little more than avoidance of the need to address the deepening impact of the EU within all the member states. Deployment of diverse notions such as Union Citizenship, fundamental rights protection, institutional transparency, respect for the *acquis communautaire*, subsidiarity and flexibility are symptomatic of circumvention of the question how the evolving polity should be characterized for the purposes of engineering trustworthy and trusted systems of accountability. They do not offer a convincing nor an appealing underpinning for the evolving process of European economic and political integration. Each deserves brief comment.

Union Citizenship

Looking at the anaemic provisions inserted into the EC Treaty by the Treaty on European Union in the name of Union Citizenship,[27] one may easily agree with the brilliant observation of my late colleague Brian Wilkinson when he paraphrased Mark Twain to observe that the Union Citizen could rightly complain that rumours of his or her birth had been greatly exaggerated.[28] Indeed, even before the Maastricht Treaty was ratified, the member states, in Edinburgh in December 1992, were rapidly clarifying, for the benefit of a highly sceptical Danish electorate then mid-way between its two referenda on whether or not Denmark should ratify the Union Treaty, that Union Citizenship in no way took the place of national citizenship. This was plain enough from the terms of the Treaty, but the very fact that it was necessary to placate the people of Denmark (and, doubtless, not only Denmark) suggests that the tokenism of the ill-prepared status of Union Citizenship was the very opposite of an attraction to the Union's endeavours. And, notwithstanding the Commission's oft-stated claim that the insertion of the citizenship provisions into the Treaty has elevated the status of the people to a new constitutional plane in the EC legal order,[29] little that has happened subsequently on either the legislative or the judicial plane[30] to the Union Citizen born on 1 November 1993 has put any flesh on these bones.

[27] Articles 8–8e EC.
[28] Wilkinson, 'Towards European Citizenship? Nationality Discrimination and Free Movement of Workers in the European Union' 1 European Public Law (1995) 417. See also Jessurun D'Oliveira, 'Union Citizenship: Pie in the Sky?' in Rosas and Antola, *A Citizens' Europe*, Sage, 1995.
[29] E.g. COM (93) 702, COM (97) 230. For up-to-date information on developments: http://europa.eu.int/comm/dg15/en/people/index.htm.
[30] The Court has been markedly reluctant to make use of the new provisions when pressed to extend the reach of EC law in order to further individual protection; Case C-91/92 *Faccini*

Fundamental rights protection

Article 6(2) TEU commits the Union to observe fundamental rights but the Court's jurisdiction to apply that provision is excluded by Art. 46. The value of this new express commitment to fundamental rights protection is less than it might initially appear. The Treaty on European Union did not weaken the system of fundamental rights protection in the EC, crafted over two decades by the Court 'in accordance with constitutional traditions common to the Member States, and . . . international treaties [of which] . . . The European Convention for the Protection of Human Rights and Fundamental Freedoms . . . is of particular significance . . .',[31] but it did not enhance the system of judicial protection in the generous manner suggested by a cursory inspection of Art. 6(2).[32] Even the Court's role in securing the development of an individual rights-based jurisprudence in the EC bears the scars of timidity at the margins of the EC's competence. Opinion 2/94 on accession to the European Convention on Human Rights[33] is one candidate for examination from this perspective, but, at a more specific level, it is hard to find explanation outside the sphere of legal formalism (or, perhaps, deference to the legislature) for the Court's abrupt refusal in *Grant v South-West Trains*[34] to maintain the receptivity shown in *P v S and Cornwall County Council*[35] to trends towards identification of equality as a constitutionally mature principle of general application.

Institutional transparency

Open government is not a slogan which has held evident appeal for the Council.[36] In recent years, gradual steps have been taken within the EU's institutions to increase transparency, notably in the December 1993 code of conduct concerning public access to Council and Commission documents.[37] The EC judicature has so far preferred not to treat access to information or institutional transparency as part of the fabric of general principles of the EC legal order. Instead, it has adopted the more cautious approach of examining individual requests for information against the standards established in relevant secondary legislation. In *Carvel and Guardian Newspapers Ltd v Council*[38]

Dori v Recreb [1994] ECR I-3325, rejecting the invitation of AG Lenz, and Cases C-64/96, C-65/96 *Land Nordrhein-Westfalen v Kari Uecker, Vera Jacquet v Land Nordrhein-Westfalen* [1997] ECR I-3171.

[31] Case 46/87 *Hoechst v Commission* [1989] ECR 2859.

[32] See Bebr, 'Judicial Protection and the rule of law' in Curtin and Heukels (eds), *Institutional Dynamics of European Integration*, Nijhoff, 1994.

[33] [1996] ECR I-1759.

[34] Case C-249/96 judgment of 17 February 1998.

[35] Case C-13/94 [1996] ECR-2143.

[36] For a biting critique, see Curtin and Meijers, 'The principle of open government in Schengen and the European Union: Democratic retrogression?' 32 CMLRev (1995) 391.

[37] *OJ* 1993, L340/41. For both directly relevant and comparative material, see *Le Citoyen, L'Administration et le Droit Europeen*, report for XVIII FIDE Congress, Stockholm, 1998.

[38] Case T-194/94 [1995] ECR II-2765.

decisions were annulled for violation of provisions of Decision 93/731 governing public access to Council documents.[39] Rather than asserting any general
principles, the ruling was in essence an instruction to the Council to apply its
own procedures more rigorously, especially in balancing institutional interests
in confidentiality against the request for disclosure. Comparable comments
may be directed at the decision in *WWF UK v Commission*,[40] a successful
application for annulment of a Commission decision refusing to release documents, based on Decision 94/90 governing public access to Commission
documents.[41] Furthermore, *Netherlands v Council* provided no suggestion of a
Court in a mood to accept the Dutch government's invitation to develop
access to information as a general right.[42] The 'Swedish Journalists' case also
generated a ruling of the Court of First Instance in which an application for
annulment was successful but the legal reasoning remained constrained by
the parameters of the Council's own Decision. The Court felt able to avoid
ruling on submissions based on fundamental principles of citizen access to
documents.[43] Transparency remains a gift bestowed by the institutions rather
than an inherent principle of good government.

It may yet prove possible to shake the EC judicature out of its grudging
attitude. The Ombudsman, Jacob Soderman, is beginning to offer an alternative route to tackle the problem of intransparency. And the Amsterdam
Treaty promises a higher profile for the matter in the shape of a new enabling
Treaty provision, Art. 255. But this is slow progress. It is doubtless true that
'transparency of the decision-making process strengthens the democratic
nature of the institutions and the public's confidence in the administration'.
But these words are taken from the Declaration on the Rights of Access to
Information attached to the Treaty on European Union. Very slow progress.

Respect for the *acquis communautaire*

It is certainly true that the Treaties are peppered with assertions that the *acquis
communautaire* is to be respected. In Arts 2 and 3, the Treaty on European
Union asserts that the union will maintain in full and respect the *acquis*. This
has been interpreted as 'une interdiction de regression'.[44] But this is only a
facade of stability. For the *acquis* is undefined and it means different things in

[39] *OJ* 1993, L340/43.
[40] Case T-105/95 [1997] ECR II-313.
[41] *OJ* 1994, L46/58.
[42] Case C-58/94 [1996] ECR I-2169.
[43] Case T-174/95 *Svenska Journalistforbundet v Council* judgment of 17 June 1998. The Court's
disapproval of the applicant's use of the Internet to publicize the Council's defence was based
on infringement of the rules of procedure, rather than any general distaste for the medium,
but nonetheless appears rather old-fashioned.
[44] da Cruz Vilaça and Piçarra, 'Y a-t-il des limites materielles a la revision des traites instituant
les Communautes Europeennes?' 29 CDE (1993), 3, 29.

different contexts.[45] It is used by the Commission to represent the obligations that must be shouldered by applicant states in Central and Eastern Europe, but the Commission treats some aspects as carrying a higher priority than others, without any obvious constitutional justification.[46] The *acquis*, as something that cannot be altered, cannot mean **all** law – for legislative reform is vital for the health of any political system – so what is being presented as something more than mere law, the *acquis*? Again, no trace can be found in the constitutional documents. The *acquis*, as a core set of values, begins to look less commanding once one interrogates its content. And, worst of all, one may even conclude from inspection of the Treaties that the promises to respect the *acquis* are put in the mouth of the Union, and not of the member states acting at times of Treaty revision, in which case the appeal to a core *acquis* becomes a great deal less valuable as a benchmark of stability and durable constitutionalism than it may first appear. In this context, as the states step outside the EU system and assert their sovereign identity, the *acquis communautaire* loses any adhesive constitutional property which it might possess in the internal political and legal institutional context.

Subsidiarity

In its first annual report on the subsidiarity principle[47] the Commission stated drily that 'one cannot help observing that principle and practice are often far apart with member states meeting within the Council often adopting positions on individual cases at variance with their respect in principle for Article 3b'. So where is the value of subsidiarity? Mary Robinson, when President of Ireland, observed that '. . . the chief advantage of [subsidiarity] seems to be its capacity to mean all things to all interested parties – simultaneously'.[48] This is the key to a slogan which may once have held the promise of focusing a constructive debate on issues of competence and the efficient and legitimate location of government, but which has long since surrendered its utility to the dismal world of the politician's soundbite. Yet the EU has not given up on subsidiarity.[49] The Amsterdam Treaty adds a Protocol on the application of the principles of subsidiarity and proportionality. Explicitly building on the 1992 Edinburgh conclusions and the 1993 inter-institutional agreement, it includes an attempt to give a sharper edge to the notion:

---

[45] Pescatore, 'Aspects judiciares de l' "acquis communautaire"', 17 RTDE (1981) 617; Curti Gialdino, 'Some Reflections on the *Acquis Communautaire*', 32 CMLRev (1995) 1089; Weatherill, 'Safeguarding the Acquis Communautaire', paper delivered at the 40th Anniversary Conference of the Europa Instituut of Leiden University, publication forthcoming.

[46] E.g. COM (95) 163, 'Preparation of the Associated Countries of Central and Eastern Europe for Integration into the Internal Market of the Union'.

[47] COM (94) 533.

[48] 'Constitutional Shifts in Europe and the United States: Learning from Each Other' (1996) 32 Stanford Jnl Intl L 1, 10.

[49] On the role of the Court, see de Burca, 'The Principle of Subsidiarity and the Court of Justice as an Institutional Actor' 36 JCMS (1998) 217.

For any proposed Community legislation, the reasons on which it is based shall be stated with a view to justifying its compliance with the principles of subsidiarity and proportionality; the reasons for concluding that a Community objective can be better achieved by the Community must be substantiated by qualitative or, wherever possible, quantitative indicators.

However, subsidiarity has some ground to make up if it is to serve a constructive function in the political and legal life of the EU.

Flexibility and closer cooperation

The provisions introduced at Amsterdam were discussed above. If used, they promise complex dimensions of integration involving different groupings of member states acting in different areas of policy integration. This is capable of causing awkwardly intricate questions of demarcation between these multi-patterned clusters. Most of all, the contours of the system will become progressively harder to grasp. In such an environment, the EU will be free of any accusation of dumbing down; but it will also look in vain for tributes paid to its intelligibility.

The slogans that have been bandied do not offer a convincing nor an appealing underpinning for the late twentieth century process of European integration.[50] This occurs not least because the member states do not know what they want of the EC/EU and are, deliberately and understandably, avoiding bolder and more decisive overt steps towards more powerful labels: there is value to them in concealing the depth of the process. 'Beyond the common market', to be sure; but this is a Union heaped with short-term compromise and muddled thinking, of which these slogans are disturbingly typical and transparently unappealing.

I have been critical of aspects of the Maastricht settlement, but let me make plain that I am not necessarily suggesting the expulsion of notions such as citizenship and subsidiarity from the debate, rather I am drawing attention to the way that they have been mishandled. Union Citizenship could have a future as a means of drawing out how to situate the relationship between individual and government in a broader context than that of the nation state; a Scot, with or without a Parliament in Edinburgh, is no less a Scot for being simultaneously British, and why not also a European aspect to that identity? So, too, the Catalans, Corsicans and so on. Citzenship has not (yet) been permitted to fulfil its potential.[51] Had subsidiarity in Art. 5 (formerly 3b) been treated as a framework for debate about competence allocation, it could have provided a helpful basis for elaborating the limits of EC rule-making and, its corollary, the outer limits of state competence. Regrettably, it was not drafted

---

[50] See also Hilf, 'Amsterdam – Ein Vertrag fur die Burger?' 32 EuR (1997) 347.
[51] Cf Weiler, 'Does Europe need a Constitution? Reflections on Demos, Telos and the German Maastricht Decision' 1 ELJ (1995) 219; Shaw, 'The Interpretation of European Union Citizenship' 61 MLR (1998) 293; Shaw, 'The Many Pasts and Futures of Citizenship in the European Union' 22 ELRev (1997) 554.

in that constructive spirit. Even though the central issue of competence allocation has not been resolved (and if it is correctly identified as a federal-type question, perhaps it never will be), subsidiarity has become contaminated with such a level of misunderstanding that it is hard to predict a constructive future for it. I am anxious too not to convey the impression that I oppose in principle the insertion at Amsterdam of new provisions such as those on closer cooperation and on institutional transparency. My concern is that they have been blithely introduced; and only once the Treaty has been agreed has serious attention been paid to assessment of their value. In this way, their capacity to sharpen and clarify the debate has been compromised.

VIII A CONSTITUTIONAL DOCUMENT

It is inevitable that there will be adjustment of the structure of the EU as it evolves. To criticize amendments to the EC Treaty because they are amendments is not useful. And the Amsterdam Treaty, for all its opaque cross-references, intricate Protocols and bewilderingly diverse Declarations, contains much which, at a detailed level, merits modest congratulation. The scope of application of the codecision procedure is expanded, thereby advancing the role of the European Parliament, and eliminating many (though not all) of the institutional and constitutional anomalies that hinged on choice between available Treaty bases for legislative action;[52] the provisions concerning fundamental rights are elaborated; the peculiar extra-EU status of Schengen has been addressed, albeit not very satisfactorily; redundant provisions are repealed, others helpfully updated by amendment; social policy will be developed by and for all fifteen member states. But, in the Amsterdam Treaty, the devil is not in the detail. The package is incapable of capturing the popular imagination. Whereas the Single European Act was framed by the 1992 project and the Treaty on European Union by EMU, the Amsterdam Treaty was bereft of a big idea. Preparing the Union's institutional structure for enlargement served for a while as a modestly inspiring lead agenda item, but even that ambition was quietly dropped once it became apparent that agreement on several key issues would not be forthcoming. Decisions on, for example, weighted voting in Council and reduction in the number of Commissioners were left for future resolution.[53] The problem lies in the accumulation of texts, breeding ever deepening intransparency. Change which is not intelligible is likely to cause alienation. Both the Maastricht and the Amsterdam Treaties are hard to absorb; and both have bred alienation.

[52] E.g. the demarcation between the internal market provision, Art. 100a, Art. 95 post-Amsterdam, and the environmental protection provision, Art. 130s, Art. 175 post-Amsterdam, so troublesome in the past because of the distinctions between the two bases relating to the Parliament's role and the voting rules in Council, is now much less significant because of the great reduction in (though not elimination of) those institutional distinctions.
[53] Protocol on the Institutions with the Prospect of the Enlargement of the European Union. See Blumann, 'Aspects institutionnels', 33 RTDE (1997) 721.

My proposal is not a new one, but it possesses a motivation distinct from what has gone before. It is for a 'Constitutional Document' produced through an open debate, which enshrines what is truly of constitutional importance, and which stipulates how, if at all, amendments may be made. The motivation for the production of a constitutional document is generated most of all by the current damaging alienation from the EU's endeavours bred in large measure by the intransparency of both the intergovernmental conferences and the finally agreed Treaties that carry the labels Maastricht and Amsterdam. Citizens were left bemused about what they were being offered a rare invitation to approve.

Although ambiguity is hugely helpful at many levels of legal drafting in national and, especially, transnational fora, the EU has reached a stage where a failure to make a more ambitious commitment than that offered by periodic intergovernmental conferences yielding ever more labyrinthine Treaties is liable to doom it to regression at the hands of a disgruntled populace. The process of elaborating a constitutional document which would stand apart from the tinkering process of revision of which the Treaty of Amsterdam is the latest instance could serve to identify what is really central to the achievements and objectives of 50 years of European integration. It could make the EU transparent. It would provide more precise standards against which interference with what I might call 'Community fundamentals' rather than the *acquis communautaire* could be judged. This would help in the assessment of the progress of an IGC 'from the outside'. Moreover, it would help to structure an IGC 'from within' and thereby to invest it with a clearer and more intelligible sense of purpose.

Such a document could serve to make clear what the EC and the EU can do and, perhaps equally important, it could make clear what cannot be done and should not be done at European level. It could depict the dynamic relationship between the 'conservatory elements' of the Union, which preserve the position of the member states, and the 'constitutionalizing elements', most prominent among them direct effect and supremacy, which have conferred such vitality on the EC's distinctive institutional and constitutional architecture.[54] At the very least, the attempt to elucidate the very fact that there is and should be such a give-and-take could do much to develop an appreciation of a cooperative and constructive relationship between two different sources of power, that of the member states and that of the EU structure. This, in turn, could begin to nudge deep rooted thinking away from perceived clashes of sovereignty and instead towards the embrace of pluralism. Nothing is more debilitating in the great European debate than the assumption that in so far as the EU acquires competence, it is robbing the member states. There is no light at the end of a tunnel in which the EU is depicted as undermining the power of the states and in which it is judged

---

[54] Dashwood, 'States in the European Union' 23 ELRev (1998) 201, in which the notion of a 'fully-fledged "constitution"' is explicitly rejected (204).

(invariably and inevitably unfavourably) with reference to the extent to which it is state-like in its patterns of democracy, legitimacy and constitutionality. Instead, the ambiguous nature of the EU should not merely be tolerated, but welcomed. The relationship between the states of Europe has been radically refashioned via the EU – for the better. Europe, then, can enjoy 'a two-dimensional configuration of legal authority'[55] in which different legal orders may, judged from the inside looking out, be incapable of reconciling themselves with the constitutional aspirations of the systems sharing their territory, yet which are nonetheless capable of coexistence. The assumptions about sources of legal authority found in EU constitutional principles may be fundamentally different from those found in the member states. Both systems have it right – on their own terms.[56] Seeking to land a knock-out blow on the other is fruitless, because the systems are not in the same ring. And both systems, aware of each other, have little incentive to go to war over their differences. Quite the contrary. They are not opponents. Mutual respect has typically characterized the relationship between the EC and national legal orders, built upon constructive dialogue both of a direct nature, via the Art. 177 preliminary reference procedure, and an indirect nature, as disquiet on either side may be transmitted by appropriately pointed judgments.

I am proposing a constitutional document that would not obstruct the evolution of this dynamic relationship. It would be short and digestible. It would be designed to convey the essential ambitions of the system, as much as its more concrete constitutional and institutional characteristics. This constitutional document would not eliminate the capacity of the member states to act 'above' EU law as masters of the Treaty. That is, I do not propose a constitutional document for a European State. I wish instead to affirm the complementary relationship prevailing between the member states and the EU.

As Sir Hugh Munro knew perfectly well, whether or not we choose to call something a mountain is quite irrelevant to its majesty. The hill is not the product of human endeavour and it will not be limited by our imaginations. Not so the European Union. Teasing notions such as citizenship and subsidiarity convey the message that integration in Europe engages much more than the economic sphere. But they also leave the accurate impression that the constitutional character of the entity remains elusive. The deepening problem is the negative interpretation popularly placed on this imprecision. It is my submission that the preparation of a constitutional document could assist in a positive portrayal of the EU and the member states drawing strength from each other, enjoying mutual reinforcement rather than struggling for hierarchical ascendancy.

---

[55] Walker, note 22 above.
[56] *Cf* MacCormick, 'Beyond the Sovereign State' 56 MLR (1996) 1; Eleftheriadis, 'Aspects of European Constitutionalism' 21 ELRev (1996) 32. See also the Special Issue on Constructing Legal Systems: '"European Union" in Legal Theory', 16/4 Law and Philosophy (1997); Special Issue on Sovereignty, Citizenship, and the European Constitution, 1/3 ELJ (1995).

2

THE IROQUOIS AT THE KIRCHBERG; OR, SOME NAÏVE REMARKS ON THE STATUS AND RELEVANCE OF DIRECT EFFECT

Christine Boch

I MENU

I have been asked to write about the status and relevance of direct effect. What could anyone have to say about direct effect which has not already been said, or which could still be of some interest?

Direct effect as a constitutional principle of the EC legal order, or as a constitutional characteristic of EC law, is no longer disputed. There is no doubt that, on accession, EC law becomes an integral part of the legal systems of the member states which their courts are bound to apply – irrespective of the national constitutional arrangements governing the relationship between international agreements and domestic law:

> the task assigned to the Court under Article 177, the object of which is to secure uniform interpretation of the Treaty by national courts and tribunals, confirms that the States have acknowledged that Community law has an authority which can be invoked by their nationals before their courts or tribunals.[1]

EC law, nowadays, is increasingly invoked by individuals before national courts.[2] Throughout the EC, lawyers are displaying the greatest inventiveness and imagination in bringing their clients' claims within the remit of EC law, thereby contributing to the expansion of the EC legal order.[3] Further, EC

---

[1] Case 26/62 *van Gend en Loos v Nederlandse Administratie der Belastingen* [1963] ECR 1.

[2] To the extent that one can actually talk of the 'paradox of success' J. Weiler: 'The European Court, National Courts and References for Preliminary Rulings – The paradox of success: A revisionist view of Article 177', in *Art. 177: Experiences and Problems*, TMC Asser Instituut, 1987, pp 366–378.

[3] K. Lenaerts, 'Interaction between judges and politicians' (1992) 12 YEL 1 at 11: 'The decision that a provision has direct effect also has the added advantage that it makes the ECJ responsible for fine-tuning the application of the provision in concrete cases which in turn leads to a judge-made gloss on the provision, determining its real content and relevance.'

21

law is invoked for the purpose of doing many different things, *inter alia* to render national law inapplicable,[4] as an aid to interpretation[5] and for the purpose of founding a claim for damages against the member states.[6] It is also recognized that EC law must be applied by national courts. Most original difficulties have been ironed out and the national courts have accepted that they are ordinary courts of EC law;[7] they have accepted their obligation to apply EC law, and that this involves carrying out a variety of tasks, ranging from the straightforward application of a legally perfect provision of EC law to an investigation of sophisticated economic evidence.[8]

Of course, it is tempting to say that direct effect no longer has much relevance since Art. 10 EC and the duty of Community loyalty has taken centre stage in the case law of the European Court, thereby relegating direct effect to a back seat. But I do not succumb to the temptation.

It is not proposed to rehearse, nor even to shed some new light on, what remains the last controversial issue for academics, namely that of the direct effect of directives.[9] There is little with which I could really enlighten you. What I will do, is look at direct effect from a very specific perspective: that of securing compliance with EC obligations. This is a very topical and highly ranked preoccupation for all EC institutions. Equally, in recent years, the member states have made regular calls for improving compliance, from the Declaration on the Implementation of Community law[10] to the Resolution on Effective Penalties;[11] or the new intervention mechanism to safeguard free trade in the Single Market.[12] The member states have even taken practical steps: *inter alia* the revision of Art. 228 and the insertion of new provisions combating fraud against the budget.[13] Even though not all actors in the EU system attach the same importance to compliance, although the meaning of compliance varies,[14] and although the member states may not have the same attachment to compliance in relation to each and every one of their EU

---

[4] Case 152/84 *Marshall v Southampton and South West Hampshire Health Authority* [1986] ECR 723 *(Marshall I)*, and Case C-271/91 *Marshall II* [1993] ECR I-4367.

[5] C-106/89 *Marleasing v La Comercial Internacional de Alimentacion* [1990] ECR I-4135.

[6] Case C-6/90 and C-9/90 *Francovich v Italy* [1991] ECR I-5357.

[7] R. Lecourt 'L'Europe des Juges', Bruxelles Bruylant, 1976.

[8] Thus, direct effect of Art. 90(2) translates as 'the duty of the national court to investigate whether an undertaking which invokes the provisions of Article 90(2), for the purpose of claiming a derogation from the rules of the Treaty has in fact been entrusted with the operation of a service of general economic interest, and if so, whether its conduct is necessary to enable it to perform its task', Cases C-114/95 and C-115/95 *Texaco* [1997] ECR I-4263, para. 46.

[9] For a comprehensive and stimulating overview see S. Prechal, *Directives in European Community Law: A Study on EC Directives and their Enforcement by National Courts*, OUP, 1995.

[10] TEU, Final Act, Part III: Declarations, Declaration No. 19 'Declaration on the Implementation of Community Law'.

[11] *OJ* 1995, C188/1.

[12] COM (97) 619 and Regulation 2679/98 *OJ* 1998 L337/8.

[13] Article 209 EC.

[14] Thus, for some, compliance with directives is secured with black letter implementation whilst the mechanisms for application and enforcement may remain grossly inadequate. On all of these points see Boch: 'Rules to enforce the rules: Subsidiarity v Uniformity in the implementation of the Single European Market Policy', in: *The Evolution of Rules for a Single European*

obligations,[15] a consensus exists with regard to the seriousness of the problem and the need to treat it as a priority. So, the first question is, to what extent does direct effect help to secure compliance in the Community system?

Secondly, from *van Gend en Loos*, the Court has reached out to individuals:

> this Treaty is more than an agreement which merely creates mutual obligations between the contracting States . . . The Community constitutes a new legal order of international law . . . the subjects of which comprise not only the Member States, but also their nationals.

Whether 'Citizenship of the Union' implies a commonality of rights and obligations uniting Union citizens by a common bond transcending member state nationality,[16] or is just high rhetoric, it cannot be denied that, in the last 35 years, efforts have been made to bring the Community, and the Union, closer to its citizens and to give expression to its character as more than a purely economic project. Therefore, the relationships between direct effect and individuals, and the role individuals have to play to secure compliance with Community obligations, will be examined as well.

II   WHY THE TITLE?

Since an anniversary is an occasion for celebration and enjoyment, the status and relevance of direct effect will be looked at with the eyes of a *bon sauvage*. It is not to Rousseau, however, but to Rivero that credit for this approach goes. Rivero wrote 'Le Huron au Palais-Royal ou réflexions naïves sur le Recours Pour Excés de Pouvoir'.[17] Rivero's article describes, in the most naïve, extremely humorous but still very serious tone – a style which should appeal to British pragmatism – the main weaknesses and pitfalls of judicial review of administrative acts. The tone adopted by Rivero's *bon sauvage*, the many references he made to what common sense dictates, are reminiscent of what one learns about useful effect, the need to make rules operative, the 'infant disease'.[18] If member states have agreed obligations, and set up an institutional structure to make common rules, it would be unfortunate if the necessary conditions for the system to work well and be operative were not in place.

Market, Part II: Rules Democracy and the Environment Mayes (ed.) Office for Official Publications of the European Communities, Luxembourg, 1995, 1.

[15] Witness the difficulties surrounding the adoption of the Directive on the burden of proof in cases of discrimination based on sex, Directive 97/80 EC *OJ* 1998, L14/6, directive for which a proposal was first submitted to the Council in May 1988 COM(88) 269.

[16] Case C-274/96 *Criminal proceedings against H.O. Bickel*, opinion of A.G. Jacobs, para. 23.

[17] J. Rivero, *Dalloz Chronique*, 1962, 36–40. The title has been adapted. First, during that part of the six years war fought in Canadian territory, the Iroquois supported the English whilst the Hurons sided with the French; le Palais Royal is the seat of the Conseil d'Etat whilst the Kirchberg is the seat of the ECG.

[18] Pescatore 'The Doctrine of Direct Effect an Infant Disease of Community Law' (1983) 8 ELR 155.

The other reason why it was thought appropriate to draw a parallel with Rivero's piece is that both the *Recours pour Excés de Pouvoir* and direct effect can be seen as instruments to secure protection of individuals against the arbitrariness of power. My first naïve remark is that direct effect would not be necessary if member states were complying with their EC obligations. It is the member states' inertia and/or resistance, because of non-compliance, because of a pathological situation, that instruments and techniques are needed. It is because of non-compliance, that some mechanism to ensure compliance with Treaty obligations becomes vital. If member states agree to dismantle barriers to trade between them, then they should do so, and not re-erect them. From this perspective, direct effect appears to be a tool destined to secure compliance, compliance with obligations willingly undertaken.[19]

The European project is about a lot more than free trade, or mere economic integration. It is a grand project, animated by the ideals of peace, prosperity and supranationality;[20] designed to bring about benefits for individuals. It is a new project: one for the benefit of the people. The people are part of the project,[21] another compelling reason to create the necessary conditions for this project to work. Creating the conditions for the project to work is tantamount to ensuring that individuals will not be deprived of the benefits which the project is meant to bring about. Thus, through direct effect, individuals secure their rights not to be deprived of the benefits the project is designed to deliver. In this way, direct effect can, naïvely, be seen as providing not only mere protection of individual rights, but as the mechanism that enables individuals to ensure the good functioning of the system. In other words, direct effect – alongside being a technique, or a means available to ensure that individuals are not deprived of specific individual rights – provides the mechanism through which individuals acquire a right to protection against member states before domestic courts for violations of Community law.

It has been said that judges in the ECJ were inspired by 'a certain vision of their own'.[22] This expression has sometimes been associated with disparaging comments about the ECJ, but should not be. Quite the reverse; it seems that no other vision could have been had. Who would not share this vision? Who would have resisted creating the necessary conditions to ensure that the system will be operative so as to deliver the benefits it was meant to bring about?

---

[19] What is really naïve about this perspective, is to regard all EU obligations as willingly undertaken. These points are however outwith the remit of this paper; see Weiler, 'The White Paper and the Application of Community Law' in Bieber and Others *1992: One European Market?* at 347 for a discussion of the case law of the Court as a source of law and obligations.

[20] Weiler: 'Fin de siècle Europe' in R. Dehousse (ed.), LBE, 1994, 203–215.

[21] Although politicians learnt on the occasions of the Danish (1st) and French referenda on Maastricht that the people are not always aware of all the benefits that accrue from integration.

[22] *Une certaine idée de l'Europe*, Pescatore *op. cit.* at 157.

III DUAL VIGILANCE REVISITED

It will be remembered that in the observations presented in *van Gend en Loos*, member states argued that failure to comply with Community obligations could only be ascertained in the context of the infringement proceedings provided for under the Treaty. Further, as the Advocate General pointed out, under Art. 234 the Court jurisdiction was limited to the interpretation of the Treaty and did not extend to its application. The Court disagreed:

> The vigilance of individuals concerned to protect their rights amounts to an effective supervision in addition to the supervision entrusted by Article 169 and 170 to the diligence of the Commission and of the Member States.[23]

The mere fact that the Treaty provided for means of redress did not preclude, or exclude, the possibility that individuals too had a role to play. Thus, two channels to secure compliance were created.

The public[24] (Art. 226) and private (Art. 234) systems of enforcement are also commonly referred to as centralized and decentralized systems of enforcement. I propose to revisit this 'dual vigilance' from two perspectives: those of effectiveness and complementarity. I propose to do so by looking at the respective merits and shortcomings of both systems 35 years on from *van Gend en Loos*. Despite lack of empirical research on the issue, we have learnt a few things about their respective weaknesses and advantages. Generally, what we read about the many deficiencies of the Art. 226 procedure might lead us naïvely to believe that perhaps we do not need dual vigilance any more. However, some of what we learned does not really stand up to scrutiny and hence might be of little use. Other findings though could be used perhaps to try and work out some formulae or strategies to ensure that Arts 226 and 234 work as complementary mechanisms.

Complementarity

What exactly is the meaning of dual vigilance?[25] Do individuals and the Commission do the same things, or do they do different things?

The questions need to be asked, not to suggest that a parallel may be drawn between Arts 226 and 234 procedures, given that, as is well-known, 'the two proceedings have different objects, aims and effects',[26] but because

---

[23] Case 26/62 *van Gend en Loos* v *Nederlandse Administratie der Belastingen op. cit.*; *Emerald Meats* [1993] ECR I-209, para. 40.

[24] The other specific enforcement procedures provided for under the Treaty, such as Art. 93(2) will not be discussed here.

[25] Member states too, by virtue of Art. 227, have an opportunity to redress breaches of EU law. However, they will be left out as they did not have much recourse to it: Case 141/78 *France v UK* [1979] ECR 2923. Instead, and although unilateral adoption or corrective or protective measures designed to obviate breaches of the Treaty is not allowed, member states occasionally feel like taking the law into their own hands, e.g. the decision to police Spanish slaughter houses Case C-5/94 *R v MAAF, ex parte H. Lomas* [1996] ECR I-2553.

[26] Case 28/67 *Molkerei-Zentrale Westfalen/Lippe GmbH* v *Hauptzollamt Paderborn* [1968] ECR 143.

it might, naïvely, be thought that through the coexistence of both systems, one could cast the net wider and correct more situations where the member states are failing to comply with their Community obligations. Indeed, while both actions are not mutually exclusive,[27] one might assume that, to be meaningful and effective, dual vigilance would mean that the surveillance mission would differ, in the sense that a division of labour would exist, and that there would be some degree of specialization.

However, it is one thing to hope for some specialization, and even complementarity, and another for such complementarity to exist. Could there be such complementarity, and to what extent could such complementarity be achieved? Is there any evidence of decentralized enforcement coming into play as a means to secure compliance or point to cases of non-compliance in instances where the centralized system might fail or vice versa? Is it the case that we have complementary mechanisms?

Casting the net wider

Does private enforcement allow detection of problems or situations of non-compliance which the Commission could or would never have been able to detect?

A naïve remark: for the Commission to take action, it has to be aware that action needs to be taken. The Commission will only take action if it is aware that some deficiency exists. Given that not every case of non-compliance is a blatant breach of EC obligations, that in many areas the Commission does not possess any powers of inspection, and that it is under-staffed and under-resourced, how does the Commission operate? It acts principally upon complaints from individuals.[28] This dependency on complaints is often criticized.[29] However, one could adopt a naïve perspective and ask: why are individuals bringing complaints to the Commission rather than to their national courts? Are they not aware that they can bring complaints before their national courts? Dependence on complaints therefore is not so much a weakness of Art. 226 as an indicator that, in a number of instances, redress in the national courts is problematic. Individuals may be unable to get access to the judicial process, or it may be the case that no remedy is available from the national court. Access to judicial process is threatened, either through a finding of lack of title and interest,[30] or because a limitation period has expired, or the

---

[27] As the coexistence of Articles 226 and 234 actions before the Court has demonstrated: e.g. Case C-221/89 *R v Secretary of State for Transport, ex parte Factortame* [1991] ECR I-3905 and Case C-246/89 *Commission v UK* [1991] ECR I-4585; but also Case C-288/89, *Gouda* [1991] ECR I-3905 and Case C-288/89 *Commission v Netherlands* [1991] ECR I-000; *R v Pharmaceutical Society* [1987] 3 CMLR 951.

[28] 13th Annual Report on the implementation of EU law COM(96) 600.

[29] Since *inter alia* individuals do not necessarily bring to the attention of the Commission those violations of EU law which have some 'Community interest'.

[30] Typically, in the field of environmental law where disputes focus on the threat to collective goods, in those member states where *locus standi* concepts are too restricted, the objective treaty violation procedure is often the only door open, Winter: 'Inspecting the Inspectors' (1996) 33 CML Rev, 689–717.

form of process is held incompetent, or a plea of no jurisdiction is sustained, or the decision sought to be challenged does not fall within the category of reviewable acts. In short, for a variety of reasons, vigilance by individuals has its limits and even on occasion just fails. Complaints go to the Commission because individuals are unable to secure compliance with Community law at national level.[31] Happily, public enforcement is there to relay private enforcement. Article 226 allows treatment of non-compliance situations which cannot be effectively dealt with by the decentralized system.[32]

On the other hand, reflecting on some unsuccessful Art. 226 actions,[33] the Commission has pointed out that some infringements would be more effectively dealt with at national level, as they involve points of facts the existence and definition of which were difficult for the Commission to establish, but might be more easily established at national level. However, it also conceded that, at present, such cases are often denied access to national courts, the complainant being unable to prove an interest. Accordingly, the Commission confirmed the need for national procedures in relation to public complaints. One may be drawn to the naïve conclusion that situations exist where even dual vigilance does not suffice to secure compliance.[34]

Another serious weakness of the Art. 226 procedure stems from the various problems associated with the Commission's discretion to bring proceedings. That such decisions to commence or not to commence proceedings will often be influenced by political considerations has been well documented,[35] and it is not disputed that limits should be placed on such discretion[36] to avoid the procedure turning into an arbitrary exercise of power. Yet, the fact that the Commission acts with full discretion can also attract the following naïve comment. The Commission's discretion could be used to further a strategy: the Commission might consider, wherever possible, concentrating on these areas where compliance with EC law may not be secured through private enforcement. It is suggested that the Commission definition of what comes under the 'Community interest' might take account of the lack of opportunities for redress at national level.

---

[31] COM (96) 600 *op. cit.* at 84.

[32] Witness also the new intervention mechanisms to safeguard free trade.

[33] In the environmental law field, COM (98) 317, 15th Annual report on the application of Community law at 76.

[34] And indeed the Commission itself acknowledges the need for initiatives in the field of enforcement mechanisms, ibid.

[35] Weiler: 'The Community system: the dual character of supranationalism' (1981) 1 YEL 267 at 299; Craig: 'Once upon a time in the West: Direct Effect and the federalisation of EEC law' (1992) 12 OJLS 453 at 456; R. Williams 'The European Commission and the Enforcement of Environmental law, an invidious position' (1994) 14 YEL 351 at 359; A.C. Evans: 'The enforcement procedure of Article 169 EEC: Commission's discretion' (1979) 4 ELR 449.

[36] The Ombudsman in its own initiative inquiry on the Newbury bypass concluded that there was a general need to review the position of complainants in Art. 226 proceedings, OJ 1997, C272/32, the CFI, is placing some limits: Case T-105/95 *WWF UK v Commission* [1997] II-313; also see P. Kunzlink: 'The enforcement of EU Environmental law: Article 169, the Ombudsman and the Parliament' (1995) EELR 336; and also R. Mastroianni: 'the enforcement procedure under Article 169 of the EC treaty and the powers of the European Commission: Quis Costodiet Custodes?' (1995)1 European public law 535.

Different functions?

Is it the case that, through decentralized enforcement, issues come before the European Court which would or could have never come before it via the Commission? It has been argued that the systematic expansion of the private enforcement function avoided many of the problems which would have arisen in legitimating the expansion of the EC legal order if public enforcement had been heavily relied upon. Public enforcement of EC law would have stressed the political dimension to the debate over the interpretation and scope of the new order, so directly exposing conflicts of perspective and interest between different institutional actors. Private enforcement, on the other hand, reduced the expansion of the new legal order to a series of legalistic disputes turning upon private rights and interests and backed by the venerable authority of the national courts.[37] Certainly, such cases as *Cassis de Dijon*,[38] and *Reyners*[39] tend to confirm this view. *Cassis de Dijon*, typically, is presented as a dispute concerning private rights and interests to trade; it is rarely described[40] as raising fundamental constitutional issues about which legal basis (Arts 28 or 94[41]) should have been used to address these fundamental regulatory issues. It can further be said, that via private enforcement, the Court has been given an opportunity to influence the course of the integration process in a way which perhaps would not have been possible with public enforcement[42] alone.

More on the effectiveness of dual vigilance

The effectiveness or lack of effectiveness of the Commission's supervisory function and the ability of the Commission to monitor the implementation of Community law depends on how much there is to monitor. Clearly, as the EU engages in more activities, the body of Community law expands, and so the more there is to monitor. Given that the Commission is under-staffed and under-resourced, the more the need therefore to rely on decentralized enforcement.

Litigation is a minor part, the 'last resort' in the Commission's role under Art. 226. As is well documented, Art. 226 is a process of negotiation and settlement of differences, and a system of cooperative contacts,[43] and only a fraction of

---

[37] Craig *op. cit.*, Walker N. [1996] PL 266–290 at 276.

[38] Case 120/78 *Rewe-Zentrale v Bundesmonopolverwaltung für Branntwein* [1979] ECR 649.

[39] Case 2/74 *Reyners v Belgium* [1974] ECR 631.

[40] For a dissident view Joerges: 'European Economic law – The Nation State and the Maastricht Treaty in Dehousse (ed.) *op. cit.* 29–56.

[41] As was argued in *Cassis* itself.

[42] Reference is made here to the debate on positive and negative integration and to the role of the Court in promoting negative integration, equivalence, mutual recognition and the new approach to harmonization. The role played by the ECJ in promoting negative integration is outwith the remit of this paper. It is well documented in *inter alia* A. Easson: 'Legal Approaches to European Integration: the role of the ECJ and Legislator in the completion of the SEM'; D. Berlin: 'Interactions between the law-maker and the judiciary within the EC' LIEI 1992/2 17–48; McGee and Weatherill: 'The evolution of the single market – harmonisation or liberalisation', (1990) 53 MLR 578–590.

[43] F. Snyder 'The effectiveness of European Community law' (1993) 56 MLR 19 at 30, A. Dashwood and R. White (1989) 14 ELR 338. Evans *op. cit.*

28

infringement procedures results in a Court judgment. This political dialogue between the Commission and the member states, and the political management of the control of the application of EC law, may in effect lead to a renegotiation of the nature and extent of the EC obligations between the Commission and the member states. This state of affairs leaves much to be desired in terms of accountability and transparency, and to this extent private enforcement appears more desirable, since a court of law is involved. That a court's involvement in the arbitration between competing interests is sufficient to redeem the democratic deficit may seem a naïve view. And of course courts may not be the ideal forum.[44] It may sound equally naïve to suggest that policy decisions are better taken in the judicial arena, rather than by the legislator. This is not what is suggested, given that in the administrative phase the settlement takes place outside the decision-making process framework agreed under the Treaty.[45] What is suggested is merely that courts might be better placed than the Commission to rule on the reasonableness or otherwise of member states' action or lack thereof (the better of two evils). Indeed, courts seem less vulnerable to the various types of pressure[46] to which the Commission is subject.

The other value of dual vigilance, the other advantage of having a decentralized enforcement system alongside the public enforcement mechanism, is that private enforcement has a legitimacy of its own as it can be assimilated to a 'social ordering in which individuals are involved in their own capacity'.[47] One may wonder how and to what extent litigation can be seen as a way to achieve social engineering. There are few studies about who goes before national courts in the EU, but by and large, only a limited category of litigants has the resources and energy to resort to litigation. Throughout the EU, impairments to litigation are built into and around the judicial system which, in different ways, all have the capacity to weed out all but the strong and hardy complainant. Certainly, the few studies relating to those cases before national courts which came to the ECJ via Art. 234[48] tend to show that so far it is mostly for wealthy or well-backed[49] players that the potential of litigation at European level is significant. This in turn carries the risk that the haphazard development of EC law which takes place in the enforcement process is rather one-sided.[50] And, as has been shown,[51] litigation

[44] The shortcomings of litigation as a means of social engineering are explored below.

[45] Although the Commission may act as an initiator of legislation, it is not acting qua a legislative organ when it discharges its monitoring function.

[46] Stemming from the inherent conflict between the Commission's dual role as initiator of legislation and guardian of the Treaty.

[47] Craig *op. cit.*, Walker *op. cit.*

[48] C. Harlow (1992) 12 YEL 213–248; C. Harding 'Who goes to court in Europe? An analysis of litigation against the European Community' (1992) 17 ELR 105–125.

[49] See the role of Maitre Vogel-Polski in the *Defrenne* litigations, or that of the EOC in the two *Marshall* sagas.

[50] See the discussion of the standard of protection of 'diffuse interests' in the EU in Weatherill: 'Compulsory Notification of Draft Technical Regulations: The Contribution of Directive 83/189 to the Management of the Internal Market' (1996) 16 YEL 129 at 197–201.

[51] Micktliz: 'The interest in Public Interest Litigation in European Courts' Micklitz and Reich (eds) Nomos Verl. Baden Baden, 1996.

so far resembles organized law enforcement more than public interest litigation. This is particularly so given that under the Art. 234 procedure, title and interest is dependent entirely on the requirements defined under national law. These requirements, for the most, favour personal, individual rights.

Public interest litigation or organized law enforcement?

Economic actors have successfully instrumentalized EC law through the Art. 234 procedure to foster the development of a Common, now Internal, Market. In the pursuit of their own special interests, economic actors have contributed to the establishment of common rules governing the market. The four freedoms translated not only into rights to trade, but also into rights to open up markets. Landmark decisions by the European Court in this field have been taken in the course of proceedings which have been described as organized law enforcement.[52] These rulings are the results of a strategic use of EC law to eradicate national rules; not only those which affect transborder trade, but also those which generally are perceived as unnecessarily curtailing commercial freedom.[53] However, one observes some changes,[54] as other actors[55] are discovering the potential for action offered by Community law.

Lack of *effet utile* of direct effect[56]

Before concluding on the assessment of dual vigilance, the fact that both systems have matured and undergone transformation must be acknowledged. Taking stock of the changes in the two systems in the last 35 years, the superiority of private enforcement might not be so blatant.

National courts decide on the ways to give effect to direct effect. The sanctions for breach of EC law are dependent on national courts, which must follow national rules. These national rules were not designed for the purpose of enforcing EC law and have proved, on occasion, ill-suited to the task. In cases where national procedural rules or substantive rules governing the remedy were challenged, the ECJ, at the request of national courts, has influenced the working of national judicial systems. This impact has been quite real, at all stages of the judicial process, from access to the domestic

---

[52] Micktliz ibid. at 29.

[53] E.g. the Sunday trading saga above.

[54] Case C470/93 *Vereingegen Unwesen in Handel und Gewerbe v Mars* [1995] ECR I-1923, and Reich: 'Public Interest litigation before European jurisdictions' in Mickliz and Reich (eds) *op. cit.* at 9. Case C-34/95 *Konsumentombudsmannen (KO) v De Agostini (Svenska) Förlag AB* [1997] ECR I-3843.

[55] Certainly in the UK the EOC is aware of this potential and has developed a clear and well organized litigation strategy. L. Fletcher: 'Enforcement of Community Sex Equality Law' in Hervey and O'Keeffe (eds) *Sex Equality Law in the European Union*, Wiley, 1996, 173–178.

[56] J. Mertens de Wilmar: 'l'efficacité des différentes techniques nationales de protection juridique contre les violations du droit communautaire par les autorités nationales et les particuliers' in 1981, Cahiers de Droit Européen (CDE) 17, 379.

courts to the final outcome of the litigation.[57] However, in the regrettable absence of harmonizing EC provisions, the ECJ can only ensure an adequate standard of judicial protection on a case by case basis. Such an approach is evidently haphazard, dependent on the financial resources and tenacity of the litigants and the willingness of national courts to cooperate.

Another weakness of the centralized system was that judgments declaring member states in breach of their EC obligations were all too often ignored. However, the reform of, and actual reliance on, the new sanction mechanisms under the amended Art. 228 are starting to show their effects.[58] Private enforcement, on the other hand, had previously equipped itself with a powerful instrument: the possibility of claims for damages brought by individuals. But this new EC remedy remains as yet undeveloped and much of its consequences for the different types of EC obligations are unclear. Given that one of the conditions is that the provision was intended to confer rights on individuals, it is dependent on the approach to the concept of individuals' rights.[59] Furthermore, its significance in practice,[60] is dependent on national courts: *inter alia* causation, questions regarding limitation periods, mitigation of loss will be assessed in accordance with the domestic rules on liability.[61] More importantly for the sake of this argument, an action in damages against the state will, in a number of instances, be a poor alternative to the direct and immediate protection of the Community claim. For example, where a directive imposes obligations on individuals, in which case by definition, the state is not the proper defendant, the plaintiff would effectively be required to bring two separate sets of legal proceedings, either simultaneously or successively, one against the private defendant and the other against the public authorities.[62]

IV PROTECTION REVISITED

Dual vigilance tells us who can be regarded as having an interest in member states complying with their Community obligations. Clearly, the Commission, as guardian of the Treaty, has an interest in member states complying with their Community obligations. In bringing administrative proceedings, the Commission need not show the existence of a specific legal interest since:

---

[57] Lonbay and Biondi (eds) *Remedies for Breach of EC Law*, Chichester, Wiley, 1997.

[58] COM (98) 317 at I.

[59] See below at page 32–36, also see J. Jans, *European Environmental Law*, Kluwer, 1995, 187–189.

[60] So far C. Harlow's prediction of 'an illusion of remedy' in 'Francovich and the Problem of the Disobedient State' (1996) 2 ELJ 199 at 222 seems accurate, and certainly was for Andrea Francovich.

[61] Provided that these conditions laid down by national law are not less favourable than those relating to similar domestic claims and must not be such as in practice make it impossible or excessively difficult to obtain reparation Case C-46/93 and 48/93, [1996] ECR I-1029 para. 67.

[62] Advocate General Jacobs at point 33 of his opinion in C-316/93 in *Vaneetveld v SA le Foyer* [1994] ECR I-763; Tridimas 'Horizontal Effect of Directives: A Missed Opportunity?' (1994) 19 ELR 621 at 633–635.

> The Commission, in the exercise of the powers which it has under Articles 155 and 169 of the Treaty does not have to show the existence of a legal interest, since, in the general interest of the Community, its function is to ensure that the provisions of the Treaty are applied by the Member States and to note the existence of any failure to fulfil the obligations deriving therefrom, with a view to bringing it to an end.[63]

This, however, does not, in itself, suffice to preclude or exclude the idea that individuals too should be recognized as having such an interest.[64] It is proposed that the true meaning and significance of dual vigilance should be an acceptance that individuals too have such an interest. It is suggested that individuals be regarded as guardians of the Community interest, in so far as overseeing actions by member states, ensuring that member states comply with their Community obligations and fulfil their duties, in turn guarantees that individuals are not deprived of the benefits that would accrue to them if member states complied with their Community obligations. In other words, private enforcement of Community obligations in the different member states and appropriate sanctions for breach of Community law are in the interests of individuals and companies, for they ought not to be deprived of the benefits which integration is meant to bring.

> The fact that under Article 12 it is the Member States who are made subject of the negative obligation does not imply that their nationals cannot benefit from this obligation.[65]

The extent to which individuals, like the Commission, are guardians of the EU public interest, are entitled to promote the EU public interest and have an interest in securing the benefits of integration, will therefore be examined. Beforehand, the relationship between direct effect and individual rights will be revisited.

V.1 PROTECTION OF INDIVIDUAL RIGHTS

In the 35 years since *van Gend en Loos* Community law has been accepted as an integral part of the legal systems of the member states. Belonging to the EU means accepting that the whole of Community law is incorporated into national law and available in legal proceedings before national courts. Individuals have been bringing claims before national courts so as to secure compliance by member states with many of their Community obligations. It is no longer disputed that EC law may be invoked before national courts – what was referred to as direct effect as a constitutional principle.[66] What remains a matter of some contention and difficulty is what litigants are entitled to expect from national courts. This problem is often couched in

---

[63] Case 167/73 *Commission v France* [1974] ECR 359 para. 15.
[64] See above.
[65] *van Gend en Loos.*
[66] See above.

terms of the qualities or characteristics of the EC law provisions invoked. The literature often contains references to concepts such as **horizontal** and **vertical** direct effect.[67] Nevertheless, it is contended that these issues and this nomenclature can often detract from an understanding of this area of law which, put naïvely, involves consideration of the different duties imposed on national judges. And, if the language of rights must be used, then it is suggested that the various duties imposed on national judges correspond to rights for individuals.

It seems essential now to make a number of remarks on the use of terminology. In an EU sufficiently sophisticated to make clear and precise distinctions between day-old chicks, breeding poultry, productive poultry and slaughter poultry,[68] some clear and precise distinctions should also be made in relation to basic and important concepts governing the relationship between EC and national law, or relating to the effects to be attached to a particular EC law provision in the national legal systems. In this respect, one can only observe that direct effect has a variety of confusing meanings.[69] To begin with, it refers to the fact that EC law is part of the national legal systems and can be invoked before national courts.[70] As daily practice suggests, EC law is invoked for a variety of purposes. However, direct effect is also used to refer to the capacity of a specific EC provision to be applied directly,[71] as it stands. In practice, few EC obligations translate into legally perfect provisions, and accordingly, national courts have to seek guidance as to the exact scope and significance of the EC provision invoked. Moreover, direct effect seems to be one of the judicial techniques available to give effect to rights[72] contained in an EC provision, rights which may be protected by other means, namely through the interpretative duty or state liability for breach of EU law. Finally, direct effect is also used to refer to the capacity of an EC provision to confer rights upon which individuals may rely. This last meaning is by far the most perplexing and is a loaded one. It is confusing, given that on occasion the conferral of individual rights is a condition for direct effect,[73] whereas in other instances the two are completely divorced.[74] It is also tricky given that direct effect is sometimes a means by which existing rights can be effectuated

---

[67] Terms which have not been approved by the European Court.

[68] D. Curtin and K. Mortelmans, 'Application and Enforcement of Community Law by the Member States: Actors in search of a third generation scenario' in D. Curtin and T. Heukels (eds) *The Institutional Dynamics of European Integration*.

[69] Notably in relation to enforcement of directives, Steiner: 'Direct Applicability in EEC law – A Chameleon Concept' (1982) LQR 229.

[70] J. Usher, *European Community Law and National Law: the Irreversible Transfer?* London, Allen & Unwin, 1981.

[71] But not J. Winter: 'Direct Effect and Direct Applicability: Two Distinct and Different Concepts in Community Law' (1972) 9 CMLRev 425.

[72] J. Steiner, 'From Direct Effects to Francovich: Shifting Means of Enforcement of Community Law' (1993) 18 ELRev. 3. J. Coppel, 'Rights, Duties, and the end of Marshall' (1994) 57 MLR 859.

[73] Case C-236/92 *Comitato di Coordinamento per la Difensa della Cava v Regione Lombardia* [1994] ECR I-483.

[74] Case C-6/90 and C-9/90 *Francovich v Italy* [1991] ECR I-5357.

and sometimes the medium through which rights are created. It is loaded because in the context of directives, even where a provision is capable of creating a right, that right cannot be effectuated[75] if the defendant is a private party.[76] The idea that, in a 'Community governed by the rule of law',[77] the outcome of litigation is determined by the identity of the defendant is puzzling.

In *van Gend en Loos*, reference is made for the first time to 'individuals concerned to protect their rights':[78]

> the objective of the EEC Treaty which is to establish a Common market, the functioning of which is of direct concern to interested parties in the Community, implies that this Treaty is more than an agreement which merely creates mutual obligations between the contracting States.[79]

When are individuals concerned? Who are these interested parties? What are those rights? When do EU rights arise?

> These rights arise not only where they are expressly granted by the Treaty, but also by reason of obligations which the Treaty imposes in a clearly defined way upon individuals as well as upon the Member states and upon the institutions of the Community.[80]

Questions as to whether and under which circumstances someone has a right under EC law are often answered by reference to the characteristics the EC provision relied upon should present.[81] Such an approach no longer appears helpful. It has nothing but limits, since, as is well known, most EC provisions lack specificity, be it the Treaty, a *'traité cadre'* which for the most part required further action, or directives which merely lay down an obligation of result.[82] The requirements of clarity, precision and unconditionality, given the essence and nature of most EC obligations, will have to be somewhat relaxed[83] and reinterpreted, since otherwise they would never be capable of being satisfied. A decision that EC obligation be enforced via private action, i.e. the decision that a provision produces direct effect, rather than referring to the intrinsic qualities of a particular provision, is in fact a policy

---

[75] Although it may be protected by other means. Case C-91/92 *Faccini Dori v Recreb srl* [1994] ECR I-3325 paras 26 & 27; C-334/92 *W Miret v Fondo de Garantia Salarial* [1993] ECR I-6911 Case C-192/94 *El Cortes Inglés SA v C Blázquez Rivero* [1996] ECR I-1281. However these various techniques of judicial protection are not of equivalent efficacy; *op. cit.*

[76] Although, to add to the confusion, private parties may have obligations imposed upon them, albeit indirectly, via the interpretative obligation Case C-129/94 *Criminal proceedings against Rafael Ruiz Bernaldez* [1996] ECR I-1829, C-32/93 *Webb v EMO Air Cargo (UK)Ltd* [1994] ECR I-3567.

[77] Case 294/83 *Les Verts v European Parliament* [1986] ECR 1339.

[78] Which is also the first case where the ECJ was called upon to examine the relationship between Community law and national law.

[79] *van Gend en Loos.*

[80] Ibid.

[81] Clarity, precision, unconditionality.

[82] Article 249 EC.

[83] For a study of the relaxation of the conditions see *inter alia* Craig *op. cit.*

decision[84] justified by the need to ensure that member states comply with EC obligations.[85] It follows that:

> direct effect appears to be in a way *l'art du possible*, as from the point of view of Community law it is to be expected that national courts are willing to carry the operation of the rules of Community law up to the limits of what appears to be feasible considering the nature of their judicial function.[86]

That direct effect is a very subjective concept is confirmed by *van Gend en Loos* itself, the Court and Advocate General Roemer reaching opposite conclusions in this respect with regard to Art. 25. Further, as the case law on Art. 25, and that on the relationship between Arts 25, 87, and 90 suggests, the Court of Justice continues to clarify and define, as is necessary, the meaning and scope of the prohibition contained in Art. 25 'as it ought to have been understood and applied from the time of its coming into force'. The conditions for direct effect are essentially matters for interpretation, which in turn explains why the question of whether a provision fulfils these requirements is exclusively a matter for the ECJ. As is well known, the criteria for direct effect have not been adhered to strictly. Thus, reference in the Treaty to implementing measures is no bar to the recognition of a certain degree of direct effect, as the case law on the direct effects of Arts 43 and 59[87] illustrates. Key Treaty articles, although basic principles designed to guide the member states, and/or the EU institutions, although intended to further implementation, have been translated into rights. Equally, and consistently with the approach in national administrative law, the existence of a discretionary power does not *per se* preclude the possibility of judicial control.[88] However, it is difficult to ascertain the frontier between conditions that prevent and do not prevent direct effect, because this is dependent on the willingness of the ECJ to set out the parameters for the operation of the conditions giving rise to judicial control.[89] The decision that an obligation is or not defined in a clearly defined way is not always readily understandable.[90] Given that the principles that guide the Court are not so apparent, its activity

---

[84] S. Weatherill, *Cases and Material on EC Law* 2nd ed. Blackstone, 1994 at 67.

[85] And the limit on the direct effect of directives is the price to pay for such justification, given that the member state is the party which failed to comply, and not the private defendant, obligations cannot be imposed upon the latter.

[86] Pescatore, *op. cit.* at 177.

[87] See Boch *op. cit.*

[88] See Case 41/74 *van Duyn v. Home Office* [1974] ECR 137; Case 51/76 *Verbond van Nederlandse Ondernmingen v Inspecteur der Invoerrechten en Accinjnzen* [1977] ECR 113; Case 38/77 *Enka v Inspecteur der Invoerrechten en Accinjnzen* [1977] ECR 2203; Case C-72/95 *Aanermersbedrijf P.K. Kraaijeveld BV and Gedeputeerde Staten van Zuid-Holland* [1996] ECR I-5403; and C. Boch: 'The enforcement of the EIA Directive: A breach in the Dyke?' (1997) 9, JEL 129.

[89] Weatherill and Beaumont, *EC Law*, London, Penguin, 2nd ed. 1995, at 340.

[90] But on occasion is readily understandable: Case 126/86 *Zaera v Institutio Nationale de la Seguridad Social* where the reference in Art. 2 EEC to the promotion of an accelerated standard of living was held incapable of imposing legal obligations on member states or conferring rights on individuals.

in this field appears to come close to picking and choosing. Thus, in *Comitato di Coordinamento per la Difensa della Cava v Regione Lombardia*[91] denying direct effect to Art. 4 of Directive 75/442, the ECJ held that the provision at issue must be regarded as defining the framework for the action to be taken by the member states regarding the treatment of waste and not as requiring, in itself, the adoption of specific measures or a particular method of waste disposal. It was therefore neither unconditional nor sufficiently precise, and thus not capable of conferring rights on which individuals might rely upon as against the state. Although it cannot be disputed that this directive does not give a right to the adoption of a particular method of waste disposal, the Court could have decided that, given its clear objective, i.e. the safe disposal of waste, it gave a right to individuals to check whether the particular method of disposal of waste chosen was in conformity with this objective, but it did not. The practical result of such a decision is that individuals are denied the right to ensure that the exercise of the discretion granted by the directive remains within the limits laid down in the directive.[92]

The question is not so much whether an obligation is defined in a clearly defined way, but rather whether or not it is considered to be so.

V.2   PROTECTION OF EU LAW BY INDIVIDUALS

When they join the EU, member states undertake to comply or fulfil a variety of EU obligations. What is proposed is that the questions 'when does some-one have a right under EC law', and 'which of those EC obligations concern individuals' be approached in a different way. If we accept that direct effect enables individuals to secure compliance with EC obligations, then 'whether individuals have a role to play in relation to all EC obligations or only a selection of them, and why', should become the subject of attention. If this proposed approach is followed, we need no longer ask: what kind of rights are we talking about? what sort of rights are we talking about? We no longer need to worry either about such issues as: are EC rights limited to individual rights, or personal rights, or subjective rights? Should the classification of a particular position under national law be abandoned for an EU definition of a subjective right?

The obligations undertaken by member states[93] vary greatly. This is par-ticularly so when one considers the obligation laid down in directives. Some directives require member states to set up procedures, while others impose obligations on member states to provide information to the EU institutions or to notify them of a proposed course of action, such as the introduction of

---

[91] Case C-236/92 [1994] ECR I-483.
[92] In contrast with C-131/88 [1991] ECR I-825; C-361/88 [1991] ECR I-2567; C-59/89 [1991] ECR I-2607 where different consequences are attached to the need not to endanger human health.
[93] Of course obligations are also put on individuals under the Treaty, but these remain outwith the remit of this paper.

new technical regulations. Some directives require member states to grant exemption from VAT, others oblige them to introduce or modify substantive provisions governing legal relationships in the private sphere. To say that EC obligations vary means that when EC claims come before national courts a variety of issues arise, *inter alia* ensuring that member states have set up adequate procedures which offer the guarantees required, or substituting a legally perfect EC provision for a provision of national law, or deciding which effects to attach to the non-respect of an obligation to notify standards or provide the relevant information, or deciding whether the sanctions attached to a failure to comply with a given EC obligation will secure proper compliance with that obligation. In other words, the duties national judges have to carry out vary.

Furthermore, the existence of different types of EC obligations also implies that topics such as to whether or not individuals may be recognized as having an interest in ensuring that member states comply with these different EU obligations will change. If direct effect can be interpreted to mean that individuals are given the right to secure compliance with EC obligations, and if it is about individuals keeping the member states in line, in the same way as judicial review of administrative action keeps the executive under proper control, then questions regarding title and interest must be approached differently. The primary focus of judicial review is not private law rights, but rather public law wrongs:

> Public law is not at base about rights, even though abuses of power may and often do invade private rights; it is about wrongs – that is to say misuses of public power[94]

In this context it is important to note that individuals are not parties to Art. 226 proceedings. The main purpose of Art. 226 is not to protect an individual who wishes to rely on EC law,[95] but to see that EC obligations are adhered to. Article 234 is not a means of redress available to the parties.[96] Its primary focus is not the protection of individual rights. The main function of Art. 234 is to secure the uniform application and interpretation of EC law, and thus to secure compliance with EC law. The fact that, on occasion, individual rights are protected is only an additional benefit.

What can be asked of the national judge?

To correct the public wrongs committed by the member states, and to force compliance by member states, what are individuals entitled to require the

---

[94] *R v Somerset County Council, ex parte Dixon* 75 P & CR 175, [1997] JPL 1030 per Sedley J.
[95] And the Commission's discretion as to whether or not it acts upon a complaint and initiates proceedings cannot be reviewed at the suit of individuals. Case 247/87 *Star Fruit v Commission* [1989] ECR 291.
[96] Case 283/81 *CILFIT v Ministero della Sanità* [1982] ECR 3415.

national judge to do? In the event that EC obligations are breached by member states which duties does EC law put on national judges? In the event that EC obligations are breached, what is the role of the individual?

Clearly, individuals are entitled to go before their national courts for the purpose of safeguarding their situation when some of their private interests have been affected. But individuals are entitled to do much more. What else are individuals entitled to do? Can they complain about maladministration and secure good administration? Is there a place for public law principles in the EU?

Clearly, EC law can be used in certain circumstances for the purpose of asking a national court to effectuate a private EC right. For example, I am entitled through Directive 76/207 to work until the age of 65, and so I can insist on my employer keeping me until then, or paying me some compensation if he/she decides to dismiss me earlier. But EC law is not only about the creation of these types of 'private' rights. In other instances, the justiciability of directives means that the national court checks whether a particular procedure has been followed and whether it afforded individuals all the guarantees it ought to have offered. The obligations the member states undertook vary; accordingly the 'rights' they may confer vary and so do duties for national judges. Alongside private enforcement of private rights we have private individuals pursuing public law claims, and title and interest should be assessed differently.

The justiciability of some EC obligations could be assimilated to, and approached as, judicial control of discretionary power. Individuals can go before their domestic courts and ask them to check that member states remain within the margin of discretion left by an EC instrument.[97] In the context of directives imposing the introduction of particular procedures, the national judge can verify only whether or not such a procedure exists, whether it is open in all required circumstances, and whether or not it offers the guarantees it ought to afford. Where no procedure has been introduced, the directive is incapable of giving individuals a right to which the judge could give effect, as national judges have no power to make a positive order providing for procedural machinery. Still, the individual has the right to invoke the directive for the purpose of seeking a remedy for the failure to respect procedural obligations. The consequences to be attached by national judges to the non-respect of procedural obligations vary.

The effects of a failure to comply with a notification procedure depends on the nature, aim and intended effect of a notification procedure, all of which are matters for the ECJ, and may alter.[98] In *CIA*, the inapplicability of an obligation of national law, adopted in violation of EU requirements,[99] was

---

[97] Case C-72/95 *Kraaijeveld BV and Gedeputeerde Staten van Zuid-Holland* [1996] ECR I-5403.

[98] Compare Case C-194/94, *CIA Security International v Signalson and Securitel* [1996] ECR I-2201 with Case 380/87 *Enichem base v Commune di Cinisello Balsamo* [1989] ECR 2491 and Case C-226/97 *Lemmens* judgment of 16 June 1997 n.y.r.

[99] Contained in Directive 83/189 laying down a procedure for the provision of information in the field of technical standards and regulations *OJ* 1983, L109/8 amended by directive 94/10 *OJ* 1994, L100/30.

sought and secured.[100] In *CIA*, the ECJ decided to enhance the effectiveness of the notification procedure. It is seen as not merely concerning relationships between, on the one hand, the member state wishing to introduce new technical standards and, on the other, the Commission and the rest of the member states. Since the directive impacts directly on the main actors in the Single Market, namely undertakings, these too must be able to prevent the emergence of new obstacles to trade and must be empowered to take action. As a result of private litigation, the validity of the un-notified specifications is affected. Private enforcement of the EC regime ensures a better level of compliance on the part of member states, a position consistent with dual vigilance. Supervision and application of EC law by member states should not be a matter for the Commission and the member states alone. Individuals too have a role to play in ensuring member states discharge their EC obligations. Thus, on occasion, individuals may acquire an EC right enforceable before national courts in order to obtain annulment or suspension of national rules adopted in breach of a notification procedure. Individuals are able to force compliance with EU obligations. Consequences flow from non-compliance with procedural obligations, and national courts must attach effects to breach of a notification procedure. In *Enichem*, by contrast, the notification procedure being merely intended to inform the Commission, did not make the entry into force of the envisaged rules subject to the Commission's approval. Accordingly it did not grant individuals any right capable of being infringed by a failure to notify. Individuals had no EC right which they could enforce before national courts in order to obtain annulment or suspension of national rules adopted in breach of this notification procedure.[101] It is certainly noteworthy that the measures challenged in *Enichem* were in fact in conformity with another objective of the directive, namely protection of the environment,[102] and so for the purpose of this argument, member states can be seen as in fact complying with their EC obligations, and so the individuals have no role to play.

In the EU we have gone a long way down the line of creating a right for individuals to secure compliance with EC law even where individuals are not directly and individually affected by the violations of EC law. EC law has affected the question of which persons are to be regarded as interested parties by the national legal systems.[103] EC law has had an influence on who should be entitled to question national decisions taken in breach of EC obligations.

The right to rely on the provisions of directive 79/7 is not confined to individuals coming within the scope *rationae personae* of the directive, other persons may have

---

[100] With a practical result for traders: they can sell products, although they do not conform with national technical specifications, since these have not been notified.
[101] The practical result for traders: they could sell **only** products complying with the un-notified measures.
[102] Para. 7 of the judgment.
[103] J. Jans, 'Legal Protection in European Environmental Law' (1993) EELR 151.

a direct interest in ensuring that the principle of non discrimination is respected as regards persons who are protected.[104]

Individuals have, in certain circumstances, been given the right to secure the application of the law to third parties; in other words, in certain circumstances, individuals have been entitled to compel public authorities to act to enforce the law.[105] Individuals have been able to go before their national courts to secure basic standards of good administration.[106] Individuals have been able to ensure that their governments act legally.[107] Individuals are now entitled to go before national courts for the purpose of preempting member states introducing measures liable to compromise the result prescribed in a directive, and perhaps even insisting that a particular course of action be followed. Given that member states are, by virtue of Art. 10, under an obligation to abstain from jeopardizing the achievement of the Community tasks, the adoption of a directive creates an obligation on the member states to refrain from taking measures which would, in due course, diminish the effectiveness of the implementing legislation or be 'measures liable seriously to compromise the result prescribed' by a directive.[108] Individuals can, in a variety of ways, ensure that member states behave in conformity with EC law.

The EU is not just about trading, moving, pursuing one's professional activity or providing services. A number of new policies have been introduced, such as consumer and environmental protection. In these fields, legal protection cannot be evaluated solely from the perspective of personal rights.[109] In relation to these new policies, new approaches to legal protection are required, for these policies too need protection; in these areas too, the obligations undertaken need to be complied with. Given that the EU is also concerned with setting environmental standards and safeguarding a high level of consumer protection,[110] have individuals any role to play in insisting that these interests are safeguarded, and that these standards are observed? Rather than wondering whether, just as we have a right to trade, a right to move around in the EU, a right to a clean environment, attention should focus on whether and to what extent individuals have been able to play a role in relation to the various fields of EU competence. Put naïvely, can

---

[104] Case C-87/90 *A. Verholen e.a. v. Sociale Verzekeringsbank* [1991] ECR I-3757.

[105] Case 158/80 *Butter-Buying Cruises* [1981] ECR 1805 para. 40.

[106] Case 222/84 *Johnston v Chief Constable of the RUC* [1986] ECR 1651; Case 222/86 *UNECTEF v Heylens* [1987] ECR 4097.

[107] *Equal Opportunities Commission v Secretary of State for Employment* [1994] 2 WLR 409.

[108] Case C-129/96 *Inter-Environnement Wallonie ASBL and Région Wallonne* [1997] ECR I-7411.

[109] J. Jans *op. cit.*

[110] Although a new and puzzling distinction seems to have been introduced between obligations undertaken by the EU and obligations undertaken by the member states. In Case C-192/94 *El Cortes Inglés SA v C Blázquez Rivero* [1996] ECR I-1281 para. 20, the ECJ indicated that Art. 129a 'merely assigns an objective to the Community and confers powers on it to that end, **without also laying down any obligation on Member States or individuals**'.

individuals play a role in ensuring compliance with environmental standards via their national courts, or are traders alone, entitled to question national environmental standards that curtail their economic activities? Has the range of circumstances where individuals have been entitled to oppose violations of Community law increased together with the increase in EU competences? Is the role of the individual the same in relation to the different fields of EU policies,[111] and if it is not, what are the reasons and are these objectively justifiable?

The extent to which individuals have been entitled to secure compliance with various types of EU obligations in the different fields of EU intervention seems to vary. The fact that, on occasions, individuals have been denied the opportunity to play a role and have failed to secure compliance with some EU obligations does not preclude continued and mounting pressure from individuals to see that more and more EU obligations are adhered to, provided of course that access to the judicial process can be secured at national level, that national courts are prepared to send references on these issues, and that the ECJ is willing to entertain dialogue in all these new areas. Among the universal aspects of constitutional law which Professor Mitchell discussed in his published work was the function of judicial control of administrative action in maintaining the rule of law[112] in today's world,[113] this observation holds good for the EU.

---

[111] Weatherill *op. cit.* note 84, and above at 40.

[112] 'L'Etat de Droit appears to be a new idealised form of democratic Society which sets up the judge as supreme arbitrator. The citizen brandishes his rights like a machette in an equatorial jungle, and the ultimate regulation of all rights and liberties is more and more in the hands of the judges' N. Questiaux [1995] PL 425.

[113] A.W. Bradley, 'Jurisdictional aspects of judicial review in Scots law', *In Memoriam JDB Mitchell*, London, Sweet and Maxwell, 1983.

3

THE COMMON FOREIGN AND SECURITY POLICY*

Alan Dashwood

I INTRODUCTION

This paper is not about the substance – critics might say the lack of substance – of the European Union's common foreign and security policy,[1] as it has developed, in fits and starts, over the period of some five years since its launching under the Belgian Presidency in November 1993. The only comment I would make is that the difficulties encountered, and the modesty of the successes gained, during this running-in phase should not have come as a surprise; nor, in my opinion, do they justify a gloomy prognosis.

Indeed, I find in the Amsterdam Treaty cause for guarded optimism about the CFSP. The Treaty surely marks the abandonment of the hope, cherished by some of those who insisted on fixing a **rendezvous** for 1996 in Art. N(2) of the TEU, that the three sub-orders of the Union would soon cohere into a single order based on the European Community model. As long as that hope survived, there was no strong incentive to make a success of the CFSP on its own terms. Now Amsterdam has confirmed that the tripartite structure of the Union is set to continue for the foreseeable future. In that context, the agreement to replace the present Title V of the TEU with a new Title containing radically revised provisions, may be taken as signifying a more whole-hearted commitment, at the political level, to creating an effective policy.

The task I have set myself is to examine the revised arrangements under Title V, to see whether they provide an adequate legal and institutional

---

* The bulk of this paper consists of material previously published in the October 1998 issue of *Common Market Law Review*, as part of an article entitled, 'External Relations Provisions of the Amsterdam Treaty'. I am grateful to the publishers of CMLRev, Kluwer Law International, for agreeing to the re-use of the material.
[1] Hereinafter, 'CFSP'.

framework for organizing the CFSP, assuming the political will exists to make the most of the opportunities offered. I shall consider how far those arrangements improve on present ones and try to identify weaknesses that remain. The matters I have selected for attention are these: the scope and objectives of the CFSP; formal and informal CFSP instruments; decision-making; strengthening the CFSP's infrastructure; international legal personality capacity of the Union; and security and defence.

Scope and objectives of the CFSP

The scope and objectives of the CFSP are defined in Art. 11(1) TEU as follows:

> The Union shall define and implement a common foreign and security policy covering all areas of foreign and security policy, the objectives of which shall be:
> — to safeguard the common values, fundamental interests, independence and integrity of the Union in conformity with the principles of the United Nations Charter;
> — to strengthen the security of the Union in all ways;
> — to preserve peace and strengthen international security, in accordance with the principles of the United Nations Charter, as well as the principles of the Helsinki Final Act and the objectives of the Paris Charter, including those on external borders;
> — to promote international cooperation;
> — to develop and consolidate democracy and the rule of law, and respect for human rights and fundamental freedoms.

There are subtle differences as compared with the drafting of the previous Art. J.1.

One difference is that the phrase 'and its Member States' has been dropped from the introductory sentence and from the second indent. The deletion will bring a gain in coherence. When acting within the framework of Title V TEU, the member states do not have an identity separate from the Union.

Another difference is that the present paras (1) and (2) have been combined in a single paragraph. This apparently cosmetic change has a bearing on an issue of some importance. Is the CFSP limited to the traditional forms of diplomatic activity, security tasks and, ultimately, some kind of defence capability? Or does it also cover those aspects of external economic relations which are not within exclusive EU competence, so that the member states retain the possibility of acting, either individually or collectively, under their own powers?

The issue has practical implications. For instance, the Court of Justice has accepted that there is no legal objection to the financing of aid under the Lomé Convention outside the EU budget, through direct national contributions to a European Development Fund.[2] The handling of the aid is organized on the basis of a so-called 'internal agreement', which has the status of

---

[2] See Case C-316/91, *Parliament v Council* [1998] ECR I-625.

an agreement binding the member states in international law. Would it be possible for those arrangements, instead, to be included in an instrument adopted by the Council under Title V of the TEU? More topically, one might ask whether a CFSP instrument could be used to organize the implementation of elements of the WTO package that were concluded pursuant to member state powers. It might, for example, be provided, in a joint action based on Art. 14, that the common position of the EU on the liberalization of services, other than those provided across frontiers or the subject of existing EU legislation, should be adopted under a procedure corresponding to that applicable, under Art. 133 EC, to trade matters.

The drafting of Art. 11 is ambiguous: on the one hand, the CFSP is described in paragraph (1) as 'covering all areas of foreign and security policy', which could hardly be more general; on the other hand, the objectives expressly listed in the present paragraph (2) are broadly political in character (though the vague reference in the fourth indent to promoting international cooperation might, perhaps, stretch to economic matters). The assimilation of the list of objectives into paragraph (1) will strengthen the case for reading them as qualifying the scope of the CFSP. It will be more difficult, in future, to argue convincingly that CFSP instruments may be used to organize external action by the member states in the economic field.[3]

II FORMAL AND INFORMAL CFSP INSTRUMENTS

Turning to the means provided by the TEU for pursuing the objectives of the CFSP, I describe as 'formal' those instruments that have specific legal consequences defined by Title V. Two such kinds of instrument, common positions and joint actions, were created by the TEU, and the Amsterdam Treaty will add a third kind, common strategies.

A preliminary question, which lawyers might be tempted to brush aside, but which my former clients on the Political Committee thought highly pertinent, is why formal acts are necessary at all. The answer, of course, is that foreign policy making within the Council is quite different from the activity at national level, where decisions are taken under the political responsibility of ministers. Decisions of the Council need to engage member states' legal responsibility, so that positions and actions of the Union do not begin to disintegrate as soon as ministers come under political pressure at home.

The price of using formal instruments to make foreign policy is that decisions cannot be reached by simple agreement between officials in foreign ministries. Common positions and joint actions are acts of the Council, which must be adopted either as an 'A' or 'B' point on the agenda of a

---

[3] The writer finds this regrettable. For a contrary view, see the Editorial Comment in 32 CMLRev (1995) at 385. The Council has shown no inclination in practice to adopt the wider interpretation of the CFSP: see Torrent 'Le "quatrième pilier" de l'Union européenne', in Bourgeois, Dewost and Gaiffe (eds), *La Communauté européenne et les accords mixtes*: 49.

meeting or in accordance with the requirements of the written procedure. This caused a good deal of irritation in the early days of the CFSP, among the diplomats accustomed to running European Political Cooperations.

The new Art. 12 is a more highly articulated version of para (3) of the previous Art. J.1 (3). Five means of pursuing the objectives of the CFSP are specifically identified, viz:

— defining the principles of and general guidelines for the common foreign and security policy;
— deciding on common strategies;
— adopting joint actions;
— adopting common positions;
— strengthening systematic cooperation between Member States in the conduct of policy.

Those provisions are further elaborated in the new Arts 13 to 16, which replace the previous Arts J.2 and J.3.

The division of labour in CFSP matters as between the European Council and the Council is spelt out by the new Art. 13. The European Council is to have the role of laying down policy at the general level: according to para. (1) of the Article, it 'shall define the principles of and general guidelines for the common foreign and security policy, including for matters with defence implications'. The Council's role will be to give concrete substance to such policy: according to para. (3), it 'shall take the decisions necessary for defining and implementing the common foreign and security policy on the basis of the general guidelines defined by the European Council' and it 'shall ensure the unity, consistency and effectiveness of action by the Union'.[4]

Under the previous Art. J.3, the Council is required to act on the basis of general guidelines laid down by the European Council only when adopting joint actions. That requirement is now, it seems, to apply to all decisions taken by the Council for the purposes of Title V TEU. The aim is, presumably, to strengthen the coherence of the CFSP; however, it may inhibit the Union's ability to react effectively to changes in the international situation, if decisions always have to be fitted into preexisting guidelines.

Another change will be the introduction of a new category of formal CFSP instruments to be known as 'common strategies'. All we are told as to the function and content of common strategies is that they are 'to be implemented by the Union in areas where the Member States have important interests in common' and that they 'shall set out their objectives, duration and the means to be made available to the Union and the Member States'.[5] To understand the significance of this innovation it is necessary to turn to the new Art. 23(2) which provides for derogations from the general rule that Council decisions for the purposes of the CFSP are taken by unanimity: the

---

[4] Corresponding provisions are found in the previous Art. J.8(2), first subparagraph.
[5] Art. 13(2).

first indent of the paragraph enables the Council to act by a qualified majority 'when adopting joint actions, common positions or taking any other decision **on the basis of a common strategy**'.[6] The primary purpose of establishing a common strategy will thus be to displace the unanimity rule in favour of qualified majority voting[7] in the policy area in question.

Common strategies are to be decided on by the European Council. This is one of several places in the Amsterdam Treaty where, for the first time since it received formal recognition in the Single European Act, the European Council has been endowed with power to take legally binding decisions.[8] That it should be given such power seems constitutionally anomalous. In the first place, the wording of Art. 4 indicates that the function of the European Council is to lay down general political guidelines, not to decide on particular matters. Secondly, the European Council is composed differently from the Council meeting at the level of Heads of State or Government: it has sixteen members, including the Commission President.[9] Can it really have been the intention to give the Commission a veto over common strategies? Thirdly, the European Council has no rules of procedure. Are common strategies to be decided on by unanimity in the sense of the new Art. 23(1) (or of Art. 205(3) EC), or must there be common accord between the sixteen members? How are common strategies to be distinguished from mere declarations of political intention? And how can anyone know when the European Council is quorate? Answers will have to be found to these and similar questions, if politically damaging disputes (incapable, under Title V, of being resolved judicially) are to be avoided.

Two further questions arise in respect of common strategies, this time concerning the role of the Council. According to Art. 13(3), second subparagraph, 'The Council shall recommend common strategies to the European Council and shall implement them, in particular by adopting joint actions and common positions'. The first question is whether the Council has been given a monopoly of the initiative. In other words, may the European Council decide on a common strategy in the absence of a Council recommendation specifically relating to the matter in question? It is submitted that the European Council may so decide, since in Art. 13(2) it is not described as 'acting on a recommendation by the Council'. The second question is prompted by the phrase '**in particular,** by adopting joint actions or common positions'.[10] Is the implication that instruments other than those mentioned may be used to implement common strategies? This, together with the reference to 'any other decision' in Art. 23(2), first indent, could be

---

[6] Emphasis added.

[7] ('QMV').

[8] See also Art. 17(1), first and second subparas. and Art. 23(2), both of which are further considered below, as well as Art. K.12(2).

[9] Ibid.

[10] Emphasis added.

read as an acknowledgement that *sui generis* Council decisions may be adopted for the purposes of the CFSP, just as they may under the EC Treaty.[11]

Turning now to joint actions and common positions, the formal instruments presently known to Title V, these will be left substantially intact, though the Amsterdam Treaty attempts to identify with a little more precision the purposes for which the two kinds of instrument are respectively appropriate.

In the practice of the Council since the entry into force of the TEU, joint actions have been used for matters having an operational aspect: the most notable example is the series of Council Decisions organizing the EU's administration of the town of Mostar in Bosnia-Herzegovina.[12] That practice is reflected in the definition of joint actions provided by the new Art. 14(1), which says they 'shall address specific situations where operational action by the Union is deemed to be required'. Another difference, as compared with the previous Art. J.3, is the new paragraph (4) of Art. 14, according to which, 'The Council may request the Commission to submit to it any appropriate proposals relating to the common foreign and security policy to ensure the implementation of a joint action'. Such a request would activate the duty of cooperation imposed by Art. 3 TEU, as amended. Joint actions may thus be complemented, where appropriate, by decisions taken in the framework of the EC Treaty, without doing violence to the Commission's right of initiative.

Common positions are formal Council acts expressing an agreed point of view. They have been used, in particular, for collectively acknowledging and giving effect to international obligations incumbent on the member states[13] or for defining the general approach and the aims and intentions of the Union in a given international situation.[14] The new Art. 15 says, 'Common positions shall define the approach of the Union to a particular matter of a geographical or thematic nature'. That definition seems unduly constraining. It surely cannot have been intended, for instance, to prevent common positions from being adopted under the two-stage process for imposing economic sanctions, as provided for by Art. 301 EC.[15]

---

[11] See, as to this possibility, Dashwood, 'The Legal Framework of the Common Foreign and Security Policy', in Emiliou and O'Keeffe, *Legal Aspects of Integration in the European Union*: 225, at 227 to 228 and the examples there cited.

[12] See e.g., Council Declaration 95/23/CFSP, *OJ* 1995, L33/1. In practice, the choice of instrument is often a finely balanced one: see, e.g., the joint action associated with the Council's Regulation on dual use goods, which might arguably have been adopted in the form of a common position: Council Declaration 94/942/CFSP, *OJ* 1994, L367/8.

[13] E.g. the obligation to impose economic sanctions pursuant to a UN Security Council Resolution. Since the entry into force of the TEU, the invariable practice has been for the political decision on sanctions to be taken in the form of a common position. This is followed up, where appropriate, by EU measures based on Art. 301.

[14] See, e.g., the common position 95/91/CFSP of 24 March 1995 on Burundi, *OJ* 1995, L72/1.

[15] The possibility of its being 'provided, in a common position . . . for an action by the Community to interrupt or to reduce, in part or completely, economic relations with one or more third countries . . .' is expressly envisaged in Art. 301.

A final point under this heading concerns the longstanding practice, inherited from the days of European Political Cooperation, of issuing purely political statements on behalf of the EU. It was a question, when the TEU entered into force, whether such statements – not in the form of a common position and so not having the legal consequences prescribed by Title V – were still permissible. Common sense suggested that the answer must be 'yes'; and there was textual support for this in Art. J.2(2) which provided, '**Wherever it deems it necessary** the Council shall define a common position'.[16] The implication of the emboldened phrase is that defining such a position is not the only option available to the Council for pursuing the systematic cooperation required by Art. 11(3). Any remaining doubts will be put to rest by the new Art. 12, fifth indent, which refers to 'strengthening systematic cooperation between Member States in the conduct of policy' as a separate means of pursuing the objectives of the CFSP.

III   DECISION-MAKING PROCESS

The Amsterdam Treaty does nothing to adjust the balance between the institutions resulting from the provisions of Title V of the TEU, which is strongly tilted towards the Council. If anything, the predominance of the Council in the decision-making process of the CFSP will be confirmed and strengthened. The Commission will continue to share the right of initiative with the member states,[17] which in practice has meant that proposals are almost invariably formulated and presented by the Presidency. The European Parliament, while it has the right to be consulted by the Presidency on the main aspects and the basic choices of the CFSP and to have its views duly taken into consideration, and while it must be kept regularly informed of developments, remains outside the formal process for deciding on particular actions.[18] Nor is there any provision for the Court of Justice to receive, for the purposes of Title V, even the limited measure of jurisdiction it will enjoy under the new Title VI on police and judicial cooperation in criminal matters.[19]

The main changes to the institutional provisions of Title V will concern the Council's voting rules, to be found in the new Art. 23. In principle, Council decisions will continue to be taken by unanimity, but this is qualified in important ways.

First, Art. 23(1) states explicitly that abstentions by members of the Council present in person or represented will not prevent decisions from being adopted. It will thus be made clear that unanimity means the same here as in Art. 205(3) EC, namely absence of negative votes: the lack of a reference to that provision in the previous Art. J.11(1) has given grounds for arguing that all decisions on CFSP matters require common accord.

[16] Emphasis added.
[17] New Art. 22(1) TEU.
[18] New Art. 21 TEU.
[19] See the new Art. 35 TEU.

Secondly, as a palliative to the unanimity rule, a principle of so-called 'constructive abstention' has been written into the second subparagraph of the new Art. 23(1). By making a formal declaration, a member of the Council may, when abstaining in a vote, avoid being bound by the decision taken, though accepting that it commits the Union. The aim is to induce member states to refrain from preventing the adoption of joint actions or common positions they do not wish to be associated with. Since the option remains of vetoing a decision which is considered positively harmful, the ultimate reassurance of the unanimity rule will be retained. The device seems well suited to building confidence in a new area of common action like the CFSP.

Thirdly, the Council is empowered by Art. 23(2) to act by a qualified majority in two cases. One such (noted above) is where the Council is operating within the four walls of a 'common strategy' laid down by the European Council. The other case is where a decision is taken implementing a joint action or a common position. That is a development of the rule in the previous Art. J.3(2) allowing the Council, when adopting a joint action, to define on an *ad hoc* basis (and by unanimity) those matters which may be decided by QMV. The replacement of this option by an automatically applicable majority voting rule will remove a source of controversy on which much political energy has been fruitlessly expended.

The rules of Art. 23(2) on QMV are subject to two exceptions.

One of these relates to 'decisions having military or defence implications'. That such decisions, even at the implementing stage, should still require unanimity was only to be expected in a polity where armed forces remain essentially national. However, it must not be supposed that decisions of the kind in question will always be easy to identify. Potentially, therefore, the exception opens up a large breach in Art. 23(2), at least in respect of actions with an operational dimension.[20]

The other exception is provided for in the following terms:

> If a member of the Council declares that, for important and stated reasons of national policy, it intends to oppose the adoption of a decision to be taken by qualified majority, a vote shall not be taken. The Council may, acting by a qualified majority, request that the matter be referred to the European Council for decision by unanimity.

This is a version of the notorious Luxembourg Compromise of January 1996,[21] elevated to the status of a Treaty provision, and with the additional feature of a *renvoi* to the European Council.

Apart from the barbarism of giving the European Council a power of decision, already considered in relation to common strategies, two main

---

[20] For a suggestion as to a voting rule that would avoid any judgment as to whether or not a decision has military implications, see *Reviewing Maastricht*, Position Paper: 227 to 229. See also the Conclusion, below.

[21] The full text of the Luxembourg compromise is published in *Bulletin of the EC*, March 1996: 8 to 10.

objections may be levelled against this 'Luxembourg Compromise Mark II'. One objection is that it may confer fresh credibility on the Compromise Mark I which, since the early 1980s, has ceased to influence the Council's everyday decision-making.[22] The other, and perhaps more substantial, objection is that, once legitimated, the Compromise Mark II is liable to be seen as a ready-made solution on any occasion when there is a dispute about extending QMV. The final phase of the Amsterdam negotiations is a case in point: having found its way into the provision that became Art. 23(2), the Compromise Mark II could be more easily accepted as part of the procedure for authorizing closer cooperation, including in the domain of the EC Treaty. An old taboo has been broken, and the extent of the threat to the coherence of the constitutional order is unpredictable.[23]

IV STRENGTHENING THE CFSP's INFRASTRUCTURE

The Presidency is confirmed by the new Art. 18 as the representative of the Union in CFSP matters and as the executant of Council decisions taken under the powers conferred by Title V. The right of the Commission to be 'fully associated' in the tasks of the Presidency, and more generally with the work carried out in the field of the CFSP, is likewise reiterated.[24] There are, however, three changes in Art. 18, as compared with the previous Art. J.5, which may be noted.

Two of the changes are relatively minor. It is provided in para. (4), second sentence, that the Presidency may be assisted in its tasks, if need be, by the next member state to hold the office, but no longer by the previous holder: the so-called 'Troika' will thus become a two-horse vehicle. Paragraph (5), provides that: 'The Council may, whenever it deems it necessary, appoint a special representative with a mandate in relation to particular policy issues': this consecrates a practice, already well established in the context of the former Yugoslavia, which might otherwise perhaps be seen as conflicting with executive function of the Presidency.

More significantly, the role of the Secretary General of the Council is to be upgraded. He or she is to be designated 'High representative for the common foreign and security policy',[25] with a mandate to 'assist the Council

---

[22] On the history and significance of the Luxembourg Compromise, see Dewost, 'Le vote majoritaire: simple modalité de gestion ou enjeu politique essentiel?' in Capotorti et al. (eds) Liber Amicorum Pierre Peseatore, 1988, Nomos: 167; Dashwood in Schwarze (ed.), Legislation for Europe 1992, 1989, Nomos: 79; Wyatt and Dashwood, European Community Law, 3rd ed., 1993, Sweet & Maxwell: 44 to 46.

[23] The writer has taken other opportunities of criticizing the 'Luxembourg Compromise Mark II'. See Dashwood, 'States in the European Union', 23 ELRev (1998) 201 at 214 to 215; Dashwood, 'The Council of the European Union in the Era of the Amsterdam Treaty', in a forthcoming collection of papers marking the 40th Anniversary of the Europa Instituut, Leiden.

[24] See Art. 18(4), first sentence and Art. 27 TEU.

[25] Art. 18(3).

50

in matters coming within the scope of the common foreign and security policy, in particular through contributing to the formulation, preparation and implementation of policy decisions, and, when appropriate and acting on behalf of the Council at the request of the Presidency, through conducting political dialogue with third parties'.[26] The more mundane task of running the General Secretariat is to be assigned to a Deputy.[27]

The new-style Secretary General will have responsibilities of two distinct kinds.

On the one hand, he or she will be a representative for the CFSP on the world stage, either acting in support of the Presidency, or directly conducting political dialogue with third parties under instructions from the Council. This should help to overcome the lack of continuity in the international representation of the Union, owing to the rotation of the Presidency, which is perceived as one of the main weaknesses of existing arrangements: not only do ministers change but also the teams of national civil servants working with them, making it necessary to rebuild relations of confidence every six months.[28] It should also be more immediately clear, to the Union's international partners and to its own citizens, when action is being taken in the CFSP framework rather than in furtherance of national policies of the Presidency.

On the other hand, the Secretary General will be 'contributing to the formulation, preparation and implementation of policy decisions'. It seems, at last, to have been realized, at the highest political level, that the Council needs to be more adequately equipped to carry out the tasks it has been given in every phase of the management of the CFSP, which is entirely different from its traditional EU role as a legislative organ.[29]

Further evidence of this realization can be found in Declaration No 6 'on the establishment of a policy planning and early warning unit'. The unit, which is to be part of the Council's General Secretariat (though with some of its personnel drawn from the member states, the Commission and the WEU) will have a remit that includes:

(a) monitoring and analysing developments in areas relevant to the CFSP;
(b) providing assessments of the Union's foreign and security policy interests and identifying areas where the CFSP could focus in future;
(c) providing timely assessments and early warning of events or situations which may have significant repercussions for the Union's foreign and security policy, including potential political crises;
(d) producing, at the request of either the Council or the Presidency or on its own initiative, argued policy options papers to be presented under the responsibility of the Presidency as a contribution to policy formulation in the Council, and which may contain analyses, recommendations and strategies for the CFSP.

---

[26] Art. 26 TEU.
[27] Art. 207 EC.
[28] See the discussion and references in *Reviewing Maastricht*, Position Paper: 221 to 222.
[29] The specificity of the Council's role under the CFSP is more fully considered in the contribution to the collection of papers mentioned above.

It is disappointing that the list of tasks does not refer expressly to the preparation of concrete proposals for decisions by the Council. Such proposals, it may be supposed, will continue normally to be framed by civil servants of the Presidency. However, the unit will at least provide the raw material of a foreign policy conceived in the broader perspective of the Union.

The smooth functioning of the CFSP should also be assisted by amendments to the financial arrangements applicable under the previous Art. J.11(2). The rule that operational expenditure be attributed to the budget of the European Union only where the Council so decides by unanimity, is to be reversed: pursuant to the new Art. 18(3), operational expenditure will automatically be charged to the EU budget, except in two cases. One is where the expenditure arises from operations having military or defence implications: here, no contributions will be required from member states whose representatives in the Council have made a declaration under the constructive abstention principle of Art. 23(1). The other case is where the Council decides unanimously against attribution to the EU budget, in which event the national contributions will be in accordance with the GNP scale. The potentially delicate issue of the classification of CFSP expenditure (as compulsory or non-compulsory, within the meaning of Art. 272 EC) has been resolved by an Inter-Institutional Agreement. Such expenditure is to be treated as non-compulsory, which is right in principle;[30] but the total amount, and the allocation of appropriations between different articles of the relevant budget chapter, will be determined annually by agreement between the European Parliament and the Council. That was, presumably, seen by the Parliament as a preferable option to the proposal of the Dutch Presidency that CFSP expenditure be formally classified as compulsory.[31]

V INTERNATIONAL LEGAL PERSONALITY AND CAPACITY OF THE UNION

Title V of the TEU contains no language that could be construed as recognizing the capacity of the European Union to enter into international agreements and otherwise behave as a subject of international law. The orthodox view is, therefore, that agreements on CFSP matters can only be concluded under national powers. To avoid the impression that the member states are acting on their own individual account, the formula, 'the Member States of the European Union acting within the framework of the Union', was invented for the purpose of concluding that strange instrument, the Memorandum of Understanding ('MOU') on the EU Administration of Mostar.[32]

---

[30] See the definitions in Art. 272(4) EC and in the Joint Declaration of 30 June 1982, *OJ* 1982, C194, point I.

[31] Thus formally giving the Council the last word on this category of expenditure.

[32] The text of the MOU remains unpublished.

The Union's lack of international capacity has severe disadvantages. It is confusing for international partners, after listening to speeches and reading declarations made by the Presidency on behalf of the Union, to find, when the time comes to discuss legal texts, that their interlocutors are fifteen member states and the Commission (whether in its role as 'associate' in the work of the CFSP or as the EU negotiator). A practical disadvantage is the necessity of securing the ratification of international agreements in accordance with the constitutional requirements of fifteen member states. This can take up to two years, because there are nearly always some member states that have to act by way of parliamentary procedures.

The Dublin II text of the Irish Presidency included, under the heading 'Endowing the Union with legal personality', a rather elaborate draft provision bringing together elements apparently inspired by Arts 281 and 282 EC, Art. 6 ECSC and Art. 300 EC.[33] The principal elements of the proposal were: the conferment on the Union of legal personality and internal legal capacity juxtaposed with those of the EC and the other two Communities; the conferment on the Union of external capacity within the limits of its functions and purposes, such as the EC Treaty omits to confer explicitly on the Community but which was recognized by the Court of Justice in its *AETR* judgment through an audacious interpretation of Art. 281;[34] and the creation of procedures for the negotiation and conclusion of international agreements on behalf of the Union, as well as for testing in the Court of Justice the compatibility with the TEU of any such agreement. The succeeding Dutch Presidency went further still, proposing a single legal personality for the Union as a whole, which would have assimilated the existing personalities of the three Communities.[35]

In the event, the Amsterdam Treaty contains no allusion to the legal personality of the Union. There is simply to be a Council procedure which may (but need not) be used where an international agreement is called for in a matter falling within Title V or Title VI of the TEU. The new Art. 24 provides:

When it is necessary to conclude an agreement with one or more States or international organizations in implementation of this Title, the Council, acting unanimously, may authorize the Presidency, assisted by the Commission as appropriate, to open negotiations to that effect. Such agreements shall be concluded by the Council acting unanimously on a recommendation from the Presidency. No agreement shall be binding on a Member State whose representative in the Council states that it has to comply with the requirements of its own constitutional procedure; the other members of the Council may agree that the agreement shall apply provisionally to them.

The provisions of the Article shall also apply to matters falling under Title VI.

[33] Cited in note 1, above. See CONF 2500/96: 87 to 89.
[34] Case 22/70, *Commission v Council* [1971] ECR 263, para. 13. See the discussion of this part of the *AETR* judgment in the writer's chapter in *Koskenniemi*: 113, at 114 to 117.
[35] Surely the only fully coherent solution.

53

The Dutch Presidency's text, if it had proved acceptable, would have had the virtue of clarifying the internal constitution by putting beyond doubt that there now exists a single legal and political entity, the European Union, which operates under different powers and procedures depending on the sub-order under which a given activity falls. However, the Amsterdam Treaty could not actually have given the Union **international** legal personality, since the existence of such personality is a matter for international law itself. All the Treaty could do would be to make manifest the intention of the member states that the Union should, in principle, be capable of acting as an independent subject of the international legal order, and that its capacity should, in particular, extend to the conclusion of international agreements. It would then be for international law to draw the appropriate conclusions.[36] In the view of the writer, applying the criteria enunciated by the International Court of Justice in the *Reparation for Injuries* case, there are solid grounds for regarding the European Union as being already possessed of international legal personality, at least as regards the functions assigned to it under Title V of the TEU. The main indications can be found in the ambitious scope and objectives of the CFSP as defined by Art. 11, which can only be realized effectively through action on the international plane, and the fact that, in the Council, the Presidency and the Commission, the Union is equipped with organs well qualified to pursue such action. Practice since the entry into force of the TEU has provided a measure of confirmation, though the message is a mixed one. On the one hand, ambassadors are now regularly accredited to the Union rather than to the Communities; and there is a tendency in CFSP instruments to refer to the Union as if it were an international actor with rights and obligations.[37] On the other hand, there are no instances to date of the Union's being party to an international agreement.

The main question raised by the new Art. 24 is whether it acknowledges the capacity of the Union as such to enter into international agreements; or whether it merely establishes a simplified procedure for the negotiation and conclusion of agreements on behalf of the member states. Unfortunately, the text itself is radically ambiguous. The fact that it is the Council acting, and not the representatives of the governments of the member states meeting within the Council, would suggest the capacity being exercised will be that of the Union. However, the reference to national ratification procedures seems to indicate the contrary. We shall have to wait and see what happens in practice. If the European Union is expressed to be the party to agreements negotiated and concluded under Art. 24, there will no longer be any room

---

[36] The leading case is the Advisory Opinion of the International Court of Justice on *Reparation for Injuries suffered in the Service of the United Nations* ICJ Reports, 1949, 174 (hereinafter the *Reparation for Injuries* case). The Opinion draws a distinction between attribution of legal personality in principle, and the scope of the capacity enjoyed by a given international organization: see, in particular, ibid. at 178 to 184.

[37] See, e.g., the joint action on the participation of the Union in the implementing structures of the peace plan for Bosnia-Herzegovina, *OJ* 1995, L309/2.

for doubt as to the intention of the member states, and international partners will be entitled to act accordingly.[38]

Other questions about Art. 24 abound, with no certain answers available at this stage. What will be the legal situation where, pending the completion of one or more member states' constitutional procedures, the other member states have agreed to be provisionally bound? Will the agreement be with those States or with the Union? And, if the former, will the Union be substituted as a party once all member state ratifications have been successfully completed? Again, how will the constructive abstention principle operate in this context? If a member state opts out of an international agreement pursuant to the principle, it must 'accept that the decision commits the Union': can that mean, for the third country concerned, that it is contracting with a truncated Union, with only fourteen members? It will be a challenging task indeed for the legal advisors of the Council to ensure that a coherent practice develops.

VI SECURITY AND DEFENCE

The provisions of Title V relating more particularly to security and defence were initially contained in Art. J.4. Pursuant to the Amsterdam Treaty, that Article will be replaced by the new Art. 17.

In the drafting of both Articles, 'all questions relating to the security of the Union' are treated as already being covered by the CFSP. Defence, on the other hand, is something for the future. While the previous Article spoke of 'the eventual framing of a common defence policy, which might in time lead to a common defence', in the new Art. 17, the word 'eventual' has been replaced by 'progressive' and the qualifying phrase 'in time' has been dropped, presumably to indicate a more certain outcome. Moreover, a procedure has also been specified for establishing a common defence. This is to be done by a decision of the European Council, to be recommended to the member states for adoption in accordance with their respective constitutional requirements. A similar procedure is to be used, in case it should be decided to integrate the WEU into the Union.[39]

The previous Art. J.4 was rather tentatively worded as a **request** to the WEU 'to elaborate and implement decisions and actions of the Union which have defence implications'. It is stated in the new Art. 17(3), first subparagraph that the Union '**will avail itself** of the WEU'[40] for those purposes, a stronger formulation implying the assertion of a right. Another change will be to make clear that, besides its future role as the defence arm of the Union, the WEU will have an immediate security role, 'providing the Union

[38] My understanding of Art. 24 was quickly assigned by debating the point at the Edinburgh Conference with Professor Weiler and other participants.
[39] These are two more examples of the conferment on the European Council of power to take decisions.
[40] Emphasis added.

with access to an operational capability', notably in tackling the so-called 'Petersburg' tasks listed in para. (2) of the Article. These comprise 'humanitarian and rescue tasks, peace keeping tasks and tasks of combat forces in crises management, including peace-making'.[41] Member states of the Union which are not full WEU members are to have the right to participate fully in carrying out the Petersburg tasks; and, if they do so, the right also to participate, on an equal footing, in planning and decision-taking.[42]

There was a view that a timetable should be set by the Amsterdam Treaty for the eventual integration of the WEU into the Union,[43] but the reference in Art. 17(1), second subparagraph to integration as nothing more than a possibility does not, it is submitted, represent a real setback. In fact, the EU/WEU relationship, as refined by Amsterdam, will function as a rather elegant flexibility mechanism. The member states of the Union which have observer status in the WEU effectively enjoy an automatic opt-out from any security action involving recourse to military means, with a right to opt in on an *ad hoc* basis.[44] This caters nicely for differing constitutional exigencies and political sensibilities.

VII   CONCLUSION

Disappointment with the product of the CFSP so far has been, I believe, largely a self-fulfilling prophecy. The era of flexibility and subsidiarity, which the Treaty of Amsterdam has made official, offers the opportunity of building on previous experience, in a legal and political framework better adapted to the particularities of foreign and security policy. However, the rather tentative approach that pervades the Amsterdam Treaty is found even in the new Title V.

This can be seen, for instance, in the changes to the Council's voting rules. QMV will apply automatically to implementing decisions; but the extension of its use has been purchased at the price of the Luxembourg Compromise Mark II and of an exception for decisions having military or defence implications which is liable to prove elastic; and unanimity will continue to be required for deciding on the principle of taking action in a given situation, unless it is one already covered by a unanimously adopted common strategy.

Such an outcome might be thought to cast doubt on the aptness of QMV, in the sense of Art. 205(2) EC, for transplantation into Title V TEU. The problem lies, as the writer has previously explained, in 'the huge disparity

---

[41] See para. II.4 of the Petersberg Declaration, adopted by the WEU's Council on 19 June 1992. On this, and the subsequent Noordwijk Declaration of 14 November 1994, see Weller, 'The European Union within the "European Security Architecture"' in *Koskenniemi*, 57 at 63 to 65.

[42] Art. 17(3), third subpara.

[43] See CONF 2500/96, cited in note 1, above, at 85.

[44] The member states in question are Austria, Denmark, Finland, Ireland and Sweden.

between the Member States in terms of influence in the world, diplomatic resources, range of international responsibilities and – most of all – military capability and the will to exploit that capability'.[45] The disparity matters, because foreign and security policy is all about pursuing objectives through the deployment of such assets. The voting system of the CFSP needs to be tailored to that unwelcome but inescapable fact. Various suggestions, inspired by the UN Security Council model of majority voting in combination with a veto restricted to certain countries, were canvassed during preparations for the IGC.[46] The objection that any such solution would entail treating member states unequally, misses the point. In the CFSP sphere there is not the fundamental equality that characterizes the legislative process of the EU, where the member states, big and small, accept a limitation of their sovereign rights which is similar, in principle, for all of them. Unless their special position is recognized, some at least of the member states whose full-hearted cooperation is most needed to make a reality of the CFSP, will continue to regard the present unanimity rule as indispensable.

Other examples of reforms that need to be taken further are those connected with the infrastructure of the CFSP. The new-style Secretary-General should help give the Union external visibility and enhance the continuity of policy; and the planning and early warning unit will, if strongly led, provide an alternative focus to the specific preoccupations of the Presidency, even if its remit ends upstream of the preparation of formal proposals. For the time being, however, the Presidency retains its grip on the levers of executive power in CFSP matters. The writer's hope for the medium-term would be that the Secretary-General develops an independent authority, under the direction of the Council, similar to that of the Secretary General of the United Nations or of NATO; and that he or she be supported by Council staff sufficient in numbers and appropriately trained, so as to be capable of managing all aspects of the CFSP 'in-house'.[47]

But, at the end of the day, there is only so much legal technicians can do. If the Union does succeed in achieving a substantive CFSP, that will be because the politicians in member state governments and in the Commission have decided that they really want one.

---

[45] *Reviewing Maastricht*, Position Paper: 227.

[46] Ibid. at 227 to 229. See also the first (and only) Report of the High-level Group established by the Commission, at point IV D.

[47] See, on the training of Council staff, the writer's contribution to 'The Council of the European Union in the Era of the Amsterdam Treaty' in Heukels, Blokker and Brus (eds), *The European Union after Amsterdam*, Kluwer Law International (forthcoming): 117.

4

THE EASTERN ENLARGEMENT OF THE EUROPEAN UNION AND THE COMMON AGRICULTURAL POLICY

Joseph A. McMahon *

I INTRODUCTION

The long-term outlook for agriculture as outlined in the Agenda 2000 document indicated that the European Union would be confronted with a number of problems.[1] First, the outlook for the existing policy was described as 'not very promising' as structural surpluses would begin to reemerge for a number of products. The traditional means of dealing with such problems, increased use of export subsidies, would no longer be available to the EU as a result of the commitments made in the context of the Uruguay Round. The successor to this round was identified as a second problem for the EU. According to Art. 20 of the Agreement on Agriculture negotiated during the Uruguay Round, negotiations for a further package of reforms would begin in 1999. This would continue the process of improving market access, reducing direct budgetary support and implementing further decreases in the levels of export subsidization which represent the core of the Uruguay Round commitments of the parties in the area of agriculture. In addition, negotiations on a range of new issues, such as environmental and social standards and consumer protection would begin. Finally, during the period of these negotiations, accession negotiations would be conducted with the applicant countries of Central and Eastern Europe and Cyprus. The resulting accession of these countries to the EU would necessitate an adaptation of the existing Common Agricultural Policy (CAP). This was the third problem.

Therefore the EU will be faced with three distinct but interrelated problems: adaptation of the existing policy to maintain the EU's position in world

---

* LLB (Hons) (QUB), PhD (Edin), Reader in Law, Queen's University of Belfast.
[1] COM (97) 2000 *Agenda 2000: Part 1, The Policies of the Union*, Chapter III.2. Also reproduced in Bull EU Supp 5/97.

trade; an element of that adaptation will involve the renegotiation of existing international commitments and the negotiation of new commitments; and, finally, the adoption of this new policy, accompanied by consequential reforms, by the six applicant countries on their accession to the EU. Any one of these problems represents a significant challenge to the EU but the combined solution to these three problems may indicate that the new CAP which will emerge will be fundamentally different from the CAP which existed at the time of the first enlargement, some thirty years earlier. This paper will examine in depth two of these particular problems, the adaptation of the existing policy and the enlargement of the EU to include the countries of Central and Eastern Europe. In this examination, it is impossible to ignore the impact which the Agreement on Agriculture and the forthcoming negotiations will have.

II ADAPTATION OF THE EXISTING POLICY

The nature of the CAP has not changed fundamentally since the inception of the policy in the 1960s. Although the range of measures available under the policy have increased significantly, the core of the policy remains the three principles of common prices, common financing and Community preference and even though a fourth principle, producer responsibility, has been added over the years, it has not yet assumed an overall level of importance equivalent to the three core principles. Likewise, although the EU has developed a structural policy for agriculture, it has not attained the status accorded to the market and price policy of the CAP.

The original principles of the CAP were designed to meet the situation where Europe was still a net importer of agricultural products. The support of farm incomes through internal price arrangements and the partial or total exclusion of imports for certain products as a result of increased protection at the frontiers of the EU ensured that the policy met the problems it was initially designed to deal with. However, once this situation had been reached, the instruments of the policy were not changed. As a result surpluses appeared in a number of areas, with a consequent negative impact on prices, and trade relations with third countries deteriorated with increases in the level of EU subsidized exports and continuing restrictions on imports. Reform of the policy was inevitable. Such reform, according to the Commission in 1980, would have to reconcile four main objectives:

(1) to maintain the positive aspects achieved, i.e. consumer security of supply, income of farmers, free trade and the contribution of farming to external trade;
(2) to set up mechanisms whereby the budgetary consequences of production surpluses may be held in check. This could be achieved by adjustment of market organisations to introduce the principle of co-responsibility or producer participation;
(3) to ensure better regional distribution of the benefits derived by farmers from the CAP; this would entail a radical readjustment of structural policy aimed at the reduction of regional disparities; and,

(4) to organise the financing of the CAP on sound foundations which will not cause disputes in future between Member States.[2]

Gradual reforms were introduced throughout the 1980s which would attempt to reconcile these four objectives. In 1982, the milk coresponsibility levy which had been introduced in 1977 was replaced by a system of guarantee thresholds.[3] In response to the failure of this measure to stem the tide of increased production in 1984 a quota and super levy system were introduced.[4] Confirming the emergence and significance of a fourth principle, producer responsibility, in 1986 and 1987, strict limits were imposed on market support for cereals and milk products and in 1988 further stabilization measures were introduced in all market organisations.[5] Also in 1988, the European Council meeting in Brussels set a maximum annual amount of expenditure, a budgetary guideline, for the market and price policy aspect of the CAP for the years 1988–1992. The basis for the guideline was the actual expenditure incurred in 1987 with expenditure not being allowed to rise by more than 74 per cent of the rate of increase of the EU's Gross National Product (GNP) over this period.[6] The discipline provided by the Interinstitutional Agreement on budgetary discipline and improvement of the budgetary procedure was confirmed and extended at the 1993 Edinburgh Summit until 1999 at which stage the share of the EU budget devoted to the market and price policy will have decreased to 45 per cent from 50 per cent in 1993.[7]

These reforms represent the beginning of a process of continuing reform of the CAP, the most significant set of reforms to date emerged in 1992 with the so-called 'MacSharry reforms'. In essence these reforms were twofold. First, there was a three year reduction in the level of prices in the arable crops and beef sectors. The purpose of such a reduction was to bring the level of EU prices closer to those on the world market, so improving the competitiveness of EU production. Some form of compensatory aid was required and this is granted under such schemes as the aid per hectare scheme and various land set-aside programmes. Likewise, in the beef sector, compensatory payments were introduced and were made payable on the

---

[2] COM (80) 800 *Reflections on the CAP*.
[3] Regulation 1183/82 *OJ* 1982, L140/1. See also Regulation 1079/77 *OJ* 1977, L131/6.
[4] Regulation 856/84 *OJ* 1984, L90/10, also Regulations 1355/86 (*OJ* 1986, L119/19) and 775/87 (*OJ* 1987, L78/5). As for the levy, see now Regulation 3950/92 *OJ* 1992, L405/1. For a discussion of the original scheme, see A. Freidberg, 'Milk Surpluses Till the Cows Come Home?' (1984) 7 World Economy 421.
[5] See for example Regulation 1094/88 *OJ* 1988, L106/28 and Regulation 1096/88 *OJ* 1988, L110/1.
[6] The per annum growth rate from 1988–1992 would be 1.9% per annum in real terms over this period in contrast to a figure of 7.5% in the period 1975–88. The discipline was incorporated by Decision 88/739 *OJ* 1988, L185/29. See also the Interinstitutional agreement on budgetary discipline and improvement of the budgetary procedure, *OJ* 1985, L185/33.
[7] Interinstitutional agreement of 29 October 1993, *OJ* 1993, C331/1. See also Decision 94/729 *OJ* 1994, L293/14.

basis of a reduction of the stocking rate per hectare.[8] The second set of reforms built on the compensatory payments by introducing a range of accompanying measures, such as the granting of aid to farmers to encourage the protection of the environment, the landscape and natural resources.[9] These latter reforms would be built on the 1988 reforms of the structural funds which had encouraged integrated rural development as part of promoting greater economic and social cohesion of the EU[10] and a range of additional measures promoting the structural aspects of agriculture.[11]

As for an assessment of these reforms, it must be pointed out that they were limited to cereals, oilseeds and the dairy and beef sectors; around 75 per cent of EU production. These were areas where the budgetary and international trade problems had become most acute; other areas such as sugar were excluded as such problems had not arisen. So the 1992 reforms were not a wholesale reform of the CAP rather a response to both internal and external problems thus raising some doubt as to what was likely to happen in other sectors of the policy in the years that would follow, where the problems were not so prominent. As was usual, the Commission's reform proposals were more dramatic than the end result; the original proposals had called for a 40 per cent reduction in cereal prices but the final figure was 29 per cent. Having said this, agreement on such a large cut did represent a significant shift in the attitudes of the member states and a symbol of the future direction of the CAP. As for the nature of the symbol, it was clear, especially with regard to the conditions attached to the set-aside provisions, that the burden of financing agricultural expenditure was being shifted from the consumer to the taxpayer. The classification of the second set of reforms as 'accompanying measures' indicated that the primary concern is, as was noted above, the preservation of farmers' income rather than pursuing environmental goals as an essential element of agricultural reform.[12]

One assessment of the reforms concluded:

> They have failed to address the fundamentally objectionable features of the CAP and they have introduced a new and unwelcome policy instrument into the CAP's operations. They have not addressed the distortions the CAP creates, they leave decision making capacity in the hands of institutions that have demonstrated their

---

[8] See Bull EC 6-1992, points 1.3.140–1.3.147.

[9] Regulations 2078/92 to 2080/92 *OJ* 1992, L215/85, 91 and 96.

[10] Regulation 2052/88 *OJ* 1988, L185/9 as modified by Regulation 2081/93 *OJ* 1993, L193. For a discussion of the 1988 reform see P. Lowe 'The Reform of the Community's Structural Funds' (1988) 25 CMLRev 503.

[11] See for example, Regulation 866/90 *OJ* 1990, L91/1 and Regulation 2328/91 *OJ* 1991, L218/1.

[12] It has been noted that: 'As environmental difficulties have emerged, the EU has attempted to tackle them in a relatively imaginative way, although never addressing (until 1992) the central problem of price support; but the response has remained reactive, rather than to turn the environment into a central feature of agricultural policy.' Ockenden and Franklin, *European Agriculture: Making the CAP fit the future*, Pinters, London, 1995, 44.

incapacity to make good decisions, and they even appear unlikely to have solved the budgetary problems that first put reform on the EC agenda.[13]

In its assessment of the MacSharry reforms, the Agenda 2000 document, the Commission noted a considerable improvement of market balances, continuing improvements in average agricultural incomes but the reforms had mixed effects on the environment and had led to increased budgetary expenditure in the sectors affected by the reforms.[14] The reforms were characterized as insufficient to meet the new demands confronting the CAP in the years to come. As the Commission indicated:

> In order to help European agriculture take advantage of the expected positive world market developments, further reform of the CAP must improve the competitiveness of Union agriculture on both domestic and external markets. Greater market orientation will facilitate the progressive integration of new member states and will help prepare the Union for the next WTO Round. It will also help the Union to reinforce its position as a major world exporter.[15]

This will involve a 'deepening and extending' of reform through a further package of reforms aimed at converting the primary support mechanism of the CAP from price support to direct payments.

The initial Commission thinking on the nature of the reforms needed in the CAP was outlined in the Agenda 2000 document. They would involve a continuation of the process of reducing support prices for those agricultural products which are expected to generate surpluses in the years to come such as cereals and beef. The existing quota scheme for milk will continue until 2006 with a 10 per cent reduction in the level of support prices over this period. This is a surprising recommendation given the acknowledgement by the Commission that dairy farmers should not be given the impression that the current system would last forever. No proposals are made for the future of the dairy regime beyond 2006, thereby adding a degree of uncertainty to the long term prospects of this sector. Moreover, no reference is made in the section of the paper on new reforms for measures which would lead to the eventual elimination of the existing quota system in the sugar sector. With respect to direct income support, the Commission acknowledged that there will be an individual ceiling for such payments, allowing member states, under commonly agreed rules, to supplement these payments. The model used in the most recent enlargement of the EU to include Austria, Finland and Sweden may therefore be extended to all the member states.[16]

---

[13] Atkin, *Snouts in the Trough*, Woodhead Publishing, 1993, 146.
[14] Above note 1, Part 1, Chapter III.1. As for the impact of the Fifth Environmental Action Programme, see also the Interim Review of the programme, COM (94) 453 and the Progress Report, COM (95) 624.
[15] Ibid., Part 1, Chapter III.3.
[16] See Articles 138–144 Act of Accession of Austria, Finland and Sweden, *OJ* 1994, C241, 45–47.

In addition to the conversion of the CAP from a system of price support to a system of direct income payments, the new CAP will also have to agree a more aggressive rural policy than the current policy which was recognised as being 'a juxtaposition of agricultural market policy, structural policy and environmental policy with rather complex instruments and lacking overall coherence'.[17] A more coherent policy is needed not only to tackle the social and economic problems of rural areas but also to reinforce and enhance the existing environmental aspects of these areas and the CAP. This latter aspect of rural policy is seen as increasingly demanded by the citizens of the Union, who at the same time, in their capacity as consumers, are also demanding greater food safety and products which are both 'environmentally-friendly' and 'culturally-significant'.[18] In addition to these objectives, the promotion of greater economic and social cohesion between the member states will also be demanded by the new CAP. The first report of the Commission on economic and social cohesion pointed out that only five of the then twelve member states received positive net transfers from the operation of the CAP; of the four cohesion countries only Portugal was a net contributor to the EU's agricultural budget.[19]

On 18 March 1998 more detailed proposals for the reform of the CAP were published by the Commission, which were intended to translate the above reforms into legal texts.[20] For arable crops, there would be a new regulation which would, in part, confirm the future role of intervention as a safety net for farmers rather than as a guarantee of price stability. To reinforce this change, the intervention price for cereals would be reduced by 20 per cent in one step. Beyond this the essential elements of the regime agreed in 1992 would continue. In the beef sector, the existing intervention scheme would be replaced with a private storage system, similar to that used in the pigmeat regime, to be introduced by 2002, by which stage the effective market support level for beef will have been reduced by 30 per cent in three equal steps. To ensure a fair standard of living for the farmers affected by these changes, the direct payments introduced in 1992 will be increased. In the dairy sector, internal prices are to be reduced by 15 per cent (in four stages), instead of the 10 per cent suggested in the Agenda 2000 document, whilst there will be a 2 per cent increase in the total reference quantity for milk under the existing quota scheme. Whilst young farmers in all member states will benefit from a 1 per cent increase in the overall quota, the

---

[17] Above note 1, Part 1, Chapter III.1.
[18] See Regulation 2092/91 *OJ* 1991, L198/1 on organic farming and Regulations 2081/92 and 2082/92 *OJ* 1992, L208/1 which establish an EU framework with respect to protected designations of origin and protected geographical descriptions and allows certificates to be issued indicating the specific character of agricultural products and foodstuffs.
[19] See COM (96) 542 final/2, 59–66. The report does note that two of the poorest regions in Portugal were net beneficiaries of transfers under the CAP.
[20] COM (98) 158 for full details of the proposed reforms.

remaining 1 per cent will be allocated to farmers in mountainous areas, so not all member states will benefit. There will also be changes to the premium paid to dairy farmers, involving the division of the farmer's quota by the average EU yield of milk per cow with payments being based, not on the number of cows they actually have, but the number they would have if they had an average yield – a virtual cow.[21]

The proposals recognise the diverse nature of the agricultural situation in the member states by promoting a new division of functions between the EU and the member states. For example, in the area of direct payments to producers, where there will be a new regulations establishing common rules, compensation will be provided in the form of national envelopes by the EU, with the member states being responsible for the allocation of this money, subject to agreed criteria, to its agricultural producers. As examples of the agreed criteria, a digressive ceiling is to be proposed on the amount of direct aid that a farm can receive and member states will be able to adjust the direct aids awarded on criteria they define relating to the number of workers employed on a farm. A similar decentralised approach is also to be taken in the area of rural development, where there will be a new legal framework which will form part of the process of the simplification of EU agricultural legislation. This simplification will also apply to the main agricultural legislation where new consolidating regulations for the common organizations of the market in beef and veal and milk and milk products are proposed.

There will also be a new EU Regulation on aid for Rural Development which would reduce the existing nine regulations under which rural development aid can be granted to one and which will govern all rural development measures to be financed by the EAGGF. Under the proposal, the Guarantee Section would finance the accompanying measures implemented as part of the 1992 reform of the CAP and aid to farmers in less favoured areas. Under the proposal responsibility for the designation of less favoured areas will be given to the member states and the regions. All other measures, for example of farm modernisation and diversification, would be financed by the Guidance Section and will form part of the EU's efforts to promote greater economic and social cohesion in the EU in the newly defined Objective 1 and Objective 2 areas. Measures in Objective 1 areas will be financed through the Guidance Section and measures in Objective 2 areas will be financed through the Guarantee Section. Beyond these areas, measures to support Objective 3, the development of human resources, will be financed across the EU from the Guarantee Section. The Regulation also proposes a simplification of the system for the delivery of aid not only from the EAGGF but from the full range of rural development measures. As a further contribution to the simplification of existing agricultural legislation, there will be a new Regulation on the financing of the CAP.

---

[21] See *Financial Times*, 4 March 1998: 3. 'Brussels offers farmers the virtual cow solution'.

Table 1

Country	Agriculture/GDP	Agriculture/Employment
Hungary	7.2%	8%
Poland	6.6%	27%
Estonia	7%	7%
Czech Republic	5.2%	6.3%
Slovenia	4.3%	7%
EC	2.4%	5%

III   THE CAP AND THE APPLICANT COUNTRIES

According to the Agenda 2000 document:

> Extension of the Common Agricultural Policy (CAP) in its present form to the acceding countries would create difficulties. Given the existing price gaps between candidate countries and generally substantially higher CAP prices, and despite prospects for some narrowing of these gaps by the dates of accession, even gradual introduction of CAP prices would tend to stimulate surplus production. . . , thus adding to projected surpluses.[22]

Such surpluses could not be disposed of by means of export subsidization, given the new rules for international agricultural trade. Moreover, extension of the existing CAP to the countries of Central and Eastern Europe would add around 11 billion ECU per annum to the EU budget. The resulting cash injections would create income disparities and social distortions in the rural areas of these countries. So, the prospect of further enlargement, would have prompted the reform of the CAP even without the emergence of problems in the existing policy.

There is no doubting the importance of the agricultural sector to the applicant countries in Central and Eastern Europe, even with the problems caused by the transition to a market economy. This is amply demonstrated by looking at Table 1 above which shows the contribution of agriculture to each of the applicant countries' GDP and the percentage of the population employed in agriculture and then comparing these figures with the equivalent figures for the existing EU.[23]

These figures can be contrasted with the equivalent figures produced in 1994 by the Commission which demonstrate an overall greater dependence on agriculture and illustrate the depth of the problems of the transition to a market economy.[24]

---

[22] Above note 1, *The Effects on the Union's Policies of Enlargement to the Applicant Countries of Central and Eastern Europe (Impact Study)*, Part 2, Chapter 1.4.

[23] Figures obtained from COM (97) 2000, 2001, 2002, 2006, 2009 and 2010.

[24] COM (94) 361 *Follow-up to Commission Communication on 'The Europe Agreements and Beyond: A Strategy to Prepare the Countries of Central and Eastern Europe for Accession'*, Annex III reveals the figures for the Czech Republic to be 8.5% and 9.9%, for Hungary 15% and 10%, for Poland 7.3% and 28.1% and for the EU 2.8% and 5.8%. No figures were given for Estonia and Slovenia at that time.

Although the structure of agricultural production varies between each of the applicant countries, a distinction can be drawn between Hungary and Poland, on the one hand, and the remaining three applicants. In the case of Hungary, it is a net exporter of agricultural products covered by the CAP and its agricultural policy is export-oriented.[25] Hungary's main crop is cereals, of which 15 per cent is exported, followed by oilseeds. It is self-sufficient in sugar and in years of high production it exports sugar. It also exports a large variety of fruit and vegetables and is a traditional exporter of wine. It is also a traditional exporter of dairy products and although production has declined in the meat sector, it continues to export pigmeat. Poland is also an exporter of pigmeat, along with fresh and processed fruit and vegetables (in particular potatoes) and is considered self-sufficient for the main CAP products.[26] In contrast to these two countries, Estonia, the Czech Republic and Slovenia are net importers of agricultural products.[27] The application of the main instruments of the CAP to these countries could lead to an overall improvement in their level of self-sufficiency for a range of products and, in some cases, to exports of any resulting surplus production.

As for the agricultural policies currently being followed by these countries, Hungary has moved towards an agricultural policy which gives direct market support for a range of products through guaranteed prices within maximum quantities. These prices are lower than EU support prices, although wholesale prices are closer to EU prices for several products. For a further range of products indirect market support is available and stability in the market is maintained through external trade measures.[28] Similar mechanisms have been introduced in Poland for major commodities and although these are similar to the instruments of the CAP, market and support prices are, like Hungary, significantly lower that the equivalent EU prices.[29] For example, the intervention price for wheat was only 79 per cent of the EU intervention price in 1995–96 and the beef prices were 46 per cent of the 1995 EU price. A significant element of the Polish agricultural budget is devoted to the social security system for farmers. Great efforts are also being made to introduce a range of rural, structural and environmental measures to promote a more modern and competitive rural sector.

As for the adaptation of existing policies by these countries to meet the demands of the existing CAP, all the countries will bring with them a range of common problems to be resolved.[30] Farm productivity falls well below existing EU levels, although this problem is not so acute in Hungary which is recognised as being the most competitive of the applicant countries. The

[25] COM (97) 2001, 64–65.
[26] COM (97) 2002, 67–68.
[27] COM (97) 2006, 67–68, 2009, 65–66 and 2010, 73–74.
[28] Above note 25, 65–67.
[29] Above note 26, 68–71.
[30] See for example, above note 25, 69.

process of land reform is causing some problems, for example, violent demonstrations occurred in 1997 in Hungary against a proposed law allowing businesses, including foreign-owned businesses, to own agricultural land.[31] Similar problems arise in the other applicant countries, for example, in Poland where the process of collectivization was never completed but where 50 per cent of farms have less than five hectares and where the privatisation process has been hampered by the lack of investment capital.[32] Each of the countries will have to make greater efforts to ensure the implementation and enforcement of veterinary and phytosanitary requirements meet EU standards.[33] Existing administrative structures will also have to strengthened to ensure the capacity of each of the applicant countries' ability to implement and enforce the policy instruments of the CAP. Hence the discussion of the preaccession regulation in the EU's proposals of 18 March 1998.

At the more specific level, Hungary is progressively adapting its policies to the CAP, but greater progress will be needed in certain sectors, notably, pigmeat, dairy quotas and cereals.[34] Equivalent problems exist in all the applicant countries, especially Poland.[35] To a greater extent than is the case with Hungary, if the problems of Polish agriculture are remedied, they will allow it to become a significant exporter of products for which the EU is already self-sufficient or an important exporter. Given the almost total absence of product support policies in Estonia, there will need to be a fundamental reform of their agricultural policy to meet the demands of membership of the EU.[36] The situation in the Czech Republic and Slovenia is only slightly better with market regulations existing for only a few essential products, with price levels significantly lower than those of the EU. In both countries, the focus of agricultural policy has not been market support rather, in the case of the Czech Republic, increasing attention has been devoted in recent years to rural development and environmental policies[37] and, in the case of Slovenia, to the achievement of sustainable rural development in the less-favoured hilly and mountainous regions of the country, to be achieved through income support rather than support prices.[38]

In each of the current and prospective assessments of the future development of the agricultural policies of the applicant countries, the Commission acknowledged that:

It is difficult to foresee at this stage how agricultural support prices in [the applicant country] will develop in the period before accession; this will depend on a

[31] *Financial Times*, 9 December 1997, Survey on Hungary, 6.
[32] Above note 26, 68.
[33] See, for example, the dispute concerning imports of Polish milk into the EU arising from hygiene problems in industrial milk premises, *Financial Times*, 1 December 1997, 7.
[34] Above note 25, 67–69.
[35] Above note 26, 71–74.
[36] COM (97) 2006, 69.
[37] COM (97) 2009, 66.
[38] COM (97) 2010, 74.

number of factors including the domestic economy, the situation in export markets, and the development of price support levels in the Union.[39]

However, it is possible to identify a number of constraints on the development of agricultural policy in each of the applicant countries over the next few years. In the case of the Czech Republic, Hungary, Poland and Slovenia, membership of the Central European Free Trade Area entails progressive agricultural market liberalization with the goal of achieving complete market integration by 1999. The countries have also made commitments under the Uruguay Round Agreement on Agriculture. For example, Hungary established a number of minimum access quotas for a wide range of products, it set a maximum level for the Aggregate Measurement of Support[40] it will grant (about 10 per cent of existing production value) and set a limit to export subsidization for its main products.[41] A similar range of commitments were made by Poland, the Czech Republic and Slovenia. As noted above, in all cases the overall level of support falls well below that of the EU, and so it would be difficult to imagine a scenario in which the commitments under the WTO Agreement on Agriculture could be reviewed upwards as part of their accession to the EU.[42]

As a further constraint all of the countries have concluded Europe Agreements with the EU, as part of the two-pronged approach to prepare these countries for accession.[43] The agreements give a limited range of agricultural concessions to these countries, which have been characterised by the Commission as leading to improvements in the level of access for these countries. It is ironic that the day before the Commission published its proposals for reform, ministers agreed to suspend preferential import tariffs on Czech pigmeat, poultry and fruit juice exports in retaliation against the introduction of Czech restrictions on the import of EU apples.[44] This particular action lends some support to other evaluations of the impact of the Europe Agreements which are not as positive as the Commission's.[45] Ockenden and Franklin note that:

---

[39] Above note 26, 68.
[40] Aggregate Measurement of Support is defined in Art. 1(a) of the Uruguay Round Agreement on Agriculture as 'the annual level of support, expressed in monetary terms, provided for an agricultural product in favour of the producers of the basic agricultural product or non-product-specific support provided in favour of agricultural producers in general.'
[41] Above note 26, 66–67.
[42] The figures for the Producer Subsidy Equivalent (PSE) for the EU was calculated by the OECD to be 49% in 1995, the equivalent figures for the applicant countries are Hungary, 16%; Poland, 21%; Estonia, 3%; Czech Republic, 14%; no figure was given for Slovenia.
[43] COM (94) 329 *The Europe Agreements and Beyond: A Strategy to Prepare the Countries of Central and Eastern Europe for Accession* and COM (94) 361 *Follow-up to Commission Communication on 'The Europe Agreements and Beyond: A Strategy to Prepare the Countries of Central and Eastern Europe for Accession'.*
[44] *Financial Times*, 18 March 1998, 36.
[45] See, for example, House of Lords Select Committee on the EC, *The Implications for Agriculture of the Europe Agreements*, Paper 57-I, 1994.

The agricultural access provided by the association agreements is not generous, thanks to the influence of farmers' lobbies and finance ministries. However, by offering only restricted access to the distorted prices of the CAP, the EU may not only have saved itself money but also have curtailed the corrosive effect of the wrong prices.[46]

This may have been a benefit to the EU but it must also be considered a benefit to the applicant countries. To have moved towards the adoption of the instruments of the CAP would have been, and to some extent continues to be, both economically and politically unrealistic. Instead, the applicant countries are attempting to resolve a number of problems in the agricultural sector, mainly social, structural and environmental, to promote a more modern and competitive rural sector. In terms of the objectives of the CAP, the focus of agricultural policy is not market or producer support as in Art. 33(1) but rural development as in Art. 33(2).

In the Agenda 2000 document the Commission considered that the existing different forms of preaccession support should be unified into a single framework. On 16 March the Council adopted Regulation 622/98 on assistance to the applicant countries in Central and Eastern Europe in the framework of the preaccession strategy.[47] The 18 March proposals end with a discussion of the preaccession Regulation suggesting an annual budget of over 500 million ECU to address the priority needs of agriculture and rural development in each of the applicant countries.[48] A long list of 'indispensable' pre-accession measures is given with a view to allowing the applicant countries to adapt to what is described as 'a rather complex EU "*acquis*" in this area'. Following the demands of Regulation 622/98, and as suggested by Agenda 2000, a series of Accession Partnerships have been concluded with the countries of Central and Eastern Europe to prepare them to meet the obligations for membership of the EU. Each of the Partnerships set out priorities and intermediate objectives to be achieved in the short and medium-term and each of the applicant countries is required to establish a national programme for the adoption of the *acquis* setting out a timetable for the achievement of the priorities and objectives. Failure to respect the general conditions for membership, the commitments of the Europe Agreement and a lack of progress in the implementation of the Accession Partnership are listed as grounds which may lead to a suspension of financial assistance. As for the details of the partnership so far as agriculture is concerned, they repeat the assessments made in the Agenda 2000 document, and noted above, of the various measures which need to be taken over both the short and medium term to ensure the adoption of the agricultural *acquis*.[49]

---

[46] Above note 12, 81.
[47] *OJ* 1998, L85/1.
[48] Above note 20, for further details.
[49] Details of the Accession Partnerships for each of the applicant countries can be found on DG1A's website, europa.eu.int/comm/dg1a/enlarge. The Annex to each of the Partnerships

IV TOWARDS A NEW COMMON AGRICULTURAL POLICY?

In December 1996, the Economic and Social Committee adopted an opinion advising against the extensive reform of the CAP in anticipation of the possible accession by the countries of Central and Eastern Europe.[50] At the same time, the European Parliament adopted a resolution urging that the broad outlines of the CAP adjustment should be drawn up before the end of the negotiations so as to enable the acceding countries to decide on accession in the light of information about future agricultural policy. The Parliament continued by acknowledging that the variegated agricultural situation in the various applicant countries warranted an 'individually-tailored, prudent and cautious approach during the enlargement negotiations'; such an approach would emerge by studying the potential impact of the new accessions on the CAP prior to enlargement. For both bodies it was essential that enlargement should not occur at the expense of the CAP.[51]

Both bodies, and indeed all the institutions, now endorse the Commission's analysis of the need to reform the CAP before the accession of the countries of Central and Eastern Europe. Having understood the arguments is not, however, the same as sharing the solutions advocated by the Commission in the Agenda 2000 document or the 18 March proposals. It is clear that transforming the proposals into legislation will not be an easy task, especially as they involve a net increase in agricultural spending of about 10 per cent of the existing agricultural budget of 40 billion ECU. The net increase may be larger if, like the 1992 reform package, there is some slippage between the Commission's proposals and the final package; to use an example already cited, in 1992 the Commission had called for a 40 per cent reduction in cereal prices and the final figure was 29 per cent. It is to be hoped that this slippage will not include the proposed digressive ceiling on the amount of direct aid that a farm can receive which was excluded from the 1992 reform package. Moreover, the 18 March proposals did not contain proposals for the reform of various Mediterranean products, such as wine and olive oil; such proposals have now been made. There is still no reference to reform in the sugar sector.

A number of the reforms proposed do raise certain problems. To take just one example, the decentralization of payments under the CAP in the form of national envelopes, raises a number of issues. The estimated size of these national envelopes is around 3 billion ECU in the beef and dairy sectors or some 30 per cent of total direct aid payments.[52] A member state will be able to adjust the direct aids awarded on criteria they define relating to the number of workers employed on a farm. By allowing the member states to define

---

details the particular EU measures to be adopted. See also *Agricultural Situation and Perspectives in the Central and Eastern European Countries* available on DGVI's website.

[50] Bull EU 12-1996, point 1.4.51. See also Bull EU 1/2-1997, point 1.3.69 for the opinion of the Committee of the Regions on the CAP and eastward enlargement.

[51] *OJ* 1997, C20.

[52] *Financial Times*, 19 February 1998, 2 'Farmers uneasy at CAP reform plan'.

these criteria, distortions in competition may arise between the member states which may threaten the integrity of the single market. It must be recognised at this point that the existence of various national quota schemes within the CAP is in effect an exception to the integrity of the single market. Distortions of competition may also arise in the area of rural development. Here the national envelopes will be devoted to the Less Favoured Areas scheme, the schemes introduced in the 1992 reform package and the modernisation and diversification programmes outside the Objective 1 and 2 areas. Under the proposal, the Guarantee Section would finance the accompanying measures implemented as part of the 1992 reform of the CAP and aid to farmers in less favoured areas. In this respect, it is worth repeating the point noted earlier that the proposal for a new EU Regulation on aid for rural development, responsibility for the designation of less favoured areas will be given to the member states and the regions.

In terms of direct support, not only will this increase by 7.7 billion ECU but there are no proposals for the abolition of this form of 'compensation'. This raises two problems. First, it is unthinkable that the acceding countries would agree not to have the same rights and duties with respect to agriculture as the existing member states, but this raises the problem of these countries receiving 'compensation' for losses which they have not suffered. Secondly, a timetable for the abolition of this form of support must be set or it should be converted into truly decoupled payments. Under Art. 13 of the Uruguay Agreement on Agriculture, the so-called peace clause, the 1992 reform measures were classified as Blue Box measures and so not subject to reduction commitments.[53] However, the peace clause expires in 2003 and, if such measures continue in their present form, they are likely to be challenged in the forthcoming WTO negotiations. To avoid a successful challenge such payments must be production neutral and must be related to the pursuit of a legitimate public policy objective to qualify as what the Agreement on Agriculture refers to as 'green-box policies'. The most obvious legitimate public policy objective is the protection of the environment, hence the reference in the Agenda 2000 document to the beginning of international negotiations on new issues, such as environmental standards. Such a reference is also a reflection of the enhanced status which environmental policy will enjoy as a result of the Treaty of Amsterdam which will add a provision that to promote sustainable development in the EU 'environmental protection requirements must be integrated into the definition and implementation' of all EU policies and activities mentioned in Art. 3.

As for the green box policies that are excluded from the reduction commitment they include: structural adjustment assistance provided through producer retirement programmes, resource retirement programmes and investment aids; payments under environmental programmes; and payments under regional assistance programmes. Annex 2(1) of the Agreement on Agriculture states:

[53] Article 6 and 5(a) Agreement on Agriculture.

Domestic support policies for which exemption from the reduction commitments is claimed shall meet the fundamental requirement that they have no, or at most minimal, trade distortion effects or effects on production. Accordingly all policies for which exemption is claimed shall conform to the following basic criteria:

(i)   the support in question shall be provided through a publicly-funded government programme (including government revenue foregone) not involving transfers from consumers; and,

(ii) the support in question shall not have the effect of providing price support to producers.

If excluded, it is up to the member to ensure that such policies remain consistent with the requirements of Annex 2.[54] The examples cited above of green box policies are all features of the EU's existing agricultural structural policy. Structural adjustment assistance provided through producer retirement programmes is provided for in Regulation 2079/92. Structural adjustment assistance provided through resource retirement programmes is provided for under the various set-aside schemes, such as those of Regulation 2328/91, which also provides payments under environmental programmes. Structural adjustment assistance provided through investment aids can be made under Regulation 866/90 and payments under regional assistance programmes are provided through Regulation 2052/88. It is for the EU to ensure that such policies have no, or at most minimal, trade distortion effects or effects on production and that the support they do provide does not have the effect of providing price support to producers.

The question of further reform of the existing agri-environmental policy is addressed in the Agenda 2000 document which notes:

> In the coming years, a prominent role will be given to agri-environmental instruments to support a sustainable development of rural areas and respond to society's increasing demand for environmental services. The measures aimed at maintaining and enhancing the quality of the environment shall be reinforced and extended.[55]

This prominent role will be assured by increased budgetary resources being allocated to these measures. It is clear from the discussion of the reform of the CAP in the Agenda 2000 document that these agri-environmental measures will remain complementary, or 'accompanying measures', to price support and production control measures. This is hardly in keeping with the enhanced status which environmental policy will enjoy as a result of the Treaty of Amsterdam which implies that greater efforts than have been made in the past will have to be made in the future to integrate environmental considerations into the operation of the CAP. Yet the Agenda 2000 document and the 18 March proposals continue to emphasize the primacy of price support and production control measures. Rural development and the

---

[54] Article 7(2)(a) provides that in the event that the measures do not meet the requirements of Annex II, they will be included in future calculations of the total AMS.

[55] COM (97) 2000 *Agenda 2000*, Part 1 *The Policies of the Union*, Chapter III. 4.

environment measures continue to be viewed as mechanisms offering some form of alternative price support or compensation for price reductions rather than an equal priority for the CAP. This is evidence of a failure to address properly the future demands placed on the policy by both amendments to the Treaty and the international dimension of the reform process.

So, the discussion of direct support in the Agenda 2000 document and the 18 March proposals ignores the need to convert blue box measures into green-box measures, so as to allow for the continuation of these measures. Equally, the discussion of price support and production controls ignores the likely impact of future tariff reductions and export subsidy reductions. Under the Uruguay Round Agreement, for the EU, the average reduction for these tariffs over the duration of the agreement will be 36 per cent. This applies not only to traditional tariffs but also to the tariffication of nearly all types of non-tariff measures, including, according to a note to Art. 4(2) of the Agreement on Agriculture, quantitative import restrictions, variable import levies, minimum import prices, discretionary import licensing, voluntary export restraints and similar border measures other than ordinary customs duties.[56] For export subsidies there is a commitment to reduce the budgetary outlays on, and the quantities benefiting from, such subsidies, to a level of 36 per cent with respect to budgetary outlay and 21 per cent with respect to export quantity below the levels in the 1986–1990 base period.

In a study of the implementation of the Agreement on Agriculture within the EU, Thomson points out that the implementation of the Agreement's provisions on domestic support and market access has been carried out 'with less than maximum rigour', but that the export subsidy reduction commitments are likely to constrain future behaviour.[57] As for the overall impact of the Agreement on the immediate prospects of reform of the CAP, Thomson concludes:

> So far, then, there seems little in [the Agreement on Agriculture] to enforce rapid or radical CAP reform. Given the exemptions, and the prospects for stronger world markets than appeared likely a few years ago, there seems enough scope in the Agreement itself, to enable the Commission to avoid even changing the CAP on this account, except in relatively minor administrative ways, at least until well into the next decade. . . .[58]

However, it is unlikely that a similar assessment will be possible after the forthcoming round of agricultural trade negotiations given the end of the

---

[56] The measures which will not be converted are limited to measures maintained under balance-of-payments provisions or under other general, non-agriculture-specific provisions of the GATT 1994 or of the other Multilateral Trade Agreements in Annex 1A of the WTO.

[57] 'The CAP and the WTO after the Uruguay Round Agreement on Agriculture' (1996) 1 EFA Rev 169. See also Scott, 'Tragic Triumph: Agricultural Trade, the Common Agricultural Policy and the Uruguay Round' in Emiliou and O'Keefe (eds), *The European Union and World Trade Law: After the GATT Uruguay Round*, Wiley, 1996, 165–180 who discusses the impact of the Agreement on the cereals sector.

[58] Ibid., 183.

peace clause, likely agreement on greater tariff reductions and further reductions in the values and volumes of subsidised exports.

The international dimension points to the need to agree a realistic set of new objectives for the CAP. The existing objectives set out for the CAP in Art. 33(1) are:

(a) to increase agricultural productivity by promoting technical progress and by ensuring the rational development of agricultural production and the optimum utilisation of the factors of production, in particular labour;
(b) thus to ensure a fair standard of living for the agricultural community, in particular by increasing the individual earnings of persons engaged in agriculture;
(c) to stabilise markets;
(d) to assure availability of supplies;
(e) to ensure supplies reach consumers at reasonable prices.

Further objectives, of a regional and social nature, are added by the second paragraph of Art. 33. The end result is a series of objectives which are conflicting and not capable of reconciliation; despite the fact that this has been recognised for a long period, Art. 33 has never been considered as an article in need of reform at the various inter-governmental conferences. To the list of objectives in Art. 33, further objectives have been added over the years and the Commission now wish to add an additional series of objectives. In essence, the Commission, in the Agenda 2000 document and the 18 March proposals, is trying to rewrite the objectives set down in Art. 33. Such a rewrite would set the objectives of the CAP as being:[59]

(a) to improve the Union's competitiveness through lower prices;
(b) to guarantee the safety and quality of food to consumers;
(c) to ensure stable incomes and a fair standard of living for the agricultural community;
(d) to make its production methods environmentally friendly and respect animal welfare;
(e) to integrate environmental goals into its instruments;
(f) to seek to create alternative income and employment opportunities for farmers and their families.

The obvious question to ask is: is a reformed CAP the best way to achieve these objectives? For example, would environmental problems be resolved in a more effective and efficient manner through an enhanced environmental policy rather than the environment being an element of a response to the problems arising from price support in the CAP?

---

[59] See 'Agenda 2000 for a stronger and wider Union', part 4 'Further reform of the Common Agricultural Policy', available on the EU's website, europa.eu.int/comm/agenda2000/overview/en/agenda.htm.

In relation to the existing Art. 33(1) the European Court of Justice has recognised the fluid nature of the objectives listed.[60] Such fluidity has allowed the scope of the CAP to expand to embrace new policy goals identified within the Treaty, such as public health, consumer protection and animal welfare issues.[61] In the event of a conflict between the objectives the Court has stated:

> In pursuing these objectives the Community institutions must secure the permanent harmonisation made necessary by any conflict between the aims taken individually and, where necessary, allow one of them temporary priority in order to satisfy the demands of the economic factors or conditions in view of which their decisions are made.[62]

The formulation has been repeated by the Court on several occasions with the result that the Court has limited itself to an examination of whether the measure in question contains a manifest error, constitutes a misuse of power or whether the discretion enjoyed by the EU institutions has been exceeded.[63] However, the statement in *Balkan* also suggests that at some stage the Court may overrule a measure of the institutions if the situation of 'temporary priority' is continued for a substantial period of time, thus jeopardizing the achievement of the other objectives of the common agricultural policy. The possibility that the Court could adopt such an approach was highlighted in *Behla-Mühle* where Advocate General Capotorti suggested that a strict interpretation of Art. 33(1) might:

> ... justify the conclusion that the whole of the market policy so far followed by the Community is illegal in view of the fact that ... its essential basis is the fixing of prices to suit agricultural products in order to assure farmers an adequate income, whereas the policy favouring the modernisation and structural improvements and, in consequence, the rational development of agricultural production has been late in gathering momentum and is now evolving slowly and with considerable difficulty.[64]

Whilst the EU institutions enjoy considerable discretion in the implementation of a policy to achieve the objectives of Art. 33(1), both individually and collectively, it is important to conclude that the discretion is not unlimited. Considerable latitude has been given to the institutions by the *Balkan* formula but as *Behla Mühle* indicated there are limits to that latitude. Perhaps,

---

[60] See as examples, Case 297/82 *Danish Farmers* [1983] ECR 3299 and Cases 36 and 71/80 *ICMSA* [1981] ECR 735; Case 2/75 *Mackprang* [1975] ECR 607; Case 281/84 *Bedburg* [1987] ECR 49; and Case 49/83 *Luxembourg v Commission* [1984] ECR 2931.

[61] On public health and consumer protection, see for example Case 11/88 *Commission v Council (Pesticides)* [1989] ECR 3799; on animal welfare see Case 131/86 *UK v Council (Battery Hens)* [1988] ECR 905.

[62] *Balkan v Hauptzollamt Berlin-Packhof* [1973] ECR 1091, at 1112.

[63] See for example Case 29/77 *Roquette Frères* [1977] ECR 1835.

[64] Cases 114, 116 and 119–20/76 [1977] ECR 1211 at 1229.

the time has now come for the Court to overrule a measure on the basis that the 'temporary priority' accorded to Art. 33(1)(b) has continued for too long a period of time, thus jeopardising the achievement of the other objectives of the CAP and the Treaty.

It must be recognized that the EU institutions have failed to secure the permanent harmonization advocated by the Court. To hope for this harmonisation occurring in the new objectives is equally implausible, given the failure of proposals to date to address the new international trade reality of agricultural policy and the changes which will result as a consequence of the Treaty of Amsterdam's dictate that 'environmental protection requirements must be integrated into the definition and implementation' of all EU policies and activities mentioned in Art. 3. This new twin reality dictates a move away from price support and production controls towards a system which rewards farmers in the pursuit of certain public policy goals, such as protection of the environment.

In November 1995 the Directorate-General for Agriculture invited a group of experts to analyse the inconsistencies and problems inherent in the existing CAP and in this light to define a series of principles which would form the basis of a new integrated rural policy. The resulting report, known as the Buckwell report, proposed that the existing CAP should be transformed into a Common Agricultural and Rural Policy for Europe whose objective would be 'to ensure an economically efficient and environmentally sustainable agriculture and to stimulate the integrated development of the Union's rural areas.'[65] The three elements of the new policy, economic efficiency (through market stabilisation), the environment (through environmental and cultural landscape payments) and rural development (through a series of incentives), would, unlike the CAP, be equally balanced. With respect to market stabilisation, common organisations of the market will be limited to intervention measures for products subject to uncontrollable market fluctuations. The policy will no longer involve market price supports. In relation to the environment, payments will be made to farmers who actively protect the environment and the landscape. Merely being a farmer will not be sufficient to attract a payment. Finally, to ensure that the abolition of market price supports do not cause the collapse of rural areas, various rural development incentives are to be introduced to stimulate the non-agricultural use of farm resources. The report makes it clear that the new policy, although revolutionary, will also be evolutionary, so allowing the policy to respond to new challenges as they emerge.

The Agenda 2000 document identified the future enlargement of the EU as one of challenges to the future of the CAP. Yet the proposals in that document, and the further details added in the 18 March proposals, represent an attempt to eliminate only some of the distortions of the existing policy before enlargement. It fails to recognize the new international trade reality

---

[65] See europa.eu.int/en/comm/dg06/new/buck_en/index.htm, Chapter 6.1.

facing the CAP which the Agenda 2000 document recognized as an equally important challenge. The alternative Common Agricultural and Rural Policy for Europe (CARPE) addresses this new reality by moving away from the concept of direct income support for farmers whilst promoting an economically efficient and environmentally sustainable agriculture. Such a policy is dictated internationally by the Agreement on Agriculture and will be demanded within the EU as a result of the ratification of the Treaty of Amsterdam. This is the message which the EU should be sending to the applicant countries, rather than the unrealistic and unsustainable message contained in the Agenda 2000 document and the 18 March proposals. If the EU is seriously committed to enlargement, it is time for it to seize the day, or, as they say in Latin, *carpe diem*.

5

ENVIRONMENTAL PROTECTION AND THE AMSTERDAM TREATY

Professor Jan H. Jans

I INTRODUCTION

In this short paper I will try to give an answer to the question to what extent, if at all, the Amsterdam Treaty will or can contribute to a more suitable system of genuine sustainable development in the European Union. After addressing a couple of central legal issues by making a comparison between the previous state of European environmental law and the changes introduced by the Amsterdam Treaty, I will try to draw some conclusions.

II SOME LEGAL OBSTACLES FOR SUSTAINABLE DEVELOPMENT

What then, under the previous Maastricht Treaty text were the main legal problems and obstacles on the road of European Environmental Protection? I will mention just a few:

1. To promote sustainable development was not mentioned as one of the key objectives of Arts 2 and 3 of the EC Treaty (old). The **constitutional** status of environmental protection therefore was still not beyond discussion. The lack of a clear provision still triggered the idea that environmental protection should or could be regarded as subordinate to economic development and economic growth.

2. A second problem had to do with the question to what extent member states are entitled to derogate from Community environmental measures taken in the framework of the Internal Market. In particular in the area of harmonization of environmental product standards there was uncertainty under which conditions member states were allowed to issue more stringent legislation than the European.

3. A third problem had to do with decision-making procedures. For some environmental measures unanimity was required:
   (a) provisions primarily of a fiscal nature;
   (b) measures concerning town and country planning, land use with the exception of waste management and measures of a general nature and management of water resources;
   (c) measures significantly affecting a member state's choice between different energy sources and the general structure of its energy supply.

   This meant that for not the least important environmental issues, for instance the introduction of a carbon dioxide tax and measures pertaining to climate change and the greenhouse effect, were subject to decision-making by unanimity.

4. A fourth problem has to do with Art. 36 of the EC Treaty (old). It provides the member states the power to take trade restricting measures, if these measures can be justified on certain grounds. Environmental protection is not mentioned as one of them. Of course I am aware of the case law of the Court of Justice in cases like *Danish Bottles* where the Court acknowledged the existence of other mandatory requirements to justify trade restrictions.[1] However, it is accepted both in case law and in the literature that these mandatory requirements cannot be applied to justify export restrictions falling under the scope of Art. 34 of the EC Treaty (old).[2] The reason for this is that Art. 34 is applicable to discriminatory measures only, while the *Danish Bottles* doctrine can only be applied in case of non-discriminatory trade restrictions. This case law could have a serious negative impact on the possibilities to control the export of waste.

5. A final problem I want to mention has to do with legal protection. Once again we can read in the preamble of the Treaty on European Union that the EU is based on the Rule of Law. Under the Rule of Law, at least in my interpretation, the exercise of public competencies should be based on legal rules and mechanism must be implemented to ensure that these competencies are being exercised within the attributed legal powers. I just want to recall Art. 3B and 164 of the EC Treaty (old). In environmental law we have the following problem. In particular, the Commission has been attributed or delegated decision-making powers, for instance in the area of the Structural Funds. These decisions can have a negative impact on the environment. In the recent *Greenpeace* judgment the Court had to deal with a decision of the Commission to subsidize the building of electrical power stations at the Canary Islands which was challenged by locals and

---

[1] Case C-302/86 *Danish Bottles*, [1988] ECR 4607.
[2] See however the recent case C-203/96 *Chemische Afvalstoffen Dusseldorp*, [1998] ECR I-4075, where the Court did discuss the environmental protection requirements in relation to Art. 34 ECT.

environmental organizations because of its effects on the environment.[3] The Court, more or less applying the standard case law on *locus standi* in action for annulment proceedings (the old Art. 173 EC Treaty), declared the applicants claim inadmissable: there was no question of **direct and individual** concern. The particular problem in environmental law is that in most cases decisions of public authorities affecting the environment are not of individual concern. They are of a general concern. This would mean that it will be virtually impossible to find an admissible claim to challenge Commission decisions affecting the environment. *De facto* this will lead to a situation that no legal control can be exercised over the way the Commission operates. In a European Union based on the Rule of Law this cannot be accepted.

Having mentioned five serious legal obstacles on the road to sustainable development, it is time to see what the Amsterdam Treaty has to say.

III SUSTAINABLE DEVELOPMENT AS ONE OF THE CONSTITUTIONAL OBJECTIVES

As you all know, the term 'environment' was introduced for the first time by the Maastricht Treaty in its key Arts 2 and 3, which set out the objectives and activities of the Community. Article 2 referred to 'the promotion, throughout the Community, of a harmonious and balanced development of economic activities, sustainable and non-inflationary growth respecting the environment', while Art. 3(k) stated that one of the activities for attaining this is 'a policy in the sphere of the environment'.

The formulation 'sustainable growth' in Art. 2 has been heavily criticized by legal writers as being a departure from the more usual formulation, at least in environmental circles, of 'sustainable development'. From the point of view of environmental protection, the concept of 'sustainable growth' seemed marginally weaker than that of 'sustainable development'. It was feared that this unusual terminology would imply that environmental protection would have a subordinate legal status compared to economic growth and development. Environmental protection as a lip-service only.

In the Amsterdam Treaty, the text of Art. 2 has been improved considerably. We can now read that the Community shall have as its task to promote a harmonious, balanced and sustainable development of economic activities. This formulation is much more in line with internationally accepted practice in the environmental policy area. The political importance of this cannot be underestimated.[4] Of course the text is still not entirely satisfactory, because

---

[3] Case C-321/95P *Greenpeace*, [1998] ECR I-1651. For a critical appraisal my annotation (in Dutch) in Tijdschrift voor Milieu en Recht 1998/7/8, nr. 67.
[4] *Cf* Geert van Caltster and Kurt Deketelaere, 'Amsterdam, the Intergovernmental Conference and Greening the EU Treaty'. In: *EELR* 1998, 13–25, at 14.

there is still a link in Art. 2 between the use of the terms 'sustainable development' and 'economic activities' and because we find a slightly different formulation in Art. 2 of the Treaty on European Union (new).[5] But as a whole we could agree that the text really has improved.

There is however a second improvement. The Amsterdam Treaty not only speaks of sustainable development, in Art. 2 it also introduces as a Community task to promote 'a high level of protection and improvement of the quality of the environment'.

As such, this 'high level of protection' principle is of course not new. Article 100a(3), included in the Treaty by the Single European Act, provided that the Commission, in its internal market proposals in the field of environmental protection would take as a base a high level of protection. This proposal was criticized as being directed only at the Commission and that the Council, as the ultimate decision-making body, could depart from the Commission's proposals. It was also doubtful to what extent the prescription in the Article was open to review by the courts. Suppose the Council were to take its decision in conformity with the Commission's proposal. Could it then be argued before the courts that the decision could be declared invalid if it did not take as a base a high level of protection? It seemed hardly conceivable. In the Amsterdam Treaty the new Art. 100a(3), now Art. 95(3), reads as follows:

> The Commission, in its proposals envisaged in paragraph 1 concerning health, safety, environmental protection and consumer protection, will take as a base a high level of protection, taking account in particular of any new development based on scientific facts. Within their respective powers, the European Parliament and the Council will also seek to achieve this objective.

This provision makes it quite clear that the high level of protection principle is not only directed at the Commission, but also at the European Parliament and Council in their legislative capacity. However, the 'seek to achieve' formulation still makes it doubtful indeed whether this principle is subject to review in a court of law.[6]

As regards the high level of protection principle and its inclusion in the objectives of the Treaty, I want to make just one other remark. One of the most welcomed, but also most criticized, judgments of the Court of Justice concerning European Environmental Law is the *Danish Bottles* case. It was welcomed as the judgment where the Court accepted 'environmental protection' as a mandatory requirement in the context of the Rule of Reason, enabling member states to restrict intra-community trade if national measures are necessary to protect the environment.

The criticism concerned the way the Court of Justice applied the proportionality principle in the case. To freshen your memory: under the

---

[5] 'a balanced and sustainable development'.
[6] *Cf* Geert van Caltster and Kurt Deketelaere, 'Amsterdam, the Intergovernmental Conference and Greening the EU Treaty. In: *EELR* 1998, 13–25, at 15.

proportionality principle, a measure must restrict trade as little as possible, in the sense that there must be no measures less restrictive, but adequate, available. As far as the requirement that producers and importers must only use containers approved by the National Agency for the Protection of the Environment was concerned, the Court's finding was not favourable to the Danish Government. The Court argued that although it was undoubtedly true that the existing system for returning approved containers ensured a maximum rate of re-use and therefore a very considerable degree of protection of the environment, nevertheless, the system for returning non-approved containers was capable of protecting the environment as well.

In those circumstances, the Danish measures were held to be disproportionate to the objective pursued. The Court accepted implicitly the Commission's view on the proportionality principle. The Commission considered that it followed from the principle of proportionality that the level of protection should not be fixed exaggeratedly high and that other solutions should be accepted even if they were a little less effective in assuring the aim pursued.

In my opinion, the inclusion of the high level of protection principle in the objectives of the Treaty will make a difference in applying the proportionality principle in the context of Arts 30 and 36, now Arts 28 and 30 of the EC Treaty. Under the Rule of Reason it must be accepted that a high level of environmental protection is considered a mandatory requirement enabling member states to justify intra-community barriers to trade. In other words: if the *Danish Bottles* case were to be decided again today it would be my opinion that the Danish legislation concerning returnable bottles would in no way violate the new Art. 28 EC Treaty (new).

Maybe there is a third improvement. According to the integration principle as stated in Art. 130r(2) EC Treaty (old): 'Environmental protection requirements must be integrated into the definition and implementation of other Community policies'. This refers to what is known as 'external' integration, in other words the integration of environmental objectives in other policy sectors such as agriculture, transport, internal market, etc.

The **text** of this principle will not be changed to any great extent. Article 6 of the new EC Treaty will only contain a reference to the activities mentioned in Art. 3 of the Treaty and the concept of sustainable development. However, this means that existing problems concerning the interpretation of the principle still remain:

- The first question which still remains is what precisely has to be integrated? The Treaty refers to 'environmental protection requirements'. What should this be taken to mean? Certainly it would seem to include the objectives of Art. 174(1) EC Treaty (new). It also seems likely that it includes the other principles referred to in Art. 174(2) EC Treaty (new), such as the precautionary principle and the principle that preventive action should be taken. And, finally, integration of the policy aspects referred to in Art. 174(3) EC Treaty (new) should not *a priori* be excluded, though it is true that the Treaty does not state that these aspects have to be integrated, but only that they should be taken into account.

- The next problem not addressed concerns the question whether the integration principle implies that the Community's environment policy has been given some measure of priority over other of the Community's policy areas. Probably it has not, at least not if priority is taken to mean that, in the event of a conflict with other policy areas, the Community's environment policy has a certain added value from a legal point of view. The text of the Treaty does not support such a conclusion. The integration principle is designed to ensure that protection of the environment is at least taken into consideration, even when commercial policy is involved or when other decisions are being taken, for example, in the fields of agriculture, transport, development aid, regional policy etc., and has to be worked out in more detail in those areas. However, the manner in which potential conflicts between protection of the environment and, for example, the functioning of the internal market should be resolved cannot be inferred from the integration principle as such.

- A third aspect which is important when evaluating the legal status of the integration principle is whether the legitimacy of actions of the Council and Commission can be reviewed by the Court in the light of the principle. Can the validity of a directive or regulation, for example in the field of transport or agriculture, be questioned on the grounds that the decision has infringed the environmental objectives of the Treaty? In other words, the question as to the legal enforceability of the principle is in fact a question as to the legal significance of the objectives, principles and other aspects referred to in Art. 130r(1), (2) and (3) EC Treaty (old). It has already been noted that the present version of the principle is formulated fairly forcefully ('**must** be integrated'). In principle, review of Community measures in the light of the environmental objectives should therefore be regarded as possible. However, it should be borne in mind that the institutions have wide discretionary powers as to how they shape the Community's environment policy, and will have to balance the relative importance of the environmental objectives and other Community objectives as they proceed. Only in very exceptional cases will a measure be susceptible to annulment (or being declared invalid) because certain environmental objectives seem not to have been taken sufficiently into account.

A final question that should have been discussed in connection with this principle is that of the possible consequences for member states. In principle, in view of the fact that the text of the Treaty expressly refers to 'Community policy', the integration principle should have no direct legal consequences for the member states. Of course, there will be indirect effects, in the sense that the Council and the Commission will observe the principle in their legal acts, which are often addressed to the member states. As these are often integrated regulations and directives, the member states will also be required to observe a certain degree of integration. On the other hand, it seems unlikely that the member states will be bound by the environmental objectives and principles of the Treaty in areas that have not been harmonized, other than by the general obligation contained in Art. 10 EC Treaty (new).[7] According to the Court of Justice in *Peralta*, national environmental laws cannot be reviewed **directly** in the light of Art. 130r(2) of the EC Treaty (old).[8]

This all leads to the conclusion that the text of the new integration principle does not as such change the law. However, there is a difference and that is that the integration principle has been shifted from the Environment paragraph in the Treaty to Part One (General Principles). This will raise the additional question: what are the legal effects, if any, of this upward movement? Although other authors have expressed a somewhat different view on the matter, I remain fairly sceptical.[9] I do not think that declaring the integration principle a General Principle of Community law makes a significant difference from a legal perspective. Let us take a closer look at the four aspects I have just mentioned:

(1) General Principle or not, the question of what exactly should be integrated is not addressed by this new provision.

(2) The question of priority? I am still of the opinion that the integration principle only states that environmental protection requirements should be taken into account, without giving a definitive answer as to **how** the balancing of different objectives and interests should be performed by the Council and EP. The integration principle has a formal, not a substantive character. In that respect, including the high level of protection principle, a principle which does have a substantive content, in Art. 2 EC Treaty (new) as one of the Community's objectives could prove of more importance.

(3) Are Community measures open to review by the Court? The European environment legislator still has a wide discretionary competence and I do not see how the integration principle's being a General Principle makes any real difference.

(4) Consequences for the member states? According to the text of the integration principle it is directed at the Community. It is indeed a General Principle, but one directed at the institutions only. I cannot see any direct consequences for the member states.

---

[7] See, with respect to Art. 5 EC Treaty (old): Case C-129/96, *Inter-Environnement Wallonie v Région Wallonne*, [1997] ECR I-7411.

[8] *Cf* Case C-379/92 *Peralta* [1994] ECR I-3453, in particular paras 55–59. *Cf* also High Court, Queen's Bench Division (Smith LJ and Farquharson LJ) 3 October 1994, *R v Secretary of State for Trade and Industry, ex parte Duddridge* [1995] Env LR 325.

[9] *Cf* Geert van Caltster and Kurt Deketelaere, Amsterdam, 'the Intergovernmental Conference and Greening the EU Treaty', in *EELR*, 1998, 13–25, at 17–19.

My conclusion is that the integration principle remains one of the more important principles of European Environmental Law. However, existing problems regarding its interpretation have neither been addressed nor resolved by the Amsterdam Treaty. Making it a General Principle and moving the principle to the beginning of the Treaty does not seem very important from a legal point of view.

IV DEROGATION AFTER HARMONIZATION

With respect to the possibilities of derogation, after harmonization, from internal market related measures by virtue of environmental protection requirements (the old Art. 100a(4) procedure), I have to admit that the new text is an improvement, not only from a substantive but also from a procedural point of view. However, the new text has introduced new legal questions on the interpretation as well.

First the improvements:

(1) Under the old version of the Treaty it was not altogether clear whether a member state, wanting to rely on Art. 100a(4), had to vote against (or at least not in favour) a directive or regulation it wanted to derogate from. The text suggested this, because it referred to the Council having voted by a qualified majority. As a result, member states were confronted with a dilemma: voting against a Community measure could mean that it could not be adopted at all; voting in favour would mean losing the possibility of relying on Art. 100a(4) in the future. Because the new text omits any reference to qualified majorities, it must be interpreted in the sense that any member state, irrespective of how they voted in Council, can in principle be allowed to rely on the derogation procedure. However, it could be argued that the principle of estoppel – recognized by the Court of Justice as being a general principle of Community law – could restrict the use of the procedure by those member states who voted against a measure.[10] I am fairly confident the Commission will try this argument out before the Court of Justice at some stage.

(2) Under the old text it was questionable whether the derogation procedure could be applied with respect to Council measures only, or if measures taken by the Commission (for instance implementing framework directives enacted by the Council) were also covered by Art. 100a(4). The current text speaks of harmonization measures taken by Council or Commission, so this problem has been solved.

(3) As a result of the judgment of the Court of Justice in the *German PCP case*,[11] where it was stated that national measures cannot be

[10] Case 148/78 *Ratti* [1979] ECR 1629.
[11] Case C-41/93 *France v Commission* [1994] ECR I-1829.

applied before the Commission has given its consent, the question was raised: and what if the Commission is not able or willing to deliver a decision in due time?[12] In other words, within what time framework is the Commission required to act? This is by no means a purely academic question. If I am informed correctly, the Dutch Government has been waiting for more than seven years now for a Commission reaction to the notification of Dutch law prohibiting the use of cadmium. The new text requires the Commission to take a decision within six months, failing which the measures are deemed to have been approved.

(4) A major improvement is the fact that, where a member state has been authorized to take national measures derogating from a harmonization measure, the Commission is required to examine the Community measure immediately with a view to a possible amendment of Community law.

(5) Perhaps the most important change has been made concerning the use of the derogation procedure for introducing new national measures. Under the old text it was not altogether clear whether derogation was only allowed with respect to existing national measures or whether the procedure of Art. 100a(4) could also be used to introduce new legislation. Legal writers debated the matter fiercely, without the battle being decided by a judgment of the Court of Justice. Paragraph 5 of the new Art. 95 finally makes it clear that it is permitted to introduce new national legislation which derogates from Community harmonization measures. In this respect I must warn against one possible consequence. The widening of the possibilities for member states to derogate from Community legislation might have serious consequences for the harmonization process itself. After all, why should the Council bother to harmonize if there are ample possibilities for member states to derogate from the results achieved? I hope that this will not be the result, because, from an environmental point of view, no harmonization at all could prove even worse.

So, from an environmental point of view, the improvements are clear and obvious. What then are the remaining problems and what possible new problems may arise?

(1) Although the **introduction** of legislation is indeed covered by para. 5 of the new Art. 95, the conditions under which this is possible are not altogether clear. First of all, para. 5 requires that member states must prove that there is 'new scientific evidence' justifying their behaviour. A mere policy change would not seem sufficient! Secondly, para. 5 requires that this evidence relates to the protection of the environment or the working environment. The 'public policy'

---

[12] Case C-319/97, Kortas, n.y.o.r.

grounds of Art. 36 EC Treaty (old) are omitted. This of course seems odd, particularly when we read that the 'public policy' grounds can be used for maintaining existing national standards. Introducing new national standards is therefore more difficult than maintaining existing ones. Looking at this from a non-discrimination point of view it could be argued that this is still problematic. This imbalance in the Treaty could result in a certain national measure being allowed in one member state (because it is existing national legislation covered by an Art. 36 ground) but not in another (because that member state wanted to introduce it).

(2) The member state must show that the new national measures are necessary to tackle a problem that is specific to that member state. In other words, there have to be circumstances specific to that member state justifying the more stringent environmental measures. This means that a simple statement: 'we want stricter environmental legislation', would not be not sufficient. This criterion cannot be found, at least not explicitly, in the text regarding existing national legislation and this seems to imply another imbalance. However, it could be argued that this condition must be met with respect to para. 4 as well. The Court's judgment in the *German PCP* case could be interpreted to imply this. Moreover, practice at the Commission, in particular its second decision on German PCP and Danish PCP legislation,[13] shows that the Commission will review all national measures in the light of such specific circumstances. In my opinion, this is the correct course. If national environmental legislation has been harmonized, the presumption must be that the level of protection resulting from harmonization is adequate. The famous *Inter Huiles* case seems to point in the same direction.[14] If member states want to derogate from a directive, either by introducing new legislation or by maintaining existing stricter standards, they have to show that this is justified on grounds specific to that member state.

(3) In para. 6 of the new Art. 95 we find a new condition which must be met before the Commission is allowed to approve national derogating measures. Besides the well known conditions of 'no arbitrary discrimination' and 'no disguised restriction to trade' we find a new one: 'no obstacle to the functioning of the internal market'. This of course raises the interesting question of what this means. In the Dutch legal literature the opinion has been expressed that the 'no obstacle' clause is a translation, admittedly bad, of the proportionality principle.[15] If this author is right, this clause is superfluous. I think

---

[13] *Cf* the second Commission Decision on the German PCP legislation in *OJ* 1994, L316/43. See also the Commission Decision on the Danish PCP legislation in *OJ* 1996, L68/32.
[14] Case 172/82 *Inter-Huiles* [1983] ECR 555.
[15] Hugo G. von Meijenfeldt, Vergroening van Verdrag van Amsterdam 'Tijdschrift voor Milieu en Recht', 1997, 174–178, at 174.

there is no doubt at all that national derogating legislation has to be proportionate. If the proportionality principle plays a role before harmonization, and as we all know it does, it must *a fortiori* play a role after harmonization! I doubt therefore whether the 'no obstacle' clause is simply another word for proportionality. If that were the case the drafters of the text would have made a reference to the proportionality principle of the old Art. 3b, now Art. 5, of the EC Treaty or they would have used the well known formulas of the Court of Justice. I am thus led to the conclusion that the 'no obstacle' clause has a meaning of its own. It shows first of all that the Commission has been given a wide discretionary power to block derogating national standards even if the national measures are justified from an environmental point of view and even if there is no arbitrary discrimination or disguised restriction to trade. In assessing the national measures the Commission can take into account any effect on the internal market and has therefore been given a power to balance different objectives and interests going well beyond the proportionality principle. Although the new provisions have been presented as a victory for environmentalists, I am not quite sure whether the real winner is not the Commission.

(4) Another problem not addressed by the Amsterdam Treaty has to the do with the status of national legislation not notified to the Commission or with legislation introduced in violation of the stand still obligation. In the *German PCP* case the Court argued that the member state is acting in violation of Art. 100a(4) EC Treaty (old) if it applies national legislation not notified to the Commission. However, the Court was not asked to rule on the possible direct effect of these obligations. The interesting question is therefore: can the Court's ruling in the *CIA Security* case be applied by analogy to the notification of measures under the new Art. 95? In my opinion this is indeed the case: the reasons underlying the *CIA Security* judgment[16] (notification and the relation with the free movement of goods) are valid with respect to this kind of notification as well.[17] National legislation derogating from harmonization measures and not notified to the Commission or national acts which have been notified but are applied before the Commission has given its consent, cannot be enforced against individuals.[18]

---

[16] Case C-194/94 *CIA Security* [1996] ECR I-2201.
[17] See also my 'National legislative autonomy? The procedural constraints of European law' published in LIEI 1998/1.
[18] See for different views the annotation by Slot to *CIA Security* in CMLRev 1996, 1035–1050, at 1045. *Cf* also Stephen Weatherill, 'Compulsory Notification of Draft Technical Regulations: the Contribution of Directive 83/189 to the Management of the Internal Market', YEL 1996, 129–204.

V THE PROVISIONS IN THE ENVIRONMENT PARAGRAPH OF THE TREATY

The provisions of the environmental paragraph, now Arts 174–176, in the EC Treaty have not been changed in their material, their substantive meaning. A major change however concerns the decision-making procedures. The codecision procedure has become the standard decision-making procedure for environmental legislation. Although codecision does not automatically lead to more environmentally friendly legislation, this change must nevertheless be welcomed. We have come a long way from decision-making by unanimity under the old Arts 100 and 235 EC Treaty to majority voting and a strong role for the European Parliament under an explicit environment paragraph in the Treaty. Perhaps even more important than the codecision procedure as such is that there is now no longer a difference in procedure between internal market legislation and purely environmental legislation. This means that time consuming interinstitutional battles fought before the Court of Justice concerning the choice of legal grounds are no longer necessary.[19] If all the time spent thus in previous years were to be devoted to policy-making instead, we could look forward to a bright future indeed. One problem however still remains: and that is that the unanimity rule still applies with respect to environmental legislation containing:

- provisions primarily of a fiscal nature;
- measures concerning town and country planning, land use with the exception of waste management and measures of a general nature and management of water resources;
- measures significantly affecting a member state's choice between different energy sources and the general structure of its energy supply.

This means that some important environmental issues, for instance the introduction of a carbon dioxide tax and measures pertaining to climate change and the greenhouse effect, are still subject to decision-making by unanimity.

VI NO AMENDMENT OF ARTICLE 36 EC TREATY (OLD)

At the beginning of this paper I argued that there was a need to amend the old Art. 36 of the Treaty, now Art. 30, and that 'environmental protection' ought to be included in the list. The transformation from a Rule of Reason type of exception to an official Art. 36 ground is, as I have stated, particularly necessary in view of a more comprehensive policy in the area of transfrontier movement of waste. It will also enable the Court of Justice to bring its judgment in the *Walloon Waste* case[20] more in line with its traditional case

---

[19] Like for instance in Case C-300/89 *Commission v Council* [1991] ECR I-2867, Case C-70/88 *European Parliament v Council* [1991] ECR I-4529 and Case C-155/91 *Commission v Council* [1993] ECR I-939.
[20] Case C-2/90 *Commission v Belgium* [1992] ECR I-4431.

law on the free movement of goods. The fact that the Amsterdam Treaty did not address this problem is a pity.

VII THE RULE OF LAW AND ENVIRONMENTAL PROTECTION

As I have said before, one of the major problems undermining the legitimacy of the Community institutions has to do with access to justice. The *Greenpeace* judgment of the Court of Justice makes it quite clear that environmental organizations, but also natural persons affected by decisions taken by the Commission and having environmental consequences, have no possibility whatsoever in standing before the Court of Justice. This is due to the Court's narrow interpretation of the 'direct and individual concern' condition mentioned in Art. 173 EC Treaty (old), now Art. 230. As a result, Commission decisions affecting the environment are in practice not subject to review by a court of law. The Amsterdam Treaty will not bring any changes here. In a European Union devoted to the Rule of Law this is a shame.

VIII SUMMING UP

From the five legal obstacles on the road to sustainable development in the European Union, two have been removed by the Amsterdam Treaty. This is not particularly good, but it is not a particularly bad result either. And it may be that conclusions can be drawn with respect to the whole of the Treaty of Amsterdam as well.

6

THE NEW EMPLOYMENT CHAPTER AND SOCIAL POLICY PROVISIONS OF THE AMSTERDAM TREATY

Noreen Burrows

I INTRODUCTION

It is possible to view the social policy provisions of the Amsterdam Treaty from a number of different perspectives. Depending on the question asked, the answer might turn out to be very different. Does the new Treaty improve the sense of coherence to European social policy, given that some of its critics find no such coherence? Does it push forward the boundaries of social citizenship? Does it help us define or redefine a European social model? Has it deepened the process of European integration or improved efficiency in the decision-making processes or does it reinforce intergovernmentalism? What does it tell us about multilayered governance? Does it redefine the competencies between the member states and the European Union or reinforce subsidiarity?[1]

This chapter seeks to analyse the social policy provisions from a different perspective although it touches upon the important questions of institutional reform, efficiency in decision-making processes and the strengthening of the process of European integration. In relation to the various Treaty amendments on social policy and employment it asks two questions. The first arises from the conclusion of Langrish that Amsterdam in all aspects except the question of justice and home affairs was merely a 'routine service' rather than a fundamental reconstruction of the European Union.[2] Was the Treaty a routine service in matters of social policy and law? The second question relates to the enlargement process. Given that one of the purposes of the Amsterdam Treaty was to assist the European Union in preparation for

---

[1] Social law and policy has been subject to analysis using all these approaches. For a discussion of the literature see, for example, T. Hervey, *European Social Law and Policy*, Longman, 1998.
[2] S. Langrish, 'The Treaty of Amsterdam: Selected Highlights' (1998) 23 EL Rev 3.

enlargement, have the amendments on social policy assisted in this process or made the process of enlargement more difficult?

In order to answer these questions the chapter will examine two areas where the Amsterdam Treaty introduced changes: the inclusion of the employment chapter and the consolidation of the Social Policy Agreement into the text of the Treaty. Other changes were made in the area of social policy and they have their own significance; the introduction of a general article expanding the forbidden grounds of discrimination; the reinforcement of the commitment of the European Union to fundamental human rights; revision of the Title on justice and home affairs. These are all matters which might be dealt with under the heading of social policy. However, this chapter concentrates solely on new Titles VIII and XI. A feature that unites these two Titles is the role of social dialogue as a means of furthering EU policy and this chapter examines the new Titles in the context of proposals to enhance the participation of the social partners. In relation to each Title, Langrish's conclusion will be examined. If these new Titles were a continuation of existing policy, without contributing to a major revision of policy, then it would seem fair to suggest that they are merely part of the routine service, an oil change rather than a new engine. If they clarify or simplify Union policy, they may make the negotiation process with the applicant states more straightforward. Furthermore, if they streamline structures and procedures, this should assist in reducing the burden faced by the applicant states when confronted with the need to translate Union policy into an existing domestic legal and administrative order.

II THE EMPLOYMENT CHAPTER; (NEW) TITLE VIII

The new Title on employment is inserted into the Treaty establishing the European Community immediately following on from the Title on economic policy. At the national level, employment and welfare policies are inextricably linked to national economic policies. In some member states, such as Germany, there is a constitutional linkage made between these policies. Chalmers and Szyszczak, unlike Langrish, view the 'acceptance of Community responsibility for the coordination of macro-economic policy vis-à-vis national labour markets' as 'a far-reaching change' made by the Treaty of Amsterdam.[3] They argue that the inter-relationship between employment policy and the involvement of ECOFIN in defining guidelines in the area of economic and monetary union put employment issues 'firmly upon the agenda of the European Council'. However, it is significant that the Treaty of Amsterdam subordinates national employment policies to the need for the convergence of economic policies as part of the project to develop economic and monetary union.

---

[3] D. Chalmers and E. Szyszczak, *European Union Law: Volume II*, Dartmouth, 1998, 509.

The objectives of the new title on employment are: to achieve a high level of employment, to develop a coordinated strategy for employment, to emphasize skills and training and to develop responsive labour markets. The role of the EU in these matters is to encourage and support national policies and to take into consideration the need to ensure a high rate of employment in the formulation of EU policies, for example, in the development of rural policy. It is not envisaged that legislation will be used as a tool to effect the coordination of national policies – instead the Council will draw up guidelines to provide the yardstick against which national policies might be measured. Member states will report to the Council of Employment Ministers who will examine these reports and may issue recommendations to member states. The Council is also empowered to adopt incentive measures to encourage cooperation particularly relating to the exchange of information and expertise. Finally, the Treaty envisages the establishment of an Employment Committee with advisory status to promote coordination of labour market policies. Its tasks are similar to those exercised by the Council of Employment Ministers in that the Committee is to monitor the employment situation and employment policies of the EU and the member states and to formulate opinions at the request of the Council, the Commission or on its own initiative and prepare for the meetings of the Council. In its tasks, it has been compared to ECOFIN.[4] The Employment Committee is to be composed of two members from each member state and two members appointed by the Commission and in carrying out these tasks it is to consult management and labour.

It has been said that these provisions 'reflect a difficult compromise between the various national views and are thus very weak'.[5] Scappucci argues that the negotiating positions of the member states during the IGC were irreconcilable given the diverse traditions on employment policy ranging from the state subsidy and intervention of the Nordic countries and France and Italy to the UK reliance on market flexibility coupled with a German reluctance to award any degree of competence to the European Union on these matters. Indeed, it could be argued that they add little to the existing Treaty provisions. The original Treaty of Rome in Art. 118 had given to the Commission the task of promoting close cooperation in the employment field and this Article is repeated in the new Art. 140. Furthermore, the Treaty on European Union recognized the need for the EU to pursue a policy of a high level of employment and social protection.

Whether the inclusion of the new Title on employment is of symbolic importance only will be seen in the context of what measures are taken on the basis of the new Title VIII. However, it should be remembered that it had been one of the anomalies of European law that a Treaty devoted to the creation of a common market, and even more surprisingly to the creation of

---

[4] By Chalmers and Szyszczak in ibid.
[5] G. Scappucci, 'Social and Employment Policy' in Glockler et al. *Guide to EU Policies*, Blackstone Press, 1998.

an economic and monetary union, had not, until Amsterdam, included substantive provisions on employment and unemployment. All theories of economic integration had predicted that the creation of economically integrated units such as common markets or customs unions would tend to create pockets of unemployment as economic restructuring threw out inefficient firms and drew investment and capital away from marginal areas. The European Coal and Steel Community Treaty made specific provision for retraining and redeployment of workers but the Treaty of Rome was not so explicit. It was based on an assumption that these problems could be solved by facilitating the free movement of labour and by encouraging economic growth. Later, the creation of the European Social Fund with its emphasis on training modified this approach slightly but European led employment policies were never seen as integral to the workings of the collective European economy.

Free movement is not the solution to the problem of unemployment in a European context and is not a reality for the vast majority of European citizens. Unlike the USA, where mass migrations were sometimes the response to economic crises, Europeans do not find it so easy to cross national borders for a variety of reasons; cultural, linguistic, bureaucratic and legal. Neither can the structural funds make a significant impact on the problem – they are inadequate to meet the task. Nonetheless, there is a significant European dimension to this problem, not least because the pursuit of policies such as economic and monetary union has required stringent financial controls on government spending.

It would be wrong to suggest, however, that the Amsterdam Treaty represents some sudden conversion to the idea that national employment policies interact with EU policies. It is perhaps more accurate to state that the Amsterdam Treaty has revitalized the debate at the European level and has attempted to respond to the criticism that EU policies do not meet the expectations of ordinary citizens. In doing so it can be argued that Amsterdam has created a shift in emphasis in terms of future policy. This shift in emphasis affects both the institutional framework in which European policy is developed as well as its content. In support of this view is the importance which seemed to be attached to the new Title VIII by the Heads of State or Government who called for the immediate implementation of the new Title prior to the coming into force of the Treaty itself. In response, the Commission proposed employment guidelines which were discussed at the so-called jobs summit in November 1997.

Amongst other things, that summit emphasized the need for a strengthened role of social dialogue in the development of an employment strategy. Until the adoption of the Amsterdam Treaty, the key institution for discussion of employment policy was the Standing Committee on Employment established in 1970.[6] That Committee was a tripartite committee bringing together representatives of the Council, the Commission and the social partners.

---

[6] Council Decision of 14 December 1970 *OJ* No, L/273 of 17 December 1970.

Its function was to determine shared objectives. In addition, a number of other committees were established bringing together national employment experts and the social partners. This proliferation of committees and the subsequent dilution of the process of consultation led the Commission to call into question the efficiency of the Standing Committee. Therefore, following the adoption of the Council Resolution on the 1988 Employment Guidelines, which called for an Employment Partnership, the Commission has proposed an amendment of the original Council decision establishing the Standing Committee on Employment.[7] The Commission is proposing a rationalization of the process of consultation by limiting the membership of the Committee, by updating its membership and by incorporating its meetings into the decision-making processes. The new Committee will be composed of either the full Council or the Troika, the Commission and sixteen representatives of the social partners – eight from the union side and eight from the employers. Its function is to ensure that there is continuous dialogue between the EU institutions and the social partners 'in order to facilitate co-ordination by the Member States of their employment policies in harmony with the objectives of the Community'. It is envisaged that the Committee will meet twice a year enabling it to feed in to the decision-making processes. One meeting will take place before the meetings of the Heads of State and Governments at the end of each presidency. The second meeting will take place after the Commission has issued its Communication on the national action plans but before the Employment Committee meets to give its opinion of the Commission's Communication.

This strengthening of the role of the social dialogue in employment matters reflects the direction of policy inherent in the new Title VIII. The emphasis on skills, training and adaptability of the workforce in the new Art. 125 reflects earlier EU initiatives. The Commission's consultation on 'Partnership for a new organisation of work' of April 1997 spelled out its views on the need for a flexible and responsive labour market characterized by equality of opportunity, a trained and responsive workforce and the need for competitiveness.[8] In some respects, the Amsterdam Treaty formalizes these ideas and in that sense provides a steer on the way in which EU and national policies might develop over the next decade. These themes certainly reappear in the Employment Guidelines adopted in December 1997. Adaptability, equality of opportunity, employability (a trained and responsive workforce) and the encouragement of entrepreneurship underline these Guidelines. This does suggest that the idea of large-scale job creation projects or other government directed initiatives have been rejected as a solution to unemployment.

If the emphasis in employment policies is to be on adaptability and flexibility then it is clear that the social partners have a key role to play in furthering the objectives of the EU. It is also clear that legislative pressure will not be

---

[7] COM (98) 322, 'Adapting and promoting the Social Dialogue at Community level', 20 May 1998.
[8] COM (97) 128 final, 'Partnership for a new organisation of work', 16 April 1997.

brought to bear to force through, for example, compulsory training. In many ways therefore the burden of solving the problems of unemployment is placed firmly in the hands of the social partners. Workers must get themselves educated and trained, employers must explore new forms of working. The role of the EU is a facilitator. The kinds of initiatives that can be taken emphasize the residual nature of EU action; incentive measures designed to ensure cooperation and to support national action; the exchange of information and good practice, the possibility of pilot projects.

It can be argued that the new Title VIII merely translates into Treaty form what has actually been happening at the European level. In that sense, it is a continuation of policy. It is also a continuation in the sense that the compromise nature of the text and the weakness of its provisions, indicate that there is not real agreement as yet on the direction of employment policy. However, what is more interesting is what has been done with the Title so far, even before the Amsterdam Treaty has been ratified. The creation of new institutions at governmental level and the reform of existing tripartite structures may provide the first step towards the real coordination of policies. This is more likely to occur where the structures themselves are coordinated. The cycle of meetings where employment policies are discussed, whether in the European Council, the Council of Ministers, the Employment Committee or the reformed Standing Committee on Employment provides an opportunity for the exchange of views that might provide the basis for coordinated EU action. Given that the current level of unemployment in the EU runs to approximately 18 million, the need for such policies is obvious. The 1998 Employment Guidelines do provide the basis for discussion and have shown some weaknesses in national employment strategies, for example, in relation to equal opportunities. Despite the weakness of the actual provisions themselves, therefore, they are producing results.

Consolidation of the Social Policy Agreement

It was clear from early drafts of the Amsterdam Treaty that there had been no agreement between the UK and the other member states on the place of the social policy provisions within the new Treaty.[9] The Dublin draft, for example, points to the desire of the fourteen member states to incorporate the Agreement on Social Policy into the body of the Treaty itself. The Dublin draft made it clear that any such decision would have to be made at a late stage in the negotiations. Following the UK general election in May, it was clear that the Social Policy Agreement could be incorporated into the text of the Treaty but that lack of time prevented a thorough reappraisal of its contents. The result of this was that the text of the Agreement was lifted almost verbatim and cut and pasted into the new Title XI, thereby repealing the Protocol on Social Policy. The legal significance of this shift is that, after

[9] N. Burrows, 'Opting in to the opt-out; the UK and European Social Policy', 1997, Web JCLI.

Amsterdam comes into force, the UK opt-out will end and any provisions adopted under the Title will apply to all fifteen member states. Up until that time special arrangements have been made to enable the UK to participate in discussions on matters governed by the Agreement on Social Policy. Directives based on the new Art. 94 have been used to apply the legislation on Works Councils and Parental Leave to the UK.[10]

Very few substantive changes were made during the process of incorporation of the Agreement on Social Policy. A paragraph was inserted into the new Art. 137 providing a legal base for a limited range of actions to combat social exclusion. Perhaps a more significant change is the amendment to the new Art. 141. This Article now provides a specific legal base for measures relating to equal opportunities and equal treatment of men and women in matters of employment and occupation. Such measures can be adopted under the codecision procedure and, hence, by qualified majority vote. The obvious aim of this amendment is to reduce the influence of any single member state who would use the veto to block the development of legislation in this area. Article 141 has also been amended to allow member states to maintain or adopt measures providing for specific advantages to make it easier for a member of an under-represented sex to pursue a vocational activity or to prevent or compensate for disadvantages in their professional careers. Such measures must be aimed at ensuring full equality in practice of men and women. This exercize in subsidiarity will allow greater flexibility to member states in devising policies aimed at achieving equality of outcome. However, it does not provide a legal base for new EU initiatives in this field. Developments will therefore take place at the level of the member states.

Given the time frame of the negotiations it is not surprising that the simple solution of integrating the Agreement into the text of the existing Treaty was the chosen option. The new Arts 136–145 retain the emphasis on social dialogue and agreement between management and labour as being the preferred procedure for developing minimum standards. Whether in fact all the participants in the process share this enthusiasm might be questioned. Just a few months after the signing of the Treaty, the process of social dialogue was reported to be in crisis with the European Commission calling for an emergency summit.[11] At that time it was reported that 'there are many industry critics who would like to see the social dialogue consigned to the history books'. As Barnard points out, the Social Policy Agreement had not resulted in a flowering of initiatives and out of the seven opportunities for negotiations between the social partners, four had been declined by the employers side by the time the Amsterdam Treaty had been signed.[12] Furthermore, the whole process was challenged, unsuccessfully as it turned out,

---

[10] N. Burrows and J. Mair, 'Catching up with European Social Law' (1998) 3 SLPQ 159 and C. McGlynn 'An Exercise in Futility: the Practical Effects of the Social Policy Opt-out' (1998) 49 NILQ 60.

[11] *European Voice*, Vol 4, number 11.

[12] C. Barnard 'The United Kingdom, the "Social Chapter" and the Amsterdam Treaty' 26 ILJ 275.

in the European Court of Justice by representatives of small businesses for an alleged failure to consult sufficiently widely[13] and the European Parliament had voiced its concerns about a legislative process from which it had been effectively excluded. The two gains emerging from the process, the directives on the rights of part-time workers and on parental leave seem perhaps to fade into insignificance against this background.

One effect of the incorporation of the Social Policy Agreement is to put an end to variable geometry in the social policy field. This 'twin-track' approach had been criticized as leading to an attack on the integrity of EU law and of creating two divisions of workers' rights.[14] From the date of ratification of the Amsterdam Treaty, therefore, the UK government will be fully involved in the development of social policy and the UK social partners will become an integral part of the social dialogue. From the UK perspective, the emphasis on dialogue and partnership is reflected in its own approach to some industrial relations issues. For example, it is clear that in matters of trade union recognition the UK government would have preferred to act as a facilitator between the TUC and CBI rather than having to impose a view on the exact details of its manifesto commitment to recognition of trade unions where a majority of workers wish to be represented by a trade union. The UK government is also supportive of partnership agreements such as that negotiated between USDAW and Tesco. The then Trade Minister is quoted as saying about the latter that the government favours 'a culture of shared values and goals'.[15] The ending of the UK opt-out is therefore a reflection of a difference in emphasis at the national level.

Given that social dialogue is not to be discarded as a means of furthering social policy and that that its importance has been emphasized in the Treaty of Amsterdam, the Commission has been seeking ways of strengthening its operation. Prior to the conclusion of the negotiations at the IGC, the Commission had issued a Communication seeking views on how improvements could be made to the process of social dialogue. It has now reported on the actions it wishes to see taken.[16] These actions essentially relate to the efficient functioning of a number of committees and institutions and the rationalization of their work.

Two distinct types of social dialogue procedures can be identified; consultation at sectoral level and consultation at cross-industry level. It is the cross-industry social partners who have a wider role to play in the negotiation of EU wide provisions affecting all categories of workers whereas sectoral consultation, via Joint Committees, is confined to specific categories within the labour market. In addition to these consultation procedures, there exist a

---

[13] Case T-135/96 *UEAPME v Council* [1998] IRLR 602.

[14] For example by J. Shaw 'Twin-track Social Europe – the Inside Track' in D. O'Keefe and P. Twomey (eds) *Legal Issues of the Maastricht Treaty*, Wiley, 1994.

[15] *The Herald*, 14 March 1998.

[16] COM (96) 322 in note 6. The description of the Commission's proposed changes in the following section is adapted from that Communication and the references to the Commission's decisions and proposals are from the same document.

number of Advisory Committees looking at specific issues. The Commission proposes changes to this whole structure.

The Commission's proposals on the sectoral dialogue are based on the need to allow a uniform participation of the various sectors of industry at the European level. In this way it is hoped that the newly established Sectoral Dialogue Committees will be able to fulfil their role of assisting in the formulation and development of policies, of identifying best practice and initiating benchmarking. The Commission also foresees a role for the Sectoral Dialogue Committees of feeding into the debate on industrial change. The argument runs that, given their inside knowledge, the members of these committees will be able to predict future developments. In its Decision of 20 May 1988 setting up Sectoral Dialogue Committees, the Commission states that it will set up a Committee in 'those sectors where the social partners make a joint request to take part in a dialogue at European level' provided that certain criteria are met. The organizations representing both sides must 'relate to specific sectors or categories and be organised at European level' and must be part of the social partner structures of the member states and have the capacity to negotiate agreements. They need not represent organizations in all the member states but should be representative of several. Finally, they must have an adequate structure to be able to play a full part in the process. These new Committees will replace all existing Joint Committees by December 1998 and any other informal working groups. Membership of each Committee is limited to a maximum of 40, with equal numbers from both sides of industry. The Commission will chair meetings at the request of both sides but otherwise each new Committee will determine the rules of procedure. The function of the Sectoral Dialogue Committees is 'to be consulted on developments at Community level having social implications' and to assist in the development of social dialogue. One possible outcome of such dialogue could be voluntary sectoral agreements. Alternatively, as the Commission points out, there is nothing in the new Title XI to prevent formal negotiations leading to contractual agreements that could be made binding through the process of EU law.

The Commission's proposals for consultation at cross-industry level are not so radical. The Commission's view is that the system appears to be working satisfactorily although, as has been noted, this view is not universally shared. Its proposals could be divided into consultation on matters falling outside the new Title XI and those falling within it. In the former case, the Commission notes that it intends to consult more widely and that it will continue to examine the representativeness of the various organizations with a view to adding or deleting organizations from its list. On matters falling within the new Title XI, the Commission stresses the need to respect the autonomy of the social partners. It reiterates the view that it is not for the Commission to determine the personality of a particular partner. However, the Commission does point out that the current composition of the social partners for the purposes of negotiating EU wide agreements 'is jeopardising future developments and that a political solution is needed to prepare the ground for the future'. It is clear that the Commission would like to see an extension to the current membership of the Social Dialogue Committee beyond the three organizations which currently make up is membership: UNICE, CEEP and ETUC. An extension of membership might result in a greater acceptance of the European level social dialogue.

In so far as Advisory Committees are concerned, the Commission proposes to retain these bodies but to rationalize them as the need arises. The amalgamation of certain of the Advisory Committees has already taken place and further improvements might be suggested. The work of the Advisory Committees will continue to complement the other processes of social dialogue.

The incorporation of the Social Policy Agreement did not seem, at the time, to present such a radical departure from existing policy. It did seem to be part of the routine service described by Langrish. Given the lack of outstanding success of the Agreement itself since the adoption of the Treaty on European Union, it might also have been viewed as a disappointment. However, it is clear that the Commission is determined to make the most of the opportunity that has now been presented. A more general consensus that social policy does have a rightful place within the EU structure has allowed the Commission to look again at what can be done within the confines of the new Title XI. Its proposals to reform sectoral dialogue are very exciting. European level collective bargaining sector by sector provides an alternative to the moribund negotiations via the more traditional Val Duchesse partners. Europe wide, cross-industry agreements are by definition going to be difficult to achieve. The multiplicity of factors which have to be taken into account mean that agreement can be reached at only the most general of levels, as has been seen with the agreements on parental leave and part-time workers. More specific agreements are possible where the range of variables is so very much more reduced.[17]

In addition, the Commission's proposals open up the possibility of initiatives from a much wider range of actors than is presently the case. In the context of the debates on a European employment strategy which relies on workers and employers to 'deliver the goods' on adaptability, flexibility, new forms of work and employability, more localized initiatives are likely to have a far greater impact than grand plans. In the context of one industry, for example, flexibility might take the form of encouraging part-time or home working whereas in another it may mean upskilling and retraining. As long as sectoral level initiatives fulfil the broader objectives of European economic and employment policy the sectoral approach is a welcome departure from the approach adopted to date in matters governed by the Agreement on

---

[17] Although sectoral negotiations are not guaranteed to succeed as is obvious from the failure of the representatives of employers and workers in the road haulage sector to agree on a limitation on working hours. It seems likely that the Commission will need to propose legislation in this area.

Social Policy. It may bring with it significant efficiency gains. This was recognized by the European Parliament which stated that the impact of regulation and deregulation on employment in the economic sectors can best be assessed within the sectoral dialogue.

The incentive to develop European sectoral organizations is significantly enhanced by the Commission's proposals. The Commission is effectively opening its doors to a whole range of new organizations and inviting them to take part in the development of policy. The processes are entirely independent of national governments and therefore need not feel the dead hand which governments sometimes impose either individually, or collectively, within the Council of Ministers. This European level empowerment poses a challenge to the present trade union and employer organizations that are often vertically integrated at the expense of any horizontal integration. Yet within the single market both unions and employers face the same problems across the market place.

The development of sectoral dialogue across European frontiers may also deepen European integration. The perhaps slightly old-fashioned term of 'engrenage' springs to mind to describe the process of Europeanization of union and employer organizations.

III TITLES VIII AND XI AND ENLARGEMENT

In one sense the inclusion of the new Title on employment makes little difference to the enlargement process. As the new Title does not significantly alter the existing *acquis*, there will be no further legislation requiring implementation on the part of the new member states. What may prove more difficult to accommodate is the shift in emphasis towards social dialogue and the 'employment partnership'. Even at the level of the existing member states, it has proved difficult for the Commission to identify legitimate social partners. The Commission itself has identified this particular problem and has explained it in the following terms:

> The social partners are different in nature from other organisations, like pressure groups or interest groups, because of their ability to take part in collective bargaining. In a European context the organisations continue to evolve. National affiliates continue to join and new groups are being set up.[18]

The social partners are not therefore readily identifiable. This problem has been highlighted by the challenge posed by UAPME in the cases that challenge the validity of legislation adopted under the Agreement on Social Policy. In these cases, UEAPME, which represents the interests of small businesses in the European Union, sought an annulment of legislation adopted by the

---

[18] COM (98) 322 in note 6.

Council in the form of a Directive but which incorporated a framework agreement on parental leave. UEAPME had been consulted as part of the prenegotiation stage provided for in the Agreement on Social Policy but was not party to the negotiations. The Court declared the action for annulment to be inadmissible but did stress the importance of the need on the part of the Commission to ensure that the participants in the negotiating process were sufficiently representative of both sides of industry. The Court stressed that this was an aspect of the principle of democracy. It held that, in the absence of participation by the European Parliament, the participation of 'the people' must be assured by the EU institutions. It is the duty of the Commission and the Council to 'verify that the signatories to the agreement are truly representative'. In this case, the Court was satisfied that the Council and the Commission had taken the necessary steps to verify this point.

Within the context of the European Union the Commission has undertaken to review its strategy for determining the identity of the relevant social partners. At the same time, the Commission has recognized the need to 'encourage the applicant countries to develop their own independent social dialogue structures'. In order for the applicant states to be able to participate in the employment chapter, therefore, not only must governments be ready and willing to assume their obligations but also the trade union movement and employers' organizations in the applicant states must be able to participate in a meaningful way. It is very difficult to assess the extent to which a concept such as 'employment partnership' or 'social dialogue' has been assimilated in any applicant country but, given that the direction of employment policy will be influenced by the social partners, it is important that assistance be given, where required, to develop these institutions of civil society within the applicant states. Some assistance is available through programmes such as PHARE but it is likely that more will need to be done to help assimilate the CEES social partners into the Union structures.

It has been argued in this chapter that the amendments brought about by Amsterdam and the inclusion of the Agreement on Social Policy may have a more profound effect on the development of social policy than might be believed by the simple terms of the Treaty. Whether it will assist in the enlargement negotiations is a more difficult question. Without doubt, the ending of the UK opt-out allows the EU and the member states to present a more united front on social policy and in that sense it strengthens the *acquis*. It would be more difficult for an applicant state to attempt to negotiate concessions on social policy now that there is a united front on the place of social policy within the EU. On the other hand, the applicant states are faced with a significant challenge to match internal EU developments relating to the social dialogue. Furthermore, given the emphasis on the autonomy of the social partners and their need to be independent of government, the applicant member states may need to foster an approach to social partnership and dialogue that may not be so easily accommodated at their present level of economic development.

The response of the Commission is to suggest a three dimensional strategy. The Commission is prepared to assist the social partners to extend their horizontal links to their equivalent organizations in the CEES. It will also encourage the applicant states to involve the social partners in their own preparations for accession. Finally, the Commission itself will assist in the education and training of members of organizations from the applicant states by bringing them to Brussels to participate in meetings. The extension of horizontal links might prove to be easier for some sectors than others since there is no uniform tradition of sector by sector arrangements as yet within the EU itself. It may well be that one of the issues for discussion in the context of a Sectoral Dialogue Committee might well be the involvement or consultation of non-EU participants. Within the Commission's Decision establishing these committees itself there is no prospect of financing for such involvement but financing might well be found elsewhere. Horizontal links must also be developed at the level of cross-industry organizations both for the purpose of assimilating the social partners of the CEES into the general consultation processes and for involving them in the negotiations of framework agreements adopted under Title XI.

With its emphasis on the importance of the social partners in these areas, it may be argued that the Commission is, indirectly, inviting a new set of negotiators to the discussions on enlargement. The invitation does not extend to participate in the final decisions but it does extend to an invitation to contribute towards finding ways of smoothing the enlargement process. The knowledge base of the EU social partners of conditions in the CEES in many sectors will be enormous because of their involvement as employers or as part of links through the international trade union movement. The social partners in the CEES are uniquely positioned in assessing the impact of EU policy and the degree of its implementation. The social partners could play a vital role in easing the transition from applicant to full membership.

IV   CONCLUDING REMARKS

If we examine events subsequent to the signing of the Treaty of Amsterdam we can see that, despite the seemingly bland nature of the new Titles VIII and XI, the new provisions have provided an opportunity to develop European Social Policy. In particular, they have led to a process of renewal of those institutional structures that support dialogue with the social partners. The reform of the sectoral dialogue process is likely to provide the most interesting and innovative of these developments. It certainly provides renewed opportunities for trade unions and employers to negotiate 'tailormade' agreements in the more flexible environment opened up by the Commission.

In terms of the enlargement process, the new Titles may prove disappointing to the applicant states if they were hoping to see a substantial financial commitment to programmes of job creation. However, the new Titles do not impose further legal obligations on the applicants. They are thus spared the need of further extensive legislation. The challenge in the process of enlargement will be to ensure that methods and techniques of social dialogue can be developed horizontally to ensure the full participation of the social partners throughout Europe.

7

THE EUROPEAN SOCIAL MODEL:
FRAMEWORK OR FALLACY?[1]

Caitríona A. Carter

I INTRODUCTION

In this chapter, I focus on social policy and the development of collective responsibility for social policy within the framework of European integration. With the signing of the Amsterdam Treaty in 1997, member states' governments agreed to a variety of Treaty reforms in the field of social and employment policy. The consequences of these reforms for common action in social policy are twofold: first, the Amsterdam Treaty creates a new social chapter (within Title XI of the Treaty – Arts 136–145) which comprises a mixture of original EEC Treaty provisions, accepted by all member states, and the provisions set out in the Social Policy Agreement, from which the UK had 'opted-out' in 1991. The result is a modest extension of EC policy competence in the social policy arena. Second, the Amsterdam Treaty ends the UK 'opt-out' from the Social Policy Agreement. Following its election on 1 May 1997, the new Labour Government in the UK was quick to express its commitment to the social policy reforms introduced by the Treaty on European Union in 1991 (and set out in the Social Policy Agreement) thus marking the adoption of a new stance vis-à-vis EC social policy. The resultant demise of the social policy opt-out and the establishment of a common Treaty base for future development of social policy was generally welcomed, in so far as the use of the opt-out as a device to allow for policy diversity in respect of social integration had been the subject of much criticism. Social Europe 'à la carte', it was argued, was against the spirit of the original Treaties and

[1] I would like to thank Andrew Scott for his valuable advice and comments on earlier versions of this chapter. I am also grateful to the editor for his comments and to the Sussex European Institute's research seminar for their feedback on a presentation of this chapter. My thanks also go to the University of Edinburgh's Law and Social Sciences' Faculty Group Travel Research Committee for their financial support.

105

a threat to the constitutional unity of the Community, entrenching a disparity of social rights as between different European societies. The restoration of constitutional unity, through the ending of the social policy opt-out, is thus a significant aspect of the Treaty of Amsterdam.

Although the constitutional unity of social policy has been restored by the Amsterdam revision, it is, however, less clear how the Amsterdam Treaty should be appraised with respect to the substance of an evolving common EC social policy. In the first instance, as stated above, the extension of EC competence is modest. In particular, one might question how realistic is the expectation that an active phase of common EC social policy development is foreshadowed by bringing the Agreement on Social Policy within the body of the Treaty proper. Indeed, given the rather limited amount of activity under the Social Policy Agreement to date, and the criticism of the Directives which have been negotiated, doubts persist concerning the substantive content of EC social policy and the direction of social policy development over the medium term. More importantly, it has become clear that, since the early 1990s, much of the economic and political substance of the social policy debate is taking place outside the formal structures of EC social policy discourse rather than within it. For some time now, member states' governments have been engaged in a debate on the future of the 'European welfare state' and how to effect the reconciliation of the European model of welfare capitalism on the one hand with the needs of a globally 'competitive' economy on the other hand – a policy dilemma encapsulated by the rather nebulous notion of devising a third way with respect to welfare policy generally. Whilst member states have often used European Council meetings to discuss such questions concerning the future of European social policy, these discussions have had little constitutional resonance within the dialogue which has shaped the legislative content of the Treaty-based common social policy. This indicates that two quite distinct dialogues on the collective responsibility for social policy have developed in parallel – one which concerns progress in common social measures within the policy competence of the EC institutional framework (involving the Commission, European Parliament and the Social Partners as anticipated by the Social Policy Agreement), and another which has been conducted at a 'higher' political level of national governments and which has focused on a wide array of issues involving the future of the welfare state in contemporary European societies.

In this chapter, I argue that serious academic discussion of the development of collective responsibility of social policy cannot be conducted without recourse to the terms and arguments produced by the broader economic and political debate on the European welfare state, hitherto conducted by member states under the banner of the 'European social model'. In the final instance it is the result of this debate which will determine the constitutional framework for the development and implementation of substantive EC social policy measures – indeed, and as I shall argue below, the European social model is presented as a quasi-constitutional framework outwith the Treaties.

If we are to understand the dynamics of the development of social policy it is thus essential that we bring together the two dialogues already referred to: dialogues which hitherto have been examined separately. Whilst accepting that this involves switching between different levels of deliberation of, **and** constitutional contribution to, the policy-process, it does provide a lens through which to examine the linkages that exist between the informal stage of (potentially radical) policy appraisal and reform proposals on the one hand, and the transposition of the conclusions from this process into substantive (common) action on the other hand.

Accordingly, in this chapter, I set out a conceptual framework in which to consider the on-going debate over the European welfare state (or the European social model) as a central part of the process of constitutionalizing European social policy. Central to my argument is that a distinction must be made between the European 'social model' on the one hand versus the European 'social bargain' on the other. The European social model (much discussed in EU policy documents) is defined as the current structured framework for generating distributional outcomes between different groups in society, and for settling disputes between the actors who have competing views about the specifics of those outcomes. The European social bargain, on the other hand, describes the original (or preexisting) negotiated agreement which defines the political aims and objectives of social policy – its normative content and distribution of entitlements – and the institutional mechanism through which these aims and objectives will be realized. Consequently, it is the bargain which establishes the framework within which the model operates. Crucially, the examination of the model through the lens of the prior bargain establishes the starting point for discussion on the constitutionalization of social policy within the process of European integration.

There are two main sections to this chapter. In the first section, I discuss the extant European social bargain, and the nature of the crisis in that bargain. The second section examines the application of the rhetoric of the European social model at the level of the EU and as revealed in the various policy documents emanating from the EU institutions. First of all, how is the 'European social model' being conceptualized in high level EU discussions and in the policy documents themselves? Second, what is significant about the way in which it is being conceptualized by the principal political actors, particularly the Commission and the European Council?

II   THE 'EUROPEAN SOCIAL BARGAIN' – THE CRISIS

The European social bargain

It is commonplace that European integration has been, since the outset, a political project driven, principally, by economic integration, with negotiations for the EEC Treaty primarily concerned with economic and social (rather than diplomatic) considerations (Milward, 1997: 7).[2] The political aspirations of the 'founding fathers' equally, are well known, involving as they did the fusing together of European society within a collective (or common) governance structure with nation states becoming increasingly interdependent as the barriers to the free movement of goods, services, capital and labour were progressively eliminated. In short, European integration was founded on the conviction – or the ideal – of establishing better governance in Europe (Wallace, 1994: 87) and of providing European peoples with a socially progressive society, underpinned by the fundamental social principle of solidarity among citizens.

Despite the conviction that European integration had something to do with creating a 'better' European society, the Treaty of Rome included very little that had a **direct** bearing on the social, or civic, welfare of individual 'Europeans'. Indeed, in devising the original Treaty, it was expressly decided to exclude from the Treaty any provisions relating to what we generally understand as 'social policy' – health care, pension rights, etc. A major concern of the German negotiators was to protect the tradition of free collective bargaining – a core component of the national social bargain (Milward, 1992). The striking of a bargain between German trade unionist positions and the others on the inclusion or otherwise of social provisions in the Treaty (inclusion finding strong favour with the French), enabled all parties to come together in the final agreement on this Treaty. It was agreed that: 're-distributive benefits used as an instrument of social policy should remain entirely a matter for member states' (Collins, 1975: 9). What became (common) EC social policy instead focused on addressing a narrow range of effects associated with the development and functioning of the common market. The Treaty set down provisions for the establishment of a European Social Fund to finance programmes to increase worker mobility and to reskill workers in the event of the anticipated industrial restructuring affected by the dynamics of regional economic integration. The Treaty also gave powers to the EC to ensure the provision of social security for migrant workers, e.g. through the coordination of social security systems, to encourage free movement of labour and mandated the application of the principle that men and women should receive equal pay for equal work – a provision included primarily on the insistence of the French to prevent distortions of competition between member states caused by different levels of equal pay legislation. In essence, the Treaty provisions held market-building rather than market-correcting objectives (Streeck, 1996: 72). Social policies directly bearing on redistribution would continue to be dealt with by individual member states.

At one level, therefore, it would appear that social policy was intended to have a minimal role in the new EC. But this is to misinterpret the original bargain of integration and the nature of the Community as a system of

---

[2] Milward argues in relation to the French position that 'the Quai D'Orsay was not on balance in favour of the Treaty' (Milward, 1997: 7).

governance. Developments in constitutional (political and legal) theory adopt a new conceptual lens for considerations of EC constitutionalism:[3]

> Recent work on the European Union in legal and political theory, not least by members of the Edinburgh Seminar, suggests that statist models may obscure rather than illuminate the present character of, and future possibilities for, the European Union. (Wincott, 1998)

This approach constitutes a departure from the political theory of the modern constitution which, it is argued, is embedded in nineteenth century constructs (Castiglione, 1996). And a core assumption underlying this new approach is that the signing of the Treaties was 'a constitutional moment' (Weiler, 1996) for the EC as a new constitutional order (R. Bellamy and Castiglione, 1996; Bellamy, Bufacchi and Castiglione, 1995). Such a constitutional moment can occur when a system of laws, institutions and customs becomes the valued and accepted 'general system':

> The constitutive function, according to which a constitution defines a people and its way of life, can therefore result either from an original and voluntary agreement or from the process of identification with a given group, its customs and traditions. (Castiglione, 1996: 422)

According to this approach to constitutionalism, social policy was **not** excluded in the original 'bargain' of European integration. On the contrary, the delivery of social welfare provisions was essential to the original social bargain of integration underpinning the Treaties. The decision to deliver social policy though national social systems – albeit 'social democratic', 'corporatist' or 'liberal' (Esping-Andersen, 1990) – entrenched two principles crucial to the social bargain – consensus and legitimacy. National welfare systems provide a clear link between the state and civil society. The notion of allegiance is well-developed by EC historians such as Milward drawing on social democratic accounts of the establishment of the welfare state.[4] Milward argues that preserving this new consensus and its related security (in terms of 'social welfare and personal benefits throughout the family life-cycle' – Milward, 1997: 14) was a key concern of the negotiators of the Treaties of Rome in order to secure allegiance to the new EC. Leaving to one side the theoretical (and conceptual) implications of Milward's overall thesis – namely that the signing of the Treaties was a constitutional moment for the nation state, rather than the EC as such – it is clear that post-1945 the welfare state formed a strong part of the new political consensus as the basis of legitimacy for the nation state.

The original **European** social bargain is thus defined – that social policy would be rooted in national social bargains, crucial in terms of legitimacy

---

[3] See *European Law Journal*, Special Issue on Legal Theory in the European Union, Volume 4, Issue 4, December 1998.
[4] See also P. Flora and A. Heidenheimer, 1981, V. George and P. Wilding, 1984.

and consensus. And this secured the legitimacy of the pooling of sovereignty in the other areas of the Treaties. This is to transpose Milward's ultimate position described above, namely that the Treaties of Rome had to be an external buttress to the welfare state (Milward, 1996: 216). This position notwithstanding, nevertheless the reverse is also true, namely that the welfare state had to be an external buttress to the Treaties of Rome. The acceptance of a **European** social bargain thus demands a qualified approach to the discussion of constitutionalism in a system of governance beyond the nation state.

A final set of observations concern the dynamics of this (EC) constitutional order. The European policy agreement (the assignment rule – as distinct from the inherent bargain) divides the model of economy and society as enshrined by the Treaties between different levels of delivery – the common market, with free movement of goods, services, persons and capital, at the supranational level; the social welfare state, with social redistributive, or market correcting polices, at the national level. One key question posed by the critiques is whether:

> one model of economy and society, enshrined in the Community Treaties, is relevant to the changing structures of the economy and society over time. (Holland, 1980: 6)

Given the specific nature of welfare states and their legitimacy and allegiance functions, the issues inherent in the process of positive integration in this policy area clearly differ from the issues concerned with the process of positive integration generally. The essentially civic nature of social policy with its link to society (and its goal to create and preserve societal cohesion) raises fundamental issues for constitutionalism in this policy area. Reassignment of social policy to the supranational level has constitutional implications which go far beyond the more narrow regulatory concerns relevant to other policy areas, for example environmental policy. Thus, any move to alter the levels of delivery of the EC model of economy and society must engage with the essential nature of the original European social bargain.

The changing context of the bargain – the crisis

Over the years, there have been many challenges to national social welfare systems – the national social bargains themselves have been challenged, e.g. by feminist and radical critiques of the values and norms underpinning the welfare state and/or collective bargaining mechanisms.[5] National systems have also faced a number of internal and external pressures for reform, such as responding to changing employment structures, increased global competition and so on. Such challenges are well-documented.[6]

[5] See for example M. Daly (1994), D. Richardson (1993).
[6] See for example V. George and Taylor-Gooby (1996), T. O'Connor (1973), C. Offe (1984).

Much of the criticism levelled against EC (rather than national) social policy has focused not on any failings on the part of the Treaty framers to incorporate provisions for the introduction of a common social policy with **re-distributive** objectives, but rather on the failure of the EC subsequently to develop such a policy (see, for example, Gold, 1993; Teague, 1989; Wise and Gibb, 1993). A standard critique is to view the restricted (regulatory) nature of EC social policy as a consequence of the decision-making arrangements of the Community, dominated as they have been in this area by intergovernmentalism as the style of negotiation, with lowest common denominator bargaining and weak law being the inevitable outcomes. Such an intergovernmentalist culture – both in terms of the constitutional process (i.e. re-assignment of policy between supranational/national levels) and the regulatory process (delivery at the supranational level) – it is argued, has encouraged the continuance of national divisions in the articulation of social group interests, preventing the emergence of a pan-European dialogue and stifling the establishment of the type of common social base essential for the emergence of pan-EC redistributive social policies.

However, it is not at all certain that the problems in social policy stem from the fact that the EC has failed to adopt at supranational level the kind of social welfare policy promoted at national level. This view relies significantly on a certain idea of the process of European integration that does not, in fact, conform to what has been the reality. It conceptualizes integration as a continuous process that inevitably culminates in the creation of a governance architecture which imitates a European federal state and which discharges social welfare programmes in the same way that nation states traditionally have done. On the other hand, a quite different conceptualization of the process of European integration – one that does not regard it culminating in the European federal state – would lead us to different conclusions. Thus:

> Social policy in Europe, this implies, can be understood only if one dissociates oneself radically from the received image of a slowly but steadily evolving European federal welfare state . . . Taking the end-point for granted, on the assumption that integration could lead only to replication of the familiar on a larger scale, resulted in the typical discussions on the 'social dimension' of integrated Europe, which essentially were about the question of whether the glass was already half full or still half empty. (Streeck, 1996: 64)

Critiques of EC social policy that locate the 'problem' as a direct consequence on the part of the EC to fail to complete the journey initially mapped out (sic) towards a federal governance structure (this being a prerequisite for formulating a, somehow defined, 'strong' social programme) can only be valid to the extent that the assumption that this preordained destination (of a federal European superstate) in itself is a valid understanding of the process of integration envisaged at the outset. And it is here that one might reasonably take issue with the critics, not on the basis of their disappointment at the

111

present state of development of EC social policy (which many might share), but because of what this approach implies is required in order that social policy can be further developed – namely greater steps to create a federal governance structure within the EC. This is to misunderstand the nature of the EC, which **is** the process rather than a state. Consequently, it is the process as such, rather than any imagined end objective, which should define our approach.

An alternative approach is to conceptualize integration as a continually renewing process. Arguably, only by understanding that the political and economic regime in Europe is a 'new kind of animal' altogether (Streeck, 1996: 65), can one begin to conceptualize the crisis of the European social bargain. Indeed, the EU's unique governance arrangement is producing a distinct pattern of social policy-making, different from that of any national welfare state (Leibfried and Pierson, 1995). And a defining feature of that policy-making arrangement is the emergence of multi-tiered governance. Multi-tiered governance is, of course, the product of European integration. Rather than the development of single policy instruments (as implied in the federal model) we have multiple instruments which are guided and coordinated through a process of local, national and supranational mediation.

A complex set of arguments is made within the literature focusing on the implications that multi-level governance holds for the delivery of national social policy. In general, the literature locates a collision between the emerging European policy and the national social policy as encapsulated in national social welfare systems.[7] The constraints on the ability of national social systems to deliver can be polarized around three key problems: first, the coordination between different levels of policy; secondly, the erosion of the effect of national measures due to policy leakage; and thirdly, the nature of the policy itself which is undermining some other policy goal given increasing globalization and the problems of 'competitiveness'.

Problems of coordination between different levels of policy, it is argued, are witnessed by competitive deregulation, regime shopping (Streeck and Schmitter, 1991; Scharpf, 1996) and joint decision-making traps (Scharpf, 1988). Furthermore, the application of technical devices to address problems of coordination – such as the application of the principle of subsidiarity – run the risk of producing '*de facto* de-regulatory consequences' when 'self-governance under subsidiarity . . . [becomes] non-governance under a self-regulating market' (Streeck, 1996: 80).[8] The result is either de-regulation,

---

[7] The strongest claims are made by Leibfried and Pierson: 'The process of European integration has eroded both the sovereignty (by which we mean legal authority) and autonomy (by which we mean de facto capacity) of member states in the realm of social policy' (Leibfried and Pierson, 1995: 44).

[8] There is much discussion within the literature on the extent to which competitive deregulation occurs. Regime competition, on the other hand, is clearly a localized process: 'regime competition takes place between different national systems at the sectoral level in one national social space rather than between whole societies occupying separate territories' (Leibfried and Pierson, 1995: 60).

'neo-voluntarism' (Streeck, 1996) or a limiting of policy options available (Leibfried and Pierson, 1995).

Erosion of the effect of national measures due to policy leakage is the second main challenge to national social policy. Leibfried and Pierson high-light three processes which can result in policy leakage: 'positive activist reform', i.e. legislative measures adopted at the supranational level which have a direct effect on national systems; 'negative reform', i.e. the imposition by the European Court of Justice of 'market compatibility requirements' which redefine and impose restrictions on national social policies:[9] and 'indir-ect pressures' i.e. pressures arising from the process of European integration itself which are **not** legally binding on member states yet 'strongly encourage national welfare states to adapt their social policies to avoid the potential negative consequences of economic integration' (Leibfried and Pierson, 1995: 45).[10] Echoes of negative reform arguments can be found in examinations of the role of EC law in the integration process (enforced by the ECJ and national courts as actors within the EC constitutional legal order). For ex-ample, Scharpf's examination of the role of EC law in the promotion of eco-nomic freedoms illustrates the strength of negative integrative forces in legal constitutionalism (Scharpf, 1996: 18); de Gier's comparative study of the influence of EC law in national occupation welfare systems locates 'a new and perhaps far-reaching trade-off between efficiency and social justice . . . [at] stake in these countries' (de Gier, 1991: 247).[11]

The third and further problem is that the nature of the policy itself is undermining some other policy goal. As Rhodes (Rhodes, 1993) clearly docu-ments, European welfare states are currently facing a number of external pressures stemming not only from economic integration but also from global market formation (or increasing international trade) and in particular com-petitive pressures arising from exchange control liberalization:

> the combination of the deregulatory pressures already mentioned plus pressures
> for the harmonisation of indirect taxes and the need to conform with EMU con-
> vergence criteria . . . will place new constraints on welfare state policies. (Rhodes,
> 1993: 20–21)

This must be clarified, however. Such constraints on national welfare states exist only in a situation when a government is also pursuing a low taxation policy. External forces may well prevent member states from deficit financing (the Stability Pact will also have such an effect): how a government achieves this goal is, however, a matter for domestic policy. Given that current Euro-pean publics are not in favour of a rise in taxation to increase social policy

---

[9] For example, ECJ rules on freedom to provide services (Leibfried and Pierson, 1995: 68).

[10] Leibfried and Pierson list a number of conditions under which the exclusivity of welfare state is lost (Leibfried and Pierson, 1995: 43–77).

[11] de Gier finds a 'clear dominance of economic policies over social policies' (de Gier, 1991: 83).

revenue, conflicting policy goals thus create a third set of problems for welfare state delivery.

In summary, a key concern of the literature is whether the systemic effect of multi-level governance is to produce a specific policy outcome (i.e. whether certain policy options are 'closed' at the national level). The debate concentrates on the 'real' amount of control which member states currently hold in devising social welfare policy and to what extent free-market neo-voluntary principles trump social welfare principles (or, for example, whether privatization of public services such as health care provision is encouraged by the needs of economic integration). In particular, it is argued that the economic aspects of the Treaties through legal enforcement processes affect the balance between economic versus social and civic rights in the domestic arena. This question of policy convergence is hard to assess.[12] Even if there is some dispute over the extent to which national systems are currently able to deliver diverse social policy outcomes in the face of similar economic pressures, nevertheless there is common ground on the perceived social effects of European monetary union. Most writers accept that the establishment of a single currency in 1999 will exacerbate erosion-related challenges to the ability of national levels to pursue their own policy goals. For example, ensuring labour market flexibility will be a requisite policy goal. In terms of the current and future state of play of social policy, therefore, things are likely to get worse (assuming European governments continue to pursue a policy of low taxation).

Importantly, such constraints on national social and welfare models create a predicament given the original bargain of the Treaties, which saw member states performing redistributive functions to offset (negative) effects of (market-driven) economic integration. Increasingly, EU member states are unable to deliver at the national level what is expected in terms of social welfare provision, and this is regarded as being a direct consequence of European integration. Moreover, the arrangements of governance at the EC level seem incapable of fashioning a response to this problem, and EC social policy simply is not developing as a replacement for national measures.[13]

Thus, if we go back to the original European social bargain as set out above, it is clear that a constitutional dilemma is posed within the EU as a system of governance beyond the nation state. The Treaties entrench (and thus formally legitimize) a multi-level system (within one model of economy and society) which ultimately cannot be delivered and therefore socially legitimized. The original European policy agreement (the allocation of competencies) was grounded in national social bargains. Any change in the European policy agreement (assignment rule) has to be underpinned by a renegotiation

---

[12] For example, Grahl and Teague (1996) and George and Taylor-Gooby (eds) (1996) find evidence of policy diversity. However, the effects on EMU are not taken into account.

[13] A number of proposals have been made within the literature to establish a variant of a supranational social welfare scheme; see Leibfried, 1993; Berghman, 1990; Keithley, 1991; Dumont, 1988.

of the European social bargain. In other words, the 'failure' to develop a European social integration policy can be explained by correctly defining the basis of national social policies as resting in national social bargains. Any tendency to shift to a common policy presupposes that a common social bargain had been established. Building institutions in itself is not enough: the underlying bargains have to be renegotiated as well. The constitutional crisis thus exists in the sense that, on the one hand, the delivery of the original bargain is being threatened at the lower level as a direct consequence of integration and, on the other hand, the original bargain cannot be reconstructed at the higher level, because at this level there is no strong state apparatus which would establish a 'Community of fate' (in Hirst's terms – Hirst, 1994). It is in this sense that we might reasonably talk of there being a European social bargain and of there being a crisis in that bargain. The key question which emerges is whether it is possible to fulfil the original bargain within a multi-tiered system of governance.[14]

III THE 'EUROPEAN SOCIAL MODEL' – THE SLOGAN

The essentially problematic EC dimension to the question of social welfare and the delivery of social policy is, then, established. In the run up to the Treaty of Amsterdam, and with the future enlargement of the Union in mind, the content of recent policy documents suggests a serious interest in social policy, encapsulated in the debate on the European social model. The appeal to the 'European social model' is made in a large number of documents emanating from various EU institutions, European-level organizations and national governments. These include, for example: the Commission's 1994 White Paper on Social Policy which devotes a whole chapter to a discussion on the preservation and development of the 'European social model'; the EP Opinion of that same White Paper confirms the EP's commitment to the 'European social model'; and the Comite des Sages Report.

The timing of the presentation of the European social model is critical. External pressures stem from global dynamics, with the emergent perception that the current European social model is outdated and needs to be fundamentally overhauled in the context of growing international economic interdependence and the drive for greater EC 'competitiveness' on a global scale. Internal pressures ensue from debates over the relation between social welfare and the convergence criteria as set out in the Treaty on European Union, with European monetary union having commenced for eleven member states in January 1999. Given the external economic pressures on member states to forge ahead with the establishment of a single currency and external

---

[14] In a key article by Scharpf the phenomenon described above, namely the challenges posed on national welfare states by economic integration, is explored from the perspective of democratic legitimacy and the reduction of the '*effectiveness* of democratic self-determination at the national level' (Scharpf, 1997: 23). There is no space to adequately address this argument in this chapter.

political and economic pressures to enlarge the Union, legitimizing the process is clearly a key issue. In the light of a recognized legitimacy crisis surrounding the ratification of the Treaty on European Union, a key concern of the 1996/1997 Intergovernmental Conference (which led to the signing of the Amsterdam Treaty) was precisely to set down Treaty provisions which would enable the development of policies which 'spoke' to the European citizen; for example, in the area of social policy this involved responding to the social consequences of integration, including unemployment (and social exclusion generally), addressing the looming pension crisis and so on (such discussions culminated in the new provisions on Employment in the Amsterdam Treaty). The Reflection Group Report – the blueprint for IGC negotiations – recognized that unless these fundamental social issues were addressed, public opinion would turn even further against the prospect of 'an ever closer Union'.

Within this debate on the future deepening of economic integration and the reconfiguration of the Union, it is understood that there is a relation between legitimacy and social policy, with the 'European social model' linked to broader discussions of the EU as a political or civil union. The matter was further aired when, in October 1995, the EC Commission convened a Comité des Sages to address the issue of fundamental rights, in particular fundamental social rights, in the light of future Treaty revision. The Comité's report referred explicitly to the 'European social model' as a way forward in that regard. Speaking to the Social Policy Forum in March 1996 on this Report, the Chair of the Comité, Maria de Lourdes Pintasilgo, stated that 'the European social model, if it is to be true to its vocation, must be original, which means innovative'. Clearly, therefore, the idea of a 'European social model' is a powerful one. But, what precisely is this 'model'? How is this model being conceptualized within these documents and political declarations alike? Is it possible even to grasp a commonality in definition?

It is possible to (re)construct both the Commission's and the European Council's definitions of the 'European social model' in a specific way. First of all, the slogan 'European social model' is an appeal to a commonality. For example, the following (minimal) definition offered by the President of the European Commission: 'it marks the fact that, over and above our historical and cultural diversity, there are certain shared ways of organizing our societies' (Santer).[15]

Secondly, close scrutiny of the policy documents reveals that the model is clearly being identified and presented as a systematic framework which aspires to certain, specified ideals in any 'future' development of policy. Intrinsic to the 'European social model' is a set of organizational principles. The Commission has categorized these and sets them out as follows in the 1994 White Paper on Social Policy: 'democracy and individual rights; free

---

[15] This is taken from a speech given by Jacques Santer speaking at a Forum on 'Working on European Social Policy', Brussels, 27–30 March 1996.

collective bargaining; the market economy; equal opportunity for all; social welfare and solidarity'. Importantly, in their conceptualization the 'European social model' is premised on three social bargains, common to all participant countries (even though the modalities of delivering these bargains may differ between one social welfare system to the next), and which therefore **must** be protected in any future policy development. The three bargains are as follows:

(1) A **system of industrial relations** based on a system of collective bargaining. Bargaining of this nature would take place within national structures, backed up by a substantial state apparatus, and can range from minimal labour legislation to extensive collective bargaining agreement arrangements, whereby collective agreements can be granted legal recognition in law.

(2) The **welfare state**. This includes a social security system, the public provision of health services, and can include minimum guarantees in law, such as a guaranteed minimum wage.

(3) The process of economic policy-making which recognizes the principle of **social partnership** in the production and distribution of wealth and in the creation of employment. Policy is devised and implemented in the spirit of consensus or social cooperation.

The 'European social model' conceptualized in this manner, is thus premised on a set of social bargains which underpin the whole system of Western European governance as it has operated in the latter half of the twentieth century, and the slogan anticipates that the 'European social model' will be able both to deliver and protect these bargains, fundamental to the continued legitimacy of European integration. The extent to which the model will be able to do this becomes a crucial question (and one which I will return to later on in the chapter).

Let us look more closely at the organizational principles set out above – 'democracy and individual rights; free collective bargaining; the market economy; equal opportunity for all; social welfare and solidarity'. It is clear that in a symbolic way the 'European social model' appeals to European **identity** in terms of societal organization. On the one hand, a common approach can refer to the way in which Western European societies emerged with democratic welfare and social market systems (albeit in different forms) at the end of the Second World War. And, given that part of the history of Europe is the history of the modern state, it is clearly the **democracy** of the contemporary nation state which distinguishes it from its predecessors (from the seventeenth century onwards). On the other hand, such an appeal to the past lies by contrast to the recent history of Eastern Europe. For, as Rose argues, Western Europe of the twentieth century has become 'the **defender** of the idea of Europe as a set of democracies' (Rose, 1996: 4 – my emphasis). The 'European social model' is thus presented as the legacy of a democratic Western Europe as opposed to a Communist-dominated East.

This 'Europeanness' is not only upheld in a symbolic sense reflecting the lessons of the recent history of Eastern Europe. In addition, the 'European social model' is upheld by contrast with the EU's main economic competitors and as distinct from US and Japanese models in particular. Critics of the 'European social model' have attributed certain 'failings' within the EU to the functioning of the 'European social model'. For example, it is argued that the high level of unemployment in the EU is being caused partly by the high level of social protection available in the EU. And high levels of unemployment in the EU are compared to lower levels in both the US and Japan. Such challenges to the 'European social model' (and there are many more[16]) thus must be defended within political rhetoric – 'must' in the sense of a political imperative not to lose a defining aspect of 'Europe'. In this sense, and at the level of values, the 'European' aspect of the 'social' is presented as being hostile to the establishment of a low wage society, characterized by an inequality of earnings and the creation of an 'underclass', where collective bargaining plays a minor role. What is stressed instead is investment in human resources which will, via increased productivity, raise industrial competitiveness. Only in this way, it is argued, will social challenges be addressed in a manner which continues to protect fundamental 'European' values which go to the heart of European society.[17]

A very strong sense of European history thus comes through in these policy documents. The constant references to the 'inheritance' of Europe in the promotion of the 'European social model' beg the question to what extent the current rhetoric surrounding the 'European social model' is simply an appeal to the past (especially given that the three social bargains are themselves challenged within a multi-level system), rather than representing a potentially radical development of policy. I would like to make a couple of observations about this before drawing any conclusions.

First, the appeal to the past is especially marked in the context of the post-Maastricht EU, and the end of the Cold War. As Hirst points out (1995: 46), the ratification crisis along with the collapse of a unifying adversary in the form of the Soviet Union gave rise to a situation in which the fundamental 'idea' of the European Union was questioned. As Hirst notes, this questioning extended also to the provision of social welfare in West European states. In this sense, the 'European social model' represents both the acclaimed past success and the future of the EU over the failure of Communism. Importantly one might, therefore, interpret the current emphasis being placed on the 'European social model' as an attempt to define a new 'ideal' for the EU.

[16] See for example J. Grahl and P. Teague (1996).
[17] In a key article by Stephen Nickell he illustrates the empirical weakness of the argument that labour market rigidities cost jobs: 'It is clear that the broad-brush analysis that says that European unemployment is high because European labor markets are "rigid" is too vague and probably misleading' (S. Nickell, 1997: 73).

Secondly, and in response to the critics, much has in fact been made in policy documents of the 'new' approach to social policy which the 'European social model' will adopt. Under attack from economic pressures, the 'European social model' has been presented as a 'third way' (Chirac) whereby the provision of social welfare can be reconciled with the harsh realities of a post-Fordist and increasingly global industrial system. It is in this sense that it was originally presented in a independent policy report written by Emerson (and published by the Commission) in 1986, whose primary concern was to suggest policy reform in order to implement the 'third way' (for Emerson this involved the exploration of policy reform to adapt income maintenance programmes and/or high expenditure on transfer payments to the unemployed to encourage employment growth and take-up). In this sense, the 'European social model' appears as an attempt to reinvent the original bargain within a changing economic environment – a new order and a new global economy.[18]

The European social model is thus presented as representing more than a policy framework. Indeed, drawing on alternative discussions of thinking about constitutionalism in a way 'other than' through national structures (Weiler, 1996), it is clearly possible to conceptualize the European social model as an attempt to construct a quasi-constitutional framework **outwith** the Treaties. The European social model is intended to operate as a constitutional 'pull' in the sense of upholding common 'European' values and rights (rooted in national structures). For, as Weiler argues, it is surely possible to conceive of a European polity whose membership is understood in civic and political terms (Weiler, 1996: 525):

> On this view, the Union belongs to, is composed of, citizens who by definition do not share the same nationality. The substance of membership . . . is in a commitment to the shared values of the Union as expressed in its constituent documents. (Weiler, 1996: 525–526)

This idea is also argued extensively by Shaw in a discussion on the European social model as one of the models presented by the Union for the creation of a European citizenship (Shaw, 1997).

As such both the European social model and the Treaties form part of the broader notion of constitutionalism of the social policy arena. But this must be qualified – the European social model has all the appearance of a constitutional framework, endorsing elements of national social bargains, crucial to the social contract. In this manner, the European social model is presented as a European political remedy for the problems facing national social welfare systems. But, as was argued at the end of Section II, the difficulty is that whilst the public may look to the EU level to provide answers to these problems, problems that member states can no longer tackle (for reasons given earlier), the multi-tiered governance structure of the EU renders the

---

[18] For a discussion on the detail of restructuring of European welfare states see V. George and Taylor-Gooby (eds) (1996).

speedy development of social welfare policies hugely problematic. Crucially, as Leibfried and Pierson argue, the nation building function through welfare states is challenged within this system (Leibfried and Pierson, 1996: 54). With pressures to reassign social policy in order to allow for renegotiation, the question still remains whether it is possible to renegotiate the social bargain in a new (constitutional) environment. At present, this very question is fudged in the political rhetoric surrounding the European social model. The nature of the constitutional crisis for social policy is thus distorted. The question still to be answered is whether the European social model can renew itself and protect the social bargain, which is clearly recognized as important in terms of constitutional legitimacy, or whether in fact what we are observing in the current debate is simply a rhetorical or symbolic discussion to pacify public concern over the social effects of integration, where the 'European social model' is upheld as being original and innovative when in fact it is only a re-statement of something old. In this latter rendition, the 'European social model' is little more than a slogan.

IV   CONCLUDING THOUGHTS

In conclusion, I would like to make some observations about the future role for EC social policy within the European framework as we move to the next millennium. EC social policy is clearly subject to political pressures driven by external events. In this chapter, I have not considered in any detail the nature of such internal and external pressures on social policy in Europe. For example, I have not discussed the processes of 'globalization' or 'competitiveness' and the arguments which have been developed concerning their consequences for social policy. To a large extent I accept that processes have posed problems for national social welfare programmes – problems surrounding social dumping; problems surrounding the balance of power between organized labour and employers; problems posed as a result of demands for greater labour market flexibility in search for enhanced competitiveness and so on. Such problems are well-documented. The chapter does not go into these in any detail – they are implicit in the discussions. The focus is rather on the **process** of policy-making and the consideration of the 'European social model' as it is being conceptualized as a framework for further development of policy.

Having said this, it is true that precisely these prevailing pressures have encouraged the development of the two distinct dialogues on the collective responsibility for social policy explored in this chapter. Viewed in this manner, the problematic issue confronting the development of EC social policy is that the current reconsideration of the normative principles of European welfare capitalism is occurring outside of the EC policy process (and its actors), despite the fact that the policy process will be shaped from the results of this debate. As a result, and notwithstanding the positive reforms of

REFERENCES

of or studying the historical development

the Amsterdam Treaty, the pace and direction of the future development of EC social policy cannot be established. A diachronic approach to the study of the constitutionalization of social policy not only reveals that the European social bargain **and** the European social model are contested, but more importantly that the social model cannot be articulated until the bargain is redefined. How the bargain is renegotiated will thus determine the next phase of development of EC social policy.

REFERENCES

Bellamy, R. and Castiglione, D. (eds) (1996) *Constitutionalism in Transformation: European and Theoretical Perspectives* in *Political Studies*, Vol. 44, No. 3, Special Issue 1996.

Berghman, J. (1990) 'The Implications of 1992 for Social Policy: a Selective Critique of Social Insurance Protection' in Mangen, S., Hantrais, L. and O'Brian, M. (eds) *The Implications of 1992 for Social Policy*, Birmingham: Cross National Research Papers, Aston University.

Castiglione, D. (1996) 'The Political Theory of the Constitution' in Bellamy, R. and Castiglione, D. (eds) *Constitutionalism in Transformation: European and Theoretical Perspectives* in *Political Studies*, Vol. 44, No. 3, Special Issue, 417–435.

Collins, D. (1975) *The European Communities: the Social Policy of the First Phase Vol. 2 The European Economic Community 1958–72*, London: Martin Robertson.

Comité des Sages (1996) *For A Europe of Civic and Social Rights Report by the Comite des Sages* chaired by Maria de Lourdes Pintasilgo, Luxembourg: OOPEC.

Commission of the European Communities. (1994) *European Social Policy, A Way Forward for the Union Commission White Paper*, Com(94)333, Luxembourg.

de Gier, Erik (1991) 'The Future of Occupational Welfare in the Netherlands' in Room, G. *Towards a European Welfare State?* Bristol: SAUS, and the *UK: A new Trade-Off Between Efficiency and Social Justice*.

Emerson, M. (1986) *What Model For Europe?* Internal Report II/402/86.

Esping-Andersen (1990) *The Three Worlds of Welfare Capitalism*, Cambridge: Polity.

Flora, P. and Heidenheimer, A. (1981) *The Development of Welfare States in Europe and America*, New Brunswick and London: Transaction Books.

George, V. and Taylor-Gooby (eds). (1996) *European Welfare Policy: Squaring the Welfare Circle*, Basingstoke: Macmillan.

George, V. and Wilding, P. (1984) *The Impact of Social Policy*, London: Routledge & Kegan Paul.

Gold, M. (ed.) (1993) *The Social Dimension: Employment Policy in the EC*, London: Macmillan.

Grahl, John and Teague, Paul (1996) 'Is the European social model fragmenting?' Ulster Papers in Public Policy and Management.

Hirst, Paul Q. (1994) *Associative Democracy: New Forms of Economic and Social Governance*, Cambridge: Polity.

Hirst, Paul Q. (1995) 'The European Union at the Crossroads: Integration or Decline?' in Bellamy, R., Bufacchi, V. and Castiglione, D. (eds) *Democracy and Constitutional Culture in the Union of Europe*, London: Lothian Foundation Press, 45–56.

121

Holland, S. (1980) *Uncommon Market*, London and Basingstoke: Macmillan Press Ltd.

Keithley, Jane (1991) 'Social Security in a Single European Market' in Room, G. *Towards a European Welfare State?* Bristol: SAUS.

Langan, Mary and Ostner, Llona (1991) 'Gender and Welfare Towards a Comparative Framework' in Room, G. (1991) *Towards a European Welfare State?* (Bristol: SAUS)

Leibfried, S. (1992) 'Towards a European Welfare State?: On Integrating Poverty Regimes into the European Community' in Ferge, Z. and Kolberg, J.E. (eds) *Social Polices in a Changing Europe*, Frankfurt: Campus Verlag and Boulder, Colorardo: Westview Press.

Leibfried, S. (1993) 'Conceptualising European Social Policy: The EC as State Actor' in Hantrais, L. and Mangen, S. (eds) *The Policy-making Process and the Social Actors*, Cross National Research Papers, Third Series: Concepts and Contexts in International Comparisons, European Research Centre, Loughborough University.

Leibfried, S. and Pierson, P. (eds) (1995) *European Social Policy: Between Fragmentation and Integration*, Washington, D.C.: The Brookings Institution.

Majone, G. (1993) 'The European Community between Social Policy and Social Regulation', *Journal of Common Market Studies*, Vol. 31, June, 153–170.

Milward, Alan S. (1992) *The European Rescue of the Nation-State*, London: Routledge.

Milward, A. (1997) 'The Springs of Integration' in Anderson, P. and Gowan, P. (eds) *The Question of Europe*, London, New York: Verso.

O'Connor, T. (1973) *The Fiscal Crisis of the State*, New York: St. Martin's Press.

Nickell, S. (1997) 'Unemployment and Labor Market Rigidities: Europe versus North America' in *Journal of Economic Perspectives*, Vol. 11, No. 3, Summer, 55–74.

Offe, C. (1984) *Contradictions of the Welfare State*, London: Hutchinson.

Pierson, P. and Leibfried, S. (1993) *The Dynamics of Social Policy Integration Mimeo Program for the Study of Germany and Europe*, Center for European Studies, Harvard University.

Rose, R. (1996) *What is Europe? A Dynamic Perspective*, HarperCollins: New York.

Rhodes, M. (1993) 'Social Policy and European Integration: The Persistence or Erosion of State Autonomy?', Manchester: European Policy Research Unit, Working Paper No. 8/93, University of Manchester.

Scharpf, F. (1988) 'The Joint-Decision Trap Lessons from German Federalism and European Integration', *Public Administration*, 66, 3.

Scharpf, Fritz W. (1996) 'Negative and Positive Integration in the Political Economy of European Welfare States' in Marks, G. *et al. Governance in the European Union*, London: Sage.

Scharpf, Fritz (1997) 'Economic Integration, Democracy and the Welfare State', *Journal of European Public Policy*, 4:1 March, 18–36.

Shaw, J. (1997) 'The Many Pasts and Futures of Citizenship' in the *European Union European Law Review*, Vol. 22, No. 6, December, 554–572.

Spaak Report (1956) *Comité Intergouvernemental Crée par la Conference de Messine*, Rapport des Chefs de Délégation aux Ministres des Affaires Etrangères, Bruxelles: Secretariat.

Streeck, W. and Schmitter, P.C. (1991) 'From National Corporatism to Transnational Pluralism: Organised Interests in the Single European Market', *Politics and Society*, 19, 2.

Streeck, Wolfgang (1996) 'Neo-Voluntarism: A New European Social Policy Regime?' in Marks, G. *et al. Governance in the European Union*, London: Sage.

Teague, P. (1989) *The European Community: The Social Dimension*, London: Kogan Page.

Toward, S. (1995) 'The impact of European Integration on the National Health Service and Health Policy', Southampton: University of Southampton, Faculty of Social Sciences – Occasional Paper.

Wallace, Helen (1994) 'European Governance in Turbulent Times', in Bulmer, S. and Scott, A. (eds) *Economic and Political Integration in Europe: Internal Dynamics and Global Context*, Oxford: Basil Blackwell.

Weiler, J.H.H. (1996) 'European Neo-constitutionalism: in Search of Foundations for the European Constitutional Order' in Bellamy, R. and Castiglione, D. (eds) *Constitutionalism in Transformation: European and Theoretical Perspectives* in *Political Studies*, Vol. 44, No. 3, Special Issue, 517–533.

Wincott, D. (1998) 'Does the European Union Pervert Democracy? Questions of Democracy in New Constitutionalist Thought on the Future of Europe' *European Law Journal*, Vol. 4, Issue 4, December, 411–428.

Wise, M. and Gibb, R. (1993) *Single Market to Social Europe: The European Community*, Harlow, Essex: Longman.

123

8

DOMESTIC IMPLEMENTATION OF EUROPEAN LAW IN THE CONTEXT OF DEVOLUTION

*T. StJ. N. Bates**

I INTRODUCTION

As well as being the 30th anniversary of the Centre for European Govern-mental Studies, subsequently reflagged in less sensitive political times as the Europa Institute, 1998 was also the 30th anniversary of the arrival in the Edinburgh University Law Faculty of a Cambridge public lawyer with an established reputation. The following year I was – and still am – very grate-ful to that Cambridge public lawyer for appointing me to a lectureship in the Department of Constitutional and Administrative Law. Then, as now, our Chairman, Professor Tony Bradley did not know what to expect. I subsequently learned elsewhere the responsibilities that go with sharing the bulk of public law teaching with relatively, or very, inexperienced colleagues – hoping that the ducklings will at least become academically acceptable ducks, if not elegant swans. To the extent that appointment to Chairs is a measure of such ornithological success – which I find an increasingly doubt-ful proposition – Professor Bradley's judgement was sure – in that the three young lecturers who in 1969 primarily shared the public law teaching burden with him have subsequently occupied a total of eight Chairs between them. I was the last to fly the nest. Apart from personal limitations, one reason for that was that the Edinburgh Law Faculty was then – and I have no doubt still is – a superb academic environment. A feature of that was the number of senior colleagues who were so supportive – and tolerant – of their younger colleagues. I would mention in particular Tom Smith, Bill Wilson, John Mitchell – all of whom had a healthy respect – and in some cases affection – for each other. Of these, I would like to pay a particular personal tribute to

* Clerk of Tynwald, Secretary of the House of Keys and Counsel to the Speaker, Isle of Man; Professor of Law, University of Strathclyde, Scotland; the author writes in a personal capacity.

the late John Mitchell who did so much to encourage and influence my continuing interest in the public law and institutional aspects of the European Union.

Turning now to my subject, this paper seeks to do no more than sketch the functions of the Scottish Parliament and Scottish Executive as examples of sub-member state institutions within the evolving institutional practice and legislative competence of the European Union. These functions will be exercised within the framework of the Scotland Act 1998, existing and evolving UK constitutional practice and emerging Scottish constitutional practice.

The prospects for the exercise of these functions have been widely examined by reference to regional parliaments and governments in other member states. However, a less exotic tack will be taken here of comparing the prospects of the devolved Scottish institutions with the realities of the different, but comparable, experience of the Isle of Man in its relationship with the European Union. The Manx experience is different because its constitutional status and its relationship with the European Union is different. The Isle of Man is a Crown dependency and thus is not an integral part of the United Kingdom, and indeed never has been. It has its own parliament, Tynwald, claiming unlimited legislative competence in respect of the Isle of Man[1] – although Westminster asserts and, in limited areas exercises, legislative competence in respect of the Island. It has its own government, judiciary (with the Judicial Committee of the Privy Council as a final court of appeal) and its own legal system. The constitutional relationship between the Isle of Man and the United Kingdom is regulated, not by written constitution or by statute, but solely by constitutional convention. Stated briefly, the contemporary formulation of the operative constitutional convention is that the Crown is responsible for the defence, external relations and 'ultimately the good government' of the Island.[2] The relationship with the European Union is also different from that of Scotland.[3] It is governed by Protocol 3 of the Act of Accession annexed to the UK Treaty of Accession. This protocol, in essence, provides that the Isle of Man is within the common customs area and that EU law with respect to agricultural and processed agricultural products applies to the Island (although there is no financial benefit from the Common Agricultural Policy). The Island may not discriminate on grounds of nationality

[1] T. StJ. N. Bates, 'The Legislative Process in the Isle of Man' [1996] *The Loophole* (Journal of the Commonwealth Association of Legislative Counsel) 5.
[2] The formulation is commonly derived from the Report of the Royal Commission on the Constitution 1969–1973, Vol. I Cmnd 5460, which nevertheless contains a degree of inconsistency (para. 1362 *cf para*. 1539) and is obviously somewhat dated; there is also a certain inconsistency, and inaccuracy, in the current UK Government formulation of the constitutional relationship between the Isle of Man and the Crown *cf* 584 H L Debs, cols 1307–9 (19 January 1998), *cf* H L Debs, cols 236–238 (30 November 1998); for a contemporary consideration see T. StJ. N. Bates, Friends of St German's Cathedral Annual Lecture, 'As free as thy sweet mountain air?', 30 October 1998.
[3] Deemster T.W. Cain, 'The Isle of Man and the European Union' (1996) 27 Manx Law Bulletin 65.

between natural and legal persons of the EU[4] – but otherwise EU law does not apply to the Island; in particular, EU law with respect to the movement of persons (with some exceptions), the right of establishment and the free movement of services do not apply. However, the Manx experience may provide a more useful comparison for Scotland than many of the regional arrangements within the European Union in that its relationship with its member state is regulated by convention which will to some extent also be true of Scotland, and its institutions are, despite the Viking origins of Tynwald, essentially based on the Westminster model operating within British constitutional principles.

I emphasize the importance of constitutional convention because it seems clear from the Scotland Act, read with the preceding White Paper[5] that constitutional convention will play a significant role in the operation of the devolved Scottish institutions.

I would make two initial observations on this. The first is the notion of the 'concordat' which has something in common with subsidiarity, in that both have a theological provenance but the scope of their influence is uncertain. The concordat featured in the White Paper[6] and was refined in guidance published by the Scottish Office in February 1998. These concordats which will regulate relations between the devolved Scottish institutions and their UK counterparts will be non-statutory and are not intended to be legally enforceable contracts between the parties. These parties will evidently be, in the main, civil servants in Scotland and south of the Border, but occasionally will be elected politicians. Most of them will be published and will represent authoritative statements of practice. However, I would expect constitutional conventions in the traditional sense also to operate both on, and alongside, concordats.

My second initial observation derives from recent Manx experience. This suggests that as conventions emerge they may operate in a somewhat Anglocentric manner, in the sense that the players may be Westminster and Whitehall and the subject matter may be the Scottish devolved institutions. Let me give a recent Manx illustration. In an arranged question for written answer the Home Secretary announced that a review of Manx and Channel Islands financial legislation and regulation was to be undertaken by Mr Andrew Edwards, a former Treasury official.[7] The establishment of the review was, in fact, officially communicated to the Isle of Man Government the day before

---

[4] Case C-355/89, *Department of Health and Social Security (Isle of Man) v Barr and Montrose Holdings Ltd* ([1991] ECR I-3479; Case C-171/96, *Roque v Lieutenant Governor of Jersey* [1998] CMLR 143.

[5] *Scotland's Parliament* Cm 3658 (July 1997).

[6] E.g. ibid. para. 2.4 (financial assistance to industry), *cf* paras 4.13 and 5.5.

[7] 304 H C Debs, cols 506–8 (20 January 1998); the Home Office is the lead UK Government department with respect to the responsibilities of the Crown for the Isle of Man. See further, 'Report of the Review of Financial Regulation in the Crown Dependencies', Cm 4109 (November 1998).

it was announced.[8] The establishment of this review, and the manner of its establishment, is difficult to reconcile with the autonomy of the Isle of Man, which is only subject to the convention which I have mentioned. As far as I am aware, and there has been no suggestion from the UK Government to the contrary, the financial legislation and regulation in the Isle of Man complies with Manx international obligations. Furthermore, Acts of Tynwald receive Royal Assent effectively on the advice of the Home Office. The Isle of Man was the first dependent territory to be granted designated status under the UK Financial Services Act which required its financial legislation and regulation to satisfy the terms of that Act, and its financial legislation and regulation has also been favourably reviewed by the Financial Action Task Force. In short, I am not aware of anything which would suggest that in this area the government of the Isle of Man had been shown to be anything less than good. Without such *prima facie* grounds that element of the convention would also not seem to be a justification for UK intervention in the domestic affairs of the Isle of Man. So, if the convention has a validity, the establishment of the review must have rested rather uneasily on Manx acquiescence to the UK intervention. In practical terms, on this occasion at least, the Isle of Man may have become the subject of, rather than a party to, the convention.

II INVOLVEMENT IN THE EU POLICY AND LEGISLATIVE PROCESS

The extent of involvement in the formulation of EU policy and in its legislative powers is an important dimension of domestic implementation. Although not always emphasized in a British political context, the governments of member states are closely involved in the development of proposed EU policy and draft EU legislation of the European Commission. At present, where the issues have a Scottish dimension, the Scottish Office contributes to the preparation of British governmental position in these processes. This will effectively continue post-devolution, whether the Commission initiatives relate to reserved or devolved matters, or to both of these categories. On one view, this will be assisted by the Scotland Act preserving a unified home civil service, serving both the Scottish Executive and the UK Government; however, the extent to which this arrangement will prove practicable where there are sharp policy differences between the two governments remains to be seen.

The Scottish Executive involvement in these activities is regulated by the Scotland Act. It provides that presentation of the UK position either in consultation with the European Commission or within the Council of Ministers and its committees, is a reserved matter as 'relations with . . . the

---

[8] House of Keys, *Official Proceedings*, 27 January 1998, K153–156; ibid., 10 February 1998, K209–211; see also Tynwald Court, *Official Proceedings*, 20 January 1998, T326–328, ibid., 21 January 1998, T373.

European Communities (and their institutions)' are expressly reserved.[9] However, the Act also provides that members of the Scottish Executive may assist UK Government Ministers in such negotiations[10] and indeed such assistance may include leading UK delegations. However, determining the policy to be pursued in such negotiations would be for the UK Government and any role which the Scottish Executive plays would have to be within policy so determined. On a strict interpretation of Paragraph 6(1) of Schedule 5, there would be no capacity for the Scottish Parliament to develop interparliamentary relationships with other parliaments outside the United Kingdom, including the European Parliament. If this is the legislative intention, it seems unlikely that it will be maintained in practice. In any event, the Scotland Act allows the Scottish Parliament to have a minor direct involvement in the EU process, as a member of the Scottish Parliament may be proposed as a member of the Committee of the Regions.[11]

However, the most important role for the Scottish Parliament will be to hold the Scottish Executive to account.

The Scotland Act wisely does not seek to limit the capacity of the Scottish Parliament to debate reserved matters. The Scottish Parliament can be expected to hold the Scottish Executive to account for the extent and manner in which it exercises influence on the UK Government in its negotiations on EU policy and legislation as they affect Scotland, whether the effect relates to devolved matters or not.[12] The Scottish Parliament is likely to exercise such scrutiny by means of question and debate on the negotiating position of the UK Government and the effectiveness of the influence of the Scottish Executive on the UK negotiating position which is adopted. It is entirely possible that such scrutiny may also be undertaken by Scottish parliamentary committees monitoring the policy and administration of departments of the Scottish Executive. It also seems probable that the Scottish Parliament will establish a committee to scrutinize draft EU legislation which impacts on Scotland, whether or not the impact relates to devolved or reserved matters.

However, the capacity for such scrutiny by the Scottish Parliament is somewhat circumscribed in respect of reserved matters. It may only require the attendance of persons and the production of documents relating to devolved matters concerning Scotland and matters where statutory functions are exerciseable by Scottish Ministers. It cannot require the attendance of a UK Government Minister or a person outside Scotland unless the person discharges functions relating to such matters and cannot require the attendance of a person discharging functions of any body whose functions relate only to reserved matters.[13] This is not to say that such persons will not

---

[9] Scotland Act 1998, Sched. 5, Part 1, para. 7(1).
[10] Ibid., para. 7(2)(b).
[11] Ibid., Sched. 7, para. 23.
[12] For a pre-Scotland Bill view of these matters see T. StJ. N. Bates, 'Devolution and the European Union' in Bates (ed.) *Devolution to Scotland: The Legal Aspects*, T. and T. Clark, Edinburgh: 1997.
[13] Scotland Act 1998, s. 28.

appear voluntarily before, say, a Scottish parliamentary committee to give evidence. European Commissioners and members of their staff, and MEPs from other member states, do give evidence to UK parliamentary committees, although Westminster has no power to compel them to do so. In practice, the European Commission is circumspect about giving such evidence, being conscious that if evidence is given to the committees of one national parliament the facility must be made available to other national parliaments. It may well be that the Commission, on these grounds, will not be enthusiastic about giving evidence to devolved parliaments within member states.

Even within the context of devolved matters, the Scottish Parliament may encounter practical difficulties with scrutiny. For example, if the Scottish Parliament were to scrutinize draft EU legislation relating to devolved matters in a manner similar to the scrutiny of draft EU legislation at Westminster it will face difficulties of obtaining information and of timing. It will be important for the Scottish Parliament to require the Scottish Executive to provide information on amendments made to draft EU legislation after it has been published by the Commission and it will have to undertake its scrutiny of such legislation in sufficient time for the Scottish Executive to reflect such parliamentary opinion as it accepts in its negotiations with the UK Government. In many respects the position of Scotland in this regard will be more attractive than that of the Isle of Man. It will be ameliorated by a unified home civil service and no doubt the operation of the 'concordats'. By contrast the Isle of Man has a civil service separate and distinct from the UK civil service. To date, there has been no suggestion that Ministers or civil servants of the Isle of Man Government should form part of the UK negotiating team in Brussels, although that has happened in other international contexts where there has been a distinct Manx dimension.[14] Like Scotland, the Isle of Man also has a long line of communication to Brussels, in that the formal channel of communication is through the Home Office to the relevant Whitehall department, and it must then rely on any distinctive Manx position being incorporated in the UK negotiating brief and maintained thereafter.

III IMPLEMENTATION OF EU LAW BY PRIMARY LEGISLATION

The legislative competence of the Scottish Parliament is limited and subject to a variety of controls. The limitations have a number of European Union

---

[14] In June 1997, given its concern with the basking shark, the Isle of Man Government was represented in the UK delegation to CITES; an Isle of Man Government capacity to conduct bilateral relations with Ireland and devolved governments within the United Kingdom is an inherent attribute of the British Irish Council established under the Belfast Agreement, Cm 3883; April 1998; the UK Government has also recognized the capacity of the Isle of Man Government to respond directly to the OECD in respect of the OECD initiative on harmful tax competition.

dimensions. An Act of the Scottish Parliament, with some qualifications, cannot relate to reserved matters.[15] Reserved matters relate to EU law in various ways. They are sometimes defined by specific reference to EU legislation[16] sometimes by a general reference to EU law;[17] sometimes by specific reference to 'the subject matter' of UK legislation which has the principal purpose of implementing EU obligations[18] and sometimes by a descriptive reference to an area of law with a significant EU law content.[19] Even with respect to devolved matters, it is outside the legislative competence of the Scottish Parliament to enact legislation which is incompatible with EU law.[20] In any event, the legislative capacity of the UK Parliament to make law for Scotland, whether with respect to reserved or devolved matters, is preserved.[21]

IV CONTROLS OVER PRIMARY LEGISLATION OF THE SCOTTISH PARLIAMENT

The Scotland Act provides parliamentary, judicial and executive pre-Assent controls over primary legislation passed by the Scottish Parliament, including that which has a European Union dimension; and there is judicial post-Assent control over such legislation. These controls may be compared with those that apply to Manx legislation.

1 Parliamentary pre-Assent controls

Section 31(1) of the Act requires a member of the Scottish Executive in charge of a Bill, on or before its introduction, to state that, in his or her view, the Bill would be within the legislative competence of the Scottish Parliament. Section 31(2) also requires the Presiding Officer to decide whether the Bill, in his or her view, would be within that legislative competence and state the decision. This role of the Presiding Office effectively issuing a warning an legislative competence replaced a much criticised procedure originally contained in the bill at a late stage that is only likely to occur at the instigation of a Scottish Government which disagrees with the opinion of the Presiding Officer. However, if the Parliament decides to override the decision of the Presiding Officer it will may well not be doing so on the basis of independent advice from a third quarter. The net effect of these provisions may tend to undermine the authority of the Presiding Officer.

---

[15] Scotland Act 1998, s. 29(2)(b), (3) and (4); cf s. 28(8).
[16] E.g., ibid., Sched. 5, Pt II, section B2(b)
[17] E.g., ibid., Pt II, section C8.
[18] E.g., ibid., Pt II, section L2; for a consideration of some of the implications of using this drafting technique see 19 Stat LR (1998) No. 2, V–V1.
[19] E.g., ibid., Pt II, section C1.
[20] Ibid., s. 29(2)(d).
[21] Ibid., s. 28(7).

2 Judicial pre-Assent controls

The Lord Advocate, the Advocate General or the Attorney General may refer the question of whether legislation passed by the Scottish Parliament is within its legislative competence to the Judicial Committee of the Privy Council.[22]

3 Executive pre-Assent controls

The Secretary of State may make a reasoned order prohibiting the Presiding Officer of the Scottish Parliament from submitting a Bill for Royal Assent on certain grounds. These include that the Secretary of State has reasonable grounds to believe the enactment would be incompatible with an international obligation, but curiously not an EU obligation,[23] but also where the Secretary of State has reasonable grounds to believe that certain such legislation would have an adverse effect on the operation of the law as it applies to reserved matters.[24] This would apply to Bills passed by the Scottish Parliament relating to EU obligations even where the Bill was otherwise within the legislative competence of the Scottish Parliament.

4 Judicial post-Assent control

In addition, the Scotland Act provides for a post-Assent judicial scrutiny of whether an Act of the Scottish Parliament, or any of its provisions, is within the legislative competence of the Scottish Parliament.[25] Where a court or a tribunal decides that an enactment of the Scottish Parliament is not within its legislative competence, it may make an order removing or limiting any retrospective effect of its decision, or suspending the effect of the decision for any period, or on any conditions, to allow the defect to be corrected.[26]

5 The Manx position

By contrast to the Scottish position, Tynwald has no formal limitations on its legislative competence. However, the limited application of EU law to the Isle of Man means that there are relatively few areas where the Island is required under EU law to implement EU law domestically. Where it does so,

---

[22] Ibid., s. 33. Were the Judicial Committee to make a reference to the European Court of Justice for a preliminary ruling in respect of the reference, s. 34 provides a procedure by which the Scottish Parliament may reconsider the legislation which would trigger a request to withdraw the reference.
[23] Ibid., s. 35(1)(a).
[24] Ibid., s. 35(1)(b)
[25] Ibid., Sched. 6.
[26] Ibid., s. 102(2).

it is commonly done by delegated rather than primary legislation under Manx statutory powers which parallel s. 2 of the European Communities Act 1972 in the United Kingdom.[27] In practice, it not infrequently implements EU law in domestic legislation where there is no requirement to do so. This may be as a result of public opinion demanding the application of EU standards, for example with respect to the environment. Or it may be as a consequence of using UK legislation as a model for Manx legislation where the UK legislation implements EU law – so that the Isle of Man is implementing EU law voluntarily at one remove. Although initial euphoria suggests that this will not be the case in Scotland, the reality may be closer to the Manx experience. Although the resources of the Scottish Parliament and Executive will be greater than those of Tynwald and the Isle of Man Government they will certainly be less extensive than those of Westminster and Whitehall. Consequently, Scottish legislation implementing EU law in devolved matters may, in practice, be quite closely modelled on Westminster legislation. There will also be, no doubt, commercial pressures which will tend to lead to such an outcome. One consequence of this may be that over a period of time such Scottish legislation modelled on Westminster legislation may not receive the parliamentary scrutiny which it deserves on the, possibly covert, grounds that it has been fully scrutinized elsewhere. It is to be hoped that this proves to be a somewhat pessimistic prediction, but the outcome may depend on the ability of the projected small number of Scottish parliamentary committees being able to undertake the rather large range of matters which it appears will fall within their orders of reference.

V IMPLEMENTATION OF EU LAW BY DELEGATED LEGISLATION

The competence of members of the Scottish Executive to make subordinate legislation, which would include subordinate legislation relating to EU obligations, is also subject to limitations and controls. In broad terms, and subject to some general and specific exceptions, it will be competent to make such subordinate legislation only if it would be within the legislative competence of the Scottish Parliament if it were included in an Act of the Scottish Parliament.[28] Section 57(2) specifically provides that there is no competence to make such subordinate legislation which is incompatible with EU law; and s. 57(1) effectively preserves the competence of UK Government Ministers to make subordinate legislation implementing EU obligations under the European Communities Act 1972.

---

[27] See the European Communities (Isle of Man) Act 1973, an Act of Tynwald which has been significantly amended; for the Act as amended, see *Statutes of the Isle of Man*, Vol. 3, 1–31ff (Juta & Co Ltd: South Africa).

[28] Scotland Act 1998, s. 54(2); *cf* ss. 53, 55, 56.

The Scotland Act contains a number of other controls on subordinate legislation made by a member of the Scottish Executive. Section 58 empowers the Secretary of State by reasoned order to require a member of the Scottish Executive to make, confirm or approve subordinate legislation, and in certain circumstances to introduce primary legislation, where the Secretary of State has either reasonable grounds to believe that a proposed action by a member of the Scottish Executive would be incompatible with any international obligation, or action capable of being taken by a member of the Scottish Executive is required to give effect to an international obligation. Like s. 35, this provision does not specifically extend to EU obligations. However, by a reasoned order, the Secretary of State may revoke otherwise competent subordinate legislation made by a member of the Scottish Executive, which the Secretary of State has reasonable grounds to believe would have an adverse effect on the operation of an enactment as it applies to reserved matters.[29] In addition, there is a capacity under the Scotland Act to make subordinate legislation which is considered necessary or expedient as a consequence a provision of an Act of the Scottish Parliament which is or may be *ultravires*; or of subordinate legislation made under such a provision.[30] Finally, whether subordinate legislation which has been made by a member of the Scottish Executive, or which such a member proposes to make, is within legislative competence is subject to judicial review. Any court or tribunal which decides that such subordinate legislation, or one of its provisions, is incompetent, may make an order in the same terms as it may make an order with respect to incompetent primary legislation.[31]

Both with respect to EU law and otherwise, the procedures by which the Scottish Parliament scrutinizes delegated legislation will be of some importance. Here, I regret to say, the Scottish Parliament will have little to learn from Tynwald. Tynwald does not have a committee which undertakes comprehensive technical scrutiny of delegated legislation and as a parliament relies on briefings which I supply as Counsel to the Speaker on these matters. This is a rather exposed position for a parliamentary officer and not one which can be recommended. Tynwald rarely refers individual delegated legislation to a committee for consideration of its merits;[32] such consideration is normally undertaken on the floor of Tynwald. It remains to be seen whether the Scottish Parliament will establish committees to undertake such technical scrutiny and committees to examine the merits of delegated legislation.

The detail of the procedure relating to subordinate legislation before the Scottish Parliament is largely left to its standing orders. There is then perhaps

---

[29] Ibid., s. 54(4)(b), (5).
[30] Ibid., s. 107.
[31] Ibid., Sched. 6; s. 102(1)(b) and (2).
[32] However, in July 1998, Tynwald did appoint a Select Committee of three members to consider and report on the Supply of Services (Exclusion of Implied Terms) Order 1998 (SD No. 190/98).

some scope here for procedural innovation. It may be that these committees could be persuaded to take rather more evidence than their Westminster counterparts. They may wish to conduct more rigorous enquiry into the nature and extent of the consultation which takes place prior to the making of such subordinate legislation. And it may even be that a Scottish Parliament would contemplate a limited abandonment of the Westminster prohibition on amending subordinate legislation, which is based on rather precious constitutional grounds. What would be most encouraging would be a procedural requirement that subordinate legislation requiring approval should not be approved before a scrutiny committee has considered it and presented its report to the Parliament.[33]

VI ADMINISTRATIVE COMPETENCE OF THE SCOTTISH EXECUTIVE WITH RESPECT TO THE EUROPEAN UNION

The Scottish Executive will exercise a wide variety of administrative functions relating to the European Union. These functions will flow from the transfer of prerogative and other executive functions presently exercised by the UK Government, of certain statutory functions conferred on a minister of the UK Government by primary and delegated legislation passed or made prior to the commencement of the Scotland Act, of statutory functions subsequently conferred on Scottish Ministers under the Scotland Act, and from functions conferred on Scottish Ministers by Acts of the Parliament of Scotland.[34] In addition, the categories of devolved and reserved matters in Sched. 5 to the Scotland Act 1998 may be modified by subordinate legislation[35] and this may result in the transfer of further functions to the Scottish Executive. Implementing obligations under EU law is specified as a matter which is not reserved[36] and this presumably includes executive as well as legislative implementation. The exercise of these functions by the Scottish Executive will be subject to parliamentary scrutiny and judicial review, in particular whether the exercise or proposed exercise of a function is a reserved matter or is incompatible with EU law, and also whether a failure to act by a member of the Scottish Executive is incompatible with EU law.[37] This may be of both legal and financial significance because, for example, in EU law there may be liability to damages, flowing from Art. 5 of the EC Treaty, against a member state for loss caused by its failure to implement EU law properly.[38]

---

[33] See further, T. StJ. N. Bates, 'The Interpretation and Review of Delegated Legislation by the Courts' in *Report of the Fourth Commonwealth Conference on Delegated Legislation*, House of Representatives, Wellington, New Zealand: 1997.

[34] Scotland Act 1998, ss. 52, 53.

[35] Ibid., s. 30(2).

[36] Ibid., Sched. 5, Part 1, para. 7(2)(a).

[37] Ibid., Sched. 6, Part I, para. 1(c)–(e).

[38] E.g., Cases C-6 and 9/90, *Francovich and Bonifaci v Italy* [1991] ECR I-5357; Case C-334/92, *Miret v Fonda de Garantia Salarial* [1993] ECR I-6911.

VII CONCLUSIONS

This *tour d'horizon* of the European Union dimension of the constitutional structures within the Scotland Act serves to emphasize that it contains quite complex arrangements to protect the United Kingdom from EU law liability as a member state. As a matter of law, these arrangements are likely to become an increasingly important dimension of the determination of the competence of the Scottish Parliament and Scottish Executive. In practical terms, the Scottish Act provides a structure in which the implementation and administration of EU obligations by the devolved Scottish institutions will require considerable attention if they are to relate effectively, as they must, both to the UK Parliament and UK Government and to the institutions of the European Union.

The practicalities of all this are reflected in the Manx experience. However, for the most part the constitutional relationship between the Isle of Man and the United Kingdom is not one of tension. The same may not be true of the relationship between the devolved Scottish institutions and their UK counterparts. Furthermore, the Manx relationship is regulated by convention, rather than the complexities of the Scotland Act and perhaps the additional complexities of 'concordats' and conventions. Despite this, the implementation of EU law in the Isle of Man is by no means free of practical difficulty. It may be that even with a general willingness to ensure the smooth operation of devolution in a European Union context, that Scotland will share something of the same experience.

9

IMPLEMENTATION OF COMMUNITY LAW IN A FEDERAL SYSTEM: THE CASE OF THE FEDERAL REPUBLIC OF GERMANY

Gisbert Brinkmann

I INTRODUCTION

The implementation[1] of Community law, in particular the accurate transposition of Community directives into national law is, as the Maastricht Conference declared, 'central to the coherence and unity of the process of European construction'.[2] The implementation of substantive Community law leads to the application of this law in administrative acts or judicial decisions in concrete cases. Apart from direct implementation by the Community itself which is only rare, e.g. in the field of competition law, the Community is largely dependent upon the effective implementation of Community law by the national administrations. This 'indirect implementation' is therefore linked to the structures, regulatory cultures and values of national law.[3] The implementation of Community law in a federal system raises problems and questions unknown to a unitary state since the implementation might be the sole responsibility of subnational entities or shared with the one of the central level. Every federal system is unique and no federal system is like the other. In the EU there are three member states – Austria, Belgium and Germany[4] –

[1] Implementation is understood as including transposition, application and enforcement. Transposition, is understood as meaning any legislative, regulatory or administrative binding measure taken by any competent authority of a member state in order to incorporate into the national legal order the obligations, rights and duties enshrined in EU Directives. Application is understood as the incorporation of EU law by the competent authorities into individual decisions while enforcement means all approaches of the competent authorities to compel others to comply with the law (*cf Implementing Community Environmental Law*, Communication from the Commission, COM(96) 500, 22 October 1996).
[2] Declaration No. 19.
[3] Shaw, *Law of the European Union*, Houndmills, Macmillan, 2nd ed., 1996: 207.
[4] In addition, the regional level of France, Italy and Spain is able to bring some influence to bear in the process of political decision-making on European affairs; *cf* the reports on Austria, Belgium, France, Germany, Italy and Spain in Straub/Hrbek (eds), *Die europapolitische Rolle*

which officially consider themselves federal. However, they differ as regards structure and powers. While Belgium experienced decentralizing tendencies with the establishment of a complicated arrangement of three cultural or linguistic communities, on the one hand, and three regions, on the other hand, whereas centralizing tendencies took place in Germany with forces pushing for greater uniformity in the provision of government services and coordinated planning for efficient use of resources resulting in greater concentration of legislative power of the Federation.[5]

This chapter discusses the problems arising in the German federal system in which different layers of government are charged with the implementation of Community law. In addition, since implementation to a large extent depends on previous involvement in the decision-making process of the law to be implemented, involvement of the *Länder* as regards the rules and practices of decision-making at national and European level will be briefly referred to beforehand.

II PARTICIPATION OF THE *LÄNDER* IN EUROPEAN LAW-MAKING

As the EC extends its responsibilities it increasingly encroaches upon powers of the *Länder* which used to be not affected by European legislation. The Community has the power to legislate in fields which, according to the internal distribution of powers in Germany, are the exclusive competence of the *Länder*, such as education and culture (*cf* Arts 126–128 TEC, to be Arts 149–151).[6] The participation of the *Länder* in European law-making not only serves to

---

der Landes- und Regionalparlamente in der EU, Baden-Baden, Nomos, 1998. In future, after the introduction of devolution in the UK regional Parliaments, Executives will be involved in decision-making on European affairs and implementation of European legislation.

[5] As regards the distribution of legislative powers between the Federation and the *Länder*, according to the wording of the Constitution (*Grundgesetz* = Basic Law), it appears at first glance that more weight is given to the *Länder* than to the Federation. Although the *Länder* have legislative power wherever the Federation does not expressly possess such power (Art. 70 Basic Law, and see the general provision Art. 30 Basic Law: 'Except as otherwise provided or permitted by this Basic Law the exercise of governmental powers and the discharge of governmental functions shall be incumbent on the *Länder*'). In fact, legislative power, however, is mainly concentrated in the Federation. First, it enjoys exclusive legislative powers according to Art. 73 Basic Law (foreign affairs, citizenship, immigration, currency, air transport). Secondly, it has exercised legislative power in almost all fields of concurring legislation according to Art. 74 Basic Law which can only be exercised by the *Länder*, as long as the Federation does not legislate; concurring legislative powers include most legislative subjects, such as civil law, criminal law, court organization and procedure, the legal profession, foreigners' residence, public welfare, economic affairs, labour relations, land law, and road traffic. Thirdly, the Federation has the right to enact skeleton or framework legislation carried out in detail by the *Länder* according to Art. 75 Basic Law which includes general principles of higher education, legal status of the press, nature conservation, regional planning. Once the Federation has exercised its power to legislate relevant law of the *Länder* becomes void (*cf* Art. 31 Basic Law: 'Federal law shall override *Land* law'. Because of the centralizing tendencies in legislation the *Länder* parliaments have become rather insignificant as legislative bodies.
[6] Other fields include police and municipal law.

protect their interests or corresponds to their desire of self-preservation but, at the same time, to secure the implementation of European legislation. Otherwise a certain unwillingness of subnational levels to implement EC legislation on whose substance they had had no influence could be expected.[7]

Although according to Art. 32 of the Basic Law external relations are the exclusive power of the Federation at national level, the *Länder* gradually could make their voice heard in European law-making. Already after the ratification of the Treaty of Rome and even more so with the entry into force of the Single European Act in 1987 the *Länder* enjoyed certain participation rights in European law-making guaranteed by an Act of Parliament. Their powers were even further enhanced with the ratification of the Treaty of Maastricht. The consent of the *Länder* in the *Bundesrat* (Federal Council – Upper House)[8] was required for the ratification of the Treaty of Maastricht which necessitated amendments of the Constitution (*Grundgesetz* = Basic Law).[9] Because of this the *Länder* enjoyed an enormous bargaining power and consequently the Federation had not much chance but to give in to the demands of the *Länder* to have their participation rights in European affairs, in particular European law-making, enhanced and enshrined in the Constitution.

The outcome of the negotiations between the federal government and the *Länder* governments was a new constitutional provision (Art. 23 Basic Law) which lays down structural parameters required for the European Union and its further development. In addition, any future transfer of sovereign rights encroaching upon the substance of the Basic Law requires a statute adopted with the qualified majority necessary for constitutional amendments. Furthermore, Art. 23 establishes the legal regime of consultation and concertation between the Federal Government and the *Länder* through the *Bundesrat*.[10] These provisions were complemented by two Acts, one of which is the Act on cooperation of the Federation and the *Länder* regarding European affairs,[11] the other one is the Act on cooperation of the Federal Government and the *Bundestag* (Federal Diet = Lower House),[12] and by an Agreement

---

[7] *Cf* Siedentopf/Hauschild, 'The Implementation of Community Legislation by the Member States', in: Siedentopf/Ziller (eds), *Making European Policies Work*, London, Sage, 1988, 1 at 45.

[8] The type of federal system in Germany is the traditional German Council principle (*Ratsprinzip*) in which the members of the upper house are delegates of the *Länder* governments bound by their instructions. This is in contrast to e.g. the US Senate principle in which the delegates of the upper house are elected by the people directly. Accordingly, in the process of the formation of political will the *Länder* representation functions chiefly as an instrument of the executive and bureaucracy.

[9] Article 28 Basic Law needed to be adapted to the right to vote of EU citizens in municipal elections (Art. 8B(1) TEC) and Art. 88 to the European Central Bank.

[10] Although the wording of Art. 50 Basic Law ('The *Länder* shall participate through the *Bundesrat* in the legislative process and administration of the Federation and in matters concerning the European Union') might be misleading insofar as it might portray the *Bundesrat* as an organ of the *Länder* it is, however, an organ of the Federation and not of the *Länder*.

[11] Gesetz über die Zusammenarbeit von Bund und Ländern in Angelegenheiten der Europäischen Union (EuZBLG), BGBl 1993 I S. 313.

[12] Gesetz über die Zusammenarbeit von Bundestag und Deutschem Bundestag in Angelegenheiten der Europäischen Union (EuZBBG), BGBl 1993 I S. 311.

between the Federal Government and the Governments of the *Länder*.[13] All instruments include further details concerning information and participation rights of the *Länder* in matters concerning EU affairs. The involvement of the *Länder* is now as follows:

- the *Länder* have to be informed (through the *Bundesrat*[14]) by the Federal Government in matters concerning the European Union,
- the *Bundesrat* has to be involved in the decision-making process of the Federation in so far as it would have to be involved in a corresponding internal measure or in so far as the *Länder* would be internally responsible,
- in case of federal legislative power, if *Länder* interests are affected the opinion of the *Bundesrat* has to be taken into account,
- if *Länder* legislative powers, the establishment of their authorities or their administrative procedures are essentially affected the opinion of the *Bundesrat* shall prevail while, at the same time, the responsibility of the Federation for the country as a whole shall be maintained,
- if *Länder* exclusive legislative powers are essentially affected the exercise of rights of Germany as EU member is transferred by the Federation to a representative of the *Länder* while, once again, the responsibility of the Federation for the country as a whole shall be maintained.

This constitutional provision means that the Federation represents the constitutional rights of the *Länder* towards the EU as trustee (*Sachwalter*)[15] except where exclusive legislative powers of the *Länder* are concerned. In this case the *Länder* directly participate in the external representation of the Federal Republic of Germany. Although the terms used in Art. 23 such as 'affected' and 'essentially affected' are vague and therefore this provision is highly likely to be subject to different interpretations by the actors of the Federation and the *Länder*. In case of dispute, however, unless a political solution is found, it will be up to the Federal Constitutional Court (*Bundesverfassungsgericht*) as the arbiter of the federal system[16] to decide in the last resort.[17]

---

[13] Vereinbarung vom 29. Oktober 1993 zwischen der Bundesregierung und den Regierungen der Länder über die Zusammenarbeit in Angelegenheiten der Europäischen Union in Ausführung von § 9 des Gesetzes über die Zusammenarbeit von Bund und Ländern in Angelegenheiten der Europäischen Union, *Bundesanzeiger* No. 226 of 1993, p. 10425; supplemented by the Vereinbarung of 8 June 1998 in order to deal in future with framework decisions of Art. 34(2)(b) TEU as adopted in Amsterdam.

[14] The *Bundesrat* can act through its Chamber for European Affairs whose decisions shall be considered decisions of the *Bundesrat* (Art. 52(3)(a) Basic Law). Likewise Article 45 provides for a Committee on European Union of the *Bundestag*.

[15] *Cf* BVerfGE 92, 203 (= Decision of the Federal Constitutional Court, vol. 92, 203).

[16] *Cf* as to the role of the Federal Constitutional Court (FCC) in federal disputes in domestic matters: P.M. Blair, *Federalism and Judicial Review in West Germany*, Oxford, Clarendon, 1981.

[17] Although Art. 23 Basic Law has not yet been tested before the FCC the FCC, however, has dealt with similar provisions on information and participation of the *Länder*, as there were

Although this strong position of the *Länder* in European law-making has been regarded as excessive[18] it could be justified by their position in constitutional law according to which they are regarded as parts of the whole state that enjoy the same status as the Federation and have a right to equal treatment by the Federation. Their powers are not derived from the Federation but recognized by it[19] since in 1949 it was the *Länder* which had founded the Federal Republic of Germany and transferred powers to the Federation. Similarly the powers of the EC are derived from the transfer of sovereignty of the member states to the EC.

Apart from the influence guaranteed by the Constitution, on the informal plane the *Länder* created already in 1959 the position of an 'observer of the *Länder*' (*Länderbeobachter*) at Brussels and Bonn and all the *Länder* have since then set up representative offices at Brussels in order to achieve **Eurofitness**, i.e. the capability to assess the implications of EU legislation for their individual *Länder*, to react to this in coherent and coordinated fashion and clearly to represent their demands to the Federal government as well as the EU institutions.[20]

The direct participation of the *Länder* in the external representation of Germany in European affairs was made possible through the amendment of Art. 146 (to be Art. 203) TEC at Maastricht that allows *Länder* ministers to be representatives in the Council. This Article already demonstrates that the conduct of relations with the EC is not necessarily reserved to the central government. In addition, Maastricht enhanced the position of the constituent parts of the member states through the creation of the Committee of the Regions composed of representatives of regional or local bodies which, although it only enjoys minimal powers in European decision-making (Arts 198A–198C, to be Arts 263–265 TEC), it serves to communicate the fact that knowledge of European issues at regional and local level is of prime importance.

III PARTICIPATION OF THE *LÄNDER* IN THE TRANSPOSITION OF EC LAW

The main Community legislative instrument to be transposed in the national legal order is a Directive.[21] According to Art. 189(3) TEC (to be Art. 249(3))

---

after the ratification of the Single European Act, in the *Television Directive* case (BVerfGE 92, 203, *cf infra*, at note 53). Certain conclusions could be drawn from this case for the interpretation of Art. 23 Basic Law.

[18] *Cf* e.g. Herdegen, 'After the TV Judgment of the German Constitutional Court: Decision-Making within the EU Council and the German *Länder*', 32 (1995) CMLRev 1369 at 1383: 'kind of overkill in the energetic quest for strengthening the position of the *Länder*'.

[19] BVerfGE 39, 96 at 119.

[20] Heichlinger, 'The significance of *Eurofitness* for regional and local administrations and how it can be achieved', 1998/1 *EIPASCOPE* 52.

[21] Regulations do not require transposition since they are directly applicable (Art. 189(2), to be Art. 249(2) TEC) they could, however, be complemented by national rules to adapt them to the national legal system.

a Directive has binding force in relation to the result to be achieved for each member state to which it is addressed but the member states are free to choose the methods and forms to implement it. Because of the supremacy of EC law over national law every member state must adapt and modify its laws in order to bring its legal system into full conformity with the objectives specified in the Directive.[22] Unless national law already conforms with the Directive it has to be transposed into national provisions in a manner which satisfies the requirements of clarity and legal certainty.

From the Community point of view the duty of implementation lies with its member states.[23] On the other hand, the Community is 'blind towards the internal structure' and does not prescribe the national distribution of powers and in particular not the institutions or levels of government in charge of national implementation measures.[24] Thus, the member states are free to decide on their internal distribution of powers which, however, does not mean that they are not under an obligation to have EC law implemented.[25] According to the European Court of Justice the duties and obligations flowing from the EC Treaty in a federal state not only bind the federal level but the federation as a whole, i.e. including the *Länder* or other entities such as local authorities.[26] It is the duty of every authority of a member state whether of federal or subnational level to guarantee compliance with EC law.[27] Any requirement that it is only the federal level which has to implement Directives can neither be deduced from Art. 5 (to be Art. 10) TEC according to which there is a general duty of Community loyalty incumbent upon the member states and even less from Art. 189(3) (to be Art. 249(3)) TEC which leaves implementation expressly to the 'national authorities' without any further specification.[28]

---

[22] ECJ e.g. Case 14/83 *Von Colson and Kamann* [1984] ECR 1891 at para. 15.

[23] The Treaty of Amsterdam underlined that the 'administrative implementation of Community law shall in principle be the responsibility of the Member States in accordance with their constitutional arrangements', (Declaration (43) relating to the Protocol on the application of the principle of subsidiarity and proportionality).

[24] *Cf* Grabitz, 'Die Rechtsetzungsbefugnis von Bund und Ländern bei der Durchführung von Gemeinschaftsrecht', 111 (1986) *Archiv des öffentlichen Rechts*, 1 at 9.

[25] ECJ Case 96/81 *Commission v The Netherlands* [1982] ECR 1791 at 1804.

[26] *Cf* ECJ Case C-8/88 *Germany v Commission* [1990] ECR I-2321 at 2359; Case 9/74 *Casagrande* [1974] ECR 733 at 779. To a considerable extent in Germany the local authorities are in charge of application of EU law such as of provisions of freedom of movement of migrant workers (e.g. Regulation 1612/68) and of federal legislation (e.g. the Act on residence of EU-nationals implementing Directive 68/360); the local authorities issue residence permits and decide on social benefits.

[27] ECJ Case C-8/88 *Germany v Commission* [1990] ECR I-2321 at 2359.

[28] The Treaty of Amsterdam has not changed the situation described although Germany, Austria and Belgium had adopted Declaration No. 3 on subsidiarity of which the Conference took note 'that action by the European Community in accordance with the principle of subsidiarity not only concerns the Member States but also their entities to the extent that they have their own law making powers conferred on them under national constitutional law'. Although it is the first time that the Treaty took note of federal structures in various member states implications for the implementation of EU legislation do not follow from this Declaration: first, the legal status of declarations in general is somewhat doubtful, in particular if adopted only by three member states – and not the Intergovernmental Conference as a whole. Secondly, this declaration concerns subsidiarity, i.e. how the powers of the EU are to be exercised (*cf* the

This EC law position, in particular as interpreted by the European Court, is in line with German legal doctrine according to which the *Länder* are under a constitutional duty to implement EC law if they have the power for a given subject according to the Basic Law. This follows from Art. 23 Basic Law which contains the commitment to Europe and, at the same time, a constitutional objective of the Federal Republic of Germany and which is directed at both the Federation and the *Länder*.[29] This follows also from the duty of the *Länder* to federal loyalty (*Bundestreue*). This unwritten legal principle derived directly and explicitly from the notion of federalism is meant to establish for the *Länder*, in their relations with each other and with the 'greater whole', as well as for the Federation in its relations with the *Länder*, a constitutional duty to be loyal and reach a common understanding. It requires that the Federation and the *Länder*, in the exercise of their respective duties, have to pay due regard to the whole interest of the Federation and the concerns of the *Länder*.[30] Therefore, federal loyalty does not simply mean 'loyalty to the federation'; but federal loyalty rather means for the federal authorities loyalty to the *Länder*.[31] This principle sets firm limits to the predominance of the whole state (*Gesamtstaat*) in the interest of its members and, at the same time, although it does not alter the distribution of powers, it could limit the exercise of those powers. This principle[32] is not only of utmost importance for European decision-making – as has been seen in the *Television Directive* judgment of the Federal Constitutional Court[33] – it is, however, of equal importance for questions of implementation.[34]

Directives have to implemented by the deadline as prescribed by the Directive. Late implementation could be due to low or even negative interest of political and economic actors, in particular if the policy area is perceived controversial and important, the complexity of the subject, the amount of

---

Amsterdam Protocol on Subsidiarity: 'The principle of subsidiarity provides a guide as to how those powers are to be exercised at the Community level') and thus does not concern the distribution of responsibilities between the EU and its member states.

[29] Rojahn, in: V. Münch/Kunig (eds), *Grundgesetzkommentar*, Vol. II, München, Beck, 1995, Art. 23 para. 3.

[30] BVerfGE 92, 203.

[31] This was clearly pronounced by the Federal Constitutional Court in its *Television Judgment* of 1961 (BVerfGE 12, 205).

[32] This principle reminds of Art. 5 (to be Art. 10) EC, according to which the member states 'shall facilitate the achievement of the Community's task'. Although, according to the wording of Art. 5 EC, it is only the member states which owe a duty to the EU and not the other way round the Court in several cases has held that the Commission owes a duty to member states to cooperate with them (*cf* e.g. Case C-56/90 *Commission v UK* [1993] ECR 1993 I-4109 at 4138, and see the Notice of the Commission on cooperation with national courts, *OJ*, C39/6 of 13 February 1993).

[33] BVerfGE 92, 203; *cf* Herdegen, above, note 18.

[34] In addition, the duty of implementation of EU legislation for the five East German *Länder* follows from Art. 10(3) of the Treaty of the Federal Republic of Germany and the German Democratic Republic of 31 August 1990 on German unification. In legal doctrine, it is an open question whether this provision applies also to the Western *Länder* (*cf* Streinz, 'Der Vollzug des Gemeinschaftsrechts durch deutsche Staatsorgane', in Isensee/Kirchof (eds), *Handbuch des Staatsrechts*, Vol. VII, Heidelberg, 1992, 817 at 839).

changes and adaptations considered necessary in the existing legal texts and in the administrative procedure.[35] Such reasons for late or insufficient implementation can be found in every member state regardless of its internal structure. They can, however, multiply or intensify in a federal system.

1 Duty of the federation to transpose

If the duty to implement lies with the Federation, problems due to the federal system can arise because of the necessary involvement of the *Bundesrat* composed of representatives of sixteen *Länder* governments in most cases. In the Federal Republic there are basically two ways of implementing a Directive: either by an Act of Parliament or by a statutory order (*Rechtsverordnung*). The latter is passed by the government executive and, like federal legislation, usually requires the consent of the *Bundesrat*. In only a few cases can a departmental minister issue a statutory order without the consent of the *Bundesrat*. Only rarely can the transposition of EU legislation be done by administrative instructions which do not require the involvement of the *Bundesrat*.

The way of involvement of the *Bundesrat* – whether it enjoys only the right of a (suspensive) veto which can be overridden by an equivalent majority in the *Bundestag* or whether it enjoys the right of an absolute veto (*cf* Arts 77 and 78 Basic Law) – depends on the subject in question and which occasionally is controversial between both Houses.[36] In case no agreement between *Bundesrat* and *Bundestag* is reached a conciliation committee (*Vermittlungsausschuss*)[37] may be convened (Art. 77(2) Basic Law). Whether or not a departmental minister is empowered to issue a statutory order depends on the relevant Act of Parliament authorizing the issue of statutory orders.[38]

In the exercise of their rights and duties the actors at federal level – the Federal Government, the *Bundesrat*, and, as the case may be, the *Bundestag* – have to

---

[35] E.g. Germany pleaded before the ECJ concerning its failure to transpose all the provisions of the Package Travel Directive (90/314/EEC) in time (Cases C-178, 179, 188 to 190/94 *Dillenkofer et al.* [1996] ECR I-4845) that the period prescribed for the transposition of the Directive was too short since, apart from legislative amendments, the government had to rely on the collaboration of third parties of the economic sector concerned. See for further examples Pag/Wessels in: Siedentopf/Ziller (eds), *Making European Policies Work*, London, Sage, 1988, Vol. II, 163 at 185.

[36] Although there have been various relevant cases before the FCC in practice the Federal Government and the *Bundestag* had generally not found it worth challenging the *Bundesrat*'s claim but had preferred where necessary to come to a political understanding. In any case there was no need for the Federal authorities to appeal to the FCC on the question provided that the Federal President was prepared to sign a law from which the *Bundesrat* has withheld its consent; a challenge would have to come from the *Länder*. The general question of the proper extent of the *Bundesrat*'s power of absolute veto remains a thorny political and legal question, in particular if the *Bundesrat* is dominated by those parties which are in opposition at federal level (*cf* Blair, *above*, note 16, 98 *et seq.*).

[37] It said that the German system served as a model to the Conciliation Committee under the codecision procedure of Art. 189B (to be Art. 251) EC.

[38] In addition, the Act itself has to comply with the constitutional requirements for delegated legislation according to Art. 80 Basic Law.

observe the (unwritten) constitutional principle of loyalty of constitutional institutions.[39] According to this principle, supreme state organs have to pay due respect to the other organs in the exercise of their respective responsibilities. In the interplay between the Federation and the *Länder* both have to observe that there is a duty to reach an understanding. Reasons put forward must not be arbitrary ones.[40]

In a unitary state there is only one government, which in the modern state is usually in control of Parliament. If there are diverging opinions on the kind and the details of implementation between departmental ministers the head of government can resolve conflicts in the last instance. Although in the German federal system, in case of conflict between Federal departmental ministers, the Federal Chancellor can exercise this role, he cannot, however, act in the same way towards the sixteen *Länder* governments. Otherwise he would interfere with exclusive responsibilities of the *Länder*. Therefore, political consideration towards the *Länder* might often be called for, in particular, if objections are raised by a *Land* whose government is of the same party-political complexion as the Federal Government.

A case in point concerned the implementation of the Construction Site Directive (92/57/EEC). The deadline for transposition could not be met since the government of one *Land* (Bavaria) had raised various objections against the Directive, in particular regarding the power of the EU[41] and compliance with the subsidiarity principle. The Federation was responsible for the transposition of this Directive through the adoption of a federal statutory order which required the consenting vote of the *Bundesrat*. Although Bavaria could have been outvoted in the Bundesrat since the *Bundesrat* can decide by simple majority, for political reasons the federal government did not want to introduce the respective Bill into the *Bundesrat* before it had secured Bavaria's consent.

2   Duty of the *Länder* to transpose

If the duty to transpose lies either exclusively with the *Länder* (e.g. as regards education, vocational training and the freedom of services of broadcasting) or is shared between the Federation and the *Länder*, it is not only one level but sixteen *Länder* governments and parliaments and, as the case may be, in addition federal institutions which have to act. A case in point is the trans-

---

[39] BVerfGE 90, 286, 337.

[40] BVerfGE 39, 96, 119; 41, 291, 310.

[41] In its *Maastricht* judgment the Federal Constitutional Court insisted upon the inapplicability of EU legislation which exceeds the powers flowing from the EC Treaty in domestic law. German authorities would have to disregard such legislation (BVerfGE 89, 155 = 1994 *CMLR* 1; *cf* Herdegen, Maastricht and the German Constitutional Court: Constitutional Restraints for an 'Ever Closer Union', 31 [1994] CMLRev 235–249). This means that legislative Acts of the EU can be challenged for lack of power to legislate (being *ultra vires*) in the same way as German Acts of Parliament. The FCC therefore can check if legal acts of the European institutions and organs remain within or exceed the limits of the sovereign rights transferred to the EU. An open conflict between the EU and Germany has not yet arisen but might, however, in a pending case before the Federal Constitutional Court (on banana quotas).

position of Directive (89/48/EEC) on a general system for the recognition of higher education diplomas.[42] While in the UK only one instrument[43] was necessary, in Germany a host of federal and *Länder* acts and statutory orders had to be adopted in order to implement the Directive.[44] The power to transpose was shared between the Federation and the *Länder* since regulation of the legal profession falls into the exclusive competence of the Federation while the responsibility for architects, engineers and teachers is with the *Länder*. And if only one *Land* fails to adopt the necessary transposition measures, the Directive has not been fully implemented.

Such failure was the case with Directive 79/409/EEC on the conservation of wild birds[45] and Directive 80/68/EEC on the protection of groundwater against pollution. The European Court had declared in 1990 and in 1991 respectively that Germany had failed to implement both directives of Justice.[46] According to German constitutional law the Federation and the *Länder* are jointly responsible for the transposition of these Directives. Although the Federation had done its share, not all *Länder* had taken the necessary measures to comply with the judgments of the Court. Following infringement procedures under Art. 171(2) (to be Art. 228(2)) TEC the Commission again brought the cases against Germany before the Court[47] and asked it to impose a penalty payment on Germany accordingly. The Commission, however, could withdraw both cases since in the meantime the two *Länder* or, as the case may be, one *Land*, had taken the necessary steps to implement the Directives.[48]

No problems arise in Germany because of lacking administrative capacity for implementation due to the size of the subnational entities in charge. Although this might be a future problem for Switzerland if it joins the EU or concludes the Sectorial Agreements currently under negotiation, since implementation of many measures will be the responsibility of the 26 cantons, some of which are not now in a position to implement federal legislation.[49] It is, however, no problem for Germany since even the smallest *Land*, Bremen, with a population of only around 660,000, has so far not experienced any serious legislative or administrative difficulties.

IV APPLICATION OF EC LAW BY THE *LÄNDER*

The application of EC legislation does not pose any problems which are due to the federal system. The application of legislation by the administration is

[42] *OJ*, L19 of 24 January 1989.
[43] Recognition of Professional Qualifications Regulation 1991.
[44] *Cf* the instruments listed on http://europe.eu.int/comm/sg/scadplus/leg/en/m19000.htm.
[45] Case 288/88 [1990] ECR I-2721.
[46] Case 131/88 [1991] ECR I-825.
[47] Cases C-121/97 and C-122/97.
[48] *Cf* 15th Annual Report of the Commission on the Monitoring of the Application of Community Law, COM(1998) 317 final, 114.
[49] *Cf* Schindler, 'Europäische Union: Gefahr oder Chancen für den Föderalismus' in Deutschland, Österreich und der Schweiz, 53 (1994) *Veröffentlichung der Vereinigung der Deutschen Staatsrechtslehrer* 70 at 76.

in most fields the responsibility of the *Länder*. Apart from *Land* legislation they also apply federal legislation. The Constitution provides that the *Länder* shall implement federal legislation either in their own right (*als eigene Angelegenheit*) according to Art. 83 Basic Law which is normally the case[50] or as agents of the Federation (*Bundesauftragsverwaltung*) according to Art. 85. Only a few fields[51] come under the administration of the Federation. And because the *Länder* are responsible for administering federal legislation they are of utmost importance in the German federal system.

Since EC law transposed by federal law becomes national law, the provisions of the Basic Law dealing with the implementation of federal legislation are directly applicable. In legal terms there is no difference to other federal law. In the case of EC law being directly applicable such as regulations or certain provisions of directives, the provisions of the Basic Law concerning the implementation of federal legislation are applicable by analogy. If the *Länder* execute federal law in their own right Art. 84(1) Basic Law stipulates that they shall provide for the establishment of the requisite authorities and the regulation of administrative procedures while, if they act as agents of the Federation, the *Länder* are only responsible for the establishment of authorities. In both cases the Federal Government may, with the consent of the *Bundesrat*, issue general administrative rules. If the *Länder* implement federal legislation in their own right the Federal Government can oversee it and has certain rights, in case of conflict with the *Bundesrat*, to ensure the proper administration of the law. If the *Länder* act as agents for the Federation the latter can issue directives that the *Länder* authorities have to comply with (Art. 85(1) Basic Law).

As far as jurisdiction is concerned it has to be noted that although only the top layer of courts[52] are federal, there are no problems of application of EC law due to the federal system either. Both, federal and *Länder* courts – as any other governmental authorities – are bound by Community law and are under an obligation to interpret national law in conformity with EC law when deciding an issue concerning a situation which lies within the scope of EC law.

Of course, all courts of law can hear proceedings dealing with whether or not actions of the government are compatible with EC law. Proceedings are directed against the authority which has issued an administrative act. If the responsibility for failure to implement is that of a *Land* or local authority it is therefore this authority which has to comply with the judgment of the court and, as the case may be, pay damages.

---

[50] According to the FCC there is a presumption in favour of the *Länder* (BVerfGE 11, 6 at 15).

[51] Articles 87 *et seq.* Basic Law: i.e. armed forces and federal defence administration, foreign service, federal financial administration, federal waterways and shipping, certain social insurance institutions.

[52] Federal Constitutional Court (Art. 93 Basic Law), Federal Court of Justice, Federal Administrative Court, Federal Finance Court, Federal Labour Court and Federal Social Court (Art. 95 Basic Law).

V PROBLEM SOLVING

Concerning European issues, there are, by and large, no major differences between neither the major political parties nor the Federation and the *Länder*. Although the *Länder* cannot necessarily be considered a monolithic bloc against the federal government. Some *Länder* could side with the federal government in case of disputes with party-political implications unless matters of powers, rights, or obligations of the two levels of government are at stake. There are political and judicial means for the settlement of disputes.

1 Co-operative federalism

EU policy has been introduced into the coordination structure of the *Länder* at national level. There is, first, cooperation between the *Länder*. The *Länder* have institutionalized their co-operation in permanent coordination bodies, even ministerial bodies such as the conferences of ministers of European affairs, of the interior, of justice, of labour and social affairs and of education, and even of the Minister-Presidents (heads of the *Länder* governments) to which representatives of the Federal Government are usually invited to attend. Secondly, this inter-*Länder* cooperation is complemented by cooperation between the Federation and the *Länder*. These coordination structures have helped to create a situation where governments and administrations of the Federation and the *Länder* have close contacts and channels for the settlement of disputes. There is a climate of consultation and compromise which might explain the general reluctance to seek a judicial solution for disputes in the federal system.

2 Constitutional provisions

Only in exceptional cases has a dispute between the two levels of government been taken to the Federal Constitutional Court. The *Television Directive* case, which related to the participation rights of the *Länder* in European law-making before the entry into force of Art. 23 Basic Law,[53] was a dispute between Bavaria and the Federal Government. It concerned the alleged obligations of the federal government towards the *Länder* in the decision-making process in cultural affairs, which is an exclusive competence of the *Länder*, leading to the Television Directive 89/552/EEC.[54] As far as implementation of European legislation is concerned so far no case has been taken to the Federal Constitutional Court. There are judicial and extra-judicial means for the enforcement of obligations of the *Länder* provided for by the Constitution.

---

[53] After the entry into force of the EuZBLG (above, note 11) the *Länder* could even force the federal government to bring an action before the ECJ to have the EU measure declared to be void (§ 7 EuZBLG).

[54] BVerfGE 92, 203; *cf* Herdegen, above, note 18.

(1) The jurisdiction of the Federal Constitutional Court according to Art. 93(1) Basic Law includes 'the extent of the rights and obligations of a supreme federal institution' which could be enforced if the *Länder* refuse their consent to federal implementation legislation and 'in case of disagreement on the rights and obligations of the Federation and the *Länder*, particularly in the implementation of federal legislation by the *Länder* . . .' which allows the Federation to go to law with the *Länder* if they refuse to apply federal law transposing EC legislation or directly applicable EC law. This procedure, however, is time-consuming and no early results can be expected. It should only be used if a question of principle is at stake.

(2) Without going to the FCC the federal government could make use of the 'Federal enforcement' (*Bundeszwang*) procedure according to Art. 37 Basic Law which means the exercise of federal authority over the *Länder*: 'Where a *Land* fails to comply with its federal obligations . . . the Federal Government may, with the consent of the Bundesrat, take the necessary steps to enforce compliance'. Such steps could include directives of the federal government directed at the *Länder* and their authorities.[55] This procedure, however, which is the most powerful weapon of the Federation against a *Land* has not yet been enforced since it can only be regarded as a last resort. Should the Federal Government introduce a respective motion in the *Bundesrat* it is extremely unlikely to be successful since the *Länder* – regardless of their party-political complexion – are likely to close ranks.

VI LIABILITY FOR VIOLATION OF COMMUNITY LAW

If a member state fails to carry out an obligation resulting from Community law it is the national government which represents it in infringement procedures under Arts 169–171 (to be Arts 226–228) EC. This is also true for federal member states. In case the Court imposed a penalty payment on the Federal Republic of Germany in accordance with Art. 171 TEC the question arises whether the Federation and/or the defaulting *Land* or *Länder* has to pay the penalty. So far, although the Court has not yet imposed a penalty payment on Germany, given the number of not or not properly implemented Directives, this question could become a real one.

In case the Federal Republic failed to transpose a Directive because the *Bundesrat* fails to give its necessary consent to the implementing measure of the Federation it is the liability of the Federation. The *Bundesrat* is a federal and not a *Länder* legislative organ.[56] Thus, its decision cannot be attributed to those *Länder* which refused their consent. The participation rights of the

---

[55] Before the federal government employs this procedure it has to use its powers under Arts 84(2) and 85(2) Basic Law (above, under note 4.).
[56] See above, note 11.

148

Bundesrat provided for by the Constitution do not create individual rights of the *Länder*.[57]

In case the subject-matter either falls under the exclusive power of the *Länder* or if the power is shared with the Federation, Art. 104(1) Basic Law stipulates that the Federation and the *Länder* shall separately finance expenditure resulting from the discharge of their respective responsibilities. This means that the duty to pay the penalty payment follows the responsibility in question. Thus, if any financial penalties were imposed on Germany, responsibility for meeting them has to be borne by the *Land* if it is responsible for the failure. The Federation can only make sure that the *Länder* pay the penalty and can urge the *Länder* to do so. If the *Länder* fail to pay the penalty and if the Federation pays in complying with its duty resulting from Arts 171(2) and (5) TEC it can request reimbursement from the *Länder*. In case the *Länder* fail to reimburse the Federation the Federation can take the *Länder* to court (administrative courts, §50(1) No. 1 Administrative Procedure Act).

VII CONCLUSION

Although 'federalism means legalism' (Dicey) it is clear that the federal system does not constitute a significant obstacle to the proper implementation of Community legislation in Germany. Although transposition of Community legislation by up to seventeen governmental actors is certainly more complicated, cumbersome and time-consuming than by only one central governmental actor it is without any significant effect on the implementation record of Germany compared with that of other member states. According to the findings of the Commission[58] as of 31 December 1997 Germany had notified the Commission of implementation measures for 93.6 per cent of all directives in force at that date. Thus, Germany's implementation record as of 31 December 1997 was only slightly worse than the Community-wide average rate of 94 per cent. It is well known that there are other more important reasons for bad performance in implementation than a federal structure.

In Germany there are several reasons for the negligible influence of the federal system on implementation. These include:

(1) Germany has been a founding member of the European Communities and its membership is supported by the overwhelming majority of the population. The positive attitude towards Europe of governmental authorities tallies with the attitude of the population. Hence, there is a serious endeavour to overcome problems in European affairs. The commitment to Europe enshrined in the Constitution is not a dead letter but has become reality.

[57] BVerfGE 94, 297, 311.
[58] 15th Annual Report of the Commission on the Monitoring of the Application of Community Law, COM(1998) 317 final, vii.

(2)   The major questions of the division of powers between the Federation and the *Länder*, of rights and duties of both levels of government have been resolved in the early years of the Federal Republic. During its almost 50 years of existence the Federal Constitutional Court has settled the major federal disputes whose judgments, due to the authority of the FCC, have been accepted by the various actors, although some quite grudgingly. In addition, through various judgments on European affairs it has cleared the air for accepting the supremacy of European law in Germany.

(3)   Intergovernmental relations took the form of cooperative federalism which achieves a balance between clear demarcation of responsibilities and a concentration of forces which guarantees the greatest efficiency in the commitment of public resources. Through the creation of institutions of cooperation and concertation and the readiness and willingness on both levels to work together in a federal spirit and in the interests of the public good, most disputes between the Federation and the *Länder* could be settled without reaching public attention.

10

USE OF SEPARATE CONVENTIONS BETWEEN MEMBER STATES IN THE CONTEXT OF THE EUROPEAN UNION ITSELF

Professor Dr Carlos Esplugues

I INTRODUCTION

My contribution to the Seminar commemorating the 30th anniversary of the University of Edinburgh's Europa Institute is necessarily restricted by its very title: 'Use of Separate Conventions Between Member States in the Context of the European Community Itself'. According to such title, we would be expected to devote the following pages to a thorough analysis, one by one, and exclusively, of the different Conventions signed by the member states of the European Communities since 1957. However, it would be convenient and necessary that, apart from carrying out that task, which will be nevertheless fulfilled in these pages, we undertake previously, albeit briefly, the study of the role played by these Conventions in the framework of the harmonization process of Private European Law. Moreover, that study will help us to understand an essential element in order to grasp the meaning and aim of all these Conventions: which role is allotted to Private International Law (Conflict of Laws) in a legally integrated environment like the European Communities.

II THE HARMONIZATION PROCESS OF PRIVATE INTERNATIONAL LAW IN EUROPE: THE ROLE ALLOTTED TO PRIVATE INTERNATIONAL LAW IN A LEGALLY INTEGRATED ENVIRONMENT

1 Private law harmonization in Europe

The process of European integration, as stated in Art. 2 of the Treaty of Rome, has had – and still has – as its main objective the creation of an integrated economic space in the European continent. The pursuit of that aim – economic integration – has brought about a process of legal unification that tries to suppress all those restrictions that may alter, or slow down, the development of transborder economic activity stemming from economic integration.[1] It must not be forgotten that, to a large extent, barriers to trade in the European Union directly result from disparities in national laws and regulations.[2]

Although this phenomenon has largely manifested itself in the realm of public law, private law[3] has also been clearly affected, albeit in a fairly smaller measure,[4] and not in a straightforward manner, but 'by induction'.

The Treaty of Rome, from its start, did not grant the EU a direct power to unify the private law of its member states. That task was carried out as an indispensable instrument to secure the building of a Common Market.[5] In so far as operations and transactions governed by rules of private law are to take place within the framework of a Single Common Market, it is essential to achieve the harmonization of those rules to help and fulfil the desired economic objectives.[6] In this vein, Art. 3(h) limits its scope to the inclusion within the activity of the EU of 'the approximation of national laws in such measure as necessary for the functioning of the Common Market'.

The mandate included in Art. 3(h) finds its complement with the statement that appears, among others, in Art. 94 (the former Art. 100) of the Treaty with regard to the adoption of Directives for the approximation of regulations and administrative rules of the member states 'having a direct influence in the establishment or functioning of the Common Market'.[7]

---

[1] See I. Maselis, 'Legislative Harmonisation and the Integration of Harmonised Legislation into the National Legal Systems, Within the European Community', *European Review of Private Law*, 1993, 138ff.

[2] See. I. Maselis, *art. cit.*, 138ff. For an in-depth analysis, see M. Fallon, 'Les conflits de lois et de juridictions dans un espace économique intégré', *R des C*, 1996, Vol. 261, 59ff.

[3] For the random differentiation between private and public law in intracommunity dealings, see G. Broggini, 'Conflitto di leggi, armonizzazione e unificazioni nel diritto europeo delle obbligazioni e delle imprese', in I. Meier and K. Siehr (Her.), *Rechtskollisionen. Festschrift für Anton Heini zum 65. Geburstag*, Zurich, Schulthess, 1995, 74–75.

[4] For extensive examples, it is convenient to consult the reports published periodically since 1985 by Professors E. Jayme and C.H. Kohler, in *IPRax*. Especially interesting, in this sense, is the one published in 1997, 'Europäisches Kollisionsrecht 1997 – Vergemeinschaftung durch "Säulenwechsel"', *IPRax*, 1997, 385ff, to which we shall later refer when dealing with the influence of the Treaty of Amsterdam in future EU developments in this field.

[5] See P.C.H. Müller-Graff, 'Europäisches Gemeinschaftsrecht und Privatrecht. Das Privatrecht in der europäischen integration', *NJW*, 1993, 13ff.

[6] This idea is self-evident from the early stages of the existence of the European Community, in that respect, see R. Savatier, 'Le Marché commun au regard du droit international privé', *Rev crit dr int priv*, 1960, 250ff. Also, see F. Rittner, 'Das Gemeinschaftsprivatrecht und die europäische Integration', *JZ*, 1995, 850; P.C.H. Müller-Graff, 'Privatrecht und europäisches Gemeinschaftsrecht', in P.C.H. Müller-Graff (Hrsg.), *Gemeinsames Privatrecht in der Europäischen Gemeinschaft*, Baden-Baden, Nomos, 1993, 204ff; P.A. De Miguel Asencio, 'Integración europea y Derecho internacional privado', *RDC*, 1997, 415ff.

[7] It has to be noted that, besides the concept of '*approximation* of national laws' used in Arts 3.h and 100, Arts 54.3.g, 56.2 and 57.2, refer to the '*co-ordination*' of national laws and Arts 99 and 117 use the term '*harmonisation*'.

It is, therefore, a function performed by way of induction. Thus, it is subordinated to its condition of being necessary 'for the functioning of the Common Market' which shows that such approximation is not an end in itself, but must be at the service of the other EU actions which are compulsory for the achievement of the Common Market.[8]

The Treaty of Rome never makes any reference to the unification of laws. It limits its scope to coordination, approximation or harmonization; these are processes of a lesser reach than that of the unification of law which by its own nature implies the adoption of common legal and procedural rules for all the member states.[9]

This situation was not greatly altered in its main design and objectives when the Treaty on the European Union was approved on 7 February 1992. The Treaty of Amsterdam of 2 October 1997, though, as we shall see further on, has affected much more directly the nature of the intervention of the EU in the field of private law, to the subjects involved and to the likely instruments that can be used to that end.

2   The harmonization mechanisms of European private law

The harmonization/approximation process with regard to national private laws is carried out through several EU instruments that were devised from the very beginning in the Treaty of Rome.[10] We are talking, basically, of Regulations and Directives. The harmonization/approximation may also be achieved, as foreseen in the former Art. 220 of the Treaty of Rome (now Art. 293 of the EC Treaty), via the conclusion of International Conventions among the EU's member states.[11]

An analysis of what has been so far the harmonization process regarding private law in the member states, shows clearly that it has been a fairly uneven process, both with regard to the instruments used and, especially, the topics covered by the said process.

---

[8] See. Art. 235 of the Treaty of Rome. In that respect, see N. Bouza Vidal, 'Modalidades de unificación y armonización de legislaciones en la Comunidad Económica Europea', in E. Garcia De Enterria, J.D. Gonzalez Campos y S. Muñoz Machado, *Tratado de Derecho Comunitario Europeo*, Madrid, Civitas, 1986, 3 vols, vol. I., 554.

[9] With relation to the meaning of these terms, see, N. Bouza Vidal, 'Significado y alcance de la aproximación de legislaciones en la Comunidad Económica Europea', *Revista de Instituciones Europeas*, 1981, 400–403; H. Patrick Glenn, 'Harmonisation of Law, Foreign Law and Private International Law', *European Review of Private Law*, 1993, 51ff; P.L. Slot, 'Harmonisation', *ELRev*, 1996, 378ff. It must be taken into account that out of the three, the first is the most limited in its function, for it does not imply any modification whatsoever of the contents of internal laws. Especially interesting when trying to find out more about the process is the article by N. Reich, 'Competition Between Legal Orders: A New Paradigm of EC Law?', *CML Rev.*, 1992, 861ff.

[10] See P. De Miguel Asensio, *art. cit.*, 417–418.

[11] See M. Desantes Real, 'España ante el proceso de elaboración de un Derecho internacional privado "intracomunitario"', in J.C. Fernandez Rozas (ed.), *España y la codificación del Derecho internacional privado*, Madrid, Eurolex, 1993, 209ff.

Regarding the instruments used, the growing recourse to the Directive as harmonization mechanism must be underlined. So far, the process has mainly relied upon the Directive,[12] perhaps as a consequence of the higher degree of uniformity that has been obtained through the use of Regulations and the inherent difficulties for the conclusion of International Conventions.

Certainly, the use of Directives has prompted difficulties and legal insecurity, directly stemming from the 'minimalist'[13] nature of the EU instrument. The Directive, not only excludes legal pluralism, it may also be subject to wrong or belated transpositions, as well as to different interpretations by the various legal operators in the member states.[14] All of these limitations have given rise to the graphic differentiation made by one author between what he calls 'droit privé national sous tutelle communautaire', which he equals with harmonized law through the use of Directives, and the 'Droit privé communautaire', that which has been generated through Regulations and Conventions ex Art. 220 of the Treaty of Rome.[15]

The criticisms that have been made against the use of this harmonization mechanism, must be contrasted, though, with a relevant fact, that allows us to diminish the weight of such criticisms: despite the two Resolutions of the European Parliament in favour of the unification of European private law,[16] it can be perceived in contemporary Europe, a very slight political and academic pressure to develop 'Codes', in the traditional nineteenth century meaning, and general legislation. The convenience of a unification has been approached by the European Doctrine with as much scepticism with respect to its effective viability – to begin with, the concept of 'private law' is unknown in some European countries – as prejudice, considering it a measure deeply impoverishing for the European legal and cultural reality.[17] Summing up, as

---

[12] In this respect, see F. Rigaux, 'Droit international privé et droit communautaire', *L'internationalisation du droit. Mélanges en l'honneur de Yvon Loussouarn*, Paris, Dalloz, 1994, 344ff.

[13] In the graphic expression of N. Reich (N. Reich, 'EG-Richtlinien und internationales Privatrecht', in P. Lagarde and B. Von Hoffmann (eds), *The Europeanisation of International Private Law*, Cologne, Bundesanzeiger, 1996, 110–111).

[14] Among many others, see P.A. De Miguel Asensio, *art. cit.*, 418; S. Alvarez Gonzalez, 'Pasado, presente y futuro del Derecho internacional privado comunitario', *Dereito*, 1996, 26; S. Grundmann, 'EG-Richtlinie und nationales Privatrecht', *JZ*, 1996, 277ff; N. Reich, *art. cit.*, 113ff; K. Kreuzer, 'Lex communis europea de collisione legum: utopie ou necessité', in J.C. Fernandez Rozas (ed.), *España y la codificación . . . , op. cit.*, 231ff.

[15] A.V.M. Struycken, 'Les Conséquences de l'intégration européenne sur le développement du Droit international privé', *R des C*, 1992-I, 287ff.

[16] Dated 26 May 1989 (*OJ*, C158, 26 June 1989, 400) and May 1994 (*OJ*, C205, 25 July 1994), respectively. The first one called 'upon the efforts to harmonise the Private Law of the Member States', requested the beginning of preliminary work to elaborate a '*Common European Code of Private Law*', and the creation of an Expert Committee in charge of determining the unification priorities. In that respect, see W. Tilmann, 'Zweiter Kodificationsbeschluss des Europäisches Parlaments', *Zeitschrift für Europäisches Privatrecht*, 1995, 534; E.A. Kramer, 'Europäische Privatrechtsvereinheitlichung (Institutionen, Methoden, Perspectiven)', *J.Bl.*, 1988, 485ff.

[17] In fact, but for a few exceptions, it can be said that there is a clear opposition of the contemporary European Doctrine to the elaboration of uniform general rules of private law, common to the whole of Europe. Suffice it to quote, R. Zimmermann, 'Savigny's Legacy Legal History, Comparative Law, and the Emergence of a European Legal Science', *LQR*,

C. Prins points in a sarcastic tone, '(U)nlike the harmonisation of procedures to the production of mincemeat and dogfood, the harmonisation of private law on a European level seems to promise little glory'.[18]

With regard to the topics covered, far from taking on a global harmonization of private law, during these years, a piecemeal approach has taken place; it has been mainly those sectors with an 'economic' importance that have been dealt with. Specifically, Regulations have been used in topics related to company law and intellectual property.[19] Directives, though, have been used for a much wider range of topics: thus, for instance, insurance, consumers' rights, advertising, employment or transport contracts, etc.[20] Anyway, the treatment 'by induction' of private law by the EU has meant that large areas of this – family law,[21] inheritance law – have been left out of the harmonization process this far.

III   THE ROLE OF PRIVATE INTERNATIONAL LAW IN AN 'INTEGRATED' ENVIRONMENT LIKE EUROPE'S

The dynamics followed so far by the harmonization process of private law lead us to consider the question of the role that can be played by private international law in a 'harmonized,' environment such as the European one. The data that have been used until now, offer us several essential keys to tackle this topic.

The doctrine does not hesitate to state that the current situation shows that 'we are dealing with no more than fragments of – more or less – uniform law, inserted rather unorganically and in a somewhat higgledy-piggledy fashion into the respective national systems'.[22] This has brought about, ultimately, a 'fragmentary uniformity'[23] which leads to an unsatisfactory state of affairs. In other

---

1996, 581–582; W. Tilmann, 'Eine Privatrechts kodifikation für die Europäische Gemeinschaft', in P.C. Müller-Graff (Hrsg.), *Gemeinsames . . .* , *op. cit.*, 485ff; P. Legrand, 'Against a European Civil Code', *MLR*, 1997, 44ff. From a more sociological perspective of the viability of such unification, see J.L. Gibson, 'The Legal Cultures of Europe', *Law and Society Review*, 1996, 55ff. As an isolated example of support for this idea, see C. Prins, 'Towards a European Civil Code: Some Thoughts on Law and Paperless Communication in a New Millennium', *The EDI Law Review*, 1995, 60ff. Also, as a favourable example for this position with regard to Procedural Law 'Public Law, after all', see E. Fazzalari, 'Per un processo comune europeo', *Riv trim dir proc civ*, 1994, 667ff.

[18] C. Prins, *art. cit.*, 60.
[19] Council Regulation (EC) No. 40/94, dated 20 December 1993, on the Community Trade Mark (*OJ*, L11, 14 January 1994), arts 93 and 94; Council Regulation (EC) No. 2100/94, dated 27 July 1994, regarding community protection of vegetable products (*OJ*, L227, 1 September 1994), Arts 101 to 106.
[20] A list thereof can be found in B. Von Hoffmann, 'Richtlinien der Europäisches Gemeinschaft und Internationales Privatrecht', *ZfRV*, 1995, 46ff.
[21] Although the integrationist dynamic itself is already making its mark. To this respect, see A. Saggio, 'Diritto Internazionale Privato e Diritto Uniforme nel Sistema Comunitario', *Riv Dir Eur*, 1996, 217ff; S. Alvarez Gonzalez, *art. cit.*, 40–44.
[22] R. Zimmermann, *art. cit.*, 581–582.
[23] 'Harmonisation of specific areas only has proved insufficient because it results in a jungle of European regulations which are implemented in an arbitrary fashion by systems of law which are still locally (nationally) oriented', C. Prins, *art. cit.*, 58.

words, the extremely reduced scope of unification, and the piecemeal and limited character of the harmonization developed within the current EU has made it possible to envisage the existence of a wide 'playground' for private international law to take part in this process. In fact, it could be said that we are driven inevitably towards it,[24] even to the point that some of the Directives passed so far have assumed this fact, and have borrowed rules of private international law, understanding that they are ancillary to the specific material topic dealt with.[25] That is, considering that the EU's competence to regulate a given sector also comprises that of adopting rules of private international law for that subject.[26]

An analysis of the current situation, reveals, though, the very limited number of private international law rules adopted by the EU until now.[27]

Having gone this far, the following question to tackle is that of the verification of how much the situation is going to change. All evidence makes us think that things are to change sensibly. The consolidation of the Single Market has made several authors openly state that 'it is likely that the last decade of the twentieth century will be, for the Private International Law of the European countries, that of European Community Law'.[28]

This bold statement must be qualified, though, taking into account the influence that several EU principles – like subsidiarity – may have on its practical effectiveness.[29] The principle of subsidiarity implies the recognition that 'expectations and desires may be different in different localities, and by taking decisions as near as possible to those involved, the decisions are most likely to comply with those needs'.[30] Article 3.b.II of the Treaty of Rome, in its latest version, after the Treaty on the European Union describes clearly the meaning of this principle:

---

[24] N. Reich, 'EG-Richtlinien . . . , art. cit., 113–114. N.H. Roth, 'The Einfluss des Europäischen Gemeinschaftsrecht auf das Internationale Privatrecht', RabelsZ, 1991, 622ff; H. Koch, 'Private International Law: A Soft Alternative to the Harmonisation of Private Law?', ERPI, 1995, 329ff.

[25] Directive 84/450/EEC on Misleading Advertising (OJ, L250, 19 September 1984) and Directive 96/71/EC concerning the posting of workers in the framework of the provision of services (OJ, L18, 21 January 1994), are good examples of it.

[26] E. Jayme and C.H. Kohler, 'L'interaction des règles de conflit contenues dans le droit dérivé de la Communauté européenne et des conventions de Bruxelles et de Rome', Rev crit dr int priv, 1995, 4.

[27] See the already mentioned chronicles by Profs. E. Jayme and C.H. Kohler, in IPRax (cit. note 4) and the collective work, C.H.Von Bar (Her.), Europäisches Gemeinschaftsrecht und Internationales Privatrecht, Colonia, Carl Heymanns, 1990.

[28] M. Fallon, 'Variations sur le principe d'origine, entre droit communautaire et droit international privée', Nouvelles itinéraires en droit. Hommage à François Rigaux, Brussels, 1993, 187.

[29] S. Alvarez Gonzalez, quoting J. Taupitz, mentions the change of perspective in the process of unification/harmonization within the EU. This change is based on three pillars: unification of bases or foundations, mutual recognition of equivalent national legislation and the principle of subsidiarity as a limit to community activity (S. Alvarez Gonzalez, art. cit., 20; J. Taupitz, 'Privatrechts vereinheitlichung durch die EG: Sachrecht- oder Kollisionsrechts vereinheitlichung?', JZ, 1993, 533ff).

[30] T.C. Hartley, 'Unnecessary Europeanisation under the Brussels Jurisdiction and Judgments Convention: the Case of the Dissatisfied Sub-Purchaser', ELRev, 1993, 509. Also see M. Rohe, 'Binnenmarkt oder Interessenverband? Zum Verhältniss von Binnenmarktziel und Subsidiaritätsprinzip nach dem Maastricht-Vertrag', RabelsZ, 1997, 58–62.

In areas which do not fall within its exclusive competence, the Community shall take action, in accordance with the principle of subsidiarity, only if and in so far as the objectives of the proposed action cannot be sufficiently achieved by the Member States and can therefore, by reason of the scale or effects of the proposed action, be better achieved by the Community'.[31]

As has been brilliantly exposed by S. Alvarez Gonzalez, the principle of subsidiarity has already had a direct influence on the harmonization process of both private law and European private international law, leading to the 're-nationalization' of several subjects, thus reducing accordingly the amount of EU-produced legislation. Equally, some voices can be heard against the 'unnecessary Europeanization' of several institutions in the judiciary sector.[32]

All that is bound to affect the role that private international law is called upon to play in the new Europe, 'revitalising its interest, even in those areas subject to unification and harmonisation'.[33] In those cases where legal unification/harmonization is not feasible, 'the unification of the rules of conflict may result in private international situations being judged in the same manner regardless of the forum (member state) where they are judged'.[34] A unification that, besides, should develop through Regulations and not through International Conventions[35] or limited Directives as has been the custom until now.[36]

Moreover, this process should take into account other principles, which – unlike subsidiarity – are not related to the **by whom** or **when** the harmonization process must be carried out, but to the **how** it must be fulfilled:[37] principles such as proportionality, mentioned in Art. 3.B *in fine*[38] of the Treaty of Rome, which plays in favour of the establishment of a minimal intervention of the EU and which in this respect would imply that harmonization would prevail upon unification, and that the harmonization of the rules of private international law would also prevail upon substantive legal harmonization.[39] Or the principle of mutual recognition that promotes deregulation[40]

---

[31] Also to be taken into account are both the Declaration of the European Council meeting in Birmingham, on 16 October 1992 and the document adopted by the European Council in Edinburgh, 11–12 December 1992 called 'General approach to the application by the Council of the principle of subsidiarity and of Art. 3.B of the EUT' (both quoted in J. Diez-Hochleitner and C. Martinez Capdevila, *Derecho Comunitario Europeo*, Madrid, McGraw-Hill, 1996, 30ff).

[32] T.C. Hartley, *art. cit.*, 509–510. Also to be considered E. Jayme, 'Identité culturelle et intégration: le droit international privé postmoderne. Cours général de droit international privé', *R des C*, 1995, vol. 251, 168ff and 195ff.

[33] S. Alvarez Gonzalez, *art. cit.*, 18ff.

[34] S. Alvarez Gonzalez, *art. cit.*, 22.

[35] See Mª. Victoria Cuartero Rubio, 'Técnicas de unificación del Derecho internacional privado en la CEE', in J.C. Fernandez Rozas (ed.), *España y la codificación...*, *op. cit.*, 251ff.

[36] K. Kreuzer, *art. cit.*, 231ff and S. Alvarez Gonzalez, *art. cit.*, 31ff.

[37] In a generic manner, see J.A. Usher, 'Principles Derived From Private Law and the European Court of Justice', *European Review of Private Law*, 1996, 109ff.

[38] *'Any action by the Community shall not go beyond what is necessary to achieve the objectives of this Treaty.'*

[39] For an in-depth analysis, see M. Fallon, 'Les conflits...', *art. cit.*, 134ff.

[40] M. Guzman Zapater, 'El principio de reconocimiento mutuo: ¿Un nuevo modelo para el Derecho internacional privado comunitario?', *Revista de Derecho Comunitario Europeo*, 1998, 139–144.

in this area, the principle of non-discrimination by reason of nationality[41] or that of the country of origin.[42] All of them, among others, will influence necessarily the procedure of marking the exact boundaries of the harmonization process.

IV SEPARATE CONVENTIONS CONCLUDED AMONG MEMBER STATES IN THE CONTEXT OF THE EUROPEAN UNION ITSELF

Having arrived at this crossroads, it is now necessary to start the analysis of the Conventions concluded among themselves by the member states of the EU. Thus, in the first place, and following the method used when examining the unification mechanisms of private law in Europe, we are bound to begin pointing out those Conventions that have been concluded under the guidelines of Art. 220 of the Treaty of Rome, an article which states the possibility for member states to conclude international treaties in different matters:[43]

> Members States shall, so far as is necessary, enter into negotiations with each other with a view to securing for the benefit of their nationals; . . . The simplification of formalities governing the reciprocal recognition and enforcement of judgements of courts or tribunals and of arbitral awards.

Based on this rule, in the last 30 years, four Conventions have been elaborated, about different subjects and with unequal significance.[44] In particular, we can speak of:

(1) The Convention of Brussels of 27 September 1968 on Jurisdiction and the Execution of Judicial Resolutions in Civil and Commercial Matters.[45][46]

---

[41] See S. Sanchez Lorenzo, 'La incidencia del principio comunitario de no discriminación por razón de nacionalidad en los sistemas conflictuales de los Estados miembros', *RCEA*, 1996, 61ff; M. Fallon, 'Les conflits . . .', *art. cit.*, 116ff.

[42] See F. Rigaux, *art. cit.*, 345. Also, N. Bernard, 'Discrimination and Free Movement in EC Law', *ICLQ*, 1996, 83ff.

[43] Naming but a few, see G. Isaac, *Manual de Derecho Comunitario General*, Barcelona, Ariel, 1995, 3ª ed., 166–167; A. Borras Rodriguez, 'Los Convenios complementarios entre los Estados miembros de la CEE', *Noticias CEE*, 1986, 115ff.

[44] In this respect, see for example, J.L. Iglesias Buhigues, 'La cooperación judicial en materia civil (CJC) antes y después del Tratado de Amsterdam', *RGD*, 1998, 5853ff.

[45] In effect since 1 October 1997 in the version given by the Convention of San Sebastián of 16 September 1989 for all the member states, with the exception of Austria, Finland and Sweden, whose Convention of Adhesion is in the process of ratification, having obtained that of the Netherlands on 4 July 1997.

[46] Note equally the existence of the Convention of Lugano dated 16 September 1988, celebrated between the countries of the Union and those of the European Free Trade Association (EFTA) and with respect to which all the signing states have accepted the petition for the adhesion of Poland. At the present moment requests for adhesion on the part of Hungary and the Czech Republic have also been formulated.

(2) The Convention of Rome of 19 June 1980, on the Law Applicable to Contractual Obligations, not foreseen in Art. 220, but which has been considered complementary to the Convention of Brussels of 1968.[47]

(3) The Convention on Insolvency Proceedings, concluded in Brussels on 25 November 1995, and for which the process of ratification has not yet begun, as it has not been signed by the United Kingdom so far. It is a Convention based in Art. 220, and complementary to that of Brussels, as it expressly excludes this matter in its Art. 1.

(4) The Convention of Brussels of 29 February 1968 on the Mutual Recognition of Corporations and Legal Entities which has never entered into force, having been abandoned definitively.[48]

These are, as it is well known, Conventions between member countries of the EU, not EU law in a strict sense, which implies, regardless of its value and significance, that Protocols of interpretation by the Court of Justice of Luxembourg should be incorporated in them.[49]

Nevertheless, not only have Conventions on international private law been concluded between the countries of the current EU based strictly on Art. 220 of the Treaty of Rome. In its day, Art. 30 of the Single European Act introduced the notions of Cooperation in Foreign Policy Matters and European Political Cooperation, direct forerunners of what are known in the European Union Treaty as the so-called Second and Third pillars. Under the influence of this European Political Cooperation, two Conventions were concluded among members states, Conventions which up to now have lacked any relevance at all. These are:[50]

(1) The Convention of Brussels of 25 May 1987, on the Suppression of the Legalization of Documents in the Member States of the European Communities[51] and,

(2) The Convention of Rome of 6 November 1990, on the Simplification of Proceedings Related to the Payment of the Debt of Alimony.[52]

As we said, these are two Conventions which for years have had very little success, although in the last year the number of ratifications seems to have revived slightly.

---

[47] Currently in effect, in the version given by the Convention of Funchal of 18 May 1992, between Germany, France, Italy, Luxembourg, the Netherlands, Portugal, Spain and the United Kingdom.

[48] For other works carried out under this precept, see M. Desantes Real, *art. cit.*, 209.

[49] See, L.G. Radicati Di Brozolo, 'Libre circulation dans la CE et règles de conflit', en P. Lagarde and B. Von Hoffmann, *The Europeanisation . . .* , *op. cit.*, 87.

[50] More extensively dealt with in A. Mangas Martin and D.J. Liñan Noguerass, *Instituciones y Derecho de la Unión Europea*, Madrid, McGraw-Hill, 1996, 706.

[51] So far ratified only by Belgium, Denmark, France and Italy.

[52] Ratified by Ireland, Italy, Spain and the United Kingdom.

The Maastricht Treaty on European Union of 7 February 1992, meant the consolidation in Art. K.1.6[53] of the idea of Judicial Cooperation in Civil Matters (JCCM), as one of the spheres of common interest in order to 'achieving the objectives of the Union'. The Treaty of Maastricht mentioned as such a designated Third Pillar concerning 'cooperation in the fields of justice and home affairs' contained in its Title VI.[54] In this sense, Art. K.3 in its Section 2, developing the mandate included in the already mentioned Art. K.1.6., indicated that,

> The Council may,
> — on the initiative of any Member State or of the Commission, in the areas referred to in Article K.(1) to (6) . . .
> (a) adopt joint positions and promote, using the appropriate form and procedures, any co-operation contributing to the pursuit of the objectives of the Union;
> (b) adopt joint action in so far as the objectives of the Union can be attained better by joint action than by the Member States acting individually on account of the scale or effects of the action envisaged; it may decide that measures implementing joint action are to be adopted by a qualified majority;
> (c) without prejudice to Article 220 of the Treaty establishing the European Community, draw up conventions which it shall recommend to the Member States for adoption in accordance with their respective constitutional requirements . . .[55]

This reference to the former Art. 220 of the Treaty of Rome directly raised the issue of the specification of the existing relationship between that article and Art. K.3 of the Treaty of the Union.[56] That is, between an article which designs a framework for cooperation exclusively intergovernmental and which solely contemplates matters connected to the Treaty of Rome and another, Art. K.3.2.C of the Treaty of the Union, which is inserted into a unique institutional context and enjoys, in addition, a higher degree of integration in institutional terms.[57]

The question is not so relevant in practice,[58] but projects itself to the actual activities of the Union in the field of private international law. Therefore,

[53] Art. K.1, 'For the purposes of achieving the objectives of the Union, in particular the free movement of persons, and without prejudice to the powers of the European Community, Member States shall regard the following areas as matters of common interest: . . . 6. judicial cooperation in civil matters.'

[54] For example, see, H. Labayle, 'La coopération européenne en matière de justice et d'affaires intérierures et la Conférence intergouvernemenmtale', *RTDeur*, 1997, 15ff; A. Mangas Martin and D.J. Liñan Nogueras, *op. cit.*, 700ff.

[55] 'Unless otherwise provided by such conventions, measures implementing them shall be adopted within the Council by a majority of two thirds of the High Contracting Parties.'

[56] In this respect, see J.L. Iglesias Buhigues, *art. cit.*, 5855. Also, A. Borras Rodriguez, 'Informe explicativo del Convenio celebrado con arreglo artículo K.3 del Tratado de la Unión Europea, sobre la competencia, el reconocimiento y la ejecución de resoluciones judiciales en materia matrimonial', (*OJ*, C221, 16 July 1998, 28 and 32).

[57] See J.L. Iglesias Buhigues, *art. cit.*, 5856; P. Beaumont and G. Moir, 'Brussels Convention II: A New Private International Law Instrument in Family Matters for the European Union or the European Community?', *CMLRev.*, 1996, 275–278.

[58] As Professor A. Borras Rodriguez points out, 'the legal base (has) consequences in relation to the process of elaboration, but not for the legal operators nor for the citizens in the enforcement of the determined Convention'(A. Borras Rodriguez, 'Informe explicativo', *cit.*, 32).

if the already mentioned Convention of Brussels of 1995 on Insolvency Proceedings, although with some doubt, is considered to be articulated on the basis of Art. 220 of the Treaty, it is clear that there exist three other Conventions, which have not come into effect yet, whose natural basis is Art. K.3 of the Treaty of Maastricht. These are:

(1) Two Conventions already concluded, the new European Convention on the Service of Documents in Civil and Commercial Matters, made in Brussels on 26 May 1997 and the Convention on Jurisdiction, Recognition and Execution of Judgements on Marital Matters of 28 May 1998 (the so-called Brussels II).[59]

(2) In the context of the revision of the Convention of Brussels of 1968, the Commission has presented to the Council a new project of the Convention of Brussels which, in the first stage, was open to suggestions until 30 April 1998.[60]

Seemingly these three will not remain as isolated texts in the near future. Recently the Commission Communication to the Council and the European Parliament 'Towards Greater Efficiency in Obtaining and Enforcing Judgements in the European Union'[61] besides proposing the reform of the Brussels Convention 'has the added purpose of generating debate and prompting reactions and suggestions from all circles interested in possible Union action to secure equivalent access of litigants to efficient, swift and inexpensive justice'.[62]

In this sense, the Communication points out a series of questions which should be the subject of study by the Commission in the future, with the goal of securing the mentioned 'access to justice'. In particular, the Commission presents what it describes as '(a)venues to be explored for an improvement in the administration of justice in the European Union', assuming that '(t)he complexity of the problems that arise, and the deep-rooted situation of procedural law in national traditions, suggest that the measures should be taken on a progressive, prudent and proportionate basis . . . The Commission wishes attention to focus on those points of divergence whose maintenance it considers to be prejudicial to the harmonious administration of justice in the Union'.[63] It specifically indicates in this manner the establishment of swift proceedings for the payment of sums of money,[64] enforcement

[59] In this respect, see P. Beaumont and G. Moir, *art. cit.*, 268ff; S. Alvarez Gonzalez, *art.cit.*, 43ff.
[60] See, 'Commission Communication to the Council and the European Parliament "Towards Greater Efficiency in Obtaining and Enforcing Judgments in the European Union"' (*OJ*, C33, 31 January 1998, 3ff).
[61] *Op. cit.* note 60.
[62] 'There are no operational proposals in this second part, which is directed solely to gathering reactions and suggestions from all interested circles on the avenues offered for exploration' (*cit.*, 4–5).
[63] Point 32, 12.
[64] II.1. Procedure for obtaining a writ of execution in the State of origin.

of judgments,[65] transparency regarding assets,[66] and exchange of information between authorities[67] in charge of enforcing the previous measures. It is necessary to insist that in these points, and just as the Communication indicates, it is a mere attempt to assess the existing atmosphere with respect to the subject, which may, or may not, finish in the conclusion of new Conventions.

V THE SITUATION AFTER THE TREATY OF AMSTERDAM 1997

The proposal for reflection made public by the Commission at the beginning of 1998 should be approached in the light of the innovations introduced by the Treaty of Amsterdam of 2 October 1997 into the Treaty of Rome, namely a new Title IV devoted to 'Visas, asylum, immigration and other policies related to free movement of persons'. This new Title will have a direct effect on the unification/harmonization of private law and private international law in Europe, in so far as this matter becomes a non-exclusive EU competence – including not only recognition and enforcement of foreign decisions but, for the first time, '*conflicts of law and jurisdictions*', instead of being a matter of pure cooperation among the member states, as it used to be in the situation previous to Amsterdam. For instance, this will have a direct incidence not only on the relevance of the Subsidiarity Principle on this matter as far as this sector becomes 'Europeanized'[68] – until now we were talking of a political principle of cooperation among the governments of the member states that now becomes a legal principle and clearly influences the whole practice of Title IV – but also, and that is specially important, on the way to reach this aim.

Article 61, included in Title IV, specifies that:

> In order to establish progressively an area of freedom, security and justice, the Council shall adopt: . . . c. measures in the field of judicial co-operation in civil matters as provided for in Article 65; . . .

This article – 65 – indicates how:

> Measures in the field of judicial co-operation in civil matters having cross-border implications, to be taken in accordance with Article 67 and insofar as necessary for the proper functioning of the internal market, shall include:

---

[65] II.2.

[66] II.3.

[67] II.4.

[68] Using the words of T.C. Hartley, *art. cit.*, 506. In this respect, notice must be taken of Protocol (No. 30) on the Applicability of the Principles of Subsidiarity and Proportionality (1997) and the Declaration No. 43 on the Protocol on the Applicability of the Principles of Subsidiarity and Proportionality (both in A. Sanchez Legido, *Unión Europea. Textos Normativos Básicos*, Valencia, Tirant lo Blanch, 1998, 401 and 442).

a. improving and simplifying:

-the system for cross-border service of judicial and extrajudicial documents;

-co-operation in the taking of evidence;

-the recognition and enforcement of decisions in civil and commercial cases, including decisions in extrajudicial cases;

b. promoting the compatibility of the rules applicable in the Member States concerning the conflict of laws and jurisdiction;

c. eliminating obstacles to the good functioning of civil proceedings, if necessary by promoting the compatibility of the rules of civil procedure in the Member States.

The coming into force of the Treaty of Amsterdam means that the earlier discussion around the relationship between Art. 220 of the Treaty of Rome,[69] and the k.3.2.C) of the Treaty of the Union in its original version of 1992, will be completely transformed, presenting itself in radically distinct terms.[70]

In the 'new' Treaty of the EU as drafted after Amsterdam, Art. 220 – the new Art. 293 – persists,[71] but it does so together with the already mentioned 65, whose reach is extraordinarily wider than the former. We must realize that the new Title IV, through Art. 65, covers completely what had been 'Judicial Co-operation in Civil Matters' (JCCM), and that also it does so permitting the adoption of Regulations and Directives, while the new Art. 293 – as previously happened with Art. 220 – is reduced to the conclusion of Conventions, whose nature, as must be remembered, is not strictly-speaking, EU Law. That means that Art. 293 is not going to have – most likely – any practical presence in the future. Through this precept there will be coverage for those matters which – technically – are outside the scope of the new Art. 65 or which either has no incidence in the internal market or lacks crossborder repercussions. And this is neither wide in scope, nor easy to be found in practice. . . .[72] [73]

All this would lead us to think of a future designed mainly around Art. 65 and not Art. 293 of the Treaty of Rome **post Amsterdam**, at least from the

---

[69] Which after the Treaty of Amsterdam has become Art. 293.

[70] Note that the new Art. 34 of the Treaty of the Union, which substitutes the former Art. K.3 is now included within the new Title VI, *'Provisions on police and judicial cooperation in criminal matters'*, which continues in the intergovernmental field. See P.A. De Miguel Asensio, 'El Tratado de Amsterdam y el Derecho internacional privado', *La Ley Union Europea*, No. 4510, 30 March, 1998, 1.

[71] As also persist, with practically the same wording as they originally had, several articles of such importance for the harmonization process of private law (and, indirectly, of private international law) as Arts 100 and 100A (Arts 94 and 95 in the 'new' Treaty).

[72] J.L. Iglesias Buhigues, *art. cit.*, 5859. As Professor Iglesias says, 'it would be a different question, for example, the possibility of drafting a convention on arbitration, a matter specifically stated in the new article 293 and not foreseen in the new article 65, (Ibid., 5859).

[73] It is a different question altogether the role played by the old Art. 100, and the current Art. 95 (included within Chapter 3, *Approximation of Laws*, of Title VI, *Common Rules on Competition, Taxation and Approximation of Laws*). Note that this is an option which depends directly on the adoption of a decision by the Council, just as is specified by Art. 67.2 of the Treaty following its reorganization after Amsterdam. An option which, definitely, 'n'a, jusqu'ici, jamais servi comme base juridique d'un acte communautaire comportant des règles de conflit' (E. Jayme and C.H. Kohler, 'L'interaction . . .', *art. cit.*, 4).

point of view of private international law.[74] In fact, rules such as that included in Art. 6 of the Directive 96/71, of 16 December 1996, on the movement of workers undertaken in the context of the rendering of services,[75] which directly modifies Art. 5.1 of the Convention of Brussels,[76] point the road to follow. A road, on the other hand, already explicitly pronounced by the Commission in its 'Communication to the Council . . .'[77] in which, after indicating that the proposals pointed out 'are based on the current judicial system'[78] recalls that 'it should be noted that the Amsterdam Treaty will allow the Convention instrument to be replaced by community instruments with the institutional effects this entails, without requiring a ratification process on the part of the Member States and potential candidates for enlargement'.[79] In particular, with respect to the Convention of Brussels the 'Communication' points out how '(t)he Commission reserves its position to take new, complementary initiatives on the subject reflected upon, or to present, at the appropriate time, a proposal within the framework of the new Treaty, consistent with transforming the Convention into a Community instrument'.[80]

This image, extremely positive and full of potential, generated by the Treaty of Amsterdam must be clarified though, taking into account several arguments arising from a detailed reading of Art. 65 of the Treaty of Rome **post Amsterdam**.

(1) First, it is necessary to consider that the new Art. 65 and Arts 94 and 95 – the successors of Arts 100 and 100 A – (all of them included in Title VI of the Treaty of Rome post Amsterdam) are conditioned to the 'proper functioning of the internal market'. However, as has been pointed out by P.A. De Miguel Asensio, para. 2 of the new Art. 95 excludes from its scope of application 'rules regarding free movement of people', which are directly included in the new Title IV.[81] The restrictive heading of this Title IV – '*Visas, asylum, immigration and other policies related to free movement of persons*' – could support the idea that the scope of Art. 65 is restricted to the fundamental rights or family law,[82] which would cut down considerably the expectations

---

[74] It is important to remember that Arts 100 and 100A survive in the Treaty of Rome **post Amsterdam** (Arts 94 and 95), and that these norms 'have been the legal base to adopt directives for the harmonisation of the Member States' Private Law' (P.A. De Miguel Asensio, 'El Tratado de Amsterdam . . .', *art. cit.*, 2).

[75] *OJ*, L18, 21 January 1997.

[76] See G. Palao Moreno, 'Directiva 96/71/Ce del parlamento Europeo y del Consejo de 16 de diciembre de 1996 sobre el desplazamiento de trabajadores efectuado en el marco de una prestación de servicios', *REDI*, 1997, 377ff.

[77] *Cit.* note 60.

[78] Numeral 13.

[79] Numeral 13.

[80] Numeral 13.

[81] To which belongs the new Art. 65.

[82] P.A. De Miguel Asensio, 'El Tratado de Amsterdam . . .', *art. cit.*, 2, who, besides, points to the limitations that have been added when interpreted by the Court of Justice of the European Communities.

arising from these new articles. This does not seem likely to take place in practice, though, especially if the breadth of the contents of the article is taken into account.

(2) Secondly, regarding the actual issues present in Art. 65, it must be noted that those appearing in section (a) have already been dealt with in several of the Conventions concluded among the member states. On the other hand, section (b) may be the most relevant of the three, when referring for the first time to the conflict of laws rules, insists on putting more emphasis, not in the unification of these rules but in the desire of 'promoting the **compatibility**', a concept which is even more generic and vague than that of harmonization or approximation. Finally, the third section (c) regarding the elimination of 'obstacles to the good functioning of civil proceedings' seems to be referring mainly to issues of procedural rules applied to foreign affairs, already taken on, some of them, by the Court of Justice of the European Communities in its most recent judgments.[83]

(3) Thirdly, it must be emphasized how, obviously, this new dimension of the 'Judicial Co-operation in Civil Matters' (*JCCM*) that has taken place following the Treaty of Amsterdam will not only depend upon the entrance into force of this Conventional instrument, but also appears to be linked to the culmination of the different – and complicated – phases designed in the new Art. 67 of the Treaty of Rome.[84]

(4) Fourthly, the competence of the Court of Justice of the Communities to know about preliminary rulings regarding the interpretation of the new Title IV is drawn up, apparently, in more stringent terms than those included, generically, in the new Art. 234–Art. 177 in the previous version prior to Amsterdam – of the Treaty of Rome.[85]

---

[83] See ECJ JJ. of 1 July 1993, (C. C-20/92), *A. Hubbard v Hamburger*, *Rec.* 1993, I-377ff; 26 September 1996, (C. 43/95), *Data Delekta Aktienbolag, Ronny Forsberg v MSL Dynamics Ltd*, *Rec.* 1996, I-4661ff; 20 March 1997, (C. C-323/95), *David Charles Hayes and Jannette Karen Hayes v Kronenberg GmbH*, *Rec.* 1997, I-1711ff; 2 October 1997, (C. C-122/96), *Stephen Austin Saldanha and MTS Securities Corporation v Hiross Holding AG*, *Rec* 1997, I-5325ff. In this respect see J.C. Fernandez Rozas and S. Sanchez Lorenzo, *Curso de Derecho internacional privado*, Madrid, Civitas, 1996, 3ª ed., 623ff; M. Aguilar Benitez De Lugo, 'La Cautio Iudicatum Solvi a la luz de la sentencia del Tribunal de Justicia de las Comunidades Europeas de 1 de julio de 1993 en el caso "Hubbard/Hamburguer"', *Boletín Informativo del Ministerio de Justicia*, 1993, No. 1689, 5310ff; A. De Miguel Asensio, 'El Tratado de Amsterdam . . .', *art. cit.*, 2–3. Also see L.G. Radicati Di Brozolo, 'Diritto Comunitario e regole processuali interne: inapplicabilità dell'art. 633 Cod.Proc.Civ.', *Riv dir int priv proc*, 1993, 607ff; M. Hoskins, 'Tilting the Balance: Supremacy and National Procedural Rules', *ELRev*, 1996, 365ff.

When assessing this statement, it must be taken into account, though, the mentioned 'Commission Communication to the Council and the European Parliament "Towards Greater Efficiency in Obtaining and Enforcing Judgments in the European Union"' (*cit.* note 60) in which, regardless of the legal base that has supported its elaboration, a series of issues suggested for the correct functioning of the justice in a united Europe can be found.

[84] See J.L. Iglesias Buhigues, *art. cit.*, 5859–5860.

[85] See J.L. Iglesias Buhigues, *art. cit.*, 5860ff, P.A. De Miguel Asensio, 'El Tratado de Amsterdam . . .', *art. cit.*, 2.

(5) Lastly, it is important to highlight how the proposals formulated in the new Title IV of the Treaty of Rome are left conditional, in as much as their application to Denmark, Ireland and the United Kingdom, to what has been stipulated in the Protocol (No. 4) on the position of the United Kingdom and of Ireland (1997) and (No. 5) on the position of Denmark (1997) which make dependent its application to a previous acceptance by these three member states.

VI   FINAL REFLECTION

At the beginning of this contribution it was pointed out that it would be impossible to limit this study to a mere analysis of the international Conventions concluded among the member states under the former Art. 220 of the Treaty of Rome. Their analysis, so it was said, should have an instrumental character: just serving to precis the role played by them in the framework of the process of legal integration that has taken place in Europe parallel to the consolidation of the Single Market. In this sense, these pages not only show the importance until now of the conventional way for the harmonization of the rules of private international law in Europe, as a valid and effective alternative to the unification of European private law but, also, the difficulties of this line of action have been highlighted, which have been reflected in the scarcity of Conventions on this matter concluded ever since 1957.

The Treaty of Amsterdam may bring about a change of the previous situation. The possibilities opened by the new Art. 65 of the Treaty of Rome may end up putting aside the conventional option. It is, however, no more than a mere possibility whose potential and scope are still far from being certain.

166

11

THE THIRD PILLAR: CRIMINAL LAW
ASPECTS OF 'CONVENTION LAW'

Peter Cullen

I INTRODUCTION

The purpose of this chapter is to consider some of the issues arising from the use of Conventions as a legal instrument for development of the policy of the EU in regard to 'Justice and Home Affairs' matters, under the Maastricht Treaty, and for the creation of an 'area of freedom, security and justice' in the EU after the entry into force of the Amsterdam Treaty. The focus will be on the implications of such Conventions for criminal justice cooperation among member states. It is necessary first of all, however, to say something about the overall Treaty framework of policy-making under the so-called 'Third Pillar' of the EU, more correctly known as Title VI of the Treaty on European Union. The starting point will therefore be a general survey of the aims of the Third Pillar and the means laid out for achievement of its objectives. A proper understanding of the role of the Convention can flow only from consideration of this broader context.

II MAASTRICHT'S THIRD PILLAR:
CREATING LAW OR FURTHERING COOPERATION?

The preamble of the Maastricht Treaty indicates that the inclusion of provisions on Justice and Home Affairs was both a reaffirmation of the member states' 'objective to facilitate the free movement of persons' and at the same time a new step towards 'ensuring the safety and security of their peoples'. This dual objective reflects a tension between the liberal idea of an opening of borders and the motivation to keep them closed to unwanted incomers, especially those who may threaten internal security or stability. The Amsterdam Treaty's desire to establish the European Union as an 'area' within which life is free, secure and just – even if chaos reigns outside? – is merely an extension of this thinking. One of the difficulties with the 'closure approach' which is now being followed in regard to the Union's external borders is that the frontiers of the EU are not fixed: enlargement looms and with it a change in those frontiers.[1] Also, at the core of the EU lie free trade and free movement of labour, i.e. strong liberal forces which make the idea of a watertight Union, closed to would-be immigrants, unrealistic. The protection of human rights is another countervailing liberal tendency, one which has frustrated restrictive national immigration policies in the past.[2] Even if it wanted to, the EU could not turn itself into a fortress.[3]

It is nevertheless the case that, quite independently of Community or Union policy, there are particularly strong bilateral and multilateral security concerns between and among EU countries and, increasingly, with countries applying for EU membership. By 'security', in this sense, is included more than just risks of criminal infiltration; the migration issue has also become a security concern, with member states attempting to impose restrictive policies towards economic migrants and asylum seekers. The opening of the borders of Central and Eastern Europe following the end of the Cold War probably also made it inevitable that questions of immigration and asylum, and the management of the external frontier – the border of chaos, as it were – would become matters of common concern, or, as the Maastricht Treaty puts it, 'matters of common interest' among the member states.

The creation of the new Treaty title on Cooperation in Justice and Home Affairs was recognition that certain phenomena, by their very nature transnational, could not be handled adequately by member states acting in isolation, at a purely national level. The fight against terrorism and the international drugs trade was the focus of cooperation among member states in criminal and police matters long before the creation of the EU.[4] Post-Maastricht, the Union recognized the need to address new forms of transborder criminal activities of a serious nature: trafficking in persons and crimes against children have been a strong focus of recent policy under the Third Pillar. Also highly topical is the fight against international fraud, referred to in Art. K.1(5). This legal basis overlaps with EU law jurisdiction, which has resulted in a dual legal approach (see below). In general, the opening of internal EU borders has operated as a catalyst to attempts to improve criminal justice cooperation. Police and other law enforcement officials were quick to point

---

[1] As to the 'changing status' of frontiers in contemporary Europe, see E. Bort's 'Introduction' in E. Bort (ed.), *Borders and Borderlands in Europe*, Edinburgh, International Social Sciences Institute, 1998: 5.

[2] See J. Hollifield, *Immigrants, Markets and States. The Political Economy of Postwar Europe*, Cambridge, Mass, Harvard University Press, 1992.

[3] D. Bigo, 'Frontiers and Security in the European Union: The Illusion of Migration Control' in M. Anderson and E. Bort (eds), *The Frontiers of Europe*, London, Pinter, 1998, ch. 10.

[4] M. Anderson, M. den Boer, P. Cullen, W.C. Gilmore, C.D. Raab and N. Walker, *Policing the European Union*, Oxford, Clarendon, 1995, ch. 1, 26 *et seq.*

to the 'security deficit' which the opening of borders could entail, if the necessary 'compensatory measures' were not adopted.[5]

In agreeing to submit matters such as asylum, immigration, control of external borders, international fraud and police and judicial cooperation in criminal matters to the jurisdiction of the EU, member states were not agreeing to hand over sovereign powers to make policy and legislate in these areas: they wished to retain ultimate control over decision-making within cooperative structures.[6] National sovereignty concerns are ever-present in the field of Third Pillar cooperation. They sometimes take the form of fears of erosion of (constitutionally-based) national standards of human rights by the weaker legislation of partner states. These are part of broader fears concerning an over-bearing European superstate which have become more common in recent years, being reflected in the EC Treaty's subsidiarity clause.[7] Reluctance to accept the loss of sovereign control over policy is particularly strong in relation to law enforcement, as it is at the core of national sovereignty. Member states have cited sovereignty concerns as their main reason for rejecting the creation of a fully-fledged European police 'force', as opposed to a European police 'office', and for opposing a system of 'federal' criminal law, created by European, as opposed to national, institutions, which such a force might be called upon to enforce.[8] The Maastricht Treaty steered a course well clear of such 'federalization' of criminal law or justice.[9]

The choice of means by which to pursue cooperation on the matters of common interest listed in the Third Pillar reflects uncertainty whether a significant legal approach – involving the stipulation of formal obligations to cooperate or even steps towards harmonization of laws in the areas concerned – should be added to executive or operational forms of cooperation among law enforcement agencies, ministries and their officials. A look at the measures designed to implement the Third Pillar indicates that they were not intended to be without legal effect. In this regard, the Convention stands out as a legal instrument for implementing policy (see below). On the other hand, it was unclear whether 'joint actions' or 'joint positions' were intended

---

[5] Ibid., ch. 4.

[6] Foreign Office, *A Partnership of Nations. The British Approach to the European Union Intergovernmental Conference 1996*, Cm 3181, London, HMSO, 1996, para. 49, referring to the matters of cooperation in the Third Pillar as 'involving questions of national sovereignty' and concerning matters of 'national sentiment or varying social and legal traditions'.

[7] Article 5, EC Treaty.

[8] H. Lensing, 'The Federalization of Europe: Towards a Federal System of Criminal Justice', 1993, 1(3) *European Journal of Crime, Criminal Law and Criminal Justice*, 212–229.

[9] Intergovernmental cooperation under the Maastricht Treaty in relation to police and criminal justice cooperation is significantly less ambitious than under the Schengen Convention of 19 June 1990 (see note 22). Even if the latter too remained intergovernmental, the forms of cooperation, coordination and harmonization of laws it envisaged represented a much clearer and more ambitious programme than the Maastricht provisions. As an 'experiment' for later EU measures, it was a fairly bold one, aided initially by the relatively small number of states involved.

to be legally binding.[10] Even in relation to the Convention, it was not immediately clear to what precise legal purpose it would be put.

The terms of the Maastricht Treaty's Third Pillar suggest member states may have been caught in two minds, or that they wished to compromise between the standpoints of those who favoured the creation of some kind of enhanced 'legal space', including moves to reduce the differences between member states' criminal laws (or immigration or asylum laws, for that matter), and those who saw the Third Pillar very much in the same light as the Second Pillar (concerning Common Foreign and Security Policy) as a field for executive cooperation, without legislation being required. These different standpoints are expressed in comments concerning the 'performance' of the Third Pillar, made in the context of discussions of its reform in the Intergovernmental Conference negotiations preparing for the Amsterdam Treaty. For example, the UK's Home Office has stated that the Third Pillar should not be judged solely 'through the adoption of high profile agreements, while much of the exchange of information and ideas on practical issues goes unseen and unremarked. The result can be a perception of a lack of results which may fail to do the Third Pillar full justice.'[11]

Clearly there are advantages in having formal rules to guide cooperation in those areas of policy covered by the field of Justice and Home Affairs. But their sensitivity may also make it easier to agree common standpoints, for example in the form of 'joint positions', which can then be translated into coordinated action at national level with the minimum of fuss and, if kept as a largely executive matter for coordination between departments, can also escape the prying eyes of legislatures. Common action under Pillar Three in the immigration and asylum fields has often taken the form of non-binding resolutions which nevertheless anticipate national implementation.[12] Several important 'Action Plans' have also been adopted as Third Pillar measures.[13] Those member states steeped in what one might now with an element of nostalgia call the 'Schengen tradition' were well acquainted with the virtues of executive action where police and security cooperation were concerned. Indeed, the primary decision-making body of the Schengen Agreements was

---

[10] Unlike with regard to the Second Pillar (Common Foreign and Security Policy), the effects of these instruments were not defined: cf Art. J.3(4): 'Joint Actions shall commit the Member States in the positions they adopt and in the conduct of their activity.'

[11] House of Lords Select Committee on the European Communities, Session 1997–98, 15th Report, *Dealing with the Third Pillar: The Government's Perspective*, HL Paper 73, London, HMSO, 1998, written evidence, 5.

[12] See, for example, the apparent contradiction in 'Council Resolution of 30 November 1994 relating to the limitations on the admission of third-country nationals to the territory of the Member States for the purpose of pursuing activities as self-employed persons': in para. 9 of the first section it is stated that the principles laid down in the resolution regarding movement of third-country nationals should 'govern' Member State policies, that they 'may not be relaxed by Member States in their national legislation', that these states are expected to take them into account in revising national legislation but that the principles 'are not legally binding on Member States' (*OJ*, C274, 19 September 1996, 7).

[13] For a breakdown of the type of measures adopted up until the end of 1997 see House of Lords Select Committee on the EU, 1997–98, *15th Report, op. cit.*, Home Office evidence, 15.

the so-called 'Executive Committee', in relation to which the Convention foresaw no means of democratic control.

It is clear that improved operational coordination of police and other law enforcement agencies in relation to serious transnational crime was an aim of the Maastricht Treaty. The success of European police cooperation is particularly dependent upon close operational ties, which are often of an informal nature, bilateral, and inherently flexible in character.[14] In addition to building upon such cooperation in a multilateral setting, the Maastricht Treaty took the extra step of proposing a European Police Office (Europol), with the initial function of information exchange and analysis. The establishment of Europol became a priority of Third Pillar policy, in fact one of the few clear objectives of Justice and Home Affairs cooperation. Legally, this objective was, however, to prove very difficult to achieve, with disputes arising as to the extent of the powers of the new agency and how it should best be controlled.

Summing up these introductory remarks with regard to the Third Pillar as a whole, it does seem to be the case that member states were unclear not only about the precise objectives of Cooperation in Justice and Home Affairs but also about what the best ways to achieve such cooperation would be. These remarks can be applied too with some justification to the fields of police and judicial cooperation in criminal justice matters. At least in relation to the former, however, the Treaty did set a specific goal, even if it was not clear how Europol would be established. In relation to the latter, there were reasons to believe that the Convention would be utilized to advance cooperation but it was uncertain whether significant legal changes to the structure or forms of such cooperation were intended, perhaps also encompassing some harmonization of criminal laws. These aspects will now be examined alongside the practice of Convention law-making in criminal matters.

III PRACTICE OF CONVENTION LAW-MAKING IN CRIMINAL LAW MATTERS UNDER PILLAR THREE

General points

Practice in Convention-making under the Third Pillar will be reviewed in an attempt to assess the importance of Convention law for the development of certain aspects of criminal law within the EU. Perhaps we should begin this section by recalling the limits of the ambitions of the Third Pillar. It does not embrace the whole of the criminal law and, even after the Amsterdam Treaty amendments, its main focus will be the enhancement of cooperation between the member states' systems of criminal law and justice, mainly by improving collaboration and the exchange of information and evidence between prosecutors, police forces and courts across the EU who, separately, must then

---

[14] M. Anderson *et al.*, *op. cit.*, ch. 2.

bring offenders to justice, in their own courts, according to their own rules of procedure. As has been stated by one of its Advocates-General, the European Court of Justice is not a criminal court.[15] It does not try criminals; it is not a court of criminal appeals; it is not, therefore, a European Court of **Criminal** Justice. Having said that, we might also note that a further limit of Pillar Three is that it is subject to the rules of EU law which do fall within the jurisdiction of the Luxembourg tribunal. The scope of 'EU criminal law', or at least the impact of EU law norms on national criminal law, may well be increasing and the Court's jurisprudence could come to inform standards of criminal justice in future.[16] These, however, are separate questions which must be distinguished from the present enquiry; they will be touched upon only in so far as it is necessary to point to certain overlaps between the two Pillars.[17]

The Convention occupied a place of legal honour or privilege under the Maastricht version of the Third Pillar. It was the only measure which stood out as being intended to be legally binding and it was the only measure in respect of which the permissive jurisdiction of the Court of Justice might apply (Art. K.3.(2)(c)). It is however unlike legislation, because although formally adopted by Council Act, it requires ratification in accordance with constitutional requirements and its entry into force is dependent upon ratification by **all** member states. Unanimity is thus required for adoption.

As the Third Pillar became established, so the number of proposed Conventions increased. It became clear that the Convention would be used, primarily, to reinforce law enforcement or criminal justice cooperation in general and not just for the establishment of Europol. It is difficult to determine precisely what significance the drafters of the Maastricht Treaty accorded the Convention, i.e. how far they saw a body of Convention law

---

[15] Advocate-General Jacobs in Case C-240/90 *Germany v Commission* [1992] ECR I-5383, at I-5408, adding that this would not in itself prevent the Community from harmonising criminal law. It may be doubted whether an appropriate legal basis exists for the latter, even in relation to Community fraud; see discussion *infra*.

[16] E. Baker, 'Taking European Criminal Law Seriously', [1998] *Criminal Law Review* 361–380.

[17] This issue of overlap is one with potentially far-reaching institutional consequences. Naturally, the European Parliament, with a very weak Third Pillar role compared to a joint legislative role with the Council under the First Pillar, would prefer to see initiatives on matters like fraud against the EU budget raised under EU rather than intergovernmental powers. Indeed, this was a bone of contention between it and the Council with regard to the Fraud Convention, signed on 26 July 1995 (discussed below). The Parliament argued against the proposal for a Council Act establishing the Fraud Convention on the basis that criminalization of fraud should be carried out on the basis of EU jurisdiction (Arts 100a and 209a). Amsterdam has attempted to tidy up this fraud issue by inserting an explicit EU competence to 'adopt the necessary measures in the fields of the prevention of and fight against fraud affecting the financial interests of the Community, with a view to affording effective and equivalent protection in the Member States'. On the other hand, the new Treaty Article also states that the Council measures 'shall not concern the application of national criminal law or the national administration of justice' (new Art. 280 of EC Treaty), which are precisely matters dealt with by the Fraud Convention. So, a dual legal approach may have to continue in this area after entry into force of the Amsterdam Treaty, whose new Third Pillar refers to 'fraud and corruption' in a general sense as particular criminal activities to be prevented and combated.

developing and in what fields. In seeking explanations for the inclusion of the Convention as a legal option one can surmise that the Treaty drafters considered the need for some elements of the cooperation between them to be placed on a legal footing which would be constitutionally acceptable from the point of view of their own legal systems. The 'constitutional acceptability' requirement is satisfied by the Convention in that it must be adopted 'in accordance with the respective constitutional requirements' of the member states. This opens up the possibility of participation, either in the form of scrutiny or actual approval, by national legislatures. Their consent would in any case be needed to secure any necessary national legislative implementation of a Third Pillar Convention.

Europol

Experience with the Third Pillar shows that the member states probably had at least one specific initiative in mind for adoption by use of the Convention, namely Europol, the European Police Office referred to in the Treaty (Art. K.1.9) as a 'Union-wide system for exchanging information'. In fact the Maastricht Treaty did not state that this office should be established by Convention. Indeed, the forerunner of Europol, the Europol Drugs Unit (EDU), which has been operating since 1994 as a point of exchange for criminal intelligence data among police forces, was set up not on such a legal basis but, first, by mere Ministerial Agreement[18] and, second, by Joint Action.[19] Europol's policy importance – it is the only concrete project outlined in the Third Pillar – warranted different treatment by a clearly legally binding instrument, i.e. the Convention, to be negotiated in the manner of an international treaty. Such an approach was also justified on constitutional grounds, especially given the sensitivity of questions surrounding Europol's access to and use of personal data. In several member states data protection is now a constitutional matter.[20] Parliamentary endorsement of the power to hold personal data centrally and to allow Europol to communicate criminal data with third states and organizations was regarded as necessary; these powers were held back from the EDU.

The Europol Convention is the product of detailed negotiations which were marked by significant differences of opinion as to the appropriate range of 'police powers' with which Europol should be conferred.[21] These negotiations

[18] Of 2 June 1993, signed in Copenhagen. A copy is annexed to the article by W.C. Gilmore, 'Police Co-operation and the European Communities: Current Trends and Recent Developments', 1993, *Commonwealth Law Bulletin*, 1960–1975.

[19] Joint Action of 10 March 1995 adopted by the Council on the basis of Art. K.3 of the Treaty on European Union concerning the Europol Drugs Unit, *OJ*, L62, 20 March 1995.

[20] See in relation to Germany the discussion with regard to Art. 2(1) of the Basic Law (*Grundgesetz*) in B. Schmidt-Bleibtreu and F. Klein, *Kommentar zum Grundgesetz*, 8th ed., Berlin: Luchterhand, 1995, 150.

[21] The Europol Convention is published in *OJ*, C316, 27 November 1995, 1–32. The most detailed account of the differing positions is provided by D. Bigo, *Polices en Réseaux: l'expérience européenne*, Paris, Presses de la Fondation Nationale des Sciences Politiques, 1996, 224–243.

remained closed to parliaments at national and European level, who, although sometimes provided with drafts, were rarely able to influence the outcome of negotiations on those documents. This is a criticism of the Convention law-making process to which we will return (below).

In terms of its impact on national criminal law or policing, Europol must be seen, looking to the Maastricht Treaty provisions and in accordance with the terms of the Convention, as essentially a supportive and coordinating central office for criminal data and intelligence. Its interlocutors will be the national law enforcement agencies of the member states, whom it will supply with criminal intelligence and analysis and from whom it will receive information on issues connected with certain forms of transnational crime. Europol will not be a police 'force' with executive powers in the nature of the US Federal Bureau of Investigation or the other US federal law enforcement agencies. It will be bound at all stages of investigations closely to national systems of criminal law and justice, given the absence both of a code of criminal law and of any European prosecution service or European criminal judiciary. These are gaps which could undermine the body's future effectiveness. They are also factors which could take Europol outside proper legal controls, controls which would be particularly necessary if Europol were to become involved in proactive undercover policing.

The Europol Convention was, thus, not used to harmonize national police powers nor to advance forms of bilateral, cross-border European police cooperation. These matters fall outside its legal basis and would in any case have brought it into conflict with the provisions of the Schengen Convention on Border Controls.[22] As for a crime strategy targetting the 'organized criminal structures' upon whose activities Europol was to focus, this was devised only in 1997. This strategy, taking the form of an 'Action Plan to combat Organised Crime',[23] immediately prompted the Amsterdam Treaty makers to review and revise the extent of Europol's powers.[24]

Fighting fraud within the EU budget

On the same day as the Europol Convention was signed, the member states also agreed the 'Convention on the protection of the European Communities' financial interests'.[25] Like the Europol Convention, this was based on the provisions of Art. K.3 of the Third Pillar. The Maastricht Treaty had also introduced a legal basis for action against EU fraud under the First or Community Pillar but member states took the view that this was too limited to allow antifraud measures which would harmonize the criminal laws of the

---

[22] Convention of 19 June 1990, 1991 *Commercial Laws of Europe*, 33–100.
[23] The 'Action Plan to combat Organized Crime' is published in the Official Journal (*OJ*, C251, 15 August 1997).
[24] *Cf* letter from the drafters of the Action Plan to the Intergovernmental Conference, *OJ*, C251, 15 August 1997, 17–18, as followed up in the new Treaty.
[25] *OJ*, C316, 27 November 1995, 48–57.

member states.[26] In 1994 the European Commission had, however, devised a new antifraud strategy, one strand of which entailed 'securing greater compatibility between national legislation with regard to punitive measures to deter fraud.'[27] The First Pillar legal basis which had been established in Art. 209a of the EC Treaty could not contribute to this strand. It was confined, first, to achieving 'assimilation' of the treatment of fraud against the EU budget to crimes of fraud against national interests, i.e. assimilation within, not between, member states' legal systems, and second, to obliging member states to coordinate their action against EU fraud by improving administrative cooperation. There was also a general reluctance – stronger in some member states than others – to accept that EU law could be used to harmonize criminal laws.[28]

On the other hand, member states were prepared in December 1995 to agree a Regulation putting in place a framework of general rules concerning 'administrative checks measures and penalties' to combat fraud against the EU's financial interests.[29] The sanctions envisaged by this Regulation are non-penal in nature; stipulated by EU instrument, they fall to be imposed by member states.[30] An additional EU Regulation of 1996 gives the Commission power to make checks and inspections 'on-the-spot' on economic operators to whom the EU administrative measures referred to in the 1995 Regulation may be applied, 'where there are reasons to think that irregularities have been committed'.[31] The Fraud Convention is, thus, part of a broader legal framework, split between the First and the Third Pillars.

The primary aim of the Fraud Convention was to ensure that a 'single uniform offence of fraud against the Communities financial interests' should be established in the legislation of all the member states.[32] Some member states, however, contested the need for a 'specific offence' of EU fraud which would have amounted to a 'unification' of national laws. In the end, Art. 1 of the Convention was drafted so as to require that each member state transpose a common definition of fraud 'into their national criminal law in such a way that the conduct referred to therein constitutes criminal offences'. Instead of

---

[26] The European Parliament begged to differ: see note 17 (above).

[27] European Commission, *Protecting the Community's Financial Interests: The Fight against Fraud, Annual Report 1994*, COM (95) 98 final, Brussels, 29 March 1995, 3.

[28] *Cf* Court of Auditors Special Report No. 8/98 on the Commission's services specifically involved in the fight against fraud, notably the 'Unité de coordination de la lutte anti-fraude' (UCLAF) together with the Commission's replies, *OJ*, C230, 22 July 1998, paras 2.7 and 2.8.

[29] Council Regulation No. 2988/95 of 18 December 1995 on the protection of the European Communities' financial interests, *OJ*, L312, 23 December 1995, 1–4.

[30] See preamble of the Regulation which states that the Regulation applies 'without prejudice to the application of Member States' criminal law'.

[31] Article 5 of Council Regulation No. 2185/96 of 11 November 1996 concerning on-the-spot checks and inspections carried out by the Commission in order to protect the European Communities' financial interests against fraud and other irregularities', *OJ*, L292, 15 November 1992, 2–5.

[32] See Proposal for a Council of the European Union Act establishing a Convention for the protection of the EU's financial interests, COM (94) 214 final, Brussels, 15 June 1994, 4.

uniform criminal offences, member states are thus able to adapt existing offences to fit the bill. The Council's explanatory report describes this as a guarantee of 'a common minimum level of penal action against fraud committed by economic agents in Member States.'[33] This limited harmonization of substantive national criminal law is accompanied by a modicum of procedural harmonization: for 'serious fraud', it is stipulated in Art. 2 that member states must provide 'criminal penalties involving deprivation of liberty'. Otherwise, penalties must be of a criminal nature and meet the test established by the European Court of Justice for the national sanctioning of breaches of EU law, i.e. they must be 'effective, proportionate and dissuasive'.

The Fraud Convention itself does not deal with the issue of corporate liability, as was proposed, but a 'Second Protocol', signed two years later, does require national law to be adapted to ensure that legal persons can be held liable for fraud committed for their benefit by persons with corporate responsibility.[34] The 'First Protocol' to the Convention relates to corruption to the detriment of the EU budget. It also requires national criminal law to be changed, where necessary, to embrace offences of 'active' and 'passive' corruption by national and/or EU officials in so far as it affects EU revenue or expenditure.[35] The same approach to penalties for such corruption is taken as in the Fraud Convention proper. There is a further anticorruption Convention which extends beyond fraud against the EU budget: in order to improve 'judicial cooperation in criminal matters' (see below), it provides for offences of active and passive corruption by national and/or EU officials without any necessary link to damage to the European Communities' financial interests.[36]

The justification used by the general anticorruption Convention is revealing: member states deliberately linked the need to harmonize national criminal laws with the legal basis for cooperation in criminal justice matters. The antifraud measures also envisage specific measures to enhance judicial cooperation in criminal matters which are relevant to the discussion in the next section. What should be apparent from this section is that the fight against EU fraud and related corruption has resulted in legal steps taken under the Third Pillar to compel alteration in national criminal law. The degree of harmonization may be limited – and in particular barely touches the sensitive realm of national criminal procedures[37] – but it forms part of a policy of 'criminal law protection' of the EU budget, an instrumentalization of national

---

[33] Explanatory Report on the Convention on the Protection of the European Communities' Financial Interests, *OJ*, C191, 23 June 1997, 1–10, at 4.

[34] As well as certain other crimes defined by European instruments: see Art. 3 of the Second Protocol to the Fraud Convention, *OJ*, C221, 19 July 1997, 12–22.

[35] *OJ*, C313, 23 October 1996, 1–10.

[36] *OJ*, C195, 25 June 1997, 1–6. White believes the anticorruption measures represent considerable progress 'towards enhancing co-operation in criminal law for the prosecution of corruption' (S. White, *Protection of the Financial Interests of the European Communities: The Fight against Fraud and Corruption*, The Hague: Kluwer, 1998, 160).

[37] Cf *Corpus Juris: Introducing Penal Provisions for the purpose of the financial interests of the Communities*, Paris, Economica, 1997, 34–38.

criminal laws for the purposes of the Union.[38] Another way of putting it
would be to say that the Third Pillar instruments concerned intrude upon
member states' sovereignty in criminal matters in so far as national legislatures are bound to comply with supranational norms of criminal law, albeit
norms adopted in an intergovernmental negotiating process.

Improving judicial cooperation in criminal matters

In relation to 'judicial cooperation in criminal matters', the official term used
by the Maastricht Treaty to encompass criminal justice cooperation, the
employment of the Convention to develop methods of cooperation can most
likely be explained by reference to the activities of the Council of Europe in
Strasbourg in cognate areas. Member states of the EU also had some experience of making Conventions among themselves to further particular EU
purposes, under the legal basis of Art. 220 (now Art. 293) EC Treaty, which,
notably, provided the basis for the Convention of 27 September 1968 on
Jurisdiction and the Enforcement of Judgments in Civil and Commercial
Matters (hereafter 'Brussels Convention'). The Maastricht Treaty stipulated
that the Third Pillar provisions on Conventions were 'without prejudice to
Article 220', to take account of possible areas of overlap.

When drafting the provisions of Third Pillar of the Treaty of Maastricht
concerning Conventions, the member states were probably most conscious of
the Council of Europe's long involvement in promoting criminal justice cooperation in Europe and, in particular, its success in drafting a large number
of Conventions in the areas of mutual legal assistance and extradition.[39] In
light of Third Pillar Convention practice as it has emerged one can see that
the member states had it in mind to build on specific Council of Europe
Conventions. Contacts between the Council of Europe and the EU have
intensified in recent years and their activities have begun to overlap. The EC
Treaty encourages a cooperative relationship between the two organizations.[40]
The creation of the Third Pillar has been used to develop some of the most
important legal instruments drafted in a Council of Europe context.

There was a perceived need to develop and refine certain aspects of preexisting Council of Europe Conventions, in any case, in light of growing
pan-European and global pressures created by terrorism and new forms of
organized crime, including money laundering. There may, however, be limits
to the ability of a much enlarged Council of Europe to make the quick
progress needed. The EU and in particular the legal framework of cooperation provided by Title VI appear to offer a more propitious legal and political
environment. The Council of Ministers' explanatory note on the Convention
relating to extradition between the member states of the EU expresses this

[38] See European Commission, *Protecting the Community's Financial Interests: The Fight against Fraud*, Annual Report, 1997, ch. 5, 47.
[39] For details see M. Anderson *et al.*, *op. cit.*, ch. 7.
[40] Article 303 of the EC Treaty, the new.

notion when it refers to member states' 'general desire . . . to adapt the whole sector of judicial co-operation in criminal matters to the needs of today and tomorrow'.[41] The modernization of the law of judicial cooperation to which the document alludes is, however, to be pursued by the traditional or 'old' instrument of Convention, whose legal effectiveness in the Council of Europe context is, at the very least, open to question.

Perhaps the most significant progress made in judicial cooperation in criminal justice matters to date has been the conclusion in 1995 and 1996 of two Conventions concerning extradition between EU member states: the Convention on simplified extradition procedure[42] (hereafter 'Simplified Extradition Convention') and the Convention relating to extradition[43] (hereafter 'Extradition Convention'). Shortly after the entry into force of the Maastricht Treaty, the Council of Ministers announced its intention to improve the efficiency of extradition procedures in the EU by building on and amending the Council of Europe Convention of 13 December 1957. The reform would not be confined to procedures: the main idea was to relax the conditions and grounds for refusing extradition and a work programme was set in place to examine the options.[44] The principal barriers to extradition between EU countries are the reluctance of several member states, for constitutional or other legal reasons, to extradite their own nationals and the so-called 'political offence exception' which enables them to refuse to extradite where the offence in respect of which extradition is requested is deemed by the requested state to be political in character. An example of the latter situation arose in 1996 when the Belgian Council of State suspended the Government's decision to extradite to Spain two presumed members of the Basque terrorist organisation ETA. The Council of State based its decision on provisions of the European Convention on the Suppression of Terrorism which was supposed to make invocation of the political offence exception more difficult in such situations. The European Parliament was prompted by this incident to call upon the Council 'to conclude a convention on extradition that will move beyond the current rules on the subject and abolish obsolete rules such as political offences in the Union'.[45] This incident had, however, revealed the persistence of a lack of trust or mutual confidence in legal systems between EU partners, a situation which one also associates with relations between judicial authorities in the United Kingdom and the Republic of Ireland.[46]

The Extradition Convention goes beyond earlier Council of Europe measures and those of the Benelux Convention,[47] in envisaging the complete

---

[41] *OJ*, C191, 23 June 1997, 14.
[42] *OJ*, C78, 30 March 1995, 1–10.
[43] *OJ*, C313, 23 October 1996, 11–23.
[44] European Commission, *Bulletin of the European Communities*, 11-1993, Brussels, Office for Official Publications, para. 1.5.9.
[45] *OJ*, C65, 4 March 1996, 161.
[46] See M. Anderson *et al.*, *op. cit.*, ch. 7.
[47] Treaty on Extradition and Mutual Assistance in Criminal Matters between Belgium, Luxembourg and the Netherlands of 27 June 1962 (as amended).

removal of the possibility of invoking the political offence exception. Article 5(1) requires that 'no offence may be regarded by the requested member state as a political offence, as an offence connected with a political offence or an offence inspired by a political offence'. The member states may declare reservations in relation to this provision but such reservations may not be in respect of terrorist offences. The new provisions do not, however, prevent extradition from being refused in order to protect persons against criminal proceedings motivated by discrimination on ground of race, religion, national or political opinion, though the Council's explanatory memorandum suggests that the likelihood of such circumstances pertaining in the EU is 'probably academic'.[48]

The Extradition Convention also addresses the issue of refusal to extradite on ground of nationality, stipulating that this should no longer be permissible but allowing member states to avoid this obligation by declaring a reservation. The reservation possibility was allowed 'since the prohibition of extradition of nationals is established in constitutional law or in national laws which are based on long-standing legal traditions, the change of which appears to be a complex matter'.[49] The declaration may take the form of a conditional statement, e.g. that the member states will extradite only for prosecution not execution of sentence. Certain time limits are imposed on maintenance of reservations. Together with the Simplified Extradition Convention, which seeks to expedite procedures in the case of consenting persons, the Extradition Convention has the potential to remove some of the traditional obstacles to extradition between member states, assuming it is promptly ratified and enters into force. The latter, however, is quite a big assumption and there must also be a concern that reservations will be used to defeat some of the innovations introduced.

The text of the explanatory report on the Extradition Convention shows that there is still some way to go before national legal obstacles to judicial cooperation are jettisoned completely. The real obstacles to such cooperation, especially where the cooperation in question concerns the vital task of gaining evidence from abroad for trial in the requesting jurisdiction, lie in the very existence of different systems of criminal law and, especially, criminal procedure. One of the biggest practical difficulties faced by prosecutors and others working in the field of mutual assistance is to obtain admissible evidence. This difficulty cannot be completely overcome while legal standards, including interpretation of human rights standards, vary across the member states, but the problems can be eased by practical steps such as improving communications and making clear to partner states who has responsibility for processing formal requests for assistance.[50]

---

[48] Text approved by Council on 26 May 1997, *OJ*, C191, 23 June 1997, 13–26, at 19. It is rather surprising to read in this section of the memorandum that 'the respect for fundamental rights and liberties is an **absolute** principle of the European Union' (author's emphasis).

[49] Ibid., 20.

[50] R.G. Stott, 'Mutual Legal Assistance – the View from the Scottish Trenches', ch. 20 in P.J. Cullen and W.C. Gilmore (eds), *Crime sans Frontières: International and European Legal Approaches*, Hume Papers on Public Policy, Volume 6, Nos. 1 and 2, Edinburgh, Edinburgh University Press, 1998.

In the framework of the Third Pillar, member states are currently engaged in negotiations on a draft Convention on Mutual Assistance in Criminal Matters which deals with some of these practical concerns by supplementing the basic European instrument on mutual assistance, i.e. the European Convention on Mutual Assistance in Criminal Matters of 20 April 1959. Updating of the 1959 Convention to take account of the possibilities of taking evidence by video conferencing is one such practical matter. There are, however, a number of provisions in the drafts so far presented to national parliaments for scrutiny that are proving controversial, because they go far beyond the 1959 Convention and provide for new forms of assistance, notably interception of terrestrial and satellite communications, controlled deliveries and covert investigations. Concern has been expressed by civil liberties organizations based in the UK about proposals to create a legal basis in the Convention for such new investigative techniques to be used in mutual assistance. It is felt that the proposed clauses would endanger privacy by opening up new possibilities for surveillance and information-gathering. The UK Government recognizes such concerns about 'appropriate safeguards for the citizen' which are 'still under discussion' in negotiations.[51]

Interestingly, there is a close link between many of the controversial proposals under discussion in connection with the Mutual Assistance draft and a section of another Third Pillar Convention which has already been concluded, namely the Convention on Mutual Assistance and cooperation between customs administrations (hereafter 'Customs Cooperation Convention').[52] This instrument is designed to strengthen a 1967 Convention on mutual assistance between customs adminstrations, partly by introducing procedural improvements to existing mutual assistance tools, in order to assist in combating infringements of national customs provisions and EU customs provisions. Where such infringements involve criminal investigations, it will be possible for national authorities to proceed under this Convention rather than under applicable provisions concerning mutual assistance in criminal matters.[53] The Customs Cooperation Convention foreshadows several of the disputed draft provisions of the proposed Mutual Assistance Convention. In particular, the section of the Customs Cooperation Convention referred to as 'Title IV: Special Forms of Cooperation', provides for particular types of cross-border operation: hot pursuit, cross-border surveillance, controlled delivery, covert investigations and joint special investigation teams. There is provision for member states' customs officers to operate on each other's territory in such operations but only for the purpose of investigation and prosecution of particular offences, mostly related to drugs, and subject to a series of conditions, notably compliance with the laws of the requested state.

---

[51] House of Lords Select Committee on the European Communities, Session 1997–98, 14th Report, *Mutual Assistance in Criminal Matters*, HL Paper 72, London, HMSO, 1998, 14.
[52] Convention of 18 December 1997, *OJ*, C24, 23 January 1998, 1–22.
[53] Article 3 of Convention.

As in the case of the Extradition Convention, it is possible for member states to reserve, by declaration, the right not to participate in mutual assistance in some matters, notably hot pursuit, cross-border surveillance and covert investigations. A more general saving clause is provided to allow assistance to be refused where it 'would be likely to harm the public policy or other essential interests of the State concerned [requested state], particularly in the field of data protection' or in circumstances where to render assistance would be 'obviously disproportionate to the seriousness of the presumed infringement'.[54] The wording of such clauses is clearly open to interpretation, and we shall consider in the next section what possibilities there might be for a uniform interpretation by the European Court of Justice. The preamble to the Customs Cooperation Convention stipulates that cross-border operations be conducted in accordance with the 'principles of legality . . . subsidiarity . . . and proportionality', principles with whose interpretation the Luxembourg court is charged by the EC Treaty in the context of EU law.

We can conclude that both the draft Mutual Assistance Convention and, more starkly, the Customs Cooperation Convention, embrace forms of operational or investigative assistance that go beyond the usual preoccupations of mutual assistance treaties. In this connection the House of Lords has noted that although the instruments concerned do not claim to harmonize criminal laws, they 'may impinge upon the civil liberties of individual'.[55] Consequently, careful attention needs to be given to issues such as data protection and other safeguards which require effective judicial supervision.

In more general terms we can conclude this section by noting that the Maastricht Treaty has by now engendered a number of significant Conventions affecting the area of criminal justice cooperation. Of those mentioned, only the Europol Convention has entered into force, an obvious problem for the credibility of Third Pillar work, which will be discussed further in the next section. The purposes and ambitions of the Conventions have varied between limited harmonization of criminal laws, measures to improve mutual assistance and extradition and significant institutional changes, all designed to assist the fight against serious forms of transnational crime. The cumulative effect of these measures is to put in place, at least on the EU 'statute book', a body of norms which represent an incipient criminal policy, a starting point for the development of the 'area of security' which is referred to in the Amsterdam Treaty. The role of the Action Plan to combat Organized Crime will be very important in structuring future legal developments, by Convention or otherwise, under the Third Pillar; its catalytic effects have already been seen in relation to Europol. Future EU criminal policy will also, however, be bound to take account of the appropriateness of the Convention as a legal instrument of that policy. The next section will survey some of the main drawbacks of Convention law-making.

---

[54] Article 28 of Convention.
[55] House of Lords Select Committee on the EC, Session 1997–98, 14th Report, *op. cit.*, 18.

IV PROBLEMS OF CONVENTION LAW-MAKING

The process of Convention law-making can be divided up into a number of stages: proposal, negotiation, 'establishment', i.e. adoption by the Council of Ministers, ratification, entry into force, implementation and enforcement (including judicial control). These stages merit separate consideration, even if there is not space here for full consideration of all the procedures.

The Maastricht Treaty sought to make clear that proposals for Conventions (or other legal instruments) in the area of criminal justice cooperation should come only from the member states. A right of initiative for the European Commission was ruled out.[56] In fact, the Commission found ways to get around this, using for example the overlap between fighting international fraud and judicial cooperation in criminal matters to introduce in its proposal for a Council Act establishing the Fraud Convention proposals regarding judicial cooperation between member states which were strictly not within its remit.[57] There is a lack of transparency surrounding member states' proposals for Third Pillar action; unlike Commission proposals, they do not appear in the Official Journal for general public scrutiny. Government practice in member states with regard to informing their parliaments about Third Pillar instruments varies according to national arrangements; national parliaments across the Union have been concerned to improve these arrangements in recent years, recognizing they must do so if citizens' interests are to be protected.[58] There seems to be no consistent practice in the UK regarding deposit of Third Pillar instruments, including Conventions: citing a number of examples, the House of Lords Select Committee on the European Communities points in a recent report to 'persistent delays in depositing documents in Parliament'.[59]

In negotiation of Conventions, the European Parliament has probably fared worse than national parliaments. It was particularly critical of member states' failure to consult it on the Europol Convention.[60] The Parliament's call for this situation to be improved has been partially met by the Amsterdam Treaty, though the provision guaranteeing consultation of the Parliament 'before adopting' Conventions or other measures may not in practice increase the chances for meaningful input.[61] Like national parliaments, it needs to be given documents for scrutiny at a much earlier stage. What the

---

[56] Under the Amsterdam Treaty the Commission will for the first time share a right of initiative with the member states in relation to police cooperation and judicial cooperation in criminal matters (Art. 34(2) of the new Treaty on European Union).

[57] Proposal for Council of the European Union Act establishing a Convention for the protection of the Communities' financial interests, COM (94) 214 final, Brussels, 15 June 1994, 16.

[58] See comparative survey and evidence provided to House of Lords Select Committee on the European Communities, *Enhancing Parliamentary Scrutiny of the Third Pillar*, Session 1997–98, 6th Report, HL paper 25, London, HMSO, 1997.

[59] Ibid., 11.

[60] See discussion in M. Anderson *et al.*, *op. cit.*, ch. 8.

[61] It is felt by some close observers of what goes on in Brussels that the Parliament is partially itself to blame for the poor treatment it has received from the Council of Ministers: House of Lords Select Committee on the European Communities, Session 1996–97, 6th Report, *op. cit.*, evidence of Mr T. Bunyan, 37.

European Parliament would like to see is an inter-institutional agreement to govern its participation in Convention and other Third Pillar law-making instruments at all stages.[62] Member states continue, however, to be more favourably disposed to accountability to national parliaments, for example with regard to early consultation on Title VI proposals under the new Amsterdam Treaty protocol.[63] In the UK, governments have adjusted bureaucratic procedures so that more effective parliamentary scrutiny of some Third Pillar instruments has been made possible. But government was reluctant to give Parliament the same rights of scrutiny over Third Pillar instruments which it enjoys with regard to EU measures.[64] The EU comparison is also held up by European Commission and Parliament. Largely excluded from input to Third Pillar policies, they compare Title VI procedures unfavourably with the EU method of policy-making, which is heavily dependent on legislation adopted at the behest of the Commission and with the participation of the European Parliament.[65] As Pillar Three, post-Amsterdam, assumes a more legal character, it will become increasingly difficult to justify such differentiation in treatment of national and European parliaments.

The Commission has identified the unanimity requirement as a major barrier to negotiation of Third Pillar measures.[66] This criticism appears dated in light of the increasing number of Third Pillar instruments agreed by member states. It is unrealistic to think that the member states would be prepared to submit to qualified majority voting in Third Pillar matters for primary decisions, given the acute sensitivity of such matters for national policy. Post-Amsterdam, unanimity will continue to dominate decision-making under the Third Pillar. So, Convention texts must command unanimous support, meaning compromise solutions must be found between competing standpoints. Measures implementing Conventions may, however, be adopted by a two-thirds majority of votes in the Council.

It may be argued that the greatest delays are occurring at the ratification stage of adoption, i.e. after the Council has acted to draw up the Convention.[67]

---

[62] Resolution on participation by the European Parliament in international agreements by the member states and the Union on cooperation in the fields of justice and home affairs, *OJ*, C44, 14 February 1994, 180–181.

[63] Protocol on the Role of National Parliaments in the European Union, *OJ*, C340, 10 November 1997, 113–114. The reference in this protocol to proposals 'made available' by the Commission may not be wide enough to capture Third Pillar proposals initially made by member states, thus reducing parliamentary review unreasonably.

[64] See House of Lords Select Committee on the EC, Session 1997–98, 6th Report, *op. cit.*, paras 52–61, in relation to the discussion of the 'scrutiny reserve'. Compare the findings of the House of Commons Select Committee on European Legislation, Session 1995–1996, 27th Report, *The Scrutiny of European Business*, HC Paper 51 – xxvii, London, HMSO, paras 91–98.

[65] For example, European Commission Report for the Reflection Group, Intergovernmental Conference, 1995, paras 117 *et seq.*

[66] Ibid., 52.

[67] For example, we saw the Europol Convention enter into force on 1 October 1998, more than three years after signature on 26 July 1995, whereas most of the negotiations, with the exception of the dispute concerning the Court, would appear to have been completed in the year 1994.

The Council 'establishes' Conventions by 'Acts' to which are annexed the texts of Conventions signed by the member states. The Acts and appended Conventions do not seem to be published with any great urgency in the Official Journal, in some cases appearing several months after signature, as in the cases of the Europol and Fraud Conventions. They are published in the 'C' series, even though they are intended to be legally binding. A Council Act is necessary to distinguish the Conventions from ordinary international treaties: the Council 'draws up' the Conventions by placing them in the form of a legal act of the EU – with reference to the legal basis for Conventions in Art. K.3 of the Maastricht version of the Third Pillar – and then 'recommends' them for 'adoption' by the member states 'in accordance with their respective constitutional requirements'.[68] There is thus a dual process of adoption (to use the term loosely): drawing up by the Council and ratification by the member states, with unanimity being required at both points. The Council may not, currently, impose any kind of time-limit for ratification but the Amsterdam Treaty introduces a clause which states that 'Member States shall begin the procedures applicable within a time limit to be set by the Council'.[69] The Treaty does not, however, and will not incorporate any jurisdiction for the European Court of Justice, at the insistence of the Council of Ministers, to compel member states to abide by this time limit. In any case, the Council will continue only to 'recommend' adoption; it cannot compel final ratification.[70]

The Achilles heel of the Convention as an instrument for effective law-making is the ratification requirement. The potential for delay is almost endless, as experience with Council of Europe Conventions has shown.[71] Here, the point should be made that the importation of Council of Europe practice into criminal justice cooperation matters under the Third Pillar is not unproblematic. Not only do they require cumbersome ratification procedures, the Third Pillar Conventions also introduce the possibility of reservations by member states, i.e. opting-out of particular legal obligations. This may be a welcome instrument of 'flexibility' in Council of Europe experience but it rather defeats the purpose of a common legal framework of uniform rules; it represents another departure from EU practice of seeking legal uniformity. A disadvantage of using Third Pillar Conventions to supplement those of the Council of Europe is that it leaves states outside the Union, but within the broader Council of Europe, trailing behind, even those states who have applied for membership of the Union. Another related consideration is that of 'legal dispersion', a proliferation of Conventions whose relationship to

---

[68] See for example the Council Act of 18 December 1997 'drawing up' the customs cooperation Convention, *OJ* C24, 23 January 1998, 1.

[69] New Article 34(2)(d) of the Treaty on European Union.

[70] The Action Plan to combat Organized Crime recommends that the Council, when it draws up new Conventions, should 'set a target date for their adoption and implementation', *op. cit.*, 10 (recommendation 14).

[71] Thirty years for the UK in the case of some Council of Europe Conventions: see M. Anderson *et al.*, *op. cit.*, ch. 7.

one another is not always clear and can be very complex.[72] The existence of
the Schengen Convention, which contains a substantial number of provisions
relating to measures of judicial cooperation in criminal matters, but is applicable among only a limited number of member states, contributes further to
this complicated 'variable geometry' of criminal justice cooperation.[73]

Some of the current delays in ratification are difficult to explain, especially
with regard to the Fraud Convention. In that case, it could be that implementation in national law is proving problematic, which would be another
reason for having proper national parliamentary scrutiny in the first place.
Not all Conventions will require national legal implementation and even if
they do this will not necessarily facilitate parliamentary control; the right to
reject treaties outright or to reject national implementation are blunt instruments. In the case of the UK, ratification of treaties is, anyway, a matter for
the executive, with the result that Parliament has no constitutional right of
rejection, or approval, for that matter.[74] At ratification stage of Third Pillar
Conventions in the UK, the 'Ponsonby rule' applies.[75]

The Amsterdam Treaty offers the prospect of some improvement regarding entry into force of Conventions: it will allow them, once adopted by at
least half of the member states, to be applied by those states.[76] The new
Treaty will also bring about a welcome simplification and standardization of
the position regarding jurisdiction of the European Court of Justice in Third
Pillar matters, a subject of vital importance to future enforcement. Some of
the current delays with ratification have clearly been contributed to by disputes over the jurisdiction of the European Court of Justice.

Maastricht's Third Pillar confines the object of European Court jurisdiction to Conventions. The Amsterdam Treaty will allow for interpretation and
legal challenge of other legally binding Third Pillar acts. Under Maastricht,
Court jurisdiction must be specifically conferred by the terms of the Convention, whereas under the amendments introduced by the Amsterdam provisions, it will proceed from the Treaty on European Union itself, provided
that this Treaty-based jurisdiction is invoked by means of a declaration.
Under the Maastricht Treaty, jurisdiction may extend only to interpretation
of Convention provisions or 'any disputes regarding their application'. Under

[72] See Explanatory Report on the Extradition Convention, *op. cit.*, 14 referring to the creation of
'a web of various complex sets of Treaty rules, not valid for all States, which will interact with
national legislation'.
[73] Schengen will, however, be incorporated into the European Union legal framework by the
Amsterdam Treaty.
[74] A notable exception to this in the European context is s. 6 of the European Parliamentary
Elections Act 1978, which provides that 'No treaty which provides for any increase in the
powers of the European Parliament shall be ratified by the United Kingdom unless it has
been approved by an Act of Parliament.'
[75] Texts of the Convention are laid before Parliament for a period of twenty-one days before
ratification. As discussed, recent UK government practice has been to supply draft texts in
advance of their establishment by the Council.
[76] Article 34(2)(d) of the Treaty on European Union, but the Conventions may rule out this
possibility.

Amsterdam, detailed heads of jurisdiction are set out, the most important one arguably being jurisdiction in references from national courts for a preliminary ruling on interpretation of Conventions (and the validity and interpretation of other measures). When a member state declares its willingness to invoke the jurisdiction of the Court – as a number of the member states did when they signed the Amsterdam Treaty – they may limit the right to refer under this head of jurisdiction to courts against whose decisions there is no further legal recourse under national law, or extend the preliminary rulings option to all their courts.[77] In each case, there is a discretion to refer; the EU model of obliging final national courts to refer open questions has not been adopted, though – to complicate matters further – a number of member states have reserved the right to legislate to require referrals in such cases.[78]

The Court's jurisdiction remains non-automatic under the Amsterdam scheme: member states must opt in to Court jurisdiction.[79] Also, the right to limit referrals departs from EU practice. The right of **any** national court to invoke European Court of Justice juridiction in case of doubt about the meaning of EU law has proved fundamental to the integration of EU law within national laws and also an important means for individuals eventually to obtain rulings on breaches of their EU rights. If the interpretation of Third Pillar Conventions is in practice left in the hands of lower courts of the member states (or of some member states), who cannot seek guidance from Luxembourg, the risk of divergent legal approaches across the European Union increases. Of course, this danger of lack of legal uniformity – and therefore of equal protection – will exist in even more extreme form if any member state refuses to accept either form of preliminary rulings jurisdiction (currently the case for the UK).

The Amsterdam solution regarding Court jurisdiction is in fact only an elaboration of the solution reached in Convention practice to date.[80] First, the failure to agree on any Court of Justice jurisdiction in the Conventions initially adopted, including the Extradition Conventions, the Europol Convention and the Fraud Convention, caused consternation in several member states and in the European Parliament. In the case of the Europol Convention, the European Parliament called upon national parliaments not to ratify until agreement to confer a preliminary rulings jurisdiction on the Court of Justice had been reached. Some parliaments apparently went along with this. Also, Belgium, Luxembourg and the Netherlands insisted they would not apply the terms of the First Protocol on the Fraud Convention before 'a

---

[77] See declarations made on the signing of the Amsterdam Treaty regarding the jurisdiction of the Court under Art. K.7 of the Treaty on European Union (referred to here as Art. 35 of consolidated text), *OJ*, C340, 10 November 1997, 308.

[78] Ibid.

[79] For some of them opting in may in effect be mandatory, viewed from the standpoint of national constitutional requirements. Jurisdiction of the European Court of Justice may be seen as a necessary guarantee of fairness and extra judicial control by some member states.

[80] H. Labayle, 'Un espace de liberté, sécurité et de justice', *Revue Trimestrielle de Droit Européen*, [1997] 33(4), 813–881, at 873–874.

satisfactory solution' to the question of European Court jurisdiction was reached, a question which was also holding up their adoption of the Fraud Convention itself.[81]

On the other hand, the UK government led by John Major objected in principle to Court jurisdiction over Third Pillar affairs; what this principle was Ministers did not always like to elucidate, but on one occasion the then Home Secretary stated to Parliament that he feared the European Court would adopt an 'expansive jurisdiction' to Third Pillar Conventions.[82] The fear of the loss of member state control over interpretation or disputes concerning Conventions, control which the UK wanted to keep in the hands of Ministers, was therefore the dominant concern, *sotto voce* perhaps also a fear that the Court would take the protection of the individual too far, say in data protection matters. This fear of the Court has apparently not been fully overcome by the present UK government, which remains reluctant to embrace Court of Justice jurisdiction in Third Pillar affairs.[83]

In the end, pressure from other member states for a solution to the *impasse* concerning Court of Justice preliminary rulings jurisdiction forced the compromise of 'permissive jurisdiction by declaration' which we find in a protocol to the Europol Convention, for example.[84] A number of Convention protocols contain specific provisions on Court jurisdiction, thus making it necessary to look at each Convention instrument separately to work out the exact terms of jurisdiction. More recent Conventions, but not all, have themselves included provisions on Court jurisdiction. An example is the Customs Cooperation Convention. This contains a further limit to Court of Justice jurisdiction in Art. 26(8): 'The Court of Justice shall not have jurisdiction to check the validity or proportionality of operations carried out by competent law enforcement agencies under this Convention nor to rule on the exercise of responsibilities which devolve upon Member States for maintaining law and order and for safeguarding internal security.' While ruling out interference by the Court in general 'law and order matters' may be relatively uncontroversial, the exclusion of Court control over the exercise of competent authorities' powers under the Convention may defeat the purpose of giving the Court jurisdiction in the first place. It runs counter to the trend to confer an extended human rights jurisdiction on the Court and conflicts

---

[81] See statements made by these states and Germany and Austria on the adoption of the Council Act drawing up the First Protocol to the Fraud Convention (*OJ*, C313, 23 October 1996, 10).

[82] House of Lords Select Committee on the European Communities, Session 1995–96, 10th Report, *Europol*, HL paper 51, London, HMSO, evidence, 95.

[83] House of Lords Select Committee on the European Communities, Session 1997–98, 31st Report, Incorporating the Schengen *Acquis* into the European Union, HL paper 139, London, HMSO, 1998, 42.

[84] Europol Convention Protocol of 23 July 1996 on Court of Justice jurisdiction is contained in *OJ*, C299, 9 October 1996, 1–14; *cf* also Fraud Convention Protocol of 29 November 1996 on Court of Justice jurisdiction (*OJ*, C151, 20 May 1997, 1–14) and similar protocol of the same date relating to the Convention on the use of Information Technology for Customs purposes (ibid., 15–28).

with its recent jurisprudence in EU matters.[85] Of course, it potentially also narrows the scope for uniform interpretation. But the Court itself may frustrate these attempts to hamstring it by reinterpreting the supposed limits in a narrow way, for example by claiming that 'interpreting' powers is not the same as 'checking' them or by using the word 'operations' in a narrow way.[86]

The Treaty on European Union repeats this type of reservation in a general clause, Art. 35(5), the limits of which will also require to be tested. The Treaty-based jurisdiction of the Court will be further tied down by denying direct effect to the new type of legal measures envisaged: framework decisions. On the other hand, the Court is not prevented from using other tools it has developed in an EU context to increase the effectiveness of legal instruments, notably the interpretative obligation principle or that of state liability for breaches of EU law obligations.[87] For present purposes, it should be noted that the Amsterdam Treaty does not rule out the possibility of the provisions of Conventions taking direct effect.

A basis for the application of EU law principles of effectiveness to the Third Pillar might be found in Art. 61 of the EC Treaty, which apparently imposes a Community law obligation on member states within the Council to take measures under the Third Pillar that will, by preventing and combating crime, achieve a 'high level of security'.

As to the question of supremacy over conflicting national laws, in relation to the Brussels Convention, the Court of Justice has held:

> The principle of legal certainty and the aims pursued by the Convention in accordance with Art. 220 of the Treaty, on which it is based, require that the equality and uniformity of rights and obligations arising from the Convention for the Contracting States and the persons concerned must be ensured, regardless of the rules laid down in that regard in the laws of those states.[88]

Although the Third Pillar Conventions do not share this legal basis, they do or will serve a 'Community purpose' in terms of Art. 61 of the EC Treaty. Also, the basic decision to open the possibility of submitting questions regarding Conventions to the Court for preliminary rulings jurisdiction can be taken as a confirmation that those member states who have so declared favour uniform interpretation, similarly implying 'equality and uniformity of

---

[85] See Art. 6(2) read together with Art. 46(d) of the new Treaty on European Union provisions and Case C-265/95 *Commission v France* [1997] ECR I-6959.

[86] For example, with regard to the clause of the Customs Cooperation Convention concerning covert investigations (Art. 23), member states may request permission to conduct such investigations in other member states 'only where it would be extremely difficult to elucidate the facts without recourse to the proposed investigative measures'. Would such requests fall outside the power of review because they are connected to operational decisions?

[87] For discussion of these principles see S. Weatherill and P. Beaumont, *EC Law*, 2nd ed., Harmondsworth: Penguin, ch. 11.

[88] Case 288/82 *Ferdinand M.J.J. Duijnstee v Lodewijk Goderbauer* [1983] ECR 3663, at 3674–3675. (Case drawn to author's attention by Editor.)

rights'. Such equality requires supremacy, so a Brussels Convention-type approach to Third Pillar interpretation appears, in this respect, quite likely. This need not mean riding roughshod over member state sensitivities. It would not be legitimate for the Court to override references to action being taken in accordance with national law under certain Convention provisions. Thus, there would be limits to the extent to which the Court could use 'inventive jurisprudence' to overcome the exclusion clauses inserted in Conventions or in the Amsterdam Treaty concerning 'law and order' in the member states. The Court would most probably be circumspect about adopting interpretations of Conventions which departed radically from Convention text. In balancing member state prerogatives against the rights and interests of individuals, the Court will be bound to have regard to the Treaty aim of a 'high level of security', probably the main aim of cooperation under Pillar Three.

Without effective Court jurisdiction, the operation of Conventions is likely to be undermined.[89] References for preliminary rulings are an essential means of guaranteeing some measure of uniformity of application as well as interpretation. Important too in this respect will be the exercise of the Court's other heads of jurisdiction, particularly in disputes between member states, or between member states and the Commission.[90]

Finally, connected to Court of Justice jurisdiction is the question how implementation of Third Pillar instruments such as Conventions will be monitored. It will be interesting to see whether the Commission will begin to undertake its own monitoring of Third Pillar instruments given the new powers it will acquire after entry into force of the Amsterdam Treaty: joint right of initiative and especially right to invoke the jurisdiction of the European Court under Art. 35(7). Member state governments in the Council are likely to discourage such monitoring, as they are developing their own methods of peer review. The Action Plan to Combat Organized Crime does not, however, rule out involvement by the Commission in this 'mutual "peer-evaluation"'.[91] A Joint Action was adopted at the end of 1997 to set in place procedures for this evaluation in the context of the implementation of, *inter alia*, 'Union acts' having a bearing on the fight against organized crime; these

[89] The strongly held view of the House of Lords Select Committee on the European Communities, Session 1994–95, 10th Report, *op. cit.*, para. 109.

[90] Some of the pre-Amsterdam Conventions such as Europol, do not envisage any jurisdiction for the Court with regard to disputes between Commission and the member states and the question therefore arises whether this jurisdiction can nevertheless be exercised in relation to such Conventions under the revised terms of the Treaty on European Union. Referring to Art. 40(2) of the Europol Convention, which provides that disputes between member states concerning the interpretation or application of the Europol Convention will first be referred for a solution to the Council, all the member states except the UK declared that they would 'systematically submit' disputes which could not be settled in this way within six months to the European Court of Justice. But no mention is made of any Commission involvement (*OJ*, C316, 27 November 1995, 32). *Cf* the last sentence of Art. 35(7) of the revised Treaty on European Union provisions.

[91] Action Plan to combat Organized Crime, *op. cit.*, 11 (recommendation 15).

procedures, modelled on experience within the International Financial Task Force on Money Laundering, will involve the delegation of national experts to the General Secretariat of the Council.[92] The process will be driven by the Council but the Commission may be involved in some of the work of the expert teams. The Joint Action is in danger of trespassing on the responsibilities of the Commission to monitor implementation of EU law instruments such as the Money Laundering Directive. The reference in the preamble of the Joint Action to 'instruments adopted within the framework of the Union' is broad enough to encompass EU law instruments. It is no doubt for this reason that the Joint Action is declared to be without prejudice to EU powers. This still leaves plenty of room for inter-institutional turf battles.

V CONCLUSION: MARGINALIZATION OF CONVENTION LAW-MAKING POST-AMSTERDAM?

Amsterdam's new Third Pillar will focus on the development and improvement of methods of cooperation between national systems of law rather than the harmonization of systems of criminal justice; the continuing reference in the title to 'cooperation' reflects this. An important qualification must, however, be entered: Art. 31(e) of the new Treaty will allow the Council 'progressively' to adopt 'measures establishing minimum rules relating to the constituent elements of criminal acts and to penalties in the fields of organised crime, terrorism and drug trafficking.' Article 30 states that such approximation of laws will be undertaken 'so far as necessary'. This is a potentially very significant legal basis, not only in substantive terms.[93] It is also important from the point of view of legal method, because the new Third Pillar links approximation to the creation of a new legal instrument, the 'framework decision', which will be used for approximation of laws or adminstrative provisions. It is modelled on the Community Directive, as it will be binding on the member states with regard to the result but will leave them with the choice of method. Unlike the Directive, it will not be capable of having direct effect, so its terms may not be invoked by individuals before national courts. This restriction does not apply to Conventions, which might mean that preliminary rulings from national courts will initially concentrate on them.

The provision for the new legal instrument of framework decisions, and another new instrument, the 'decision', stated to be capable of use 'for any other purpose consistent with the objectives of the Title', marks what one might call a 'juridification' of the Third Pillar. Both new instruments, like the Convention, will be of binding legal effect, removing the doubt which hangs over the joint positions and joint actions of the Maastricht Treaty. The new

---

[92] Joint Action of 5 December 1997 adopted by the Council 'for evaluating the application and implementation at national level of international undertakings in the fight against organized crime', *OJ*, L344, 15 December 1997, 7–9.

[93] The theme of gradual approximation of laws is taken up by the Action Plan to combat organized crime, *op. cit.*, 12 (recommendation 17).

Third Pillar is, thus, of a more explicitly legal character than its predecessor. At least, there will be greater **potential** to pursue the Treaty objectives by legally binding methods. This would enhance legal certainty, a concept which has been endangered by a proliferation of Third Pillar resolutions and other non-legally binding means. The requirement for legal certainty in criminal law matters is particularly pressing.

The changing legal context of the Third Pillar possibly signals changes in the role of the Convention. It implicitly limits the use of the Convention in approximating national criminal laws, though Art. 31(e) does not encompass all areas of criminal law and in particular, beyond the mention of penalties, does not refer to procedures.[94] It is likely that the Commission, in particular, will formulate proposals for framework decisions in preference to Conventions, given the problems with adoption of the latter which have been referred to. Yet the Treaty has also sought to streamline procedures for adoption of Conventions. Member states may maintain that they offer more flexibility than other instruments and that they can be useful in supplementing Council of Europe measures. So Conventions will not necessarily be 'marginalized' as a means of developing legal policy. In any case, there will be a substantial body of Convention law in place before the Amsterdam Treaty is ratified.[95] How effective this body of law will be will probably dictate the future of Convention law-making. The first step to such effectiveness – apparently a big one for many member states – is ratification. Attention will then move to implementation, accompanied by monitoring, and, if necessary, judicial enforcement. Mechanisms are being put in place for these steps, but not the usual EU methods. As we have seen, there are several drawbacks of Convention law-making and a number of open questions about judicial control. In particular, the scope for uniform interpretation and application of Third Pillar Conventions may be too limited.

The method of law-making, of whatever instruments, under the revised Title VI provisions will remain of an executive character, prepared with more Commission input certainly but continuing to involve strong input by national officials and with outcomes determined by member state governments. National parliaments should gain increased opportunities to scrutinize draft proposals as a result of the new Amsterdam Treaty protocol and the European Parliament's status has been enhanced. So there will be a certain limited democratization of the Third Pillar, which has been widely criticized

---

[94] Recent Third Pillar practice has tended to stress the use of the Joint Action as an instrument for approximating laws: see Joint Action of 24 February 1997 adopted by the Council on the basis of Art. K.3 of the Treaty on European Union concerning action to combat trafficking in human beings and sexual exploitation of children (*OJ*, L63, 4 March 1997, 2–6) and Joint Action of 17 December 1996 adopted by the Council on the basis of Art. K.3 of the Treaty on European Union concerning the approximation of the laws and practices of the member states of the European Union to combat drug addiction and to prevent and combat illegal drug trafficking (*OJ*, L342, 31 December 1996, 6–8).

[95] The Home Office counted twenty-five 'Convention (and related)' instruments (presumably including protocols) in its evidence to the House of Lords Select Committee on the European Communities, Session 1997–98, 15th Report, *op. cit.*, evidence, 15.

for its secretive and highly bureaucratic character. In essence, however, member states have taken matters in their own hands where criminal justice co-operation in the European Union is concerned. It is now basically up to them to make this system of intergovernmental law-making effective. For once, 'Brussels' will be able to avoid the blame if things go wrong.

12

THE EUROPEAN UNION'S ROLE IN INTERNATIONAL COMMERCIAL DIPLOMACY

*Stephen Woolcock**

I INTRODUCTION

There is an opportunity for the European Union to play a leading role in international commercial diplomacy by virtue of its economic importance. Indeed, it can be argued that the international trading system needs the active involvement of the EU to at least share leadership with other major economies, such as the United States and Japan. The need arises from the fact that the United States is no longer able or willing to provide, by itself, the leadership required to steer the GATT/WTO system into the next millennium.[1] For the past decade the EU has progressively grown in stature as an actor in international commercial diplomacy, casting off what had been a reactive and often disunited image. There are clear indications that the EU has become more outward looking, more multilateral and more proactive in international commercial diplomacy. But it is not certain that this trend towards a more liberal, multilaterally oriented commercial policy will endure. Whether it does or not will depend to a large extent on whether current trends are based on genuinely 'common' policies or simply a transitory phase in which a more liberal, proactive policy has prevailed in the aggregation of a series of still fundamentally separate national policies.

This chapter will argue that the EU has on balance moved markedly towards a more multilateralist, liberal commercial policy position. However,

---

* Stephen Woolcock is Lecturer in International Relations at the London School of Economics. He studied at the Europa Institute from 1976–78 (then the Centre for European Governmental Studies) before studying, researching and working in the field of European and international trade and industrial policy.
[1] The WTO is the institutional setting in which GATT rules, as well as rules on trade in services GATS and intellectual property rights are negotiated and enforced. The term GATT/ WTO system is therefore intended to include both the institution and the system of rules.

it points to a number of important internal tensions, which can easily damage the credibility of the EU as an actor in commercial policy. These tensions will have to be carefully managed if the EU is to share in the leadership of the international trading system.

The chapter first briefly outlines some of the features of the current international trade system, focusing on the pressures created by globalization and the decline in the US leadership role. It should be made clear from the start that investment as well as a range of regulatory issues are included in the definition of 'commercial diplomacy' or the 'world trading system' used here. The chapter then discusses trends in EU policy making the case that the EU has moved towards a more liberal position. It then considers the potential negotiating leverage of the EU stemming from its economic importance and other factors, before discussing EU decision making on commercial policy and the internal tensions that could damage its credibility as an actor in commercial diplomacy.[2] For reasons of space there is no discussion of the use of commercial policy instruments in the pursuit of foreign policy in this chapter. The link between foreign policy and commercial policy has, however, become closer in the post Cold-War period and poses an additional challenge for EU policy makers. Nor does the chapter discuss possible reforms of decision making.[3]

II FEATURES OF INTERNATIONAL COMMERCIAL DIPLOMACY

Widening versus deepening

A quite helpful way of characterizing the challenges facing the multilateral system is to use the concept of widening versus deepening used in European integration. In the case of the GATT/WTO system one is not concerned with the same degree of policy integration as in Europe, but as numerous authors have pointed out, increased international economic interdependence has meant that negotiations are now focused on deep integration. This has been defined in the GATT/WTO context as negotiations on behind the border issues, i.e. non-tariff barrier issues including national regulatory policies (Lawrence, 1995).

In the fifty years since the formation of the GATT in 1948 there has been a progressive 'deepening' of the commercial policy agenda. The initial rounds of the GATT were almost exclusively concerned with tariffs. By the late

---

[2] The EU practice is to refer to commercial policy. This is more suitable than trade policy as the current international policy agenda includes trade, investment and national (or regional) regulatory policies. There is no equivalent term at the international level, although the WTO/GATT (the multilateral trading system) includes elements of investment and regulatory policies. In this chapter reference will be made to international commercial diplomacy/or policy which includes conventional trade (i.e. border measures), investment, and regulatory issues.

[3] For a discussion of possible reforms see Woolcock, 1996 and Johnson, 1998.

1950s the agenda also included some of the more obvious non-tariff barriers, such as subsidies and anti-dumping policies. It is not therefore surprising that the definition of commercial policy in Art. 113 of the Treaty of Rome was limited to tariffs and non-tariff barrier issues such as subsidies and anti-dumping. By the time of the Kennedy Round of the GATT (1964–67) efforts, largely unsuccessful, were undertaken to strengthen the GATT rules on non-tariff barrier issues as well as reintegrate agriculture following the decision, taken by the US and European governments, to waive GATT rules for this sector in 1952. By the early 1970s there was a growing perception that progress in removing tariff barriers meant that non-tariff barriers had become more important (Baldwin, 1970). The Tokyo Round (1973–79) therefore included substantive negotiations on a number of qualified most favoured nation (MFN) status codes covering non-tariff barriers such as subsidies and countervailing duties, government procurement and the regulatory barriers in the form of technical barriers to trade. These were qualified MFN codes because only those Contracting Parties that were willing to sign them benefited from the enhanced market access opportunities they brought with them.[4]

The beginning of the 1980s saw pressure, from the United States, to deepen the GATT agenda to include negotiations on services, investment and high technology products. Although no multilateral negotiations were started on these new issues until 1986, work on them was undertaken in other fora, such as the OECD. The new issues included in the Uruguay Round negotiations in 1986 were trade in services, trade related investment measures (TRIMs) and trade related intellectual property rights (TRIPs). The trade related qualification was a result of developing country opposition to including any of these new issues. The inclusion of these issues took the GATT rules well beyond border measures and into national (and regional) regulatory policies.

The Uruguay Round was after many delays and false dawns, finally completed in 1994.[5] As part of the final agreement, it was decided to establish a World Trade Organization, as an international organization for trade equivalent to the IMF and World Bank. Equally important was the Understanding on Dispute Settlement (UDS), which significantly strengthened the enforcement mechanism of GATT/WTO system. These institutional measures along with the inclusion of new issues and the strengthened multilateral rules on other non-tariff and regulatory issues, constituted a significant deepening of the GATT/WTO system. But the Uruguay Round was the response to the commercial policy agenda of the 1980s. By the time it was concluded in 1994, other issues had already been pushed onto the agenda.

These issues of the 1990s have been called the 'trade ands' indicating the pressure to take account of other policy objectives in the 'trade' rules of the GATT/WTO. To put it another way increased economic interdependence

---

[4] For detail on the evolution of the GATT see Hoekman and Kosteki, 1996.
[5] See Coombe, 195 for a general treatment of the Uruguay Round.

has created pressure for an integration of trade policy with other policy areas. The policy areas concerned included: investment, which is intrinsically linked to trade and trade policy; (international) competition policy which is important because the relevant market for many sectors is now global and some 60 per cent of foreign direct investment takes the form of international mergers and acquisitions; environmental protection which environmental groups see as being undermined by narrow interpretations of trade principles in the WTO; and labour standards because organized labour does not see why the WTO should be used to enforce international standards for the protection of intellectual property rights but not protect core labour standards.[6]

The first ministerial meeting of the WTO in Singapore in December 1996 considered the calls for such a further deepening of the GATT/WTO system. It agreed to continue the work of the Committee on Trade and Environment (CTE), which had been set up in 1994 but which had produced no agreement by 1996. The meeting also established two new working groups on investment, which was also the subject of the plurilateral negotiations in the OECD, and competition. Developing countries with the backing of international business and some developed governments, such as the UK, resisted pressure to include core labour standards in the WTO agenda and kicked it back into the ILO, where the issue has been for the past 75 years.

The GATT/WTO system has also been under constant pressure to widen. The initial GATT was signed by 23 Contracting Parties. A progressive increase in membership, starting with countries like Germany (1951) and Japan (1955) and continuing with a large number of newly established independent states, characterized the first three decades of the GATT. More recently the end of east–west ideological confrontation and the acceptance of a liberal paradigm for the world by all but a few countries, has also meant that countries in transition from central planning have also joined or are seeking accession to the WTO. By 1999 there were 135 members of the WTO with 34 countries, including Russia, China and Saudi Arabia currently in accession negotiations. The GATT has therefore grown from a narrow 'capitalist club' dominated by the United States and is on the verge of becoming a truly global system of rules governing international trade and investment.

The deepening and widening of the GATT/WTO system constitutes a significant success and one that has contributed considerably to economic growth over the past fifty years. Trade and more recently investment has consistently grown more rapidly than output. Foreign direct investment has grown considerably faster than output. This increase in trade and investment has contributed to economic growth and prosperity, although one might debate whether the increase in wealth could not have been more evenly spread between countries. The success of the GATT/WTO brings with it considerable challenges. First and foremost, should the focus of the next

[6] For a critical treatment of these new issues see Bhagwati and Hudec, 1996.

196

phase of negotiations be on widening, to establish the WTO as a single global trading regime. Such an objective has important strategic, as well as economic and commercial, importance. But should widening come at the cost of accepting the lowest common denominator when it comes to the more sensitive issues, especially those touching upon national regulatory or even political sovereignty? On the other hand, should the focus be on deepening in order to ensure that the GATT/WTO keeps pace with the globalization of markets and thus retains its relevance. If widening comes at the price of deepening, the GATT/WTO system will cover trade and non-tariffs issues but may not keep up with the development in services, electronic commerce and investment. The vacuum left is then likely to be filled by regional or bilateral agreements as firms and governments seek to ensure some stable legal framework for trade and investment. Such regional and bilateral approaches will then in time undermine the multilateral order. In this respect the history of international rules on investment is salutary. In the vacuum left by the absence of effective international rules governing investment, more than 900 bilateral investment treaties have been concluded, many in the last few years.

The decline of US leadership

The second feature of the international trading system is the decline in the ability and willingness of the United States to provide leadership for the multilateral trading system. Unlike the floating of the US dollar in 1973 and the closure of the gold window which linked the dollar to the value of gold, the US move away from (hegemonic) leadership of the trading system has been less dramatic. The process has arguably been going on ever since the GATT was established, but there were clear signs in the early 1970s that the US, then suffering its first post-war trade deficit, was qualifying its support for multilateralism. In the 1973 Trade Act the US Congress gave the administration powers to act against the 'unfair' trade practices of others. During the 1980s, under the added pressure of massive trade deficits created by the imbalance in US fiscal policies, the US Congress acted again. This time in a more aggressive fashion in seeking not simply to defend US industries from unfair subsidies or industrial targeting, but to change the national regulatory policies of other countries. The 1988 Omnibus Trade and Competitiveness Act also reduced Presidential discretion, which Congress believed had been mainly used to block actions against foreign unfair trade practices. The point here is not that the US ceased to be a major economic and commercial power, it did not. What occurred was a shift away from multilateral means of resolving trade and other commercial disputes, towards unilateral or bilateral means.

US support for multilateralism was further qualified by the move, also in the 1980s, to embrace the idea of regional free trade agreements. In the early post-war years when the US was leading in establishing the open multilateral system, it was adamantly opposed to any form of preferential agreement. The move to regional agreements was taken in the 1980s, with the 1983 US–Israel free trade agreement. This was followed by the negotiation of the Canada–US Free Trade Agreement (CUSFTA) between 1986 and 1988 and by the effective extension of the CUSFTA to include Mexico in the North America Free Trade Agreement (NAFTA) which was ratified in 1993. By 1993 the US had also given a major push to the idea of a Free Trade Agreement for the Americas (FTAA) was well as liberal trade throughout the Asia Pacific region through APEC (Asia Pacific Economic Cooperation).

Compared to the multilateralist drive of the US in the 1950s, US commercial/trade policy is today therefore supported by three main pillars, unilateral, regional and multilateral. When multilateral negotiations appear to be too slow the US has pressed for plurilateral agreements, such as in the case of the 'Multilateral Investment Agreement' (MAI). US leadership has also been qualified in the sense that US commercial policy is now shaped by short-term results rather than longer term systemic objectives. The US is competing in the multilateral system rather than providing systemic leadership (Krueger, 1998). The US interests in developing and preserving the multilateral system come second to US sectoral interests. For example, if multilateral rules do not offer sufficient market opening for US companies, the US will seek to use the leverage it has by virtue of its large domestic market in bilateral or unilateral negotiations. This was, for example, the case in 1994 and 1995 in the financial services sector.

The US position on a rules-based multilateral system is also influenced by foreign policy considerations. Economic sanctions are not a new phenomenon by any means, but in recent years the US, at both federal and notably at state government level, has made increased use of them. The end of the Cold War left the US as a superpower in terms of its military and political authority. Consequently, the US is if anything under greater pressure to respond to acts of aggression, abuses of human rights or to perceived challenges to its national security. This has led to the use of commercial sanctions against Iraq, Miranma (by state government), Cuba, Iran, Libya, etc. and on occasions brought the US into conflict with WTO rules when sanctions have not had UN backing. The EU has generally made much less use of sanctions.[7]

For the reasons set out above the GATT/WTO system needs effective leadership in order to strike the right balance between widening and deepening. This leadership cannot be expected to come from the US alone. As the most powerful economic actor in the international commercial system the EU should, indeed must at least share in leadership. Before discussing whether the EU is capable of fulfilling a leadership role, the chapter first discusses whether the EU has the economic power to lead.

---

[7] Sanctions policy is decided upon by the member states under Common Foreign and Security Policy (CFSP). Once agreement has been reached (by unanimity) on common action under CFPS the sanctions may be implemented under commercial policy using qualified majority voting.

III   TRENDS IN EUROPEAN COMMERCIAL POLICY

Assessing whether the EU is pursuing 'liberal' or 'protectionist' policies requires a balanced assessment of policy in all sectors over a period of years. Interpretations will clearly differ depending on the interests and starting point of those making assessments. The case here is that the EU, along with many other actors in the international economy, has moved towards more liberal policies during the 1980s.[8] In the case of the EU internal liberalization led the way towards international liberalization. Concern about the fragmentation of the European market and its impact on the ability of the EU to compete internationally provided impetus for the Single Market initiative in the mid 1980s. But should the EU extend this internal liberalization to other countries or ask for strict reciprocal market access from its trading partners for the opening the European market resulting from the SEM?

The critical juncture in this debate came towards the end of the 1980s when the debate on 'fortress Europe' was at its peak. This debate was, by and large, resolved in favour of liberal interpretations of reciprocal market access. The EU did not, for example, apply reciprocity provisions in key service sectors, such as financial services. Most areas of the internal market contained no reciprocity measures, so that benefits from efforts to open non-tariff barriers within the EU were extended on an MFN basis to other countries. Trade diversion that could have resulted from the deepening and widening of European integration was, as in the past, compensated by multilateral liberalization within the Uruguay Round of trade negotiations (The Single Market Review, 1997). An indication of the EU's shift to accept multilateral discipline can be found in the endorsement of strengthened WTO dispute settlement procedures and the establishment of the WTO itself. Before the 1980s the majority of EU member states had favoured negotiated over adjudicated settlement of trade disputes. In the Uruguay Round the EU endorsed a significant move towards adjudication. This reflected the wider acceptance of European Court of Justice adjudication of disputes within Europe and a desire to discipline US unilateralism.

Examples of the EU becoming more proactive in commercial policy can be found in the EU's policy in sectoral negotiations on financial services in the GATS in which the Commission led efforts to reach agreement when the US withdrew from negotiations in 1995. The EU has also proposed multilateral, as opposed to unilateral or plurilateral solutions to new commercial issues, such as trade and the environment, investment and competition. Contrary to the 1970s and 1980s, when the US was pressing for new multilateral negotiations, it is the EU that has first called for a new comprehensive round of multilateral negotiations; the millennium round.

This more proactive, multilateral approach goes hand in hand with continued bilateral and unilateral policies, as in the case of the US. For example, the EU still retains commercial policy instruments such as anti-dumping

[8] See Johnson, 1998.

duties. The 1994 revision of the EU's 'fair trade' instrument also includes a more proactive approach to market opening.[9] This instrument is modelled on the US 'fair trade' powers in s. 301 of the US Trade Act, but even here there is a commitment first to exhaust all multilateral options before resorting to unilateral action.

The EU has been proactive in regional agreements concluding association agreements with most central and east European countries as well as negotiating with Mercosur (Brazil, Argentina, Uruguay and Paraguay) and South Africa. The EU also initiated bilateral negotiations with the US on strengthened commercial relations in 1994 and again in 1998. There is a tension between such regional approaches and the desire to promote multilateralism. This tension exists within the European Commission itself.[10] With those responsible for multilateral trade and investment policies stressing the need for the EU to ensure that regional agreements are consistent with GATT Art. XXIV and GATS Art. V, and those responsible for relations with the regions concerned wishing to promote closer relations. Considerable effort has gone into making the EU preferential trade agreements, such as Lomé, consistent with the GATT rules. Great care has also been taken to ensure that the EU proposals on closer EU–US commercial relations are also consistent with, at least the spirit of the GATT/WTO.[11]

In some sectors the EU like other major trading entities retains protectionist policies. In agriculture it only reluctantly agreed to accept GATT discipline during the Uruguay Round. In textiles and clothing it has fought a rearguard action against liberalization of quotas in the shape of the Multi-Fibre Arrangement. But in 13 of the 15 negotiating groups the EU was not the laggard and was often helping to strengthen the multilateral rules.[12]

The main point is not that the EU has adopted *laissez faire* policies but that it has shifted towards a more liberal, multilateralist line. Whether this will endure remains to be seen. Much will depend on whether the current policy is a genuine common policy or simply the result of the internal balance of power within the EU resulting in a policy aggregation that favours liberal policies.[13] There is a reasonably stable blocking minority that would prevent overt protectionist policies. But there is equally a blocking minority that can check liberalizing initiatives.[14] Common EU commercial policies are more likely if a number of conditions to be satisfied. First, do the member

---

[9] The so called Trade Barriers Regulation Council Regulation (EC) 3286/94.
[10] Mortensen Jens 'The institutional challenges and paradoxes of EU governance in external trade: coping with the post-hegemonic trading system and the global economy' in A. Cafruny and P. Peters (eds) *The Union and the World*, 1998.
[11] See Statement on The Transatlantic Economic Partnership (TEP) May 1998.
[12] See Hodges and Woolcock, 1996.
[13] There is a reasonably stable blocking minority that would prevent overt protectionist policies. But there is equally a blocking minority that can check liberalizing initiatives.
[14] Votes are seldom if every taken on commercial policy issues and there is a clear practice of seeking consensus, but the chair of the 113 Committee will be guided by whether those member states speaking for or against a particular policy would have a qualified majority (see Johnson, 1998).

states share a common (liberal) ideology, or do existing common positions, mask differences in the underlying predisposition of national policies, such as, for example, between British liberalism and French mercantilism?[15] Secondly, do the member states of the EU have sufficiently similar economic and industrial structures to allow the common commercial policies to endure? Third, have EU wide policy communities developed across the EU to replace the previously national policy making processes of the past. In short has there been a convergence or approximation of commercial policy based on long-term common interests.

IV THE ECONOMIC AND COMMERCIAL POWER OF THE EU

The European Union accounts for more than 20 per cent of world merchandise trade, about 30 per cent of services trade and much more if one includes intra-European trade. As important, however, is the EU's share of outward foreign direct investment flows, which stood at about 40 per cent in 1997. As a trading and investing entity therefore the EU is larger than the US and any other actor. The importance of the EU has also grown with the progressive deepening of European integration, which has resulted in the EU having competence over more areas of policy and negotiating 'with a single voice' in more areas of commercial diplomacy. A single unified market in Europe gives the EU greater leverage in international commercial diplomacy than when competence is shared between the member states and EU and there is no unified market. The 1992 programme has therefore enhanced the EU's commercial power. Enlargement of the EU has also increased its leverage. But more members also complicates the process of decision making further by adding to the heterogeneity.

New members of the EU adopt the *acquis communautaire* and thus fall into line with all established EU positions on commercial policy. But the influence of the *acquis* goes beyond existing member states. Applicant states, such as Poland, Hungary, the Czech Republic, Estonia, Slovenia and Cyprus, as well as countries that have association agreements with the EU (most of central and eastern Europe and the Mediterranean) or form a customs union with the EU (Turkey) are more or less obliged to adopt the *acquis* if they are to gain effective access to the Single European Market. This means that the EU shapes the policy of other WTO members, especially in the smaller neighbouring countries.

The EU also has an influence on the multilateral trading system by providing a model for how to accommodate national policy differences whilst removing barriers to market access. As noted above the international commercial agenda has moved progressively into areas of national regulatory policy. These are also the barriers to market access that the EU has addressed in seeking to establish a single market. The best example, of how lessons

---

[15] For a discussion of the roles of the national governments in policy making see Hayes, 1993.

from European integration have influenced the international commercial agenda is in the use of mutual recognition. Developed in the EU in order to find an alternative to harmonization as a means of overcoming national technical barriers to trade, mutual recognition has been subsequently applied in different forms in other regional agreements and encouraged in the WTO agreement on technical barriers to trade. EU experience in opening services markets has also provided a model for multilateral rule making. European integration provides examples of the successful integration of trade and environment policy and trade and competition policy. It is unlikely, of course, that the EU approach will be fully applicable at the WTO level because of the implications for sovereignty, but the more the GATT/WTO rules move behind the border the more the EU will have relevance as a model.

Finally the introduction of a single currency, the Euro, from 1999 will further enhance the EU's economic leverage and influence. Although the Euro is unlikely to supplant the US dollar as the main international reserve currency, at least for some time (Henning, 1997) a single voice in international monetary relations will be important, because of the close links between international trade and monetary relations. The EU therefore has the economic power to enable it to provide leadership in international commercial diplomacy, the question to which we now turn is whether the EU decision making processes are up to the challenge.

V DECISION MAKING PROCESSES

The EU has been criticized from a number of quarters for its commercial policy, for being unable to negotiate without internal agreement and incapable of negotiating with one, because the mandate is so constraining. Such criticism has come from the EU's trading partners and in particular the US and has been largely focused on the EU's position on agriculture. These views sometimes confuse an inability to negotiate with not adopting positions the US wants. EU commercial policy has also been criticized by liberal economists for its protection of agriculture and use of administrative protection in the form of anti-dumping duties. This criticism has also been echoed by consumers and some industries and governments within the EU. There will inevitably be differing views on EU commercial policy and a thorough analysis goes beyond the scope of this chapter. Work on the Uruguay Round suggests, however, that although there is something in the criticisms noted above the EU has, in general, performed as well as most of its trading partners in developing and articulating common positions (Hodges and Woolcock, 1996; also Johnson, 1998). The EU's policy making processes have worked remarkably well given the diversity of interests within the EU, even if, inevitably, the policies it has produced have not been to everyone's liking.

The EU decision making process is, however, coming under increasing strain as a result of the growth of the commercial policy agenda or the deepening of the multilateral system. This strain is creating tensions in EU decision making on issues of competence (EU verses national), control (who controls negotiations, the Commission or the member states through the various Councils and council committees and working groups) and a growing tension between efficiency and accountability in decision making.

VI COMPETENCE

Article 113 of the Treaty (now renumbered with the Amsterdam Treaty to Art. 133) established the exclusive competence of the European Community (EC) for common commercial policy. But Art. 113 contained no comprehensive definition of commercial policy. At the time the Treaty of Rome was drafted commercial policy, as noted above, consisted primarily of tariff negotiations with some efforts to devise rules for anti-dumping, subsidies and countervailing duties. As the international commercial diplomacy agenda has expanded, so new issues have been added to the scope of the EU's commercial policy. This has created tensions at every stage between EU and national competence, with the Commission arguing that the EU should have competence in order to facilitate a single negotiating position, and the member states seeking to limit loss of national sovereignty and competence.

To date the EU has dealt with this competence issue in a pragmatic fashion. When new issues have been added to the commercial diplomacy agenda, the member states have let the Commission be the sole negotiator in order to benefit from the added leverage a single voice brings. But they have done so without prejudice to the issue of legal competence. In the Tokyo Round there were differences over competence on public procurement, subsidies and technical barriers to trade. At the conclusion of the negotiations a political agreement was reached between the Council and Commission on competence questions, which facilitated ratification of some agreements as mixed agreements. In the Uruguay Round the member states again gave the Commission the green light to negotiate on services and intellectual property over which there was equally a different view on competence. At the conclusion of the Uruguay round the Council favoured another political arrangement between the Commission and Council, but the Commission with some member state backing sought a European Court of Justice ruling on the issue. The ECJ's decision (1/94) was a disappointment for the Commission in the sense that it found most services and intellectual property to be of mixed or national competence. This was a disappointment because the ECJ had in previous decisions (*AETR* 22/77 and *Rhine Navigation* 1/76) had supported the Commission's expansive definition of EC competence. The ECJ ruling may also complicate future pragmatic solutions to the issue of competence.

Differences over competence have created much legal debate, but the impact of tensions have, to date, created no insurmountable problems. In negotiations on services and intellectual property in the Uruguay Round the

EU agreed on coherent negotiating objectives and was able to pursue these effectively. In July 1995 the European Commission was even able to be proactive in building an international coalition to keep sector liberalization of financial services on track. All this was done in areas of disputed competence. The policy areas in which the EU had difficulties in the Uruguay Round, namely textiles and clothing at the mid term stage in November 1988 and agriculture at all times, were areas in which EC competence has existed for many years.

In the 1996 Intergovernmental Conference (as in the previous IGC) the Commission pressed hard for all services and intellectual property to be added to EC competence, but this was rejected by member states. Tensions over competence will therefore continue and will be present in EU decision making on the new commercial agenda, items such as investment and labour standards. In the case of the former, negotiations are proceeding in the OECD, where national governments speak and the Commission has difficulty in establishing its authority. In the case of labour standards, tensions over the EC's competence in international negotiations will probably continue despite Britain's signing of the Social Chapter of the Maastricht Treaty. There will also be tensions over the representation of the EU in the WTO. For example, the enhanced dispute settlement procedures of the WTO provide for what is called 'cross retaliation'. Cross retaliation means that failure to comply with GATT/WTO rules in one area, such as inadequate national laws on the protection of intellectual property rights, can ultimately lead to retaliation in other sectors, such as by denying the country concerned benefits in the field of trade in goods. If the EU is involved in such a case, non-compliance by a member state in IPR, which is national competence, could result in retaliation in goods, which is EC competence.

To sum up on the competence question. There has been more or less continuous tension between the EC and member states over the scope of EU competence in commercial policy. The continued deepening of the GATT/WTO rules will ensure that this tension continues. But on past experience a pragmatic approach should enable tensions in this area to be managed. The Amsterdam Treaty amendments provide the legal means of pursuing such a pragmatic approach. The new para. 5 to Art. N allows for EC competence to be extended to services, intellectual property or 'other agreement' if the Council so agrees by unanimity after consultation with the European Parliament. Competence is therefore likely only to be a real stumbling block when policy differences lead member states to dig in their heels.

VII   CONTROL

The question of who controls EU negotiating strategy or policy has caused serious difficulties in the past and is likely to do so in the future. Treaty provisions and established practice give the Commission the right of initiative

in areas of EC competence. Thus the Commission makes proposals on negotiations and policy positions. These are then discussed in the 133 Committee
or COREPER and finally adopted by the General Affairs Council. The Council
decision, formally on a qualified majority, authorizes the Commission to
negotiate in consultation with the 133 Committee, a Council committee
chaired by the Council Presidency. This authorization is sometimes called a
mandate. Article 133 also provides for the Council to issue directives at any
time to the Commission on the substance of negotiations. In other words the
Commission is the sole negotiator, but the member states have plenty of
opportunity to intervene in negotiations as they progress. There is also scope
for differing interpretations of mandates. This has led to tensions over negotiating tactics, and differences between Commission and Council have emerged
at critical times inflicting considerable damage on the credibility of the EU's
negotiating position.[16]

A second issue which affects relations between the Commission and Council
is the *de facto* practice of only adopting agreements by consensus. The Treaty
provides for a qualified majority vote on the adoption of commercial agreements under Art. 133. But in practice the Council has felt obliged to seek
consensus on all major commercial policy issues. The expectation that consensus will be required, clearly has an impact upon the EU's negotiating
position, since the Commission must ensure that all member states are in
agreement with any position. If the Council applied the Treaty and voted by
qualified majority on the adoption of commercial agreements, there would be
more flexibility in negotiations. For example, during the Uruguay Round the
Commission, with the backing of a qualified majority of member states negotiated the so called Blair House agreement with the US on the inclusion of
agriculture in GATT disciplines. This agreement would have formed the key
element in conclusion of the Uruguay Round at the end of 1992. France
rejected the Blair House agreement and insisted on further modifications
which meant that a further eighteen months were needed before the round
could be concluded. Agreement could only be finally reached when both the
Belgian Presidency of the Council and the Commission accepted that the
results of the round would only be adopted by unanimity (Devuyst, 1995).

Tensions over the control of EU commercial policy have therefore created
real difficulties and undermined the EU's negotiating credibility at critical
moments. Such tensions can only increase with increased membership of
the EU. Some suggestions have been made to ease the management of
such tensions. For example, various member states have suggested that the

---

[16] An example of such a conflict over negotiating tactics is the EU's position in the critical
agricultural negotiations at the Ministerial Meeting of the GATT in 1990 which was due to
complete the Uruguay Round. The Commission, seeking to break a deadlock in negotiations
engaged in informal talks with its leading negotiating partners. In the course of these talks the
Commission discussed EU concessions which went beyond the restricting mandate laid down
by EU agricultural ministers. When national ministers learnt of the move they called the
Commission to task, denounced any such concession and thus undermined the credibility of
the EU's negotiating position.

Presidency of the Council should be present in the room when the Commission negotiates in order to ensure that the Council is involved in any negotiating stance the Commission adopts during meetings. The EU's position is, of course, agreed before negotiations. But the Commission has opposed this reduction in its power and argued that it would result in the removal of any negotiating flexibility for the Commission and thus the EU. An alternative approach would be for the Council to desist from intervening in negotiations and give the Commission scope to negotiate. The Council still retain ultimate authority to accept or reject the outcome, but the Commission would have scope to negotiate a package. This approach is rejected by the Council, because it would reduce the ability of the Council and individual member states to shape negotiations. In the absence of any reform, the only means of avoiding damaging conflicts between Commission and Council is for continuous efforts by both to ensure that communication is effective.

VIII   EFFICIENCY VERSUS ACCOUNTABILITY

If, as argued above, the EU has been relatively efficient in its commercial policy making, despite the difficulties reaching a common position among the sometimes diverging interests of fifteen member states, this has come at the price of democratic accountability. Decision making in EU commercial policy is predominantly technocratic in nature. EU commercial policy is steered by a technocratic core comprising the officials in DGI and national trade officials. The General Affairs Council provides nominal political and democratic legitimacy to the process, but given the technical nature of commercial policy and the wider interests of foreign ministers, it is not surprising that the full General Affairs Council seldom debates detailed technical issues. To put it more graphically Foreign Ministers are, rightly, more concerned with developments in Bosnia then on the permissible level of BST (hormones) in beef and whether science can be used to determine this level. The latter is more often than not the substance of commercial policy, and is therefore inevitably dealt with by officials rather than politicians.

The concept of a democratic deficit in EU decision making is well known and some efforts have been undertaken to address the problem. In the area of commercial policy difficulties are accentuated by the technical nature of many of the negotiations. National ministers reporting back to national legislatures tend to limit their comments to the overriding objectives of policy, but in so doing effective scrutiny of the negotiations is lost. National parliaments also have difficulties following the detail of negotiations and the fact that negotiations take place at two steps removed from national parliamentary control (one in Brussels and the second in Geneva) means national politicians do not believe they can influence the outcome of negotiations. The end result is that national legislatures tend not to undertake any effective scrutiny of EU commercial policy. For example, the House of Commons, which has made more of the need for democratic control of EU policy making than many other national parliaments, provides no systematic scrutiny of EU commercial policy. Plenary debates in national parliaments are generally at a high level of generalization and final endorsement of major trade agreements such as the Uruguay Round sometimes occurs without a vote. The only time detailed points are made are when a significantly powerful interest group takes the effort to brief a number of relevant MPs, i.e. MPs from constituencies affected by potential increased import competition.

At a European level the European Parliament does its best to provide some scrutiny of EU commercial policy, but is hindered by the simple fact that it has only very limited powers. The Parliament must give its assent to bilateral agreements under Art. 238, such as between the EU and South Africa or the Europe Agreements, but it has no power under Art. 113, the main multilateral instrument of the EU. Nor does the European Parliament have a say in changes to EU commercial instruments such as anti-dumping measures. The Council and Commission have reached informal agreements with the EP on consultation, but the EP's views are often not sought until the Commission has reached a deal with the EU's trading partners and it has been endorsed by the 133 Committee if not the Council.[17] At this stage the chances of the EP having any impact on the substance of the agreement is close to zero. The assent of the EP is required when a commercial policy agreement has budgetary implications, when there are institutional implications for the EU and when policy areas are concerned in which the EP has codecision rights. As codecision making is increasing this suggests that the EP may have to give its assent to more international commercial agreements.

In addition to accountability via public representative bodies such as the national and European Parliaments, accountability and legitimacy can be achieved through contacts with representative interest groups, such as producer groups, environmental and consumer non-governmental organizations (NGOs), trade unions and other such organizations. Unlike the US, which has a specific formal system of advisory committees including NGOs for commercial policy making, this is not the case in Europe. The Economic and Social Committee is consulted on important policy initiatives by the Commission and feeds its opinion, along with that of the European Parliament, into the policy debate. But consultation by the Commission with the ESC is intermittent. The Commission has consultations with bodies such as UNICE, the Union of European Confederations of Industry and Employers organizations as well as sector organizations and individual companies. The effectiveness

---

[17] The Luns-Westerterp Procedures were developed for association agreements (Luns) in 1964 and international commercial agreements (Westerterp) in 1973. These provide for the Council and Commission to provide information to the relevant committees of the European Parliament on the content of an agreement and for a debate to be held in The European Parliament before the negotiations begin. The Council is also to provide information to the relevant EP committees after an agreement is signed but before it is concluded. During the Uruguay Round the Commissioner with responsibility for commercial policy, Sir Leon Brittan, made special efforts to inform the European Parliament of developments in commercial policy.

and intensity of these consultations will depend on the resources deployed by the business or other NGO interests and the inclination of the Commission officials. Such representation is not always transparent, although the Commission does hold hearings from time to time on commercial policy topics. National interests still lobby their national governments, but the trade off between interests or the balancing of one issue against another, which is carried out at the European level is not subject to any close scrutiny. Active NGOs such as environmental NGOs see the Art. 133 Committee as closed and undemocratic. National and Commission trade officials resist the 'politicization' of EU commercial policy.

To sum up on efficiency versus accountability, the EU policy process may have been relatively efficient to date, but has not been especially open. There is also no scrutiny of decision making outside the nominal structures of accountability through the Council, which for reasons given above, is less than effective. As the GATT/WTO agenda deepens and intrudes more and more into 'domestic' policy making, the number of interested parties expands. For example, linking trade and environment means that the environmental policy communities in the EU will have an active interest in trade policy in order to ensure that their policy preferences are not undermined by EU commercial diplomacy. It is unlikely that the *status quo* in decision making will be able to withstand pressure for greater accountability. On the other hand the extension of scrutiny or inclusion of more interests in decision making could make EU policy less effective. Given the trends in international commercial diplomacy this tension between efficiency and accountability can be expected to increase.

IX CONCLUSION

The EU has an opportunity to play more of a leading role in international commercial diplomacy thanks to its economic and commercial power. Indeed, the multilateral system needs the EU to share in leading the GATT/WTO into the next millennium. The EU, and especially the European Commission, has shown that it has the aspiration to provide this leadership, but its capacity to do so depends on its ability to manage or at least contain a number of internal tensions.[18]

Of the three internal tensions identified in this chapter competence appears to be less of a threat to the EU than the question of control over EU commercial negotiations. In the longer term there will also be a need to reform and strengthen the scrutiny of EU commercial policy by national and

[18] The EU and US appear to be seeking a form of joint leadership of the multilateral system. This has taken the form of the joint statements on EU–US cooperation in commercial relations, the most recent of which has been the 18 May Statement on a Transatlantic Partnership. Contrary to some proposals this partnership appears to place as much, if not more, emphasis on promoting multilateral liberalization as it does on promoting bilateral market opening.

European Parliaments as well as open channels of communication with a wider policy making community in non-governmental organizations. Although such an opening of policy appears to run counter to the short run need to ensure the efficiency of EU policy, neglect of the democratic deficit will be more costly in the long run because the legitimacy of EU commercial policy will be challenged.

REFERENCES

Baldwin, Robert. (1970) *Non-Tariff Distortions of International Trade*, Brookings Institution, Washington DC.

Bhagwati, Jagdish and Hudec, R. (1996) *Fair Trade and Harmonization.*

Coombe, John. (1995) *Reshaping the World Trade System: a history of the Uruguay Round.*

Devuyst, Y. (1995) 'The European Community and the Conclusion of the Uruguay Round' in Rhodes, C. and Mazey (eds) *The State of the European Union – building a European polity.*

European Commission Communication from the Commission. *The Global Challenge of International Trade: A Market Access Strategy for the European Union*, COM(96)53, 14 February 1996.

Hayes, J.P. *Making Trade Policy in the European Community*, Trade Policy Research Centre, 1993.

Henning, C. Randell. (1997) *Cooperating with Europe's Monetary Union*, Institute for International Economics, Washington DC.

Hoekman, Bernard and Kosteki, M. (1995) *The Political Economy of the World Trading System: from GATT to WTO.*

Krueger, Ann. (1998) *The WTO as an International Organization*, University Press of Chicago.

Lawrence, Robert. (1995) *Regionalism, Multilateralism and Deep Integration*, The Brookings Institution, Washington DC.

Macleod, I. Hendry, I.D. and Hyett, Stephen. (1996) *The External Relations of the European Communities*, Clarendon Press.

Maresceau, Marc. (1993) *The EC's Commercial Policy after 1992: the legal dimension.*

Single Market Review Subseries IV, Vol. 4, *Impact on Trade and Investment*, 1997.

Woolcock, S. and Hodges, M. (1996) 'The European Union in the Uruguay Round: the story behind the headlines', in Wallace, H. and Wallace, W. *Decision Making in the European Union*, Oxford University Press.

13

EMU AND ITS IMPACT AT THE REGIONAL LEVEL: MECHANICS AND CONSEQUENCES

Andrew Scott

I INTRODUCTION

In this chapter, we examine a number of the issues that European economic and monetary union (EMU) raises for the process of regional economic development in the European Union (EU). The focus of the chapter is monetary union rather than economic *and* monetary union. To a large (although possibly exaggerated) degree, the economic union element of EMU has been achieved with the implementation of the Single European Market (SEM) programme. That programme was launched in 1985 with the publication of the Commission's White Paper, which listed almost 300 common legislative measures that would be required to eliminate the existing impediments to the free internal movement of goods, services, capital or labour. These measures, together with the requirement that member states applied the principle of 'mutual recognition' with respect to products and factors of production originating elsewhere in the EU, combined to create a (more or less) genuinely EU-wide 'common market' by 31 December 1992.[1] While the single market programme itself dates from 1985, it is of course the case that the objectives of that programme – namely, establishing the free movement of goods, services, capital and persons – represented the foundational elements of the Treaty of Rome.

Creating a monetary union within the European Union is a more recent objective. Although monetary union was first attempted in the 1970s, following the blueprint for a 'staged' transition to EMU set out in the Werner Report,[2] the incorporation of monetary union as an explicit, Treaty based, objective dates only from the entry into law of the (Maastricht) Treaty on

---

[1] It remains the case that a number of specific internal market measures have yet to be implemented.
[2] See Werner Report (1970).

European Union (TEU) in 1993.[3] Like the Werner Report before it, the TEU envisaged EMU being achieved over three stages. Each stage would be characterized by a combination of domestic monetary and fiscal policy convergence, with member states obliged to meet objective criteria with respect to indicators of monetary and fiscal policy before being admitted to the monetary union, along with the development of a European Central Bank which would supersede national central banks and assume responsibility for conducting monetary policy once the monetary union was in place. The TEU stipulated that the final stage in the process – the launch of the monetary union – would begin no later than 1 January 1999.[4] Countries that did not meet the stipulated prerequisites for progressing to monetary union at that time (the so-called 'convergence criteria'[5]), would be given a derogation from the relevant Treaty provisions until these criteria were met. In the event, and following a decision by the European Council, it was decided that eleven member states were eligible to proceed to the single currency stage from the outset, with only Greece and Sweden being deemed ineligible to proceed to the final stage.[6] Both the UK and Denmark had secured opt-outs from monetary union at the outset, while Sweden had made clear it would not participate in the single currency at that juncture.

Despite the political success that the launch of European monetary union in accordance with the TEU timetable undoubtedly represented, the economic consequences of monetary union remain a hotly contested issue. In large part, the economic debate has focused on the prospective macro-economic repercussions of monetary union that arise with the loss of monetary policy as an instrument of national economic management. It is self-evident that the introduction of a single currency is incompatible with monetary policy (exchange rate and interest rate determination) being conducted at the level of the member state. Indeed, it is the loss of national competence for monetary policy which accounts for the importance ascribed to member states meeting the convergence criteria before being permitted to proceed to full monetary union. The introduction of a common monetary policy, to be determined solely by the European Central Bank (ECB), has two principal macro-economic consequences for member states. First, the common monetary policy stance adopted (i.e. the interest rate) may not conform to that which is desirable from the perspective of an individual member state at any given moment. This is especially likely if the economic cycles in the participating countries are not moving uniformly. Secondly, the loss of monetary policy as an instrument of domestic economic management inevitably places a much greater burden on national fiscal policy as a means of achieving

---

[3] See TEU Title I, Art. 2; and Title II, EC Treaty Arts 2, 4(2).

[4] TEU, Art. 121(4).

[5] These being the avoidance of an excessive budget deficit; achieving price stability; convergence of long term interest rates to the lowest levels; and maintaining exchange rate stability.

[6] Greece failed to meet the criteria on price stability, fiscal policy, the exchange rate, and long term interest rates.

domestic economic objectives. As we discuss later in this chapter, it is precisely these concerns which have led some critics of monetary union to question both the timing of the transition to full European monetary union, and the specific provisions of **this** monetary union especially with regard to the provisions for national fiscal policy set out in the Stability and Growth Pact agreed in July 1997.[7]

Rather than reviewing the entire EMU debate, in this chapter we examine the implications of monetary union at the regional level. This has been a somewhat neglected aspect in the literature. There are at least three reasons for this. First, it reflects the weak constitutional position of regions in the decision arrangements of the EU. It is presumed that member states will reflect the concerns of their regions when striking intergovernmental bargains. Secondly, the arguments compelling the EU towards monetary union implicitly ranked the long term collective economic interests of the EU – especially with regard to the construction of a single financial area – above any short term regional economic disadvantages that may arise from the loss of national monetary policy autonomy.[8] Finally, because monetary policy in individual member states was not used principally as an instrument of regional economic policy the regional consequences of monetary union were regarded as an extraneous consideration in the context of the EMU debate.[9] Recently, however, a greater emphasis has been placed on the regional dimension of monetary union. This is explained principally because the provisions of the Stability and Growth Pact (SGP) introduced constraints to the conduct of fiscal policies in EMU member states hence weakening the role that fiscal policy can play in pursuing national – including regional – economic objectives. At the same time, it has become clear from the 'Agenda 2000' debate that the arguments for strengthening the EU's regional policy instruments to compensate member states for the loss of monetary, and the restrictions imposed on fiscal, policies with the move to EMU – arguments that are endorsed in the MacDougall Report of 1977 and the Delors Report of 1989[10] – are unlikely to prevail.

The remainder of the chapter is organized as follows. In the next section we review the principal economic issues raised by the move to monetary union from the perspective of the macro-economic policy process. In the thirty section we examine the adjustment dynamics within this monetary union before going on to examine, in the fourth section, the specific regional development issues that may well arise within the European monetary union. In section five the options facing the EU level of governance in devising a suitable policy response to the problems highlighted are reviewed. Our conclusions are presented in the final section.

[7] See Resolution of the European Council on the Stability and Growth Pact, 97/C 236/01.

[8] For a statement of the arguments that ultimately led to the proposal that European monetary union be established, see the Report by T. Padoa-Schioppa (1987), especially 74–77.

[9] From reading some of the papers accompanying the Delors Report of 1989, there is clearly an expectation that the instruments of EU regional policy should be strengthened as EMU unfolded. See especially Doyle (1989) and Delors (1989).

[10] See MacDougall (1977) and Delors (1989).

II POLICY COORDINATION AND MONETARY UNION

Following the decision taken by the EU Heads of Government and State on 2 May 1998 that eleven member states would participate in EMU from the beginning of the third stage on 1 January 1999, the debate over 'whether EMU' has given way to a debate on 'managing EMU'. The preoccupation of policy-makers is now focused on ensuring that the introduction of a single currency does not bring in its wake serious economic difficulties for particular member states (or regions therein), or political instability for the EU as a whole. The changing nature of the EMU debate is not one purely of emphasis. Prior to the launch of the single currency, much of the economic (and political) debate was conducted solely in national terms, and centred on the impact that the convergence programmes were having on the level of economic activity and employment in individual member states.[11] In particular, controversy surrounded the fiscal policies being implemented in member states to enable them to meet the excessive budget deficit criteria set out in the TEU. These criteria stipulated that, for the reference year preceding the beginning of stage III, a member states' annual budget deficit must not exceed 3 per cent of its Gross Domestic Product (GDP), and its stock of debt not exceed 60 per cent of GDP. Only under exceptional circumstances, as defined by Art. 104(2) EC Treaty would a breach of these deficit ceilings be deemed compatible with participation in EMU.[12] Difficulties arose because the period in which fiscal consolidation was undertaken (1994–99) coincided with recessionary phase in the economies of the majority of member states.[13] In such a situation, it was inevitable that the implementation of measures to curtail national budget deficits was criticized as reducing further the level of aggregate demand and exacerbating the already deep-seated problems of high unemployment and slow economic growth. This resulted in calls for the postponement of Stage III until the EU economies had recovered their economic momentum. In the event, however, the move to Stage III was not postponed, and monetary union was introduced on schedule. With the launch of European monetary union, the substance of the debate has shifted to questions surrounding the management of the single currency. Two closely related issues have been given particular attention.

The first relates to the determination of the appropriate macro-economic policy-mix within the European economic and monetary union, given the underlying economic conditions and the objectives of policy-makers, and in the context of the institutional provisions of this monetary union as set out in the TEU. The 'policy-mix' in conventional macro-economic theory describes

[11] That is, macro-economic policy-mix designed to ensure that the convergence criteria set out in the TEU were met thus enabling a member state to proceed to the third stage of EMU.

[12] The ceilings could be breached where the excessive deficit-to-GDP ratio was exceptional or temporary but still close to the target, or where the debt-to-GDP ratio was sufficiently diminishing and approaching the reference value at a satisfactory rate.

[13] Between 1991–93 EU GDP grew by only 0.6% per annum, during which the level of unemployment rose 8.2% to 10.7%. Following a sharp upswing in 1994, the rate of economic growth declined once again throughout 1995–96 before beginning to recover in 1997. However, the rate of EU unemployment remained high at 10.7%.

the respective roles assigned to fiscal and monetary policies in attaining the objectives of policy-makers. It is axiomatic that an 'efficient' policy-mix is one in which each instrument is assigned to a particular objective, or set of objectives, and that the instruments themselves operate in a manner that is mutually consistent with respect to these objectives being met. In conventional economic and monetary unions, the policy-mix commonly is jointly determined within the context of a unitary government and the coordination between the relevant agencies involved is assumed to take place relatively easily.[14] The institutional architecture of the EU's economic and monetary union departs radically from this 'unitary' model. Instead, we have an independent ECB responsible for monetary policy (setting money supply targets and the common interest rate and which has its primary objective as maintaining price stability in the single currency area[15]) sharing responsibility for the overall macro-economic policy-mix with national governments who retain exclusive competence for national fiscal policies. Given that monetary policy is assigned principally to delivering price stability, the burden of achieving the remaining objectives of macro-economic economic policy is bound to pass to national fiscal policy. However, the provisions of the SGP as agreed at the Amsterdam European Council in June 1997 requires Euro-area governments to continue observing the excessive budget deficit criteria stipulated in the TEU other than under 'exceptional' circumstances.[16] Adherence to the SGP will limit the ability of national governments to use fiscal policy to achieve these other policy goals. In large measure the provisions of SGP reflect the prevailing orthodoxy that economic growth, job creation and price stability generally will only obtain within the context of sound public finances at a national level. It also reflects concerns that the unrestricted growth of a budgetary deficit in any single (or group of) member state may well 'spill-over' and jeopardize economic stability in other member states. Taken together, the monetary and fiscal policy assignment under European monetary union, and the Treaty rules designed to keep apart the authorities responsible for each, constitutes a radical break with arrangements for macro-economic policy coordination in prevailing monetary unions. And while this does not preclude enhanced coordination between the respective macro-economic authorities, it certainly makes it difficult. As we

[14] Even in countries with strongly independent central banks there is a significant degree of cooperation between the monetary and fiscal authorities which need not jeopardize the policy integrity of either body.

[15] Article 105(1) EC Treaty. The independence of the ECB is provided for under Art. 108 EC Treaty. Also relevant in this regard is the prohibition on the ECB from purchasing national debt instruments directly from member state authorities (Art. 101(1) EC Treaty).

[16] Council Regulation No. 1466/97. Exceptional circumstances are defined as; '. . . an annual fall of real GDP of at least 2%'. However, under a European Council Resolution, excessive deficits may be permitted where the annual fall in real GDP lies between 0.75% and 2% (see Resolution of the European Council on the Stability and Growth Pact, OJ, No. C236). It is worth noting that over the period 1961–96, and for the EU 15, there were only 45 instances (out of 240 observations) in which annual real GDP actually fell. On 30 occasions this fall exceeded 0.75%, but there were only seven occasions where the fall exceeded 2% over one year (European Commission, 1997a).

will discuss in the next section, it is fairly straightforward to demonstrate conditions under which this could lead to economic (and political) difficulties in particular areas within the European monetary union.

The second issue arises from the specific European model of monetary union and relates to coordination between the independently constructed fiscal (and other) policies of the member states, especially those within the euro-area. As we have noted, the (new) policy assignment rule within European monetary union matches a centralized monetary policy – to be used to deliver price stability – with a decentralized (though SGP-constrained) fiscal policy targeted at achieving other objectives of macro-economic policy – which presumably include maximizing the rate of economic growth and ensuring a high level of employment. However, within a unitary market in which goods, services, capital and labour are free to move across national borders, national fiscal measures are subject to a high degree of 'leakage'. This problem is well documented within the public finance literature, and describes a situation in which the impact of a change in fiscal policy in one jurisdiction spills over to neighbouring fiscal policy jurisdictions as a consequence of the integration of product and factor markets.[17] This type of leakage is particularly problematic in respect of the efficacy of stabilization policy – i.e. tax and spending policies aimed at influencing aggregate demand and, through this, the total level of economic activity (income and employment) – and is most acute in a single currency area with multiple and independent fiscal jurisdictions. The consequence of 'leakage' for the EU member states is that the magnitude of any national fiscal measures (especially stabilization policy) required to achieve a given outcome is bound to increase with the implementation of economic and monetary union. Accordingly, the incentive for a government to engage in such (stabilization) measures will be reduced, leading to concerns that, in the event of a downturn in the level of economic activity, the fiscal authorities collectively will fail to deliver an adequate (stabilization) policy impulse and hence will impart a deflationary bias to the EU as a whole. Consequently, partial centralization of fiscal policy may be a more economically efficient arrangement within EMU even where there are provisions for coordination between the independent national fiscal authorities.[18]

To an extent the problems caused by the policy assignment rule implicit under EMU have been addressed by the EU policy makers. While it is clear that a move towards a common EU fiscal policy is not on the agenda, provision for a gradation of national economic policy coordination has been incorporated into the EU economic policy process.[19] Article 99 EC Treaty

[17] These leakages operate both on the expenditure side and the revenue side of fiscal policy.

[18] The direct route for achieving intra-EU fiscal policy coordination is via fiscal federalism, where a common fiscal policy (i.e. stabilization policy and income distribution) is managed by a single EU fiscal authority. The conclusion is demonstrated, classically, by Oates (1968).

[19] The conclusions to the December 1997 Luxembourg European Council stress the need to develop close macro-economic cooperation between member states and observe, 'ministers of the States participating in the euro-area may meet informally among themselves to discuss issues connected with their shared specific responsibilities for the single currency'.

215

states that member states are to regard their economic policies as a matter of 'common concern'. This exhortation is given a tangible expression under Art. 99(2) which requires 'broad economic policy guidelines' for each member state to be adopted by the Council of Ministers, following discussions within the European Council.[20] Although the purpose of these 'broad guidelines' is not made explicit in the TEU, they can be assumed to play a dual role. In the first place, by providing a forecast of medium-term budgetary developments in member states the guidelines help ensure that national policy is consistent with the excessive deficit criteria stipulated in the TEU. Secondly, the broad guidelines provide an opportunity for establishing general intra-EU coordination of a range of policy instruments which collectively shape a member state's overall economic performance. Specifically, Art. 99(4) EC Treaty empowers the Council of Ministers to make recommendations to member state governments to amend national budgetary policies where these are deemed not to be consistent with the agreed-upon guidelines for economic policy, or where they jeopardize 'the proper functioning of economic and monetary union'. The TEU provisions for joint determination of, and multilateral surveillance over, national fiscal policies were reinforced by Council Regulation 1466/97 agreed upon at the Amsterdam European Council in June 1997. This requires member states to establish (and update annually) stability (for those in the euro-area) and convergence (for those outside the euro-area) programmes with respect to national budgetary policies that are consistent with the deficit ceilings stipulated in both the TEU and the SGP.[21] Under this Regulation, the principle of mutual surveillance of national policies is reasserted, with Arts 6 and 10 empowering the Council of Ministers to monitor the implementation of stability and convergence programmes, and to recommend measures to member states if it is thought likely that a programme will result in a divergence of the budgetary position from the medium-term objective. Although the Regulation stops short of providing the Council with the power to enforce the recommendations it makes, it does enhance the arrangements for budgetary policy coordination between member states. The need to achieve coordination over a broader range of national economic policies was made explicit in a Resolution of the European Council in its Luxembourg meeting in December 1997 which called upon the member states to apply the Treaty instruments to ensure policy coordination:

> To this end, the broad economic policy guidelines adopted in accordance with [Article 99(2)] should be developed into an effective instrument for ensuring sustained convergence of member states. They should provide more concrete and country-specific guidelines and focus more on measures to improve member state growth potential, thus increasing employment. Therefore, more attention should

[20] Article 99 EC Treaty does not make explicit which policies are included under the rubric 'economic policies'. While this is certain to refer minimally to budgetary policies, it is unclear whether it extends to national wages policies, industrial policies, etc.
[21] Under Regulation 1466/97, Art. 3(2a), the medium-term objective for a member state is a balanced budget, or one in surplus, permitting some scope for a budget deficit in the future.

henceforth be paid in them to improving competitiveness, labour-, product- and services-market efficiency, education and training, and to making taxation and social protection systems more employment friendly . . . Enhanced co-ordination should be aimed at securing consistency of national economic policies and their implementation with the broad economic policy guidelines and the proper functioning of economic and monetary union.[22]

Here the European Council is reaffirming its commitment to a collective strategy towards greater job creation that concentrates on measures that impact directly on labour markets, rather than through the operation of the conventional macro-economic levers of policy. It is an approach which is elaborated in greater detail in the European Council Resolution on growth and employment[23] where considerable emphasis is placed on the need to ensure that labour market developments – including wage rates – proceed in a manner consistent with EU-wide price stability and job creation.

Whereas recent pronouncements by the Commission and the European Council have stressed the importance of policy coordination between member states, coordination between the EU's fiscal and monetary authorities has received less attention. Coordination in this respect matters in so far as a trade-off exists between price stability on the one hand, and the stabilization of output (and employment) on the other hand.[24] This trade-off can arise where the independent central bank values price stability more than it values output stability, and therefore would be unwilling to ease its monetary stance in the event of a downswing in economic activity if this is considered to be incompatible with achieving the prevailing inflation target. Assuming that money wages are inflexible in a downward direction, the outcome is likely to be a rise in unemployment. Of course, precisely this difficulty arises in any monetary union featuring an independent central bank. However, because monetary unions generally tend also to be fiscal unions, the possibility exists for the unemployment consequences of (a non-accommodating) monetary policy to be compensated by appropriate (re)distributive fiscal measures. Clearly, the scale of this policy trade-off is likely to decrease if money wages become more flexible, a feature which itself may be improved as the credibility of the monetary authorities increases. In this respect, euro-area policymakers face two problems. First, the policy of the monetary authorities must be seen to be credible and therefore non-contestable by, and invariant with respect to, other economic agents (including member state governments).[25] Secondly, economic agents across the euro-area must adjust their wage-bargaining behaviour speedily to the new monetary policy regime should the 'new' output-inflation trade-off differ from that prevailing prior to currency

[22] European Council Resolution on economic policy coordination in Stage Three of EMU and on Treaty Arts 111 and 113, Luxembourg, 1997.
[23] European Council Resolution on Growth and Employment (OJ, 97/C236/02).
[24] See D. Begg (1997).
[25] This is ensured as the ECB is prohibited from taking instructions from any member state (Art. 108), and by virtue of the 'no bail out' provision of the EC Treaty (Art. 101).

unification. Otherwise the domestic level of unemployment will increase as money wages continue to rise at a faster rate than inflation, raising real wages. It remains true that a member state can respond to any unemployment consequences of ECB policy by implementing offsetting fiscal measures. In practice, however, the scope for this is restricted by the SGP, increasing the likelihood of a conflict arising between the ECB and a particular member state with respect to the conduct of the euro-area monetary policy.[26]

It remains a moot point whether or not the delegation of monetary policy to an independent central bank will lessen or increase the EU-wide trade-off between price stability and output. It is straightforward to devise scenarios that lead to either conclusion. What is clear, however, is that the TEU provides no mechanism whereby the independence and policy autonomy of the ECB legally can be tampered with by member states, regardless of the policy stance it adopts. While it is only reasonable to expect the ECB to accommodate the interests of member states in so far as this does not compromise the aim of price stability, scenarios readily can be devised in which conflict between an individual national government and the ECB will arise and which may lead to a degree of political instability for the EU as a whole.

III ADJUSTMENT DYNAMICS WITHIN EMU

The economic problems that are likely to confront the members of the European monetary union principally derive from the macro-economic consequences of surrendering national control over monetary policy to an external and independent central bank while, at the same time, restricting national fiscal policies within the constraints imposed by the SGP. While it is acknowledged that these costs must be viewed in the context of the potential economic gains which accrue to a monetary union, the concern is that the sum of (micro-economic) gains will be too small to offset the likely (macro-economic) costs involved.[27] The principal catalyst for revealing the costs of monetary union is an asymmetric economic shock. This describes a situation in which one economy – or region – within a monetary union is subject to an unanticipated economic disturbance which does not affect the monetary union as a whole. The shock can be either a sector-specific, such as a global downturn in the fortunes of a particular industry, or specific to one region or country within the monetary union, for instance as a consequence of a recession in a dominant trading partner, or a combination of the two. The shock will be asymmetric where one country within the monetary union has a significantly higher economic dependence on the 'shocked' industry, or where the reduction in demand for exports affects disproportionately one country

[26] See Masson (1996) for a fuller discussion of this.

[27] The gains from monetary union involve the elimination of transaction costs, seignorage benefits, and investment and trade gains that derive indirectly from the price stability that it is assumed the ECB will be capable of delivering. See European Commission (1990).

within the monetary union. In the event of an asymmetric shock, there is no incentive for the central bank to alter the stance of monetary policy in that economic conditions across the monetary union in general have not altered. Consequently, the burden of the adjustment to the shock will be borne predominately by the 'shocked' country or region.[28] Four adjustment routes are available to the shocked area.

First, the economic shock may lead to a reduction in money wages in the shocked economy thereby opening up a differential between wages in that economy, and the EU average. To the extent that the business investment responds to prevailing wage rates, lower wages may spark an inflow of investment capital which will restore some part of economic activity to the shocked economy and lower the level of unemployment. However, experience has demonstrated money wages within a single currency area tend towards equality rather than greater inequality. If we are to rely on widening national – or regional – money wage differentials as a mechanism for offsetting unfavourable shocks, then we must have some idea of the specific mechanics whereby this will occur. The risk for the monetary union is that an adverse political reaction will result before the necessary wage adjustment occurs, and this could lead to political instability in the monetary union.[29]

Secondly, the labour made unemployed by the external economic shock could move to member states or regions of greater economic prosperity and so better employment opportunities. The problem is that intra-EU labour mobility is not well developed. Despite a legal framework which permits the free movement of labour, substantial informal obstacles to labour mobility across the EU remain. Moreover, even were this to occur, labour mobility on any significant scale may result in problematic – and unacceptable – economic and political consequences within the prosperous areas of the monetary union.

A third adjustment route in the face of an adverse economic shock is through an active fiscal policy, aimed at ameliorating the immediate impact of the shock by short term stabilization measures and at enhancing the longer term economic prospects of the shocked region by funding structural programmes of regional economic development.[30] The first difficulty in this response involves the constraints imposed by the excessive budget deficit provisions of SGP which may render inoperable both of these elements of fiscal policy activism. To the extent that the current budget deficit or public debt positions are close to the SGP-ceilings, a country may have little or no scope to engage in an active fiscal policy. Moreover, to the extent that the impact of the economic shock is widespread, a country in this situation

---

[28] If the external shock impacts evenly on all parts of the monetary union, a relaxation of monetary policy is likely in so far as this is not inconsistent with price stability, and this will ease the adjustment problem.

[29] See Feldstein (1997).

[30] These take the form of investment in economic infrastructure and a variety of labour market (education and training) programmes.

actually may have to cut current and capital account items of public spending in the face of a shock-induced fall in government revenue and rise in social policy expenditure. At the same time, the prevailing arrangements governing intra-EU fiscal transfers (i.e. from the prosperous to the shocked regions) as a mechanism to alleviate the symptoms of asymmetric shocks are wholly inadequate to address this type of problem. Indeed, it is the non-existence of a common fiscal facility that distinguishes the EU model of monetary union from virtually every other example of a functioning monetary union and which is, arguably, its most significant weakness. The second problem in relying on domestic fiscal policy arises because of the 'leakage' problem noted earlier. This implies that the magnitude of the stabilization measures required are higher under monetary union than previously, placing a disproportionately greater adjustment burden on fiscal interventions.

Finally, member states may respond to the consequences of an asymmetric shock by seeking to block imports and encourage exports; that is, attempt to engage in protectionist policies in response to the rise in unemployment. While such a response would be extremely difficult to effect in the current environment – principally because of the Single European Market (SEM) rules and the enforcement of these by the European Court of Justice – the point remains that political pressures to restrict freedom of trade are likely to intensify if domestic employment and output levels are falling while economic conditions elsewhere in the EU remain relatively buoyant.

It is difficult to make any definitive predictions concerning the adjustment properties of the EU economic system under monetary union and, therefore, impossible to estimate the extent to which asymmetric shocks will prove damaging to the member state economies. Indeed, the very shift to monetary union itself may well induce a shift in the parameters of the underlying economic system – a possibility that is particularly relevant in the context of labour market responses (i.e. wage setting behaviour) to the new policy environment.[31] To the extent that the monetary policy stance adopted by the ECB is interpreted both to be credible and to be following a well understood 'rule' with respect to achieving price stability, proponents of EMU argue that economic agents will adjust speedily their wage bargaining behaviour to incorporate the correct expectations of future price movements. Accordingly, actual money wages should not differ significantly from that required to yield a real wage rate consistent with a particular level of employment, even in the context of unexpected external shocks. There is evidence in support of the claim that a high degree of central bank independence not only is consistent with greater price stability, but that it does not appear to generate any greater output (and so employment) volatility in the countries concerned.[32] However, inevitably this empirical evidence is drawn from countries which have a tradition of (a specific type of) central bank independence, and which may

---

[31] This will also be the case in countries where national monetary policy has been the principal source of asymmetric economic shocks.
[32] See D. Begg (1997).

boast central banks which enjoy a low-inflation 'reputation'. Arguably it is the inherited reputation, rather than the independence *per se*, of the central bank which explains this outcome. Clearly the newly created ECB has no inherited reputation, notwithstanding an institutional structure that corresponds closely to the Bundesbank, and this suggests that the ECB may seek to pursue an overly rigorous monetary policy in the first instance to allow it to acquire such a reputation. Despite these reservations, it is possible that the introduction of monetary union will encourage greater flexibility in EU labour markets and lessen the adjustment problems arising in the event of an asymmetric shock. Accordingly, the macro-economic costs of monetary union may be lower than euro-pessimists suggest.

Similarly, it is misleading to imply that countries which have used most actively the twin levers of macro-economic policy are those that can boast the greatest stability in output, or the lowest unemployment–inflation trade-off. If this is not the case, then the 'cost' of restricting member state use of these policy levers may be lower than the critics suggest. Advocates of monetary union argue that policy-active governments have frequently failed to achieve either greater economic stability or higher employment than their less interventionist counterparts, and that their attempts to do so have only introduced further distortions to the economic system. This is especially evident in countries which have created large, and unsustainable, budgetary deficits as a result of fiscal policy activism and which can be serviced only by incurring even more public debt – raising even more the level of domestic interest rates. In this regard, advocates of European monetary union have some ground for claiming that the fiscal rules of the SGP, and the process of member state fiscal consolidation required to meet these rules, are necessary features of a prudent budgetary policy which member states should adhere to regardless of the advent of monetary union. Notwithstanding this defence of fiscal consolidation, the feature of the SGP that has received most criticism is its requirement that budgetary deficits should remain within 3 per cent of GDP on an annual basis, rather than on average over the course of the economic cycle. Critics argue that measures which yield an 'excessive' deficit during a cyclical downswing are tolerable providing that offsetting measures are applied during the cyclical upswing leading to a balanced budget over the course of the economic cycle. Instead, by restricting a government's room for manoeuvre during the economic cycle, the SGP will both deepen the downswing, and lengthen the duration, of the cycle.[33]

A third response to the EMU 'pessimists' is to question the extent to which asymmetric economic shocks actually occur. If the incidence of such shocks is low, then it may be asserted that their spatial implications are modest and that the costs of EMU have been overstated. To the extent that all external shocks are symmetric in their impact, it is to be expected that

---

[33] Stabilization policies are appropriate only where the economic shock has a temporary effect. If the shock is permanent, adjustment within the 'real' economy is required.

monetary and fiscal policies will jointly respond and that the problems arising from excessive dependence upon the latter in the adjustment process will be avoided. It is reasonable to assume that the ECB will be prepared to relax monetary policy if required, providing this does not jeopardise price stability. In the final instance the question of incidence and scale of asymmetric shocks is an empirical one, and only in time can the importance of this problem for the EU be established. However, it is possible to offer a few general remarks. To the extent that economic and monetary union leads to a situation in which individual member states' economic profile becomes more rather than less diverse, the likelihood that an economic shock will have a country- or region-specific impact diminishes. However, should deeper economic integration result in a greater intensity of sectoral specialization along national or regional lines, the likelihood that an external shock will have an asymmetric impact increases. There is no consensus in the literature on the question of EU-wide patterns of specialization. On the one hand, modern theories of international trade which analyse the growth of intra-industry trade tend to conclude that, as trade barriers fall, economic activity within a country will become more diverse and it will be less vulnerable to an asymmetric shock rooted in a sectoral downturn. Consequently, the incidence of asymmetric shocks should fall.[34] On the other hand, recent contributions to the 'new economic geography' literature imply that in industrial economies, and particularly where factors of production are internationally mobile (as in the EU), the pattern of industrial location and activity – and, by extension, the spatial distribution of production and employment – is essentially arbitrary and may, or may not, produce a greater or lesser degree of sectoral specialization on a national or regional basis.[35] Indeed, there is some evidence to show that the degree of specialization in production has increased in the EU since the single market programme was launched.[36]

It is clear from this review that considerable uncertainty surrounds the precise impact that European monetary union will have on the macro-economic policy and performance of euro-area member states. In the next section we examine how these macro-economic uncertainties translate into issues confronting regional economic development across the EU.

IV THE REGIONAL DIMENSION OF EMU

In the preceding sections we have established the principal mechanisms through which monetary union will impact on the individual economies of the EU. In this section we bring together these themes to focus specifically on the regional dimension of these mechanisms. The political and economic

---

[34] For a useful discussion of this, see European Commission (1990), chs 6 and 9.

[35] For a full discussion of these issues, and a review of the empirical record, see Brulhart (1998a, 1998b).

[36] Brulhart (1998b).

significance of the regional dimension of monetary union derives largely from the predominant position that the principal of 'economic and social cohesion' occupies in the hierarchy of common EU policies. If it can be shown that there is a tendency for regional economic inequalities across the EU to be exacerbated with the arrival of monetary union, it follows that policy makers can expect to find themselves under political pressure to devise common policies which counteract this tendency. Otherwise the shift to monetary union may generate significant political instability.[37]

The immediate impact of monetary union on the EU regions is likely to be modest as neither interest rate policy nor exchange rate policy typically have been used by member states as instruments of regional economic management. Over the longer term, however, the loss of national monetary policy autonomy may have a discernible effect on regional development. This will arise if the post-monetary union policy-mix yields a lower rate of economic growth that was achieved previously, reflecting the fact that regional economic convergence tends to accelerate in periods of strong economic growth and to recede in periods of low economic growth, or stagnation. This tendency is explained by the fact that weaker regions frequently contain a higher proportion of sensitive sectors and only marginally efficient firms which are among the first to be affected by recession than do stronger regions. Similarly, monetary union may impact indirectly on regional economic development if EU-wide interest rates under monetary union are higher than previously. This is likely to be the case where the ECB is seeking to build a reputation for monetary discipline, and will affect industrial location decisions to the extent that the yield from private sector investment varies between regions at different stages of economic development. Generally, however, these effects of monetary union will be weak and could readily be offset by modest changes to regional economic development support measures.

A more controversial aspect of European monetary union concerns the regional consequences of the fiscal rules to be applied under the SGP. To the extent that asymmetric shocks continue (and possibly become more frequent), these rules clearly will restrict the capacity of a national government to assist the 'shocked' regions where labour and product market adjustments prove inadequate to offset the employment and output effects of the shock. It is also pertinent to note that a symmetric economic shock may well generate asymmetric effects if euro-area countries are characterized by different initial conditions with respect to their budgetary positions. If the great majority of member states are running a budget surplus, or are only marginally in deficit, it is conceivable that the ECB may not relax monetary policy following the symmetric shock and leave member states' governments to address its economic impact through expansionary fiscal policies. However, for those countries whose fiscal position already is close to the SGP ceilings this response

---

[37] Here we concentrate on the economic issues. However, the political issues are likely to include, *inter alia*, the impact of regional economic disparities on EU-wide 'regional politics'.

will not be possible. This situation will replicate the conditions of an asymmetric shock. It is clear that asymmetric shocks have the potential dramatically to affect regional economic performance. Moreover, where national fiscal policy is unable to respond, or can respond only partially, the consequences of the shock may persist and fundamentally alter the long term growth prospects of the region concerned. This is not to claim that an active fiscal policy is always the appropriate response to an external shock – this will depend on the nature of the shock. However, it is to suggest that curtailing the capacity for national fiscal policy to be used to assist the adjustment process following an economic shock substantially reduces the scope for policy-makers to offset the longer term consequences of that shock. These longer term effects might include a rising incidence of long term unemployment, a deskilled labour force and a low rate of business start-up.

In addition to the direct regional consequences that may arise as a consequence of the implementation of the SGP, it is also important to consider the longer term dynamics of regional economic development if governments find themselves (wholly or partially) unable to use fiscal policies (such as regional economic assistance measures) to promote the adjustment process in the 'shocked' regions. Although advocates of monetary union stress the role that enhanced regional wage flexibility can play in offsetting the consequences of asymmetric economic shocks, this is to assume, implicitly, that the principal issue in securing 'economic and social cohesion' in the EU is the actual level of employment, and that this responds directly and proportionately to changes in the real wage rate. Of course, neither proposition is necessarily true. Regional economic growth rates are determined also by the quality of employment available, not the quantity, weakening the connection between wage flexibility and maintaining 'cohesion'. To the extent that higher rates of economic growth are associated with knowledge – and skill-based high technology industries, a reduction in money wages in a 'shocked' region may do little to persuade high growth industries to move to the now disadvantaged regions. Instead, public investment in training and education programmes may be required to attract industries for whom access to a pool of skilled labour is a more powerful locational inducement than is a supply of low wage labour. If such investment is not forthcoming, it is conceivable that some regions will be able to attract only labour-intensive industries which, typically, have modest rates of economic growth. The outcome in that case may well be a widening of regional economic disparities.

Thus far, we have examined the regional consequences within a monetary union arising from an external economic shock which has an uneven impact across the EU. However, the provisions of the SGP also raises issues concerning the continued viability of prospective member state policies that are aimed at promoting regional economic development within the less prosperous areas of the EU. This is particularly relevant to the four so-called 'cohesion' countries – Spain, Portugal, Greece and Ireland (although Ireland is set to graduate from this group as a consequence of the high rates of economic

growth recorded during the last few years). These member states are characterized by a low level of per capita GDP, and face serious economic and
social problems arising from regional under-development – a feature acknowledged by the EU in its structural (regional development) actions. Notwithstanding the operation of the Structural Funds, however, the fiscal
conditions attached to monetary union may well further compromise the
extent to which of the governments in those countries are able to finance
domestic regional economic development programmes.[38] Indeed, it was precisely this concern which led to the establishment of the Cohesion Fund in
December 1993, which allocated ECU 15,150 million (1992 prices) from
the EU budget to assist environmental and transport infrastructure developments in the cohesion countries. This Fund was established precisely because
of the consequences that fiscal consolidation (in line with the TEU convergence
criteria) had for those countries with respect to their regional economic
development needs. And although the intention was that the Cohesion Fund
would end when monetary union began, at least for those cohesion countries
eligible to proceed to Stage III, it has now been agreed that the Fund will
continue to provide assistance to those member states where per capita GNP
falls below 90 per cent of the EU average. Notwithstanding the (modest)
fiscal assistance this facility provides to the least prosperous member states, it
remains likely that if the fiscal rules of monetary union imply a diminution of
regional development efforts in the EU's poorest member states, and if the
consequent expenditure-deficit is not made good by an increase in the scale
of EU structural operations, political dissatisfaction with the consequences of
monetary union is set to intensify.

V   A POLICY RESPONSE

In considering the regional implications of monetary union, the dominant
theme running through this chapter has been that the loss of national control
over monetary policy in conjunction with the binding constraints imposed on
national fiscal policy by the SGP may force member states both to diminish
their stabilization efforts on the one hand, and to curtail publicly financed
regional support measures on the other hand. Should this occur, and even in
the context of a greater measure of labour market flexibility, it is quite
possible that EU-wide regional disparities in income and employment levels
will increase as economic and monetary union proceeds. Not only will this
conflict with the Treaty commitment to promote greater economic and social
cohesion across the EU, it will also raise political questions as to the costs of
European integration. By way of conclusion, therefore, it is worth considering how the problems alluded to in this chapter may be resolved. Assuming
that the institutional arrangements of monetary union remain as they are,

---

[38] Generally the EU structural operations require some element of national cofinancing,
although the scale of this varies between 25% and over 50%.

with ECB independence constitutionally protected and the SGP remaining in force, attention turns to the likelihood of 'flanking' measures being devised directed towards offsetting the adverse effects of monetary union in individual member states. Further, we assume an increase in the capacity of the EU institutions to use fiscal policy for stabilization purposes to be unlikely at this time. Therefore, we consider the potential for development in two other policy areas which may be capable of bringing stability to the European monetary union should this be necessary – the structural funds, and common measures geared to creating employment across the EU.

The Single European Act paved the way for a fundamental overhaul of the EU structural funds. These reforms which followed, and which were implemented in 1989, effectively transformed the hitherto disparate common instruments of regional policy into a coherent framework for addressing the problem of uneven economic development across the EU. Two features of the reforms were notable. First was the considerable increase in the resources allocated from the EU budget to regional economic development at the EU level. Between 1989 and 1992 the combined budget for structural measures was effectively doubled in real terms, indicating the political importance assigned to attempts to improve the economic development prospects in the EU's weaker regions in the context of the single European market programme. The additional resources involved in the reformed funds flowed principally from the introduction of a 'fourth' financial resource linked to member state GDP to augment the traditional sources of EU income. Secondly, the reforms prioritized assistance to the EU's most disadvantaged regions, particularly those in which economic development was lagging (Objective 1, defined as regions in which per capita GDP was less than 75 per cent of the EU average) and those suffering from structural problems (Objective 2, defined by reference to levels of unemployment and dependence on 'declining' industries). It is worth remarking that these reforms marked the first instance in which objective economic criteria were used in determining the distribution of assistance under the EU's regional development operations. The objective of the structural operations post-1989 was to finance measures designed to improve the medium- to long-term growth prospects of the disadvantaged regions. They were not intended to be instruments of economic stabilization, where this involves a direct and automatic fiscal transfer to compensate individuals for a loss in their income and which may have a regional element, especially in the context of an asymmetric shock. Indeed, the stabilization element of fiscal policy will only be effective where the fiscal authority is able to incur a budgetary deficit – i.e. where its expenditure exceeds its income. As is well known, the EU is required to present a balanced budget. Notwithstanding the inappropriateness of the structural funds at present to respond to the consequences of asymmetric shocks – that is, to fill the 'policy gap'[39] – likely to accompany European monetary union, they do remain the only

---

[39] In using this terminology I follow I. Begg (1998).

common policy instrument at the command of the Commission which might be developed in order to buttress monetary union. Presently the prospects of this are not good. The current review of the structural funds will produce new Regulations to guide their operation from January 2000. It is clear from the Commission's proposals that, with the exception of the Cohesion Fund, no adjustments to the Funds are being sought to render them capable of responding to the regional or national economic difficulties that may arise with monetary union.[40] Two points are worth noting. First, the Commission is not proposing altering the own-resources ceiling over the next financial period (2000–2006) for the EU budget beyond its present maximum of 1.27 per cent of EU GNP. While the resources at the Commission's disposal for the structural operations will depend on the rate of economic growth that the EU records over this period, it is evident that no greater priority is to be assigned to structural operations despite the fundamental change in the EU's economic architecture that will accompany the move to monetary union. Secondly, because the overwhelming part of the structural funds will be preprogrammed to the beneficiary regions for a seven year period, the funds will be no better placed than previously to respond discretely to the regional economic consequences of an asymmetric shock. This is not necessarily to suggest that the prospective beneficiary regions – and these remain principally those regions in which economic development is lagging – are not deserving of assistance, but rather to criticize the proposals generally as lacking the degree of flexibility in application which would enable the Commission to respond to unexpected economic disturbances.

The second policy area worthy of mention in this respect concerns the EU's putative employment policy, a policy which may well have a relevance to the economic dislocation which results from an asymmetric shock. Employment policy has attracted particular attention following the introduction of a new Title on Employment (Title VIII) to the EC Treaty as a consequence of the Amsterdam treaty revision. The introduction of this new text indicates – correctly or otherwise – that a new emphasis is to be given to job creation in the scope of common, EU, activities. This is evident in the revised Art. 2, Title I (ex-Art. B) and reflected forcefully in the revised Art. 3(i) (Title II) which states that the activities of EU shall include:

> the promotion of co-ordination between employment policies of the Member States with a view to enhancing their effectiveness by developing a co-ordinated strategy for employment[41]

In addition, the Amsterdam revision also includes a new Title VIII Employment (Arts 125–130) which pronounces that member states; 'shall regard promoting employment as a matter of common concern',[42] and that, crucially,

---

[40] For a review of these proposals, see Agenda 2000 (European Commission, 1997b).
[41] Amsterdam, Art. 3(i).
[42] Amsterdam, Art. 126(2).

(T)he objective of a high level of employment shall be taken into consideration in the formulation and implementation of Community policies and activities.[43]

The Amsterdam text also provides for the creation of an Employment Committee to have an advisory capacity and to 'monitor the employment situation and employment policies in the Member States'.[44] However, it is clear from reading the Amsterdam text that the nature of the employment policy envisioned by the Council in adopting this text is essentially microeconomic in focus. That is, the types of policies over which intra-Union coordination is to be encouraged relate to 'promoting a skilled, trained and adaptable workforce and labour markets responsive to economic change'.[45]

There is, therefore, no suggestion in the Amsterdam text that member state macro-economic policies should be geared towards securing progress towards 'full' employment, despite calls on the part of some member states that indeed this should have been the case. Nonetheless, the introduction of clauses to the treaty that focus specifically on the promotion of employment may fuel expectations that the EU collectively is set to address the employment consequences over the entire range of its policy deliberations, **including** the common monetary policy and that ancillary job-creation policies may be expected if required.

VI CONCLUSION

The arguments set out in this chapter point to the potential problems for member states and regions as a consequence of the transition to monetary union. The principal conclusion from the analysis is that the institutional and policy provisions of European monetary union do not appear to offer adequate insurance against external asymmetric shocks adding to the regional economic problems presently confronting the European Union. Should these problems emerge, it is conceivable – if not probable – that an adverse political reaction will follow. To that extent, the economic gains that are likely to arise from the introduction of a single currency will be offset by potentially greater costs in terms of the credibility of integration as a whole. Moreover, to the extent that an adverse political reaction does appear, member state governments may find themselves under pressure to undermine the single market conditions of the EU. Clearly this would generate material economic losses for the affected countries. This leads us to conclude that additional flanking measures are required to attend the move to monetary union. At the very least a greater measure of fiscal policy coordination between independent member states is required. However, beyond this it may be necessary for the EU to strengthen the instruments of 'economic and social cohesion' as

---

[43] Amsterdam, Art. 127(2).
[44] Amsterdam, Art. 130, second indent.
[45] Amsterdam, Art. 125.

required to assist the adjustment process in regions which find themselves at a more disadvantaged economic position post-monetary union than before.

REFERENCES

Begg, D. (1997) 'The Design of EMU', *IMF Staff Studies for the World Economic Outlook*, December 1997.

Begg, I. (1998) 'The regions and EMU: examining the "policy-gap"', Paper to RSA Annual Conference, September.

Brulhart, M. (1998a) 'Economic Geography, Industrial Location and Trade: The Evidence', *The World Economy*, Vol. 21, No. 6, 775–802.

Brulhart, M. (1998b) 'Trading Places: Industrial Specialization in the European Union', *Journal of Common Market Studies*, Vol. 36, No. 3, 319–346.

Delors, J. (1989) 'Economic and monetary union and relaunching the construction of Europe', in Delors Report (1989), 63–66.

Delors Report (1989) *Report on Economic and Monetary Union in the European Community*, Office of Publications of the European Communities, Luxembourg.

Doyle, M.F. (1989) 'Regional Policy and European Economic Integration', in Delors Report (1989), 69–80.

European Commission (1990) 'One Market, One Money', *European Economy*, No. 44.

European Commission (1997a) *Economic Policy in EMU, Part B: Specific Topics* (Brussels).

European Commission (1997b) *Agenda 2000: For a stronger and wider Union*, Bulletin of the European Union, Supplement 5/97.

Feldstein, M. (1997) 'The Political Economy of the European Economic and Monetary Union: Political Sources of an Economic Liability', *The Journal of Economic Perspectives*, Vol. 11, No. 4, 23–42.

MacDougall, D. (1977) *The Role of Public Finance in European Economic Integration*, Vols 1 and 2, Commission of the EC, Brussels.

Masson, P. (1996) 'Fiscal Dimensions of EMU', *The Economic Journal*, 106, 996–1004.

Oates, W. (1968) 'The Theory of Public Finance in a Federal State', *Canadian Journal of Economics*, 1, 37–54.

Padoa-Schioppa, T. (1987) *Efficiency, Stability and Equity: A Strategy for the Evolution of the Economic System of the European Community*, OUP, Oxford.

Werner Report (1970) *Report to the Council and the Commission on the Realisation by Stages of Economic and Monetary Union in the Community*, Bulletin of the European Communities, Supplement 11/70.

14

ECONOMIC AND MONETARY
UNION – A LAWYER'S VIEW

John A. Usher

I INTRODUCTION

While the main focus of this paper is on economic and monetary union (EMU), it may nevertheless be seen as a discussion of the questions of flexibility and fragmentation raised by Professor Weatherill in his opening paper, given the special treatment of the UK and Denmark, and the fact that Greece and Sweden were found not to meet the criteria to participate in the third stage of economic and monetary union.[1] On the other hand, unlike many of the papers presented at this conference, there is little mention of the Treaty of Amsterdam, since that Treaty did not amend any of the provisions relating to economic and monetary union, even if there were contemporaneous important non-Treaty developments, notably the enactment of Council Regulation 1103/97[2] on certain provisions relating to the introduction of the euro. The term 'euro' is nowhere to be found in the EC Treaty, but at the meeting of the European Council in Madrid on 15 and 16 December 1995, the decision was taken that the term 'ecu' used by the Treaty to refer to the European currency unit was a generic term, and the Governments of the fifteen member states reached the common agreement that this decision was 'the agreed and definitive interpretation of the relevant Treaty provisions' and that the name given to the European currency should be the 'euro'. Thus, without changing the Treaty, the Treaty term was changed. The use of the term 'euro' was in fact judicially challenged by a member of the European Parliament,[3] but the action was held inadmissible since he attempted to challenge the proposal which eventually became Regulation 1103/97

---

[1] Council Decision 98/317 of 3 May 1998 (*OJ* 1998, L139/30).
[2] *OJ* 1997, L162/1.
[3] Case T-175/96 *Berthu v Commission* [1997] ECR II-811.

230

rather than a binding legal act. In a second action, Case T-207/97 *Berthu v Council*,[4] the annulment of Council Regulation 1103/97 itself was sought, but this action was held inadmissible on the ground that the Regulation was not of individual concern to the applicant. Regulation 1103/97[5] was adopted in June 1997 under Art. 308 of the EC Treaty, and under Art. 2 of this Regulation, every reference in a legal instrument to the ecu as defined under EC law is to be replaced by a reference to the euro at a rate of one euro to one ecu. By its terms, Art. 308 may only be used to achieve an EC objective, which raises the issue of economic and monetary union as an EC objective.

II EMU AS AN EU OBJECTIVE

While political discussion of EMU dates back to the decision in December 1969 to draw up a plan with a view to the creation of an economic and monetary union,[6] leading to the creation of the Werner committee, an express Treaty objective was only introduced by the Maastricht amendments as Art. 4(2) of the EC Treaty (now Art. 4(2)). Questions of flexibility and fragmentation are immediately apparent from the fact that under the Protocol[7] this provision is not binding on the UK once it has given notice, as it did in November 1997, that it will not participate in stage three of EMU. Article 4(2) states that as provided in the Treaty and in accordance with the timetable and the procedures set out therein, the activities of the member states and of the EC shall include the irrevocable fixing of exchange rates leading to the introduction of a single currency, the ecu, and the definition and conduct of a single monetary policy and exchange rate policy, the primary objective of both of which shall be to maintain price stability and, without prejudice to this objective, to support the general economic policies in the EC, in accordance with the principle of an open market economy with free competition.

While this provision might seem to be of academic interest to the UK lawyer, it should be remembered with regard to the UK's special treatment in the context of EMU, that the EC Treaty has from the outset required, under the original Arts 99 and 105, coordination of economic policy and exchange rate policy, that the Single European Act added a Chapter heading on cooperation in monetary and economic policy, and that in Opinion 1/91[8] the European Court also suggested that the attainment of EMU was already an EC objective. It might therefore be submitted that exclusion from Art. 4(2) does not necessarily mean exclusion from the objective of EMU, but rather from the mechanisms to achieve that objective set out in the Maastricht amendments. It should therefore hardly be a surprise that the ecu was defined

---

[4] [1998] ECR II-509.
[5] *OJ* 1997, L162/1.
[6] Compendium of Community Monetary Texts 1974, 13 at 15.
[7] Para. 5.
[8] [1991] ECR I-6079.

in a series of Regulations enacted under Art. 308.[9] Furthermore, legislation expressly intended to give effect to the first stage of EMU had already been enacted, following the decision of the European Council in Madrid in June 1989 that that stage should begin on 1 July 1990. Attention might particularly be drawn to Council Decision 90/141 on the attainment of progressive convergence of economic policies and performance during stage one of emu,[10] and Council Decision 90/142 amending the previous legislation on the Committee of Governors of the Central Banks of the member states of the European Union.[11] Indeed, as was mentioned above, although it was adopted before the UK gave its notice, Council Regulation 1103/97 on certain provisions relating to the introduction of the euro,[12] was adopted at a Council meeting attended by ministers from all the member states under Art. 308 of the EC Treaty. Rather unusually for a Regulation, the statement of reasons explaining the need for the legislation (and hence the justification for the use of Art. 308) is somewhat longer than the substantive text. It may be wondered whether there may be future occasions where use is made of Art. 308 in the general area of EMU.

To the extent that the Maastricht provisions on emu may be regarded as laying down a mechanism to achieve what was already an EC objective rather than creating a new objective, the question arises as to the legal effect of limiting the previous Treaty obligations of certain member states. This is a problem which arises more starkly in the context of the new Title in the EC Treaty on free movement of persons, asylum and immigration introduced by the Treaty of Amsterdam. Under the Maastricht version of the EC Treaty, certain aspects of visa policy fell within the EC Treaty by virtue of Art. 100c of the EC Treaty, which was binding on all the member states, and by virtue of which a common visa list has been enacted. Under the new Title on free movement of persons, asylum and immigration, Art. 100c has been repealed and replaced by provisions which in principle will not be binding automatically on the UK, Ireland and Denmark. This raises interesting questions as to the future status of the common visa list, particularly if it should be amended by those member states participating in the new Title.

In the case of monetary union, differentiation arises not just from the special treatment accorded to the UK and Denmark in the Protocols relating to those countries, but also from the fact that it was appreciated that not all member states would meet the rather strict criteria for economic convergence laid down as the precondition for participation in the monetary union; such states are referred to as 'Member States with a derogation',[13] and would, *inter alia*, be excluded from the decision-making process on certain matters.[14]

[9] From Council Regulation 3180/78 (*OJ* 1978, L379) to Council Regulation 3320/94 (*OJ* 1994, L350/27).
[10] *OJ* 1990, L78/23.
[11] *OJ* 1990, L78/25.
[12] *OJ* 1997, L162/1.
[13] Art. 122 of the EC Treaty as amended by the Maastricht Treaty.
[14] Art. 122(5).

Such states (including Denmark and the United Kingdom following their notice that they will not join the third stage when it begins) are not fully involved in the institutional structure of the European Central Bank (ECB) or of the System of Central Banks (ESCB), and are not bound by all its acts. In one sense, the status of a member state with a derogation is the obverse of a finding that other member states fulfil the conditions for the adoption of a single currency. The status of a member state with a derogation is however envisaged as being transitional rather than permanent. In this context, it may be observed that the responsible Commissioner, M. de Silguy, took to referring to member states with a derogation as 'pre-ins'.[15]

Under Art. 122(2), the Treaty provides that at least once every two years, or at the request of a member state with a derogation, the Commission and the European Central Bank must report to the Council on the progress made by such a member state in the fulfilment of its obligations regarding the achievement of EMU. After consulting the European Parliament and after discussion in the Council, meeting in the composition of the Heads of State or of Government, the Council shall, acting by a qualified majority on a proposal from the Commission, decide which member states with a derogation fulfil the necessary conditions on the basis of the convergence criteria set out in Art. 121(1), and abrogate the derogations of the member states concerned. The convergence criteria are therefore of continuing relevance.

III CONVERGENCE CRITERIA AND THEIR CONTINUING RELEVANCE

The convergence criteria may be regarded as illustrative of a different kind of flexibility in that they make reference very largely to factual situations and soft law, with the result that their nature could be regarded as having changed during the period between the signature of the Maastricht Treaty in February 1992 and the assessment which was made in May 1998. The assessment was based on a system of reports by the Commission and the European Monetary Institute to the Council. These reports included an examination of the compatibility between each member state's national legislation, including the statutes of its national central bank, and Arts 108 and 109 on the independence of the ECB and of national central banks and the Statute of the ESCB. The reports also examined the achievement of a high degree of sustainable convergence by reference to the fulfilment by each member state of the following criteria:

(1) The achievement of a high degree of price stability; this is stated to be apparent from a rate of inflation which is close to that of, at most, the three best performing member states in terms of price stability.

(2) The sustainability of the government financial position; this is stated to be apparent from having achieved a government budgetary position

---

[15] Speech to Vienna Stock Exchange, 25 September 1998 (RAPID documents Speech 98/182).

without a deficit that is excessive as determined in accordance with Art. 104(6).

(3) The observance of the normal fluctuation margins provided for by the Exchange Rate Mechanism (ERM) of the European Monetary System, for at least two years, without devaluing against the currency of any other member state.

(4) The durability of convergence achieved by the member state and of its participation in the ERM of the European Monetary System being reflected in the long-term interest rate levels.

With regard to the achievement of a high degree of price stability, the Protocol on Convergence Criteria defines closeness in terms of not exceeding the rates of the best three states by more than 1.5 per cent, which in 1992 may have seemed a tight target. However, in the year ending in January 1998, the arithmetic average of the three best performing member states was 1.2 per cent,[16] and to exceed that by 1.5 per cent gives a range of error of more than 100 per cent. The figure used was in fact 2.7 per cent.

On the other hand, the Treaty provisions on the sustainability of the government financial position themselves illustrate an element of flexibility. Under Art. 104(2), the relevant criteria relate to the ratio of the planned or actual government deficit to gross domestic product and to the ratio of government debt to gross domestic product. These criteria are further refined in the Protocol on the Excessive Deficit Procedure, according to which government deficit must not exceed 3 per cent of GDP, and government debt must not exceed 60 per cent of GDP, but they are not absolute. A member state which breaches the deficit ratio will not be regarded as having an excessive government deficit if the ratio has declined 'substantially and continuously' and reached a level that comes close to the reference value, or, alternatively, the excess over the reference value is only 'exceptional and temporary' and the ratio remains close to the reference value.[17] Furthermore, a higher ratio of government debt will not be regarded as excessive if the ratio is 'sufficiently diminishing' and approaching the reference value 'at a satisfactory pace'.[18] Thus both Belgium and Italy had a ratio of government debt to GDP above 120 per cent when the assessment of compliance with the convergence criteria was made[19] yet were not regarded as having an excessive deficit. However, this is not just a hurdle to be jumped over to gain admission to the third stage of EMU; the obligation to avoid an excessive government deficit remains in perpetuity,[20] and its enforcement is the subject of the Stability and Growth Pact.[21]

---

[16] Commission Recommendation of 25 March 1998, recital 6.
[17] Art. 104(2)(a).
[18] Art. 104(2)(b).
[19] Commission Report of 25 March 1998 on Progress towards Convergence, 1.3.1 and 1.3.7.
[20] See Hahn, 'The Stability Pact for European Monetary Union: Compliance with Deficit Limit as a Constant Legal Duty' (1998) CMLRev 77.
[21] Council Regulation 1466/97 on the strengthening of the surveillance of budgetary positions and of the surveillance and coordination of economic policies (OJ 1997, L209/1); Council

So far as the fluctuation margins under the ERM are concerned, reference is made to the 'normal' fluctuation margins and not to the 'narrow' margins. Until 1993 it was the case, as is well known, that the normal margin was 2.25 per cent, with an exceptional band of 6 per cent. The decision taken on the night of 1–2 August 1993 by Ministers and Central Bank governors adopted on a 'temporary' basis a general margin of fluctuation of 15 per cent, subject to a bilateral arrangement between Germany and the Netherlands to maintain a 2.25 per cent margin between their currencies.[22] Leaving on one side the view that such a wide band hardly represents a margin at all, it may be submitted that the 15 per cent band became the 'normal' margin of fluctuation. However, whether or not this interpretation is correct, it shows very clearly how the content of a binding Treaty provision which refers to 'soft' law may effectively be amended by a change in that soft law. The attitude taken by the Commission in its Report and Recommendation of 25 March 1998 was on the one hand to say in its Recommendation[23] that the widening of the margins of fluctuation 'modified the framework' for assessing exchange rate stability, while stating in its Report that it had used the margin of 2.25 per cent as the basis for its assessment, and seems to have been satisfied if a currency had 'almost always' traded within that margin.[24] The Treaty however refers to staying within the normal margin for two years, which gave rise to particular issues in relation to Finland, Italy and Sweden. Italy was one of the original participants in the exchange rate mechanism of the EMS, albeit initially with a wider band of fluctuation of 6.25 per cent. However, like the UK, it found itself having to leave the system in September 1992, and did not rejoin until November 1996, less than two years before the assessment was made. However, in its Report,[25] the Commission stated that 'although the lira has participated in the ERM only since November 1996, it has not experienced severe tensions during the review period and has thus . . . displayed sufficient stability in the last two years'. Finland, which only joined the EU in 1995, entered the ERM in October 1996, and in its Report[26] the Commission used wording virtually identical to that used in relation to Italy. However, Sweden, which also joined the EU in 1995, had not participated at all in the ERM, and was known politically not to wish to participate in stage three of EMU, but did not have the benefit (if such it be[27]) of a special protocol like the UK or Denmark. There is no mention of this last point in the Commission's Report, which instead observes that the Swedish crown

---

Regulation 1467/97 on speeding up and clarifying the implementation of the excessive deficit procedure (OJ 1997, L209/6).
[22] See Agence Europe 2/3, August 1993, No. 6034, 3–4.
[23] Recital 8.
[24] See e.g. Commission Report 1.3.11 in relation to Portugal.
[25] Para. 1.3.7.
[26] Para. 1.3.12.
[27] At a time when the rate of interest declared by the ECB for operations in the euro is 3%, and the UK bank rate is over 5.5%, the present author is not inclined to regard the UK's position as a benefit.

had never participated in the ERM, and that during the relevant two years it had fluctuated against the ERM currencies, 'reflecting, among other things, the absence of an exchange rate target', and the formal Council Decision[28] uses very similar wording. Both then conclude that Sweden did not fulfil the third convergence criterion. The conclusion may therefore be drawn that while this criterion has not been interpreted literally, a member state which does not participate at all in the ERM will not be regarded as meeting the criterion, at least if it has suffered currency fluctuation (which is highly likely to be the case). The practical consequence therefore may be said to be that to the extent that membership of the ERM is voluntary, participation in the third stage of EMU is also voluntary, even if no new member states are offered the special treatment given to the UK and Denmark.

So far as latecomers are concerned, compliance with this criterion at first sight poses problems, because the ecu (in the guise of the euro) will have become the single currency of a number of member states, so that the original ERM simply could not operate; rather, it would appear that the currency of a member state with a derogation would have to stay in a defined relationship with the ecu as a foreign currency in order to qualify for admission to the third stage. However, the Treaty itself fails to deal with the question of an ERM in relations between member states which participate in EMU and those which do not.

The European Monetary Institute prepared a draft framework for that relationship (a European Monetary System Mark II),[29] and this formed the basis of an agreement in principle on its structure at the Dublin European Council in December 1996. This framework was adopted in a European Council Resolution of 16 June 1997,[30] following exactly the same pattern as the 1978 Resolution of the European Council on the original European Monetary System.[31] It is thus an undefined act of an institution of the EU, even though monetary policy is clearly and expressly an exclusive EC competence – at least for the participants in stage three;[32] by way of contrast, in the context of the convergence criteria, Arts 121 and 122 are very careful to refer to the 'Council meeting in the composition of Heads of State or of Government' rather than to the European Council.

The main features of the European Monetary System Mark II include the fact that, like the first version, participation in the ERM is voluntary for the member states outside the euro area, so that the Swedish precedent appears to remain valid. Nevertheless, it is stated that 'Member States with a derogation can be expected to join the mechanism'.[33] The ERM is based on central rates against the euro. The standard fluctuation band is plus or minus 15 per cent

---

[28] Council Decision 98/317 (*OJ* 1998, L139/30).
[29] Report of the EMI to the informal ECOFIN Council, Verona, 12–13 April 1996.
[30] 'Rapid' Information Service, 18 June 1997.
[31] European Council Resolution of 5 December 1978 (EC Bulletin 1978, No. 12, Point 1.1.11).
[32] See Louis, 'A legal and institutional approach for building a Monetary Union' (1998) CMLRev 33 at 70.
[33] European Council Resolution of 16 June 1997, para. 1.6.

around the central rates,[34] as in the original system after 1993, but 'on a case-by-case basis, formally agreed fluctuation bands narrower than the standard one and backed up in principle by automatic intervention and financing may be set at the request of the non-euro area Member State concerned'.[35] In fact, in September 1998, agreement was reached between the finance ministers of the euro-11, the ECB and the ministers and Central Bank governors of Denmark and Greece that Denmark would participate in ERM II within a narrow band of fluctuation of 2.25 per cent, and that Greece would participate within the standard band of plus or minus 15 per cent.[36] However, it is also stated that 'the standard and narrower bands shall not prejudice the interpretation of the third indent of Art. 121(1) of the EC Treaty',[37] a singularly unhelpful provision given the doubts discussed above. It may be suggested, following the language of the Commission Recommendation of 25 March 1998 and the Council Decision of 3 May 1998, that what will really matter is whether the currency has suffered 'severe tensions'.

So far as the interest rate criterion is concerned, it might finally be observed that under the Protocol on Convergence Criteria it is stated that average nominal long-term interest rates should not exceed those of the three best states by more than 2 per cent. By the time the assessment was made, the figure derived from the three best states was 5.8 per cent,[38] so that again a margin of 2 per cent allows for a wide margin of error in relation to that norm, whatever may have been the situation in 1992.

IV   THE EUROPEAN CENTRAL BANK AND SYSTEM OF CENTRAL BANKS

1   Institutional nature

Differential integration is perhaps most obvious in the structure of the European Central Bank and System of Central Banks. One of the fundamental differences between the proposals of the Delors Committee and the text adopted in the Maastricht Treaty is that Delors recommended that the European Central Bank should come into being in the second stage of EMU, whereas the Treaty provided for an interim body, the European Monetary Institute, to operate during the second stage. The reason for this may be found in the structure of the European Central Bank. By virtue of Art. 112 read with Art. 122(3) and the Statute of the ESCB, the Governing Council of the Central Bank comprises the Executive Board of the ECB and the governors of the central banks of the member states without a derogation (i.e. the 'ins'). Article 112 further provides that the Executive Board of the

---

[34] Para. 2.1.
[35] Para. 2.4.
[36] Bulletin Quotidien Europe No. 7310, 28 and 29 September 1998.
[37] Para. 2.5.
[38] Commission Recommendation of 25 March 1998, recital 9.

ECB shall comprise the President, the Vice-President and **four** other members. The President, the Vice-President and the other members of the Executive Board are to be appointed from among persons of recognized standing and professional experience in monetary or banking matters by common accord of the Governments of the member states without a derogation at the level of Heads of State or of Government. It is therefore clear that the Executive Board of the ECB need not be representative even of all the participating member states. Indeed, it is provided that if there are member states with a derogation, the number of members of the Executive Board may be smaller than provided for in Art. 11.1 of the Statute of the ESCB (a President, a Vice-President and four others), but in no circumstances may it be less than four. On this basis it would be difficult to envisage all member states being involved during the second stage, only for some of them to drop out because the could not participate in the third stage; hence the European Monetary Institute. However, if there was not to be a representative of every participating state on the Executive Board of the ECB, it was difficult to envisage that one of those seats would be left unfilled for the representative of a state which **might** join later. Indeed, no seats were left unfilled when the initial appointments were made (although the duration of the appointments was staggered). It further may be observed that the meeting which made the appointments, although it was held during the British presidency, was chaired by an Austrian minister.[39]

The system derives from Art. 8 of the EC Treaty which provides for the establishment of a European System of Central Banks and a European Central Bank in accordance with the procedures laid down in the Treaty; these bodies should act within the limits of the powers conferred upon them by this Treaty and by the Statute of the ESCB and of the ECB annexed to the Treaty. The basic framework is set out in Art. 107 of the EC Treaty, under which the ESCB, the Statute of which is laid down in a Protocol annexed to the Treaty, is composed of the ECB and of the national central banks, it is to have legal personality, and the ESCB is to be governed by the decision-making bodies of the ECB which are the Governing Council and the Executive Board. This should however be read with Art. 123(3), to the effect that if and as long as there are member states with a derogation, the General Council of the ECB referred to in Art. 45 of the Statute of the ESCB shall be constituted as a third decision-making body of the ECB.

This framework is fleshed out in Art. 112 and the Statute. The Governing Council of the ECB comprises the members of the Executive Board of the ECB and the Governors of the national central banks of member states without a derogation.[40] The Executive Board comprises the President, the Vice-President and four other members. Under Art. 112(2)(b), which does not in any event apply to member states with a derogation,[41] the President,

---

[39] Decision 98/345/EC of 26 May 1998 (*OJ* 1998, L154/33).
[40] Art. 112(1); Statute Art. 10.1 read with Art. 43.4.
[41] Art. 122(3).

the Vice-President and the other members of the Executive Board are to be appointed from among persons of recognized standing and professional experience in monetary or banking matters by common accord of the Governments of the member states without a derogation[42] at the level of Heads of State or of Government, on a recommendation from the Council, after it has consulted the European Parliament and the Governing Council of the ECB. Their term of office is to be eight years and may not be renewed, though as envisaged in the Statute, the first appointments were made for four (the Vice-President), five, six, seven, and eight years.[43] It must finally be emphasized that only nationals of member states without a derogation[44] may be members of the Executive Board.

A requirement of independence similar to, if not stronger, than that imposed on members of the Commission by Art. 213(2) of the EC Treaty is laid down by Art. 108. When exercising the powers and carrying out the tasks and duties conferred upon them by the Treaty and the Statute of the ESCB, neither the ECB, nor a national central bank, nor any member of their decision-making bodies may seek or take instructions from EC institutions or bodies, from any government of a member state or from any other body. Conversely, the EC institutions and bodies and the governments of the member states undertake to respect this principle and not to seek to influence the members of the decision-making bodies of the ECB or of the national central banks in the performance of their tasks. The consequential 'democratic deficit' has been a matter of much discussion.[45]

Nevertheless, formal links with other EC institutions are established under Art. 113. This provides that the President of the Council and a member of the Commission may participate, without having the right to vote, in meetings of the Governing Council of the ECB, and that the President of the Council may submit a motion for deliberation to the Governing Council of the ECB. Conversely, the President of the ECB must be invited to participate in Council meetings when the Council is discussing matters relating to the objectives and tasks of the ESCB. It is further provided that[46] the ECB is to address an annual report on the activities of the ESCB and on the monetary policy of both the previous and current year to the European Parliament, the Council and the Commission, and also to the European Council. This report is to be presented by the President of the ECB to the Council and to the European Parliament, which may hold a general debate on that basis. The President of the ECB and the other members of the Executive Board may also, at the request of the European Parliament or on their own initiative, be heard by the competent Committees of the European Parliament.

---

[42] Art. 122(4).
[43] Decision 98/345/EC of 26 May 1998 (*OJ* 1998, L154/33).
[44] Ibid.
[45] See e.g. Gormley and De Haan: 'The Democratic Deficit of the European Central Bank' (1996) EL Rev 95.
[46] Art. 113(3).

The responsibilities of the decision-making bodies are set out in Art. 12 of the Statute. Under Art. 12.1, which does not confer any rights or obligations on member states with a derogation,[47] the Governing Council must adopt the guidelines and take the decisions necessary to ensure the performance of the tasks entrusted to the ESCB under the Treaty and the Statute. It is to formulate the monetary policy of the EC including, as appropriate, decisions relating to intermediate monetary objectives, key interest rates and the supply of reserves in the ESCB and must establish the necessary guidelines for their implementation.

The Executive Board, on the other hand, is to implement monetary policy in accordance with the guidelines and decisions laid down by the Governing Council. In doing so the Executive Board must give the necessary instructions to national central banks of the member states without a derogation.[48] In addition, the Executive Board may have certain powers delegated to it where the Governing Council so decides. It also has responsibility for the preparation of meetings of the Governing Council.[49] There may therefore be seen to be analogous with the relationship between the Commission and the Council in that the Council normally legislates on the basis of a Commission proposal and in that wide powers are delegated by the Council to the Commission.[50] However, the analogy is far from perfect – in particular the whole Commission does not participate in Council meetings! From the perspective of legal acts, furthermore, the Treaty does not distinguish between acts which emanate from the Governing Council and those which may emanate from the Executive Board; the only reference is to acts made by 'the ECB',[51] whereas in the general Treaty texts mention is made expressly of acts of the Council and European Parliament, acts of the Council and acts of the Commission.[52]

So far as the 'System', i.e. the relationship with national central banks, is concerned, Art. 12.1 provides that to the extent deemed possible and appropriate and without prejudice to the other provisions of Art. 12, the ECB shall have recourse to the national central banks to carry out operations which form part of the tasks of the ESCB. More particularly, under Art. 14.3 of the Statute, which also does not confer any rights or obligations on member states with a derogation,[53] the national central banks are an integral part of the ESCB and must act in accordance with the guidelines and instructions of the ECB. This may be seen as an express incorporation of the duty of cooperation set out in Art. 5 of the EC Treaty. It is for the Governing Council to take the necessary steps to ensure compliance with the guidelines and instructions of the ECB and to require that any necessary information be given to it. However, under Art. 14.4, national central banks may perform functions other

[47] Statute Art. 43.1.
[48] Statute Art. 43.4.
[49] Statute Art. 12.2.
[50] Under Art. 202 of the EC Treaty.
[51] See Arts 110, 230, 234 and 288.
[52] Arts 230 and 249.
[53] Statute Art. 43.1.

than those specified in the Statute unless the Governing Council finds, by a majority of two thirds of the votes cast, that these interfere with the objectives and tasks of the ESCB. Such functions are to be performed on the responsibility and liability of national central banks and shall not be regarded as being part of the functions of the ESCB.

Linked to this, Art. 109, which by virtue of the notice given under the Protocol will not apply to the UK,[54] although recent legislation has moved towards an element of independence, imposed the obligation on each member state to ensure, at the latest at the date of the establishment of the ESCB, that its national legislation including the statutes of its national central bank is compatible with the Treaty and the Statute of the ESCB, an obligation with which Sweden was found not to have complied.[55]

More specifically, Art. 14.2 of the Statute, which does not apply to the UK,[56] requires that the statutes of the national central banks should, in particular, provide that the term of office of a Governor of a national central bank shall be no less than five years. Furthermore, a Governor may be relieved from office only if he no longer fulfils the conditions required for the performance of his duties or if he has been guilty of serious misconduct. A decision to this effect may be referred to the Court of Justice by the Governor concerned or the Governing Council of the ECB on grounds of infringement of the Treaty or of any rule of law relating to its application – a unique example of a national official becoming subject to EC jurisdiction.

A further example of the involvement of the ECB at the national level may be found in the requirement in Art. 105(4) that the ECB should be consulted by the national authorities on any draft legislative provision in its fields of competence, a requirement implemented in Council Regulation 98/415.[57] Article 2(1) of the Regulation lists the relevant fields as including currency matters, means of payment, national central banks, the collection, compilation, and distribution of monetary, financial, banking, payment systems and balance of payments statistics, payment and settlement systems and rules relating to financial institutions 'in so far as they materially influence the stability of financial institutions and markets'. This provision applies even to the non-participants, except the UK,[58] and they have the additional burden of consulting the ECB on any draft legislative provisions on the instruments of monetary policy, under Art. 2(2) of the Regulation.

For the member states which are not able or willing to participate immediately in the third stage of EMU, the only decision-making body of the ECB in which they are represented is the General Council referred to in Art. 123(3) of the Treaty and Art. 45 of the Statute. Under Art. 45.2, it consists of the President and Vice-President of the ECB and the Governors of all the

---

[54] Protocol 11 Art. 5.
[55] Council Decision 98/317 of 3 May 1998 (*OJ* 1998, L139/30).
[56] UK Protocol Art. 8.
[57] *OJ* 1998, L189/42.
[58] Protocol 11 Art. 5.

national central banks. The other members of the Executive Board may however participate, without having the right to vote, in its meetings. Apart from certain advisory and consultative functions, its principal role is to take over those tasks of the EMI which, because of the derogations of one or more member states, still have to be performed in the third stage, and to give advice in the preparations for the abrogation of the derogations specified in Art. 122 of the Treaty.[59] With regard to the latter function, the General Council is to contribute to the necessary preparations for irrevocably fixing the exchange rates of the currencies of member states with a derogation against the currencies, or the single currency, of the member states without a derogation, as referred to in Art. 123(5) of the Treaty. Otherwise, under Art. 47.4 of the Statute, 'the General Council shall be **informed** by the President of the ECB of decisions of the Governing Council' (emphasis added).

Given the structure outlined above, it may be understood why the ECB as such could not be established on a provisional basis during the second stage.

2 Functions

The basic objectives and tasks of the ECSB and the ECB are set out in Arts 105 and 106 of the EC Treaty, neither of which apply to the UK,[60] with one exception, and most of which do not apply to other member states with a derogation,[61] with two exceptions. There is one exception in common, i.e. a provision which applies to all member states, which is Art. 105(6), a provision of considerable importance to the commercial banking community. Under this, the Council may, acting unanimously on a proposal from the Commission and after consulting the ECB and after receiving the assent of the European Parliament, confer upon the ECB specific tasks concerning policies relating to the prudential supervision of credit institutions and other financial institutions with the exception of insurance undertakings. If this power is used, it could have considerable consequences for the 'general good' provisions of the Second Banking Directive, for example.

The provision from which only the UK is excluded is Art. 105(4), discussed above, under which the ECB is to be consulted on any proposed EC act in its fields of competence and by national authorities regarding any draft legislative provision in its fields of competence;[62] it further provides that the ECB may submit opinions to the appropriate EC institutions or bodies or to national authorities on matters in its fields of competence.

Otherwise the objectives and tasks listed are of direct interest only to member states without a derogation. Under Art. 105(1), the primary objective of the ESCB is to be to maintain price stability; without prejudice to that

---

[59] Statute Arts 47.1 and 44.
[60] UK Protocol Art. 5.
[61] Art. 122(3).
[62] But within the limits and under the conditions set out by the Council in accordance with the procedure laid down in Art. 107(6).

objective, the ESCB is also to support the general economic policies in the EC with a view to contributing to the achievement of the objectives of the EC as laid down in Art. 2. It is further required that the ESCB should act in accordance with the principle of an open market economy with free competition, favouring an efficient allocation of resources, and in compliance with the principles set out in Art. 4.

The basic tasks[63] to be carried out through the ESCB are to define and implement the monetary policy of the EC; to conduct foreign exchange operations consistent with the provisions of Art. 111; to hold and manage the official foreign reserves of the member states, without prejudice to the holding and management by the governments of member states of foreign exchange working balances; and to promote the smooth operation of payment systems. The ESCB may also[64] contribute to the smooth conduct of policies pursued by the competent authorities relating to the prudential supervision of credit institutions and the stability of the financial system.

Article 106(1) sets out what would perhaps be the most important monetary function of the ECB, going to the heart of what has been traditionally regarded as a function of the State:[65] for the participant member states, the ECB has the exclusive right to authorize the issue of bank notes within the EC. The ECB and the national central banks may issue such notes and the bank notes issued by the ECB and the national central banks shall be the only such notes to have the status of legal tender within the EC. However, while the euro may become the currency of the participating member states in 1999, euro banknotes and coins will not be introduced until January 2002.[66] During the intervening period, and for up to six months thereafter, national notes and coins will remain in use, but their legal nature will change: under Art. 6 of the Regulation they will become divisions of the euro rather than continuing as currencies in their own right. They will only be legal tender, however, within their territorial limits as of the day before the commencement of EMU.[67] The Regulation provides that where in a legal instrument reference is made to a national currency unit, 'this reference shall be as valid as if reference were made to the euro unit according to the conversion rates'.[68] Furthermore, the substitution of the euro for the currency of each participating member state does not in itself have the effect of altering the denomination of legal instruments in existence on the date of substitution.[69] Banknotes denominated in euros, and coins denominated in euros or in cents, are to be put in circulation in the participating member states as from 1 January 2002[70] and, subject to a changeover period of up to six

---

[63] Art. 105(2).
[64] Art. 105(5).
[65] See the judgment of the European Court in Case 7/78 *R v Thompson* [1978] ECR 2247.
[66] Council Regulation 974/98 on the introduction of the euro (*OJ* 1998, L139/1) Art. 10.
[67] Art. 9.
[68] Art. 6(2).
[69] Art. 7.
[70] Art. 10.

months,[71] will be the only banknotes and coins which have the status of legal tender in all of these member states. Nevertheless, issuers of national banknotes and coins are required to continue to accept the banknotes and coins previously issued by them against euros at the conversion rate.[72] With regard to coins, Art. 106(2) permits participating member states to issue coins subject to approval by the ECB of the volume of the issue. The Council may, acting in accordance with the cooperation procedure[73] (which remains operative in this area following the failure of the Amsterdam Treaty to amend any provisions relating to EMU) and after consulting the ECB, adopt measures to harmonize the denominations and technical specifications of all coins intended for circulation to the extent necessary to permit their smooth circulation within the EC; this resulted in the enactment of Council Regulation 975/98 on denominations and technical specifications of euro coins intended for circulation.[74] From this it appears that there will be coins ranging from one cent to two euros, which will have to meet standard specifications with regard to diameter, thickness, weight, shape, colour, composition and edge, but which will have one 'European' and one national side.

Although it is a prohibition rather than a task, it might finally be observed that Art. 101, which appears to apply to all member states, forbids overdraft facilities or any other type of credit facility with the ECB or with the central banks of the member states in favour of EC institutions or bodies, central governments, regional, local or other public authorities, other bodies governed by public law, or public undertakings of member states, and also forbids the purchase directly from them by the ECB or national central banks of debt instruments. However, this does not apply to publicly-owned credit institutions which, in the context of the supply of reserves by central banks, shall be given the same treatment by national central banks and the ECB as private credit institutions.

Although it may be a bank, it is foreseen in Art. 110 (which again does not apply to member states with a derogation[75]) that the ECB may issue binding legal acts similar in nature to those listed in Art. 249 which may be issued by the Council and Parliament together, by the Council or by the Commission. It is provided that in order to carry out the tasks entrusted to the ESCB, the ECB shall, in accordance with the provisions of the Treaty and under the conditions laid down in the Statute make regulations to the extent necessary to implement certain tasks defined in the Statute in the acts of the Council;[76] it may take decisions necessary for carrying out the tasks entrusted to the ESCB under the Treaty and the Statute; and it may make recommendations and deliver opinions.

---

[71] Art. 15.
[72] Art. 16.
[73] Art. 252.
[74] *OJ* 1998, L139/6.
[75] Art. 122(3); UK Protocol Art. 5.
[76] See Art. 107(6).

In terms remarkably similar to those of Art. 249, Art. 110(2) states that a regulation shall have general application and shall be binding in its entirety and directly applicable in all member states; recommendations and opinions shall have no binding force; and a decision shall be binding in its entirety upon those to whom it is addressed. It is further provided that Arts 253 to 256 of the EC Treaty (on reasoning, publication and notification, and enforcement) shall apply to regulations and decisions adopted by the ECB. While under these provisions, publication is only obligatory for regulations, the ECB may decide to publish its decisions, recommendations and opinions. However, these are not necessarily the only legal acts which may emanate from the bank: Art. 12 of the Statute refers to the governing Council adopting 'guidelines' and to the Executive Board giving 'instructions' to the national central banks and it has been suggested that these may give rise to third party rights and that they may be regarded as reviewable acts.[77]

Finally, rather like the Commission in the context of the general competition rules, the ECB is given a policing role by Art. 110(3): within the limits and under the conditions adopted by the Council,[78] the ECB is entitled to impose fines or periodic penalty payments on undertakings[79] for failure to comply with obligations under its regulations and decisions.

The power to issue binding legal acts is no doubt one reason why the ECB is made subject to, but also able to benefit from, the full range of judicial remedies under the EC Treaty. Without wishing to repeat them all here, it might merely be observed that the action for annulment, references for preliminary rulings and liability in damages are likely to have considerable practical relevance in relation to the ECB, given the wider range of binding acts which it is empowered to issue.

V THE 'INS' AND THE 'OUTS'

With hindsight, the Maastricht Treaty introduced two different forms of flexibility or differentiated integration. The Social Protocol took the form of a permission by all the member states to a group of member states to use EC institutions and legislation, which can be seen as the precursor of the general provisions on 'closer cooperation' in the Amsterdam Treaty. On the other hand, the provisions on EMU provide for some member states to receive opt-outs or derogations from binding Treaty obligations and thus provide the model for the new Title of the EC Treaty on visas, asylum and immigration introduced by the Amsterdam Treaty. A further way in which the EMU provisions have to be regarded as different in nature from the general provisions on closer cooperation is that under Art. 11(1)(a) of the EC Treaty,

---

[77] See e.g. Louis, 'A legal and institutional approach for building a Monetary Union' (1998) CMLRev 33 at 54–58.
[78] Under the procedure laid down in Art. 107(6).
[79] *Quaere* whether a national central bank could be regarded as an undertaking.

closer cooperation must not concern areas which fall within the exclusive competence of the EC. It may be suggested that in the third stage of EMU, matters such as monetary policy and exchange rate policy will be areas where those participating in a single currency will not be able to have divergent national policies and which will be regarded as a matter of exclusive EC competence irrespective of the extent to which EC rules have been introduced. Indeed Art. 4(2) expressly states that there shall be a 'single' monetary policy. It may also be suggested that here, as in the fisheries sector,[80] participating member states will be regarded as acting as agents of the EC – a situation effectively institutionalized in the European System of Central Banks. Intriguingly, however, it will be a matter of exclusive competence only for those who participate, which may lead to new aspects of the question of mixed competence in international negotiations or to a situation in which international obligations are entered into by a 'Community' which does not include all its members.

By way of example, the need (or hope) for an exchange rate policy is envisaged in Art. 111 of the EC Treaty; it should however be emphasized that this provision does not apply to member states with a derogation[81] or to the UK following its decision not to participate.[82] Article 111(1) operates by way of derogation from Art. 300, which sets out the general procedure for the negotiation of international agreements between the EC and non-member states or international organizations; it empowers the Council to conclude formal agreements on an exchange rate system for the ECU in relation to non-EC currencies – which seems to contemplate a return to something like the former IMF system – and lays down a special procedure for this to be achieved. The Council is required to act unanimously on a recommendation from the European Central Bank or from the Commission (which indicates that the power of initiative in this area is as much, if not more, with the ECB as with the Commission) after consulting the ECB in an endeavour to reach a consensus consistent with the objective of price stability and after consulting the European Parliament. The procedure for negotiation is laid down in Art. 111(3), which provides that where agreements concerning monetary or foreign exchange regime matters need to be negotiated by the EC with one or more states or international organizations, the Council, acting by a qualified majority[83] on a recommendation from the Commission and after consulting the ECB, shall decide the arrangements for the negotiation and for the conclusion of such agreements. It is stated that these arrangements must ensure that the EC expresses a single position, and that the Commission must be 'fully associated' with the negotiations. The implication of this is that whereas negotiations under the general Art. 300 are conducted by the

---

[80] Case 804/79 *Commission v UK* [1981] ECR 1045.
[81] Art. 122(3) and (4).
[82] UK Protocol Art. 5.
[83] Though it will be recalled that under Art. 111(1) it needs to act unanimously to conclude the resultant agreement.

Commission, the same is not necessarily the case under Art. 111, and the negotiations could, for example, be entrusted to the ECB. It is, however, clearly laid down that agreements concluded in accordance with Art. 111(3) are to be binding on the institutions of the EC, on the ECB and on member states (but, of course, only those participating in monetary union).

What however the Treaty failed to provide for is an exchange rate relationship between the 'ins' and the 'outs' – hence the development of the European Monetary System Mark II by a Resolution of the European Council, as discussed above.

Although it may in practice be a more theoretical question, it may be wondered if a similar problem is not hidden in the safeguard measures permitted by the provisions on free movement of capital introduced by the Maastricht Treaty. Unlike any other Treaty freedom, Art. 56 provides that movements to and from third countries are to be treated the same way as movements between member states. More specifically Art. 56(1) states that within the framework of the provisions set out in that Chapter, all restrictions on the movement of capital between member states and between member states and third countries shall be prohibited and Art. 56(2) states that within the same framework, all restrictions on payments between member states and between member states and third countries shall be prohibited. However, the safeguard clause for defending the EMU in Art. 59 relates only to third countries, stating that where, in exceptional circumstances, movements of capital to or from third countries cause, or threaten to cause, serious difficulties for the operation of EMU, the Council, acting by a qualified majority on a proposal from the Commission and after consulting the ECB, may take safeguard measures with regard to third countries for a period not exceeding six months if such measures are strictly necessary. There is no provision for parallel measures in relation to non-participant member states, even though all such states may remain entitled to take or be authorized to take measures to protect their balance of payments under Arts 119 and 120. While it is perhaps unlikely that the Euro 11 will need to defend themselves against the four non-participants, it is unusual to find such an imbalance in the Treaty provisions.

VI THE COMPOSITION OF THE COUNCIL

Variable participation within a single Treaty, and linkages between separate Treaties outlined above, raises the question of how far a single institutional structure may operate at all levels. The present writer has taken the view that under the Maastricht provisions, the Council of Ministers varied from its basic composition under the Social Protocol and does vary from that composition in the third stage of EMU; in both those cases it has contained or will contain representatives only of the participant governments. On the other hand the Amsterdam provisions on closer cooperation make it clear that institutionally the non-participants would not be totally excluded. It is provided in the new Art. 44 of the Treaty on European Union that all the members of the Council would be able to take part in deliberations on the matters concerned. However, only the participants would be able to take part in the adoption of decisions and vote. This contrasts with the apparent practice of the UK not to participate in meetings under the Social Protocol, and what may perhaps be expected to be the practice under the third stage of EMU. Evidence on this last point may be gleaned from the European Council meeting in Luxembourg in December 1997. A Resolution was agreed there on economic policy coordination under Art. 99 of the EC Treaty in Stage 3 of EMU,[84] Art. 99 being a provision with regard to which there is no derogation or opt-out. Article 6 of the resolution recognizes that the ECOFIN Council (including everyone) is the only body empowered to formulate and adopt 'the broad economic policy guidelines which constitute the main instrument of economic coordination' but at the same time accepts that 'the Ministers of the States participating in the euro area may meet informally among themselves to discuss issues connected with their shared specific responsibilities for the single currency'. If they wish to do that in this context, it can hardly be imagined that they would wish non-participants to be present in discussion of what to them would be their domestic monetary policy. Furthermore, even where ministers representative of all the governments do meet in the Council, it may be observed that the eleven states participating in EMU total 65 votes between them, which is more than the number required (62) for a qualified majority, and the four 'outs' together have only 22 votes, which is not only insufficient to block a decision but is also not enough (23–25 votes) to trigger the 'Ioannina compromise' to delay a decision.[85]

VII   OTHER INSTITUTIONAL ISSUES

On the other hand, the Commission, Parliament and Court of Justice do not vary in their composition or their internal voting rights in the context of closer cooperation. Since 1979, the European Parliament has been elected directly by the citizens of the EU, albeit not by uniform methods. The seats are nevertheless allocated to each member state in a way which is not directly proportionate to population but which gives the bigger member states more seats than the smaller ones. However, in the context of EMU, the situation will arise where representatives of the citizens of member states which do not participate in those policy areas will be involved in the decision-making process in relation to EC acts which will not apply in the geographical area they represent. Examples include Art. 111(1) on exchange-rate agreements and Art. 112(2)(b) on the appointment of the Executive Board. It might simply be observed that this is not an unfamiliar problem in the UK and is of

[84] Annex I to the Conclusions of the Luxembourg European Council, 12–13 December 1997.
[85] See Usher, 'EC Institutions and Legislation', Longman, 1998, 23–25.

particular importance in the context of the establishment of a separate Scottish Parliament.

The question whether the same institutions can act at all levels and for different combinations of participant States arises most clearly where the institution is not necessarily meant to be representative. While the members of the Commission must neither seek nor take instructions from any government or from any other body,[86] only nationals of member states may be members of the Commission, and the Commission must, under the Treaty in its present version, include at least one national of each of the member states, but may not include more than two members having the nationality of the same state. In practice there are currently twenty Commissioners, two from each of the big countries (which for this purpose include Spain) and one from each of the other member states. However, the second paragraph of Art. 213 provides that the number of members of the Commission may be altered by the Council, acting unanimously. One of the matters frequently discussed in political circles is whether the number of Commissioners should be reduced to one per state, and there have been ideas floated of grouping some of the smaller countries together to have a rotating Commissioner between them, which essentially is the system used for selecting Advocates-General before the Court (other than those who come from the four biggest countries). This debate puts clearly into focus the question whether the Commission should be regarded as a representative body or simply in terms of its operational needs.

The Treaty of Amsterdam does not directly respond to any of these proposals, but it contains a Protocol on the institutions with the prospect of enlargement of the EU which links the size of the Commission to the weighting of votes in the Council. Under this Protocol, at the date of entry into force of the first enlargement of the Union the Commission is to comprise one national of each of the member states, provided that, by that date, the weighting of the votes in the Council has been modified, in a manner acceptable to all member states, notably compensating those member states which give up the possibility of nominating a second member of the Commission. Here, therefore, the Commission is clearly treated as part of the representative equation and not as a body whose composition is determined according to its operational needs.

If the membership of the Commission is finally to be determined by its functional needs rather than (indirect) national representation, then it clearly should be able to function at all levels, and it may be submitted that given the legal duties of its members that that should be the situation and is the situation in the context of Stage 3 of EMU. The Commission, for example, plays a leading role in the excessive deficits procedure under Art. 104, and a Commission proposal is required under Art. 106(2) with regard to the issue of coins and may be required under Art. 111 with regard to exchange rate policy.

[86] Art. 213.

With regard to membership of the European Court, the Treaty is not specific as to the representation of each member state; it merely states that the Judges and Advocates-General are to be chosen from persons whose independence is beyond doubt and who possess the qualifications required for appointment to the highest judicial offices in their respective countries or who are jurisconsults of recognized competence. However, the current Court of fifteen judges is composed of one from each member state, and until the enlargement of the Court shortly after Greek accession, if one took the judges and Advocates-General together, there were always two members of the Court from the big member states. However, since then there has been more of a trend towards meeting the Court's manpower needs, as exemplified in the number of Advocates-General (in principle eight but currently nine) rather than proportionate representation of the member states.

In the case of the Court of First Instance, the Treaty provisions merely required that its members should be chosen from persons whose independence is beyond doubt and who possess the ability required for appointment to judicial office, and in its initial proposals on the matter, the European Court suggested that the Court of First Instance could be a small body with e.g. five judges. However, the Council eventually decided on the creation of a body with twelve judges (which turned out to have one judge from each member state), and it has been enlarged to fifteen following the 1995 accessions, with its three new members coming from each of the three new member states.

VIII   ROLE OF THE EUROPEAN COURT OF JUSTICE

In the context of variable geometry, it is at the level of the Court of Justice and of the Court of First Instance that serious issues arise which do not so far appear to have been addressed in the Treaty texts or in the Amsterdam amendments. Put very simply, can member states which do not participate in a particular area of joint activity, and their citizens, exercise EC judicial remedies in relation to acts adopted in that area? There is a general statement in relation to closer cooperation in Art. 11(4) that 'the acts and decisions necessary for the implementation of cooperation activities shall be subject to all the relevant provisions of this Treaty', but it may be argued that this still leaves a number of issues open to debate, and in any event it does not apply to EMU.

With regard to actions for annulment, the established situation is that in so far as rights of action are conferred upon them by the substantive Treaty provisions, and with regard to the acts susceptible to challenge under the provisions, no real problems of *locus standi* would appear to arise with regard to actions for annulment brought by member states, the Council or the Commission. Indeed, in Case 166/78 *Italy v Council*,[87] it was held that Italy

---

[87] [1979] ECR 2575, 2596.

was not barred from seeking the annulment of a Council Regulation by the fact that its representative at the relevant Council meeting had voted in favour of that Regulation; the implication appears to be that, within its express limits, the right of action conferred upon member states to seek the annulment of an EC act is unconditional. It is also clear that the member states and these institutions do not have to show that they have an interest in bringing the proceedings,[88] although it would appear that like other litigants[89] they need to show that they have an interest in the grounds for annulment that they put forward, i.e. that the alleged breach would have made a difference to the outcome.[90]

On the other hand, it may be observed that a government, even the government of an area falling within the EC, which is not that of a member state as such, is treated on the same basis as a natural or legal person, as happened to the government of Gibraltar in Case C-298/89 *Gibraltar v Council*,[91] i.e. it has to show that the act at issue is of direct and individual concern to it. Does a non-participant government therefore have an absolute right to bring an action for annulment in relation to an act of the ECB or of a Council comprising the Euro 11, or does it have to show direct and individual concern?

Serious arguments can be put both ways, but if I could repeat a point made in my Edinburgh Inaugural Lecture,[92] a related problem has in fact already arisen in the context of references for preliminary rulings, under the 1971 Protocol on the interpretation by the Court of the 1968 Judgments Convention, where the Court took an approach not mentioned in the Treaty texts. The background is that the first reference under that Protocol, Case 12/76 *Tessili Como v Dunlop*[93] was heard in 1976, before the member states which had joined the EC in 1973 had signed the Accession Convention to the Brussels Convention, which occurred in 1978 (and was eventually introduced into the legal systems of the UK by the Civil Jurisdiction and Judgements Act 1982). In the course of the proceedings, the question arose as to whether the UK and Ireland could exercise the right to submit observations with regard to the interpretation of a Convention to which they were not parties. The answer given by the European Court was that under the 1972 Act of Accession, the new member states were **legally obliged** (emphasis added) to accede to the 1968 Convention, and that they therefore had an interest in expressing their views when the Court was called upon to interpret a Convention to which they were required to become parties.

In the specific context of references for preliminary rulings, the Amsterdam Treaty does deal with the matter in relation to the voluntary system of

---

[88] E.g. Case 45/86 *Commission v Council* [1987] ECR 1493.
[89] See Case 90/74 *Deboeck v Commission* [1975] ECR 1123.
[90] Case 259/87 *France v Commission* [1987] ECR 4393.
[91] [1993] ECR I-3605.
[92] Usher: 'Variable Geometry or Concentric Circles: Patterns for the European Union' (1997) *International and Comparative Law Quarterly*, 243–273.
[93] [1976] ECR 1473.

references under the revised Third Pillar in Art. 35(4). This lays down that any member state, whether or not it has made a declaration accepting the jurisdiction of the Court, shall be entitled to submit statements of case or written observations to the Court. However, the Treaty is silent with regard to references in the context of other areas of flexibility.

If the test laid down in *Tessili Como v Dunlop*[94] were to be applied more generally, in particular in the context of direct actions for annulment, it would produce some interesting results in the current areas of variable geometry. In the context of EMU, the 'Member States with a derogation' remain bound by the obligation to achieve that objective[95] and therefore would be able to challenge acts of EC institutions representing the participant states and ostensibly binding only on those states. On the other hand, now that the UK has given notice that it will not participate, it will not be subject to the basic Treaty obligation, and under the Court's test would not be able to exercise its special rights as a member state, but would rather be left to show direct and individual concern. It may however be submitted that it would be preferable if the matter were to be settled in an express provision of a revised EC Treaty.

With regard to private actions for annulment, it may be suggested that the requirement to show direct and individual concern circumvents the problem: there is a long history of actions for annulment being brought by applicants who are neither citizens of nor resident in a member state.[96] However, given that the third stage of EMU will commence without the participation of the UK, could a UK court faced with a dispute relating to an ECB decision relating to the use of the euro make a reference as to its interpretation? To the extent that the decision is to be regarded as an EC act and the court is a court or tribunal of a member state, it may be suggested that this question should be answered in the affirmative. What if the UK voluntarily adopted domestic rules which reflected the ECB decision? While the analogy is not perfect, there are a number of instances where the Court has been willing to interpret EC acts where what was at issue before the national court was not the EC act as such but national legislation which made reference to or used the language of the EC act.[97]

IX CONCLUSION

Admiration must be expressed for the very considerable achievements of those member states which have met the criteria for participation in Stage 3 of EMU. However, a structure which allows both for derogations and opt-outs, whatever its merits in terms of political realities, creates a whole range of novel legal problems.

[94] [1976] ECR 1473.
[95] Art. 122(3) does not exempt them from Art. 4(2).
[96] See, to take a couple of random examples, Case 60/81 *IBM v Commission* [1981] ECR 2639; or Case C-49/88 *Al-Jubail Fertiliser v Council* [1991] ECR I-3187.
[97] Cases C-297/88 *Dzodzi* [1990] ECR I-3763, and Case 231/89 *Gmorzynska-Bscher* [1990] ECR I-4003.

INDEX

non-governmental organizations
(NGOs), 207–8, 209
non-tariff barriers, 194, 195, 199
North America Free Trade Agreement
(NAFTA), 198

OECD, 195, 196, 204
opt-outs, 5–8, 245
United Kingdom, 5, 97, 98, 102,
105–6, 211

parental leave, 97, 98, 100, 102
part-time work, 98, 100
payments, direct aid, 63, 64, 70–1
peace-making and peace-keeping, 56
'Petersburg' tasks, 56
Poland, 65, 66, 67, 68, 201
police cooperation, 169, 170, 171,
173–4
policy leakage, 112, 113
Ponsonby rule, 185
Portugal, 63, 224
pre-emption, 3
price stability, 217, 218, 220, 222, 231,
233, 234, 242
prices, agricultural, 59, 60, 61, 62, 63,
66, 72, 73, 74
private international law, harmonization
of, 151–66
private systems of law enforcement, 21,
24, 25–31, 32, 36–41
producer responsibility, 59, 60
production, specialization in, 222
proportionality principle, 16–17, 81–2,
88, 157
protectionism, 200, 202, 220
public enforcement of Community law,
25–31

qualified majority voting (QMV), 12,
46, 49, 50, 56, 205

redistribution, social, 110, 111
Reflection Group Report, 116
regional commercial policy, 197–8, 200
regional impact of monetary union, 210,
212, 222–9
rights of the individual, protection of,
14, 18, 24, 32–6, 116

rule of law, and environmental
protection, 90
rural development, 64, 66, 67, 71,
72–3, 76
Russia, 196

Saudi Arabia, 196
Schengen system, 6, 7, 18, 170–1, 174,
185
Scotland
administrative competence of Scottish
Executive, 134–5
implementation of EU law, 124–35
involvement in EU policy and
legislative process, 127–9
Scotland Act (1998), 125, 127–8,
130–3
Secretary General of the Council, 50–1,
57
sectoral dialogue, 98, 99, 100–1, 103
security and defence, 55–6, 167–9
see also Common Foreign and
Defence Policy (CFSP)
services sector, 195, 197, 202, 203–4
single currency, 114, 202, 211, 213,
230–2, 236, 243–4
Single European Act (SEA), 12, 18, 81,
138, 231
Single European Market (SEM), 210,
220
Slovenia, 65, 66, 67, 68, 201
social bargain, 107–15, 120, 121
social dialogue, 97, 98–101, 102, 104
Social Dialogue Committee, 100
social model, 105–21
social partnership, principle of, 117
social policy, 5, 91–2, 96–104, 105–21
Social Policy Protocol-plus-Agreement,
5, 11
social security, 108
South Africa, 200
sovereignty, national, 169, 203
Spain, 224
specialization in production, 222
Stability and Growth Pact (SGP), 113,
212, 214, 215, 216, 218, 219,
221, 223, 224, 225, 234
Standing Committee on Employment,
94–5, 95, 96